Michael Adams has worked as a magazine journalist and editor, and a television scriptwriter, producer and presenter. He is the author of fifteen books, including *Hanging Ned Kelly*, and is the creator and host of the podcast *Forgotten Australia*.

THE MURDER SQUAD

MICHAEL ADAMS

affirm
press

affirm press

First published by Affirm Press in 2023
This edition published in 2024
Bunurong/Boon Wurrung Country
28 Thistlethwaite Street
South Melbourne, VIC 3205
affirmpress.com.au

Affirm Press is located on the unceded land of the Bunurong/Boon Wurrung peoples
of the Kulin Nation. Affirm Press pays respect to their Elders past and present.

10 9 8 7 6 5 4 3 2 1

 A catalogue record for this
book is available from the
National Library of Australia

ISBN: 9781923046504 (paperback)

Cover design by Steph Bishop-Hall © Affirm Press
Typeset in Garamond Premier Pro by J&M Typesetting
Printed and bound in China by C&C Offset Printing Co., Ltd.

MIX
Paper | Supporting
responsible forestry
FSC® C008047

For everyone who helped to save the National Library of Australia's Trove database, without which this book would not exist.

This book retains pre-decimal usage of miles for distance and pounds for weight.

1 mile = 1.61 kilometres.

1 pound = 0.45 kilograms.

Contents

In Australia there now exists ... a period of financial depression, with concomitant unemployment, starvation and misery. It is only natural that there should be a series of crimes against property ... But murder is another matter: especially as, in the recent horrifying murders, robbery has not been a direct motive ... One characteristic of them, in any case, is a total disregard for human life.

— 'Grim Riddle of the Murder Wave', *The Sun*, 1 May 1932

All records for endurance investigations are likely to be smashed by the C.I.B. squad which, since December 10, has been probing the murder of May Miller, the inquiries into whose death were additional to those incidental to the killing of Bessie O'Connor ...

— 'Never Let Up – Murder Squad Has Busy Life', *The Sun*, 11 January 1933

Author's Note

The detectives look for all the world like tough cops from a Warner Bros. gangster film – and they've just caught a murdering monster who might have slunk from the shadows in a Universal horror flick. But this isn't the movies. It's real life. And now, with the bloodthirsty killer dubbed 'the Park Demon' safely behind bars, the hard men of the Murder Squad are off to the pub.

The 1933 street photograph on the cover of this book is not the sort of image we associate with Australia during the Great Depression. Instead, this period conjures other tragedies and triumphs: unemployed men on the bush track looking for work; Phar Lap thundering past the post to put pennies in the pockets of poor punters; families by the wireless listening to the first broadcast of the ABC; Don Bradman and his cricketers bravely facing the Bodyline onslaught; the Sydney Harbour Bridge finished at great sacrifice, only for its opening to be usurped by a slashing fascist crank. But what's forgotten about those dark times is that Sydney and New South Wales – Australia's biggest city and biggest state by population – also suffered a succession of horrific killings that beggared belief and shocked the entire nation.

These mysteries and murders – concurrent with rampant unemployment, immense poverty and dislocation, and unprecedented political upheaval that engendered fear of a communist revolution and spawned the rise of the right-wing New Guard – were investigated by an elite group of detectives at a time when the police force in New South

Wales was being transformed by changes in leadership, organisation, communication, technology and science. They were also working in a very different physical landscape. Sydney then had a population of 1.25 million – it has 5.25 million today – and even inner-city suburbs had pockets of scrub and vacant land, while outer suburbs were dotted with farms and surrounded by bush.

This book focuses on the worst years of the Great Depression – 1929 to 1934 – and largely, but not exclusively, on investigations led by Detective-Sergeant Thomas Walter McRae, the biggest man on the cover photograph. One, known as the Pyjama Girl case, is still infamous, while the rest have fallen into obscurity, even though the Bungendore Bones, the Moorebank Murders, the Park Demon, the Hammer Horror and the Human Glove mysteries were very well known at the time. Some of their notoriety was due to the fiercely competitive tabloid newspapers. While they often had genuine scoops based on insider information, they just as regularly printed wild speculation or even outright fabrication, turning up the pressure on police while also compromising accused people's right to a fair trial.

Detective McRae would be celebrated by these newspapers as one of Australia's foremost murder experts as he rose to be chief of the New South Wales Homicide Squad. His evidence-gathering methods – and those of his colleagues who made up the 'murder squads' assembled to tackle challenging cases – were seen as ingenious at a time when even science-fiction writers wouldn't have dreamed of computer databases, surveillance cameras, DNA or GPS as crime-fighting tools. But McRae and his fellow officers also worked in a period when fists, batons and even revolvers were used, with few or no consequences, against ordinary citizens, locked-out coalminers, striking timber workers, marching communists and ranting fascists.

With such brutalities committed in the open, and even in front of press cameras, what could cops get away with inside police stations when they were questioning men and the occasional woman whom they believed to be guilty of horrific murders? Though detectives denied such practices, defence solicitors and barristers regularly argued that their clients had been subjected to prolonged and unfair interrogations that resulted in 'voluntary statements'. Threats and promises might be used: 'If you're convicted of murder, you're going to hang, but if it was only manslaughter, you'll be out in a few years ...' Meanwhile, these suspect interviews could be reshaped into narratives: an answer of 'Yes' to the question 'Were you driving the car that night with Bill?' might then be presented as a statement: 'I was driving the car that night with Bill ...' Such practices were pervasive. Yet accusations of frame-ups were also falsely made by desperate culprits, who would say anything to avoid the death sentence.

What happened? Who did what? Who's telling the truth? Where's the evidence? What can be proved? These are questions central to solving any murder, but we can also ask them in relation to how these homicide investigations were conducted. This book presents numerous cases where we have a chance to weigh the main evidence, assess the character of the accused, ponder the fairness of police testimony, consider the justness of punishments and assess the effect of newspaper hysteria. There aren't always answers beyond reasonable doubt, even in cases where killers were found guilty, and several murderers got away with their crimes, leaving fascinating enduring mysteries.

McRae's career is a fitting lens through which to examine this era, not only because he worked on so many major crimes, but also because his own fate would ultimately hinge on how these questions were answered. In 1886, the year of McRae's birth, Friedrich Nietzsche published *Beyond Good and Evil: Prelude to a Philosophy of the Future*, which included lines that have often been applied to homicide detectives around the world – and they're cetainly as fitting to the men of *The Murder Squad*: 'He who fights with monsters should be careful lest he thereby become a monster. And if thou gaze long into an abyss, the abyss will also gaze into thee.'

Prologue
The Pyjama Girl

Cutting off the young woman's head would be the wrong move.

Detective-Sergeant Thomas Walter McRae knows this. For the past week, hundreds of people have flocked to the Albury morgue to gaze at the girl in the ice bath to see if they recognise her. While she's a terrible sight, at least she's in one piece. But her features are beginning to contort and she can't be kept on ice indefinitely. Thus the suggestion to decapitate.

But will ordinary citizens be able to handle a face staring out from a jar of formalin? Earlier this year McRae put away a murderer where the vital evidence was the entire epidermis of the victim's right hand preserved in this way. Those floating, spongy fingers were a revolting spectacle in court. Better, in this case, that potential witnesses not be confronted with a head in a jar. Better that they expect to look upon the face and full body of the woman now known as 'the Pyjama Girl'.

Whoever she is, the newspapers have given her the allure of a fairytale: the beauty lying in repose, awaiting someone to utter the magic words – her name – that will solve the mystery of her death and bring a killer to justice. It's true she'd been attractive in life: creamy skin, blue eyes, fine features, fashionably bobbed hair dyed light brown, a small and slender figure. The image of her being killed in her yellow silk pyjamas is also haunting.

For the police, all of this is good news: the greater the public interest, the greater the chance someone will come forward with information. But anyone expecting to gaze upon Sleeping Beauty is in for a shock. The girl was bludgeoned, leaving her with multiple skull fractures and a severe wound to the forehead. Her body was bent into a sack, dumped in a culvert on a country road, doused in kerosene and set ablaze; only rain had prevented her corpse from being burned up entirely.

Remarkably, the Pyjama Girl's facial features are intact. In the past week, millions have read about the case and seen an artist's impression of how she looked in life. The story is the biggest murder mystery in years, which is really saying something, given what McRae has seen since the world slid into the Great Depression. Yet despite all the publicity, no one has identified her.

That's why McRae has been sent to Albury. He's made his name solving headline cases where the victim's identity had to be established from bits of bone or flaps of skin.

As good as he is, McRae doesn't work alone. Today he is conferring with his frequent partner, Detective-Sergeant Frank 'Len' Allmond, and their chief at the Criminal Investigation Bureau (CIB), Detective-Inspector William Prior. These colleagues and others form an elite group of investigators who regularly have their names and photos in the papers as they try to solve bloody murders and bring monsters to justice. These men have seen the New South Wales force evolve from the time when mounted constables still chased bushrangers to a modern organisation that uses cars and motorbikes, fingerprints and forensics, telephones, radio and even moving pictures. Individually, these detectives are minor celebrities. Together, they're the Murder Squad – and McRae, the chief of the Homicide department, is first among equals.

Now McRae's idea is that the Pyjama Girl be kept in one piece. Embalm her and she'll be easier on the eye for witnesses and she'll be preserved for as long as it takes for that crucial witness identification. McRae's recommendation is approved and the delicate process is undertaken, heralded in the newspapers as the first time in policing history that a murder victim has been mummified to solve a mystery. Soon the Pyjama Girl will be moved to the University of Sydney and kept in a zinc-lined coffin filled with formalin, able to be hooked from the fluid whenever she needs to be shown to someone who might know her name.

What McRae can't know is that by preserving the Pyjama Girl, he's cementing in place one piece of the path that will lead to his professional and personal destruction.

1

From Strathalbyn to a Sydney Slaying

Death could come at any moment.

Tom McRae learned this as a twelve-year-old lad in Strathalbyn, a Scottish settlement on the Angas River in South Australia, about forty miles south-east of Adelaide. For the town's children, summer meant having a splash or catching some fish. Yet few could venture safely into water of any depth, because most of the town's population, young and old alike, couldn't swim.

On Friday 9 December 1898, Tom's eight-year-old brother, Donald, and a younger mate were crayfishing at Kings Waterhole, where the water was eleven feet deep. Hauling in his net, Don overbalanced and fell in. His friend screamed and ran for help. A local man jumped into the water, grabbing Don as he went under again. But the rescuer couldn't swim either, and when the panicking boy thrashed, they both sank. The man let go and struggled to the surface. Another bloke dived into the depths and found Don at the bottom, trapped beneath rocks. He couldn't free him, but a third man succeeded and brought the boy to shore. This rescuer and a local doctor tried to resuscitate the lad. But Don was gone. Having received a 'full report', the coroner ruled there was no need for an inquest and released the body for burial.

The tragedy cast a pall of gloom over Strathalbyn. The McRaes were a pioneering family in the district. Tom, his five siblings and other Presbyterian Sunday School children headed a long funeral procession to the cemetery and sang a hymn at Don's grave. A week later, a swimming association was formed in the town to teach children how to save themselves in such situations.

Don's death surely had Tom asking big questions. How could God let this happen? Was everyone telling the truth? Had the little mate knocked or pushed his brother into the water, either accidentally or intentionally? Was the first rescuer to blame for not hanging on? Could anyone have saved Don? These were mysteries he could not solve – and without an inquest no further answers would be forthcoming. In the decades ahead, Tom would ask similar questions as he stood over dozens and dozens of bodies – and the answers he found would inform the testimonies he gave on behalf of these dead at inquests and trials. But McRae would also ask himself the hard questions again in a personal capacity, over the mortal remains of two more of his nearest and dearest.

Tom grew to stand half an inch shy of six feet. He was a sturdy twelve stone, with blue eyes, brown hair and a fresh complexion. After finishing school, he became a bootmaker, as would his younger brother Archie. Outside of work, Tom was a sporting man, good at athletics, and active in raising money for local charities.

Around 1909, he moved 525 miles east to Yackandandah, in north-eastern Victoria. This put him in the orbit of Mildred House, five years his senior, whose family lived in nearby Albury. Tom and Mildred moved to Sydney and tied the knot in Paddington in February 1911. On their marriage certificate, he listed his residence as Victoria Barracks and his occupation as soldier.

Early the following year, McRae signed up for the New South Wales police instead and began his training at the Bourke Street Academy in

Redfern. Recruits got three weeks of instruction, including classroom studies and physical exercise. After their passing-out parade, probationary constables started their real education under sergeants at city or country stations.

McRae was posted to the little village of Cooma, in the Snowy Mountains, gateway to the ski resorts and no hotbed of crime. The modest highlights of his first year included a local who poisoned himself with arsenic and the alleged theft of whisky belonging to the Railway Commissioner. But, beyond protecting life and property, McRae had his hands full, because with no union to protect their interests, police were expected to work unlimited hours, seven days a week and without scheduled time off – and do it all on a minimal salary while paying their own expenses.

Officers had an astonishing array of duties dumped on them by government departments. These included: inspecting slaughterhouses, theatres and public halls, dairies and butter factories, fisheries and tobacco; acting as agents for the Government Savings Bank; having charge of the electoral, mining, aliens and small debts registers; completing returns of jury lists and agricultural estimates; registering dogs and licensing motorcar drivers; assisting pensioners with their enquiries; and keeping records of rations given to local Indigenous people. While city police might not be called on to fulfil each of these roles, country coppers could expect to do most of them and many others besides. If there was an upside to such overload, it was that it gave McRae a wide understanding of different people, places and processes – good training for any aspiring detective.

Constable McRae would have done his duties on foot, bicycle or horseback, or in a sulky. In 1912 the New South Wales police had just one motorcar: a single-seater roadster for the personal use of the all-powerful inspector general in Sydney. Communications were also primitive – it'd be another six years before the Cooma police station had a telephone connection.

When McRae wasn't working, he and Mildred were active in the Presbyterian Church and in community affairs. He was a skilled marksman, winning rifle-shooting competitions for Cooma, and entertained locals with his singing, performing with the Male Chorus Musical Society.

When the Great War broke out in 1914, McRae's occupation meant he wasn't expected to enlist. But amid the patriotic fervour, 206 other New South Wales policemen did sign up. A quarter of them would never return, the depletion of the force so great that in August 1915 the new Inspector General, James Mitchell, banned further enlistment. A particular loss to the force's rank and file was Ted Larkin, a former Sydney police officer who, before enlisting, had become a member of the state parliament, where he had advocated for a police association. The hopes of many coppers for better pay and conditions – and even the simple ability to request a transfer to a more amenable location – died with Larkin at Gallipoli. They wouldn't be revived until well after the war.

In autumn 1916, the inspector general transferred McRae from Cooma to Queanbeyan. Relocating 60 miles north over country roads was a hassle, but Tom and Mildred soon settled into their new home and again became active in church and community affairs. In what perhaps felt like an uncanny echo of his own childhood tragedy, soon after McRae took up his new post, toddlers Eric Lee and Percy Oldfield, both just two years old, wandered unseen from a house to a nearby river. Only Percy returned. A frantic search recovered Eric, his body still warm, but efforts to revive him were in vain. As the *Queanbeyan Age* and *Queanbeyan Observer* reported:

> Constable McRae proceeded to the residence of Percy Oldfield, with the intention of questioning the little fellow. His childish prattle was not altogether intelligible to others than his mother, but the constable understood the facts of the case from the tiny boy's own lips. Questioned by the officer thus: – 'Where is

Eric Lee?' the child replied, 'Eric fell in the river and cried.' The pathetic statement only too truly told its own tale.

This time there was an inquest, McRae giving the evidence that confirmed it had been a tragic accident. It'd seem reasonable to assume he sympathised deeply with the grieving family.

At some point around this period, though the timing and circumstances aren't known, he and Mildred had their own sorrow when she became pregnant but lost the baby – either as a result of miscarriage or soon after the birth.

Six months after relocating to Queanbeyan, McRae was bounced to Eden, on the far South Coast. There was a note of frustration in the wording of the ad he placed in a local newspaper to sell all his and Mildred's furniture and effects – right down to their forty pot plants. Perhaps it was better to start afresh rather than haul everything 160 miles south-east.

Eden could hardly have been further from the Great War, where McRae's brother Archie, having survived a gunshot wound at Gallipoli, was now serving on the Western Front. Yet McRae's first notable policing triumph, in July 1917, was connected to the conflict. About ten miles out to sea, the SS *Cumberland* became the first ship to fall victim to an enemy mine in Australian waters, the explosive laid by the German raider *Wolf*. Crippled, the ship beached at Gabo Island, where some cargo washed ashore and was pinched by a trio of local fishermen.

With these plunderers based in Eden, McRae was on the case, despite Gabo Island officially being under Victorian jurisdiction. He motored out to the crime scene, where he got a confession from one crook that led to him and his mates being convicted and fined. Given the criminal spoils had included tins of preserved rabbit, it wasn't like McRae had caught Jack the Ripper. But his work got him noticed by senior police in Sydney. This included rising star William 'Billy' MacKay, who noted that McRae was to be 'commended on the splendid manner in which he tackled the job'.

The Great War expanded the police's already onerous workload in New South Wales. In February 1916, 5000 Australian soldiers protested conditions at their Casula camp by commandeering trains and going on a drunken riot around Sydney, with the fallout being the introduction of early closing times for pubs and the start of the 'six o'clock swill'. The task of ejecting rowdy drunks who refused to leave bars at closing, and of charging publicans who kept serving illegally, thereafter fell to the constabulary. More pressingly, the New South Wales force henceforth had to tackle sly-grog merchants, the most powerful of whom organised into violent gangs and presented tempting corruptions to officers.

The state's police were also put to political uses, being arrayed against communists, unionists, peace activists and anti-conscriptionists. The most notorious instance of such suppression, offering a rare public glimpse into the force's by-any-means-necessary mentality, was the September 1916 arrest on treason charges of a dozen members of the Industrial Workers of the World (IWW), an international labour union, with the cops allegedly using lying informants, planting evidence and concocting confessions.

McRae got a taste of city policing when he was seconded to Sydney during the Great Strike of 1917, the bitterest conflict in Australian industrial history. The work of the constables was hard and hazardous, with men often on duty from four in the morning until midnight. There were also conflicting emotions for the many police who wanted their own collective representation, so they could negotiate better pay and conditions, and yet they found themselves protecting 'scabs' undermining the activities of unionists battling to protect their workplace rights. Wanting to ensure the loyalty of cops who'd been on these frontlines, the inspector general authorised a special allowance for all officers who did strike duty. McRae would get an extra three shillings for each day he was in Sydney – and an extra week of annual leave. Around this time, he was also promoted to constable second class.

But the inspector general giveth and the inspector general taketh away. In April 1918, the McRaes were uprooted yet again – this time to Burrinjuck, some 240 miles to the north-west, in the Riverina district. *The Twofold Bay Magnet* reported that the locals sent them off with all good wishes: 'Never had Eden had a more popular officer than "Mac".'

McRae soon endeared himself to his new town. In July 1919, Burrinjuck – like most of Australia – was ravaged by the Spanish flu; when the local Kershaw family was hit particularly hard, with the father and a son dying and other members of the household seriously ill, McRae organised a charity drive to assist them.

In January 1921 a new life for the couple beckoned in Sydney when McRae, by this time promoted to constable first class, was transferred to the No. 1 station in Clarence Street. Given his beat was now the big bad city, he'd be working in plain clothes and learning from the best. These included Detective-Inspector William Prior, the rising man of the CIB, and Detective-Sergeant Billy MacKay, a fiercely proud Scot who had direct charge of No.1 and took an interest in officers of Caledonian heritage.

In the decade since McRae had joined the force, there had been many changes in Sydney policing. Most visible was a new dark-blue, military-style uniform worn with leather boots and a flat-topped cap with a shiny nickel badge. Officers now carried leather batons, filled with sand for extra socking power, and revolvers or semiautomatic pistols, which they kept beneath their tunics in leather holsters. The force had appointed its first female police officers, Lillian Armfield and Maud Rhodes. More and more stations had electric lights and telephone connections. Cars, vans and motorbikes were increasingly used, and in the not-too-distant future a few powerful cars would be equipped with wireless radios so patrols could receive real-time orders and speed to crime scenes.

Yet for the rank-and-file cops, the most significant change – spearheaded by MacKay, who picked up where the late Ted Larkin had left off – came in 1921 with the formation of the Police Association of New South Wales, which meant members had a body to represent their interests and defend them against arbitrary judgements from the higher-ups. This organisation quickly represented 80 per cent of the 2400 eligible officers. This was real progress, although it'd be another five years before the police won a forty-four-hour working week that included a scheduled day off.

McRae's city work was more exciting and varied than it had been in the country. He came up against illegal abortionists, bigamists and burglars, jewel thieves and child molesters. But he also knew that making an arrest was no guarantee that justice would be served. In December 1921, he was one of the officers to collar a man for fatally fracturing another bloke's skull during a scuffle, only for the jury to acquit the accused of the charge of manslaughter and set him free. Such cases weren't uncommon.

McRae's promotion and new posting meant he and Mildred could now expect to remain in Sydney, and they lived in a house called Oakleigh, in Keith Street in the beach suburb of Clovelly. This settling-down seemed complete in July 1921 when Mildred, who was now forty-one, fell pregnant again. Their baby daughter was born two months premature on 13 February 1922 at the Royal Hospital for Women in Paddington. Tom and Mildred named her Joyce. Sadly, she lived just ten days. Like Tom's little brother's death, it was unfair and unfathomable. Mildred was overwhelmed by grief, likely now believing she'd never have children. With bereavement leave for state employees still decades away, Tom went straight back to his demanding workload.

Frustrating cases abounded. In July 1922, McRae arrested a returned soldier who'd recklessly driven a bus and killed a music teacher crossing a street, but the judge ruled there wasn't enough evidence of negligence and directed the jury to return a verdict of not guilty.

In October 1922, a man was bashed to death in Centennial Park. McRae was one of the first on the scene, and would be part of the team to arrest Sylvester Patrick O'Reilly for this killing, although the Crown eventually dropped the case because there wasn't enough evidence to secure a murder conviction. For McRae and his colleagues, this had to be infuriating. They were privy to O'Reilly's sorry record: in the army he'd been court-martialled and sentenced to eighteen months for striking an officer, and he also had recent convictions for unprovoked violent assaults. The man clearly had form, but none of this would have been admissible evidence in the murder trial and O'Reilly was out on the streets again.

While it had been more than a year since Mildred and Tom had buried their daughter at Rookwood Cemetery, Mildred couldn't escape the depression that engulfed her. On Thursday 8 March 1923, she was found partially dressed in wet clothes on the rocks at Gordons Bay, not far from the couple's home in Keith Street. Mildred was reported as having become deranged by grief. Where was McRae? What could he do? Had his wife tried to drown herself? Could she be calmed or committed to care? Newspaper articles provide no insight into what happened after Mildred was found in this distressed state, but the next morning she went into her kitchen, turned on the oven's gas and lay down to die. It wasn't reported whether McRae found her body; it's possible he did upon arriving home from work.

The coronial inquest concluded that Mildred had committed suicide. *The Sydney Morning Herald* reported: 'Mrs McRae had suffered from nervous attacks since the death of her only child 12 months ago.' Yet her despair might not only have been about her dead children. McRae would later admit that, while his wife was still alive, he had 'known' a single woman who lived nearby.

In 1923, after Mildred's death, and while he was on duty, McRae became 'lost' with this lady friend in Frenchs Forest. How, why and for how long they were 'lost' wasn't revealed. But his police bosses took a dim view of the matter. McRae made a report about his 'absence' and 'asked' to be put back into uniform while an inquiry was carried out. This penance came with a pay cut, because he no longer received the plainclothes allowance. No further disciplinary action was taken. But McRae was to say he spent two months in hospital after the incident, his description suggesting he'd suffered a mental breakdown.

By August 1924, McRae was back in action, running through the city streets, chasing two thieves he'd seen do a smash-and-grab at a jewellery store in George Street. He nabbed both perps in Hyde Park, but, as he was walking them back to the No. 1 police station, one of the blokes escaped and took off. McRae didn't forget his face. The following month, patrolling on Elizabeth Street, he saw the bloke riding a tram. McRae jumped aboard and collared the crook. Such derring-do saw him feature in the papers as a brave crime fighter.

Another strange case from this time likely stuck in McRae's memory. In October 1925, eighteen-year-old Robert Audley – well spoken, well educated and from a well-to-do family – went missing in Sydney; his father believed someone had induced him to leave. While a missing persons notice appeared in the *Police Gazette*, it wasn't until the following April that the father appealed to the newspapers. They published Robert's photo and a tantalising update: since the boy had disappeared, a small fortune had been left to him. Robert resurfaced, revealed he'd run away to work in the bush, and reunited with his dad.

But this spoiled young man was soon in trouble again, this time for stealing a car. Yet no one could've imagined the ghastly death and destruction that Robert Audley would one day wreak in McRae's old beat of Cooma.

In July 1926, McRae was back in plain clothes, investigating a series of jewellery robberies, the case culminating with him and his colleagues digging up loot the suspect had buried beneath his house. In November, McRae's keen observational skills saw him crack a smuggling syndicate that involved a disgraced police officer who'd been drummed out of the force. Teaming up with Billy MacKay, McRae set up a sting in which he and other officers hid in a premises while this crooked ex-copper stitched himself up with a lengthy confession. *Smith's Weekly* headlined its admiring article about this case: 'Sydney Constable's Curiosity Leads to the Downfall of Big Wharf-Pillaging Gang'.

McRae used similar methods when a middle-aged creep and a young woman conspired to frame a businessman for rape, the sting in the intended victim's house allowing police to overhear one of the extortionists making demands. Surveillance, sex and sleaze: the newspapers lapped up the story, even if, frustratingly, the accused pair weaselled their way out of convictions. McRae's photo featured in the papers – an increasing occurrence as his profile grew.

By October 1928 McRae was promoted to detective-sergeant third class. He'd now work out of the CIB at Sydney's police headquarters and report to its new boss, Inspector Billy MacKay. McRae regularly investigated city killings. Mostly, they were spur-of-the-moment murders and manslaughters. In the space of a few weeks in early 1929, a boarding house feud between two old men led to a fatal stabbing, while a street fight led to yet another unintended death from a fractured skull.

But then McRae was on the case of Vera Stirling – a macabre murder mystery like so many macabre murder mysteries to come – right as Sydney, New South Wales, Australia and the world began the descent into the darkness of the Great Depression.

2

Death Among the Lilies

While history records that the Great Depression began in Australia after the Wall Street Crash of October 1929, the political titan and former New South Wales Labor premier Jack Lang believed its shadow loomed far earlier, and far closer to home.

'The Big Fella' dated the troubles to the slump in the coal industry and its moguls locking miners out of their Hunter Valley collieries in March 1929, because unionists working under a federal award refused to accept reduced pay and conditions. Overnight, 15,000 men were thrown out of work, and their families plunged into poverty, their only hope lying in solidarity against the owners and the conservative state government. At the same time, in Sydney, timber workers were locked out for refusing to obey a new industrial award that cut their pay while increasing their work week from forty-four to forty-eight hours. Thousands of these men and their families were similarly thrown on the breadline.

The miners and timber workers were bellwethers of troubles to come. But life was still humming along as usual for most Sydneysiders on the evening of Thursday 21 March 1929. Yet if people rushing home from work through Hyde Park cared to look around, they were afforded another preview of conditions that would soon be far more common. There, right in the heart of the city, people were camped amid the bushes.

Their clothes were tattered and they had newspapers for bedclothes. Many were mired in alcoholism and vulnerable to violence. Yet the how and why of their desperation was likely of little concern to commuters still confident in their own employment and Australia's economic stability.

As a denizen of this demimonde, Vera Stirling wouldn't have elicited much sympathy. She looked older than her forty-seven years, and with her dark eyes and short black hair might have seemed like a faded flapper. Originally from New Zealand, with a 'refined' way of speaking, it was said that Vera had once been well-to-do in England. Yet she'd fallen far, working as a street prostitute, steeping herself in methylated spirits, sleeping in the city's parks, and racking up more than forty convictions for drunkenness and vagrancy.

Early on Thursday night, Vera was near the Hyde Park fountain and in a blur of noisy, drunken motion. Wrapped in her brown coat, lank hair bouncing under a black hat, she did a jig on emaciated legs in torn black stockings as she stridently belted out Irish songs. Taking a break, Vera stopped another down-and-outer and produced a bottle from her bosom, asking the man, 'Have a drink of meths?' The chap waved her off and continued on his way to a shelter for the unemployed. But Vera would be dossing in the bed of newspapers she'd made in the eastern part of the park. As far as it went, this was a pleasant enough spot, in a triangular garden, off the path in the dark and amid canna lilies.

John Duncan was trying to get by as a bottle gatherer, paid a penny or so from the breweries for each empty he returned. Hyde Park early in the morning might offer pickings from the previous night's careless drunks, and the eagled-eyed collector was there at six-thirty on Friday. Walking towards Oxford Street, he spied a brown coat with fur trimmings in a garden bed. Crossing the lawn, perhaps thinking the garment might bring a few shillings, he stopped short when he saw it was still wrapped around its owner. There was no doubt the woman was dead: her open eyes stared into the morning sky from a blue and distorted face. Her empty meths bottle lay nearby.

As traffic lights were still a few years in Sydney's future, constables were seldom far from any given point in the city, directing cars, horses and carts, trams and trucks. The bottle collector rushed from Hyde Park to the nearest officer and related his gruesome discovery. He and the policeman hurried back to the garden, where a crowd was already forming. Fellow derelicts – dubbed 'Domain dossers' – muttered that this sure was a sad end for poor old Vera. A well-meaning onlooker, done with his morning newspaper and its stories about the coal lockout at Rothbury, another suicide at the Gap and the first all-talkie movie, placed its pages as a shroud over the dead woman.

Other uniforms from the Clarence Street station arrived on the scene. Even with the bruise over Vera's left eyebrow and the dried blood at the corner of her mouth, her bedraggled state might have made it seem she'd died from drink and hard living. But what *was* sinister was that this poor creature's hands had been tied – one over the other at the wrist, in the shape of a cross – with a flesh-coloured silk stocking.

The cops summoned their superiors, among them Tom McRae and his immediate boss, Inspector Prior, one of the state's longest-serving and most respected officers.

~

Originally from the South Coast, William Parker Prior enlisted as a cop soon after Federation, having missed that historic event because he was serving in the Boer War. In 1903, Prior, like his future colleague McRae, married a slightly older woman. He and his wife, Lily, lived in Newtown, where Prior was stationed as a constable.

One of the biggest developments in policing came that same year when Sergeant Walter Childs established the Fingerprint Division. In early 1904, a Sydney burglar became the first person convicted in Australia using such evidence. But Prior's own work was more likely to involve fists than fingerprints, because Newtown's streets were among Sydney's meanest. His cases ranged widely: a hamper baby, a stolen skeleton, a deserting boxer, shop thieves, park prowlers, cat burglars, bogus doctors, opium dealers. There were also rapists, manslaughterers, murderers and insane killers.

Like McRae, Prior experienced professional frustrations. One, in February 1911, was a case against an accused paedophile that failed despite his testimony and that of a former cop. In such acquittals, the implication was that police had lied. *Truth* newspaper characterised this particular verdict with the headline: 'The Jury Think Ex-Constable Taylor and Constable Prior Were Guilty of Perjury'.

Whenever police testimony fell under a shadow – and it happened a lot – the central questions were broadly the same. What had the accused said after the arrest and during questioning? Who had witnessed any alleged admissions? Officers would give their comrade-corroborated assurances that the accused had made statements voluntarily. The accused and their defenders would argue that any 'admissions' were made under threat or inducement, or that their words had been maliciously misconstrued or even entirely fabricated. Judges would weigh whether police testimony was admissible. If deemed so, then a jury was to decide whether it was credible and supported by other evidence. The scales were tipped in the favour of the police and the prosecution, but verdicts didn't always go their way.

Like McRae, Inspector Prior had also experienced personal tragedy. While McRae's brother Archie had survived the Great War, Prior's brother Claude had been killed in France in February 1917. Just over two years later, when a new daily mortality record for Spanish flu was set in Sydney, Prior's forty-year-old wife, Lily, was among the eighteen to die. Then, in June 1920, young constable Roy Prior, who'd followed his older brother into the Sydney police, was on duty when he was knocked from the running board of a tram and suffered a fatal skull fracture. Like other officers killed or injured doing their jobs in the days before the Police Association of New South Wales was established, Roy wasn't covered by insurance.

Professionally, though, Prior had risen during his time of grief. As a result of the royal commission into how police had handled the IWW cases, the inspector general recommended five officers be punished with transfer out of the CIB, and Prior filled one of the vacancies. His personal life brightened too when he remarried in May 1922. As the decade progressed, Prior enjoyed further promotions and became acting inspector in September 1928.

~

Now, in Hyde Park, with Vera Stirling dead at his feet, Prior was disturbed that the crime scene had been trampled by citizens and the first cops to arrive. They had likely obliterated clues, such as footprints, and their presence had tainted other potential evidence, such as cigarette butts.

Newsmen were also circling, sharks to blood in the water, a city murder promising a sensational read in a cut-throat market. Vera would make that afternoon's edition of *The Sun* – which boasted the biggest circulation in Australia – and she'd be all over tomorrow's *Daily Telegraph*, *Evening News*, *Labor Daily* and *Sydney Morning Herald*, before getting a weekend run in *The Sunday Times* and scandal sheet *Truth*.

McRae and Prior noted Vera's facial injuries, and an abrasion and slight bruising on her neck. They found three shillings hidden in her ripped black stockings. 'About all old Vera ever had at one time in her life,' a vagrant mused. It seemed unlikely the motive was robbery. Maybe it had started as an argument between drunks? Vera could've been knocked down with a punch and then strangled. She was so frail it wouldn't have taken much to finish her off. But why tie her wrists? That her clothing was disarranged suggested the restraints had been used in a rape that ended in murder. Yet, contradicting this, there was no sign of a struggle – or that she'd resisted being bound.

The detectives beat the bushes for clues. A few feet away they found another bottle containing a little whisky. McRae also discovered the 'mate' of the flesh-coloured silk stocking used to bind Vera. While a man might carry such finery as a gift for a paramour, this hosiery was old, worn and torn. Perhaps a female vagrant had taken off her own stockings to render Vera helpless?

By 10am the crowd had grown. Whenever there was a crime, Sydneysiders gathered. Kept back by a uniformed constable, men, women and the inevitable barefoot children stood on the lawn and gazed at the dead woman in the bushes. Photographers captured the onlookers, the detectives scrutinising the scene and Inspector Prior escorting the city coroner, Mr Edwin May, to examine the body. The coroner had only last year been promoted to his position, having previously been a police magistrate at Tamworth. Over the next few years, May would have his work cut out for him as he presided over inquests into some of the state's grisliest deaths.

After May had made his necessary observations, Vera's body was sent to the city morgue, where government medical officers (GMO) Dr Arthur Aubrey Palmer and Dr Stratford Sheldon, who would also figure in many cases to come, conducted the post-mortem. They concluded that Vera had died of asphyxia six to eight hours before she was found, likely of strangulation. That officially made this a murder investigation.

The paucity of physical evidence meant this mystery would likely only be solved with the help of witnesses. Police had to find someone who'd seen something in the park. That was easier said than done, when it had been so dark and most everyone so drunk. Prior, McRae and other detectives scoured Hyde Park and walked Darlinghurst, Surry Hills, East Sydney and Woolloomooloo. Heads bent to notebooks, they stood beside garden beds, outside cheap hotels and corner stores, interviewing the underclass. They heard that Vera's husband had been an English sea captain; that she sometimes got large, unexplained sums of money; that she was ladylike when sober but on the meths was rowdy; and that she'd sunk so low that she'd go with foreigners and 'coloured men'.

For the past three nights Vera had slept on her newspaper bed amid the lilies. Before she'd retreated to this haunt for the final time, the detectives learned, she'd been talking with two men near 'Mount Stokes', a huge, unsightly pile of muck excavated from the underground railway loop being built to connect with the Sydney Harbour Bridge, whose arches were slowly reaching for each other over the waterway that divided the city. McRae and his colleagues located and cleared these blokes. They were back at square one.

With an official media unit decades away, detectives and reporters developed informal relationships, trading information at crime scenes, police stations and over beers at the early-opening pubs frequented by cops coming off the night shift. The papers usually depicted detectives in glowing terms, faithfully issued their calls for public assistance and suppressed information that might hinder the hunt for a murderer. *The Sun*'s police roundsman, Bill Carrick, was held in such esteem that when he died in 1947, Billy MacKay, by then the commissioner of police, ordered a special police motorcycle escort for the funeral, which was attended by CIB detectives and uniformed men.

The Sydney Morning Herald's reporter Selwyn Speight – who would cover 122 murders in his career – characterised the relationship in this way:

> If you deal with a policeman and he'll trust you, and over years and years and years, you never let him down, you can get almost anything you want out of him. But there is a danger there, of course, that you get so friendly with the police you almost get in their pocket.

The cops 'rewarded' reporters by sharing with them various theories under consideration. Articles often contained all these speculations – no matter how contradictory – plus whatever the journalist or his rewrite man conjured up for maximum sensation. Newspapers also undermined each other whenever possible.

Vera Stirling got this treatment. When *Truth* made much of the torn skin-coloured silk stockings and suggested a woman was the killer, *The Sun* scoffed because it had learned Vera collected odd garments – the leggings that bound her wrists had likely belonged to her. When *Truth* raised the chilling possibility that Vera was killed by whoever left another 'woman of ill repute', May Anderson, 'frightfully mutilated and maltreated' in the scrub near Long Bay Gaol in May 1924, *The Daily Telegraph* came back with the possibility that Vera hadn't even been murdered, reporting the police's new theory: she'd fallen down drunk and suffocated in the garden, some other derelict 'with a spark of religion still smouldering' tying her hands 'in the shape of a cross'. This would mean the police didn't have a murder to solve. Besides, who'd want to kill Vera? The *Herald* put it bleakly:

> Then, so far as can be ascertained, there could be no motive for such a crime, for the woman, while she had no friends, also had no bitter enemies, indeed, nobody cared about her. She, with her companions of the parks, had touched the depths. It seems that the circumstances of her death will remain a mystery.

The Sunday Times flirted with criticism of the cops. Recently, it reminded readers, the government had sent Chief Inspector MacKay and two other detectives to Scotland Yard to learn the latest investigation techniques. The paper had called this trip an unnecessary and expensive 'joy ride'. Though MacKay was still away, the other senior men, Detective-Sergeant James Quinn and Detective-Constable Walter Lawrence had returned to Sydney. So why hadn't one or both of these men been assigned to the Vera Stirling case? Failure to do so had contributed to the public impression the police weren't doing everything they could to solve the murder because of the victim's lowly status. But the problem was solved in mid-April at the inquest, when Coroner May ruled that while Vera had asphyxiated, he couldn't say how it'd happened, so it wasn't officially murder.

Vera Stirling had straddled society's lower and upper echelons before she'd been found dead in a bush camp in the middle of the city, the victim of either luck so bad it resembled murder or of a cold-blooded killer who might strike again. Thus, her case contained many elements that would confront McRae, Prior, their fellow detectives, Mr May and other magistrates and judges as they faced some of the most sensational criminal investigations of the Great Depression. But, for the moment, Vera was forgotten in her pauper's grave.

Until, on 7 May 1929, she was briefly resurrected – at least in the press – when the body of seventy-year-old alcoholic and vagrant Selina Stanley was found in a vacant lot in Erskineville. Nearby were the remains of her last lonely meal and a handbag containing a flask of meths and half a quid in coins. Though her body was bruised, it was at first thought she'd died from natural causes. But Dr Palmer's post-mortem revealed that her killer or killers had used a weapon to inflict shocking internal injuries.

Selina, per *Truth*'s headline, had been the 'Derelict Victim of Vile Human Monster', sacrificed to the 'bestial instincts of a sexual maniac'. Detectives found no murder weapon and no other evidence at the scene. While a local had seen an odd-looking man apparently watching Selina, no one had any further information of use. CIB men – including lead investigator Detective-Sergeant Quinn, recent Scotland Yard student – came up against the same problems their colleagues had six weeks earlier: most of the people who'd known Selina were drink-addled drifters.

Reporters asked: had Vera been murdered, and had this monster now killed again? Detectives dismissed the idea, saying that even if Vera had been strangled, it was unlikely the killer would know about Selina's

Erskineville haunt. In any case, such a pervert would surely have come under their scrutiny already. Both were thin arguments. An opportunistic killer might seek out such lonely spots knowing he'd find vulnerable victims and could go about his dreadful business with less fear of being disturbed or detected. And only an omniscient police force could be aware of every demented suspect.

Looking further back, the newspapers said Selina's horrific death most resembled the 1924 rape-murder of May Anderson. Detectives didn't want to consider that possibility either – at least publicly. They appeared vindicated in mid-May, when they arrested a sixty-three-year-old labourer and held him on a vagrancy charge. But at the inquest at the end of the month, Mr May set him free for lack of evidence. He delivered an open verdict: Selina Stanley had been murdered by a person or persons unknown.

By the time Detective-Sergeant Quinn had hit that brick wall, Inspector MacKay had returned from his overseas study tour. He'd learned not only from Scotland Yard but also from police peers in Europe, Canada and the United States. MacKay was about to shake up the New South Wales police force, for better and for worse.

3

MacKay, Moxley, and Cops as Killers

Billy MacKay would become a policing legend – not least thanks to glowing newspaper accounts of his background, adventures and achievements. He was also prone to mythmaking. 'I was born in a police station,' he told one audience, 'brought up in a police station, and have done police work morning, noon and night.'

William John MacKay came into the world in 1885 in Glasgow, and followed his veteran police inspector father into the force in 1905. The youngster, who stood six-foot-two and was nicknamed 'Big Bill', made detective-constable within two years. He would boast that he'd been instrumental in the 1909 apprehension of a murderer, but this was almost certainly false – and it was curious that MacKay continued to make this claim even after it was shown that the police had fabricated evidence in that case, and the accused was exonerated, set free and given hefty compensation.

MacKay's real career in Glasgow was far more modest. He quit the force in January 1910, migrated to Sydney in April and joined the New South Wales police force in June. MacKay came up with another origin story about how he again embraced the uniform in his new home. He claimed that he first worked as a clerk in Sydney. One day, he was standing on a city street when he saw two pickpockets preying on a man. MacKay weighed in with his fists, collaring the crooks, helping a uniformed constable and a plainclothes detective take them to the station. When MacKay gave evidence, the detective was mightily impressed and suggested he join the NSW force. He signed up that day – and never looked back.

While he'd supposedly started with a punchy citizen's arrest, MacKay was at first a paper-pusher, serving as clerk, but he soon became personal assistant to Inspector General James Mitchell, this powerful Scotsman becoming his mentor. MacKay's shorthand skills were less exciting than his yarn about fisticuffs but they were what made his mark as a crime-fighter. In 1916, MacKay was involved in the IWW case, which became infamous because police were suspected of framing these twelve 'Wobblies', as members of this union were known. The men faced court for sedition, arson and conspiracy. While MacKay's official role was limited, in the leftist press he was later blamed for this anti-worker frame-up happening in the first place. In their account, MacKay and his partner Constable George Ferguson had been first to report to their superiors that IWW members were 'spreading sedition and selling the pamphlet *Sabotage* in the Domain on Sundays'. Ferguson had then recruited an IWW member who lied and perjured himself to say Wobblies were planning arson attacks on Sydney. MacKay took shorthand notes at IWW speeches; he'd testify the radicals knew he was doing so and made jokes like 'Hello, Mack, have you got your notebook with you?' MacKay read his notes at trial – and identified signatures from one of the accused on allegedly seditious letters. But MacKay had nothing to do with the evidence – allegedly planted and fabricated in 'confessions' – used to convict the men of arson and conspiracy. While some of the IWW convictions would be upheld in a 1920 inquiry, key witnesses were also found to be liars and perjurers. It was ruled the Wobblies had been given excessive punishments and they were all released. Enquiries revealed that five senior officers had accepted clothes from one of these dodgy witnesses, who himself hoped to avoid prosecution for forgery. These police – one of them was Detective Jacob Miller, who'd figure in many later major murder cases – were shunted from the CIB. As we have seen, Detective Prior filled one of the vacancies and another went to Detective James Comans, also prominent later in homicide investigations.

Despite this murky outcome, the IWW case put MacKay on the fast track. In 1917, Inspector General Mitchell cited him as having been instrumental in the IWW convictions and recommended his promotion to sergeant third class. Long after the dust settled, Sydney's leftists remembered MacKay as the villain of the IWW case, a man who'd built his career on the injustice he'd perpetrated. *The Workers' Weekly* would say: 'MacKay had an excellent training in stop-at-nothing service against militant workers.'

But MacKay also united workers. As a man whose rise was often described as 'meteoric', in 1920, he used his influence with the inspector general and his support from the rank and file to help push for the formation of the Police Association of New South Wales the following year. Through the decade, MacKay's ascent continued and promotions followed, with him promoted to acting inspector third class in 1925. Big Bill's most public success came after 1927, when Mitchell – his title by then changed from inspector general to police commissioner – gave his protégé the job of reporting on Darlinghurst, or 'Razorhurst', as it was known. Gangs controlled by Kate Leigh, Tilly Devine and other mobsters had made a battleground of eastern Sydney and surrounds, as they slashed with razors and shot with revolvers to control the drugs, sly-grog and sex trades. MacKay endorsed calls for more police and more police powers – including draconian consorting and vagrancy laws – and set about busting down doors. In a period of press hysteria, he was lionised as the two-fisted senior copper taking the fight to the villains of the vice underworld.

A later *Daily Telegraph* profile provided a neat summary of this perception:

By day MacKay did his office work in his frogged coat like a good inspector. At night he changed into a lounge suit and led a series of raids which began the end of the razor gangs. He raided brothels, sly-grog joints, and stand-over men's houses. The judges were in spirit behind him. A thug who saw MacKay's shoulder come splintering through his door knew he could look forward to a seven stretch.

For his efforts in suppression, in 1928 Big Bill was made detective inspector and given charge of the CIB. While he was well known to Sydneysiders, some of his methods were only revealed decades later. One was that, in the early to mid-1920s, he'd turned a Paddington probationary constable named Frank Fahy into 'The Shadow', Australia's first permanent undercover man. Fahy's recruitment and his work were so secret that for many years they apparently weren't known even to the premier or chief secretary.

The Shadow would pose as a burglar, a drunk, a gambler – whatever would get him into criminal dens, sly-grog shops, two-up schools. Dirty and unwashed, he blended with the faces in the streets or on the wharfs, listening, observing and reporting back to MacKay. While Fahy's undercover work resulted in arrests and convictions, it also revealed the brutality of his fellow officers. Scooped up with other vagrants, or rounded up in raids, he was regularly beaten by comrades who had no idea of his identity. On one occasion, a blow split his lip and knocked out two teeth.

These tales wouldn't be told until the 1950s. When they were, Fahy would also recall that, upon his recruitment, MacKay had revealed one of the other secret weapons in the fight against crime – his roll call of 'fizgigs', or informants. One of these dark stars was a minor crook named William Cyril Moxley. 'Moxley is one of the best leaks we have,' MacKay said. 'That would give the underworld a shock, wouldn't it?'

It would – and Moxley was to become inextricably linked to MacKay.

~

Moxley had actually been born Silas William Moxley in Rockhampton in March 1899. His father, Walter, was a hawker who was shot in the stomach during a pub altercation in 1902. While the bullet couldn't be removed, Walter recovered and received £100 compensation, which his wife, Julia, according to reports of their 1904 divorce, squandered before kicking him to the kerb and embarking on a spree of drunken adultery. Moxley's mother then moved young William and his siblings to Redfern in Sydney.

In January 1910, William, then ten, and his six-year-old brother Donald were visiting a relative's house when they found a shotgun leaning against a fence. The younger boy said: 'Point it at me for fun.' Moxley did and, thinking the gun unloaded, pulled the trigger and blew little Donald out of this world. An inquest cleared him of blame but his mental trauma was likely significant and long-lasting. The next year he learned his father had finally died as a result of that bullet in his belly.

For about eighteen months from April 1912, Moxley worked as telephone attendant at Sydney University and left with a good reference. As an adult, he had a distinctive look – he stood a little under five-foot-ten but was very slender, with a narrow face, wavy fair hair, big ears and slightly buggy grey eyes. In 1917 he worked as a 'scab' tram conductor for the duration of the Great Strike.

In May 1918 Moxley enlisted in the AIF, shipping from Sydney in July aboard the transport *Borda*. He didn't even make it out of the country before getting in trouble for being absent without leave in Western Australia, fined ten days' pay for his transgression. While at sea there was more trouble, when he disobeyed and insulted an officer. Moxley disembarked in London at the end of September 1918, arriving too late to see action. Awaiting return to Australia, he married an English waitress named Ada Murphy in August 1919. Perhaps feeling entitled to a honeymoon, he took off for a couple of months from October. Caught in December 1919, he was returned to Sydney in March 1920 and discharged as permanently unfit for further service – not surprising, given his undistinguished record. Shortly afterwards, Ada gave birth to a boy they named Douglas.

Moxley embraced peacetime by embarking on a new career as a crook, being convicted on two counts of theft in October 1920 in Glebe and fined £6. In April 1921, trying his hand in Brisbane, he was arrested for 'stealing with actual violence', having pushed a female cashier to the ground to grab £115 in a store and collided with a mother and child as he escaped through the streets. Moxley was caught under a bed in a suburban house, with an unloaded revolver in his pocket. He tugged on the magistrate's heartstrings, saying he'd come up from Sydney looking for work to support his English wife and baby son, and, after failing to get a job, had committed the crime in a sudden fit of temptation. 'I did not realise at the time what I was doing,' he pleaded. Convicted only of larceny, the magistrate gave him a three-year suspended sentence on a £100 bond.

But when Moxley was soon afterwards arrested on the Sunshine Coast on an outstanding warrant from New South Wales, he escaped and went on the run, making news again before he was recaptured and extradited to Sydney. There, he faced various charges for stealing and false pretences and was sentenced to two years – only to be allowed to go free on another probation.

Moxley's luck held in January 1923. Following a Chippendale break-and-enter, he was hiding out at a Redfern house with Ada and some members of his gang when it was raided by police. *The Sun* described the action thrillingly: 'Moxley made a dash across the roof, jumped the partition fence, and bolted, with two policemen in pursuit. He got away, though the police tried to stop him by revolver fire.'

This chase apparently led to Moxley becoming MacKay's fizgig. Told much later, in a fawning *Daily Telegraph* profile based on an interview with the police legend, the story went that the rising star of the NSW force felt he owed the small-time crook. He'd been after Moxley, when the fugitive had pulled a gun:

> [Moxley] stopped, turned around, and raised his hand to fire. Moxley saw it was MacKay who was on his heels, wavered, and threw the gun over the fence. Moxley escaped that day. A few months later, when under arrest, MacKay asked him why he hadn't fired: 'I couldn't do it, Mac,' he said. 'I just couldn't do it.'

When Moxley was caught, he faced twenty charges of breaking, entering and stealing goods worth £3000. But he was no criminal mastermind, having sold much of the loot for pennies on the pound. Moxley played the sympathy card again in court, saying he couldn't get work and so it was a case of 'steal or starve'. The judge gave him three years.

Moxley was released in July 1925 – and the very next day began a string of cat burglaries around Sydney, stealing from places in Bellevue Hill and Point Piper in the east, Camperdown and Hurlstone Park in the west and Roseville and Waitara in the north. If nothing else, the man knew the city.

But Moxley didn't know how to stay free. In court in November, he claimed to have 'lost his head' since coming back from the war. After being released from gaol, he said, he'd been offered a job in Queanbeyan but couldn't get there because he had no money for a rail ticket and the Prisoners' Aid Society and Prisons Department wouldn't cough up. So he'd been forced to stay in Sydney and had lapsed back into these sorry ways.

His police record detailed how he'd force doors, break windows and even hide in premises he was going to burgle. On one occasion, he got away with £1500 worth of goods. Moxley was noted as an 'expert house and shop breaker' and 'a very agile and cunning thief' who 'consorts with vagrants' and 'frequents hotels and billiard-rooms'. He was sentenced to two years. But Moxley was also declared a 'habitual criminal', which meant the authorities could keep him inside indefinitely once he'd served his time. For his sins, he was to remain behind bars far longer than his sentence required. But Moxley was no use as a fizgig inside.

~

MacKay – the 'comet of the State Police Force', as *Truth* styled him – arrived back in Sydney from his overseas tour in April 1929. He was glad, as he put it, to 'get back into [the] harness', which included taking charge of police activities against the timber workers. In July he personally supervised the raid on Trades Hall in which seven union leaders were arrested, and the subsequent warrantless searches of the Labor Council's offices and the men's homes. The seven were charged by MacKay with conspiracy to threaten and assault 'volunteer workers' – otherwise known as strike breakers. This was a constant refrain from the cops and conservatives: that unionists deployed 'basher gangs' against 'scabs'.

Among those charged by Big Bill was Jock Garden. A fellow firebrand Scot, he'd been kicked out of the Labor Party as a communist and been a thorn in Lang's side during his first stint as premier from 1925 to 1927. But Garden had become disillusioned with communism and rejoined Labor, and was becoming one of the Big Fella's greatest allies as he campaigned against Nationalist premier Thomas Bavin in a bid to once again be state leader. While MacKay's trumped-up charges against Garden and the others were dropped, the government's use of the police against the timber workers remained ferocious. As Ray Blissett, then a constable and later a superintendent, would recall fondly of MacKay's 'flying squads':

> They were known among the timber workers as the basher gang,
> see, because they weren't above jumping out of a car and giving a

couple of pickets a hiding somewhere if they were causing a bit of trouble. And if they objected to getting a bit of a thumping, they'd say, 'Don't you swear at me,' and lock 'em up for using indecent language … In those days they did it and they got away with it.

A headline in *The Workers' Weekly* on 2 August 1929 read 'Sydney Police Run Amok Among the Pickets', the article depicting MacKay on the frontlines, him and his cops trying to provoke violence at a protest outside a Pyrmont timber yard:

Inspector MacKay, head of the Criminal Investigation Bureau – who is applying the mystic knowledge he acquired at Scotland Yard, not to running the dope gangs to earth, but to directing anti-picket squads – made himself particularly conspicuous. He loudly greeted one official of the Labor Council, for instance, with every filthy expression in the language.

In September 1929, Bavin's government signalled it was giving quasi-legal cover for police to break up even small groups of timber workers and coalminers by introducing an unlawful assemblies bill. That same month, MacKay was promoted to first-class inspector. Since returning from overseas, he had in fact been applying his 'mystic knowledge' to more than union suppression; he was working on a report that would reshape policing in New South Wales. But before it did, MacKay would stand accused of unleashing his cops to become killers.

~

Since February 1929, northern coalminers had remained locked out because they refused to accept that owners and the Nationalist state and federal governments could arbitrarily reduce their wages and conditions.

When the Labor Party's James Scullin won the federal election in October, it was on the back of a campaign that included promises to put the men back to work and lock up Rothbury colliery owner and caricature capitalist John 'The Baron' Brown. But a week after Scullin was sworn in as prime minister, Wall Street crashed.

With economic chaos looming, the new federal government wanted conciliation via a conference between themselves, the New South Wales government, mine owners and union officials. When this produced no solution, another was scheduled. But Premier Bavin wasn't willing to wait on the outcome of further federal gabfests. He struck a deal with mine owners to use 'volunteer workers' to open their collieries – starting with Rothbury – and sent his despised minister for mines and forests, Reginald Weaver, to the Hunter region to stir up trouble with the unionists and set up a camp for the scabs and the police who'd guard them. The battlelines were drawn.

In the early hours of Monday 16 December 1929, some 5000 miners assembled for a mass picket at Rothbury. When they marched on the colliery and tried to go over the fence, police rushed from the scrub and attacked with batons. Miners rained stones down on the cops. The battle raged until police started shooting and the miners retreated, some savagely beaten as they tried to escape, three suffering minor gunshot injuries.

After a stand-off, some miners attacked a car approaching the colliery because they believed it contained Weaver. Police rushed to defend the car, a battle erupted further down the fenceline and constables opened fire as miners scattered. This time the bullets did far more damage. Young miner Norman Brown took a bullet through the stomach as he tried to escape, and died before he arrived at Maitland Hospital. One man was hit in the throat, another in the spine and six others suffered serious wounds. More than a dozen more men were reportedly hit and sought treatment in secret.

The police had fired 122 shots and would claim, without evidence, that they'd only done so after being fired on. Their argument that they'd only shot into the ground or into the air was equally dubious. A new battle for Rothbury – this one for the truth – began in the days that followed.

The conservative newspapers lined up behind the police's version of events, praising their 'unflinching courage' and 'remarkable forbearance' in holding off before using their revolvers and in 'taking deliberate aim to ensure that no serious injury should be done to anyone'. In the New South Wales parliament, Labor opposition leader Lang railed against the Bavin government and said the 'swashbuckling minister' Weaver, 'with an army of police, went among the miners while they were yet peaceful, rattling the sabre'. As if on cue, Weaver entered the parliament to cries from one opposition member: 'Here comes the murderer!'

Tens of thousands of unionists and their supporters assembled in Hyde Park that night. Norman Brown's death, Jock Garden told the crowd, was 'wanton murder'. With the speeches over, there was a call for a march on state parliament. Most filtered away, but many made for Macquarie Street and were confronted by several hundred police.

Even the conservative newspapers painted a brutal picture. *The Sun* reported: 'Nothing happened, till the police, as though tired of being kept about for so long doing nothing, made their first sudden raid on the crowd. They drew their batons, which they did not hesitate to use on any who loitered.'

The Sydney Morning Herald said police 'struck at the heads and shoulders of those who were resisting them. There were several further baton charges and forays to chase pickets into laneways.' This was clearly offensive policing by officers unafraid of consequence.

The Lang-controlled paper *Labor Daily* reported: 'In one of the fiercest baton charges ever staged by police in Sydney, innumerable people were struck down in Queens Square last night. Excited constables, their conception of the position enlarged by the happenings at Rothbury, ruthlessly batoned men and women.'

The conversative press reported that a few people were hurt badly enough to seek treatment. *Labor Daily* put the injury toll far higher, naming citizens treated at Sydney Hospital and listing their injuries, including a husband and wife, he with concussion and her with shock and abrasions. All night, the paper said, people had visited the office to show their wounds and describe the beatings – including a well-known female journalist bashed for no reason. Several victims made official complaints. But New South Wales chief secretary Frank Chaffey said the police were 'to be commended for the way they stopped a determined attempt to rush on parliament house'. Reports of brutality were 'one-sided', and he simply didn't believe any women had been hit. In state parliament, Labor's whip labelled Bavin's regime a 'government of bashers, baton-wielders and batterers'.

Although MacKay wasn't at Rothbury on 16 December, he departed Sydney to take control the next day. With the mine operating again, a large number of police were camped inside to protect its scab workforce, and hundreds more were deployed around the coalfields. Their stated purpose was to keep the peace. In reality, this was a brutal campaign of intimidation and suppression, aided and directed by MacKay's infiltrators and agents provocateur.

Big Bill himself was in the thick of it. In the first week of January 1930, MacKay had his coat off and his sleeves up as he led two carloads of police in a warrantless raid on a unionist's house in search of a non-existent Gatling gun. Days later, MacKay and his men stopped a car carrying six miners. The inspector allegedly took one aside, punched him in the jaw and threatened: 'We are not going to shoot for fun next time.' Miners organised to protect themselves, with 400 war veterans establishing the Labour Defence Army. But Bavin wasn't going to tolerate such defiance. MacKay was given free rein to recruit seventy Sydney officers to form a flying squad that would go north and camp at Cessnock Racecourse.

On 15 January, 2000 unionists gathered in Kurri Kurri for a protest march. They'd obtained a permit, so this was a legal gathering. Twenty-four local police walked beside the men to ensure the proceedings remained peaceful. The march ended without incident and the miners were about to head home when the police basher gangs descended. *The Sun* reported:

> The flying squad arrived from Cessnock, and, jumping from the lorries and motorcycles which brought them, batons were drawn and the men charged. There was a wild scamper, men rushing in all directions. Women screamed, and a couple fainted, while the excitement lasted. The attack lasted about ... 10 or 15 minutes and then all was quiet again.

Tellingly, there were no arrests. Through the rest of that day, the flying squads roved around the coalfields, breaking up marches with violent and unprovoked baton attacks that injured a lot of people – and struck terror into an entire region.

Relief was also used as a weapon. During the Depression, the dole comprised food ration orders, which were handed out by police. Chief secretary Chaffey ordered that on the coalfields these only be given to 'persons who observe the law'. This, of course, was at the discretion of constables, who could thus deny sustenance to men for any perceived slight or infraction. At Kurri Kurri the same week of the bashing attacks, one quarter of the 800 men who applied for rations went home empty-handed, suffering inflicted not only on them but also on their wives and children – as had been the case during the entire lockout.

When the inquest was held in February to establish how Norman Brown had been fatally shot at Rothbury, the coroner found it had been a tragic accident that resulted from a stray police bullet – even though the police had laudably *not* fired into the crowd. Despite getting no federal legal relief, the miners held out for the next four months, as intimidation and deprivation continued on the coalfields. But in mid-1930, facing a second brutal winter amid ever-worsening economic prospects, the Miners' Federation voted to go back to work, accepting the cut pay and reduced conditions.

MacKay had been in the papers day after day while the coalfield battles raged, a hero to the right wing and centre, a villain to the left wing and radicals. When Lang's *Labor Daily* printed an article headlined 'Bavin Wants Bloody War!', it listed MacKay's crimes as including murder, grievous bodily harm, assault, warrantless searches and conspiracy to frame leaders. Yet, strangely, the paper also saw fit to comment: 'Mr MacKay cannot be wholly blamed. His is a dirty job, but it is his job, and men have done even worse in their time ...'

A cynic might have wondered whether Lang was looking to a future in which he would be the one to wield a weapon as formidable as MacKay.

~

MacKay's report to Walter Childs, father of fingerprinting in Australia and now CIB superintendent and acting commissioner, ushered in big policing changes starting from New Year's Day 1930. The biggest might make tainted crime scenes – like Vera Stirling's – a thing of the past. As *The Sydney Morning Herald* explained:

> The present system whereby detectives operate from headquarters, and are summoned after local police have already inquired into a crime and realised its seriousness or difficulty, has permitted a great deal of overlapping. Upon countless occasions detectives have been summoned to investigate major crimes after some of the main clues have been handled or obliterated. First on the scene have been the local police, then have come the detectives, the inquiries of each militating against the possibilities of success against each other.

Sydney policing would now work on an area system – A, B, C and D – roughly corresponding with the points of the compass. Each was under the command of an inspector, with those men supervised by MacKay, and each had its own senior detectives and uniformed men, who were expected to know every inch of their turf and to be capable of handling serious investigations. But a crew of specialist detectives – including Tom McRae – were at the CIB and ready at a moment's notice to join squads assembled to solve major crimes.

The CIB got new, larger offices at Central Police Station, in a lane between George and Pitt streets in the heart of the city. New investigative protocols were instituted and the Modus Operandi section was established. Under the 'Modus Operandi' record-keeping and retrieval system, when a crime was committed, clerks could quickly pull the records of all crooks known to operate in a similar way. Detectives then reviewed these rap sheets to narrow down potential suspects. The fingerprint and photographic branches also had their own CIB offices, so when criminals were brought in they could be promptly inked and have their mugs shot. Central's radio operators got the latest equipment to broadcast orders to the powerful wireless cars assigned to constantly patrol the city's four areas. Police boxes would start to be placed on the streets. These functioned as mini-stations for beat cops, who could use them to temporarily detain a prisoner until a 'Black Maria' van could collect them. When urgent action was required, CIB telephone operators would make calls to the boxes to advise patrolmen to be on the lookout for this or that suspect or car. There were a few boxes at first but it wouldn't be long before there were hundreds. As far as possible, these changes sought to throw a police net over Sydney.

But MacKay went further for his CIB detectives, who'd begun as young cops without any rights or perks. Central Police Station didn't only have a billiard room and library, it also had a first-floor cafe serving hot dinners. In a nice touch, this was run by Giuseppe 'Joe' Mucci, who claimed to be the son of the late crowned head of Italy, meaning the top cops were getting meals fit for a king and cooked by a prince.

Sydney policing really was entering a new age thanks to Big Bill.

4

McRae on the Murder Trail

Although Detective-Sergeant Third Class Thomas Walter McRae was stationed at the CIB, Commissioner Walter Childs and Inspector Billy MacKay increasingly made his unofficial 'area' the rest of the state – at least when there was a suspicious death. It made sense: he had spent nearly a decade as a country copper.

At the end of March 1930, McRae was off to Barraba, near Armidale, where two unemployed men camped by the river had been attacked by an unknown assailant. One chap survived the bashing. The other, Thomas O'Brien, died from suffocation, having inhaled his false teeth, broken as his head was kicked in. Within days, McRae nabbed a local roughneck named Edwin Campbell, taking the man's incriminating statement that he'd hit a man 'a few times' when drunk.

While the accused was in the Armidale lock-up, his relatives left packages for him. Showing a startling lack of initiative, the local police reportedly asked McRae what to do. Open them, he ordered. The parcels contained razors and a bottle of strychnine. Denied the chance to suicide, Campbell stood trial for manslaughter. McRae's testimony, witness accounts and the physical evidence saw him sentenced to seven years.

McRae was next in Berry, on the South Coast, investigating the murder of labourer Arthur Wornes. Working with the local police, McRae learned Wornes had been out riding when he met his best mate, Charlie Laurence. Smelling rum on his chum, he asked for a belt from Laurence's flask. Wornes then rode home, where he told his wife, Martha, he was sick from drink given to him by his friend, and thought he'd been poisoned. She summoned a doctor but her husband died soon afterwards, the post-mortem analysis revealing he'd been killed with strychnine.

McRae interviewed Laurence, who denied everything. Then he cracked. 'The thing has been worrying me ever since I did it and I want to get it off my mind,' he allegedly said. 'I want to tell you the lot.' He signed a statement saying he'd put strychnine in his flask, knowing that he'd encounter Wornes and what would happen. Laurence told McRae where he'd hidden the flask and the tin of poison.

Why had Laurence done it? At the inquest, McRae said the accused told him Wornes had given him 'permission' to visit his home whenever he liked – whether he was there or Martha was by herself. During the proceedings, Laurence sat listlessly – except when the attractive widow gave evidence, upon which he buried his head in his hands and sobbed convulsively. Martha testified that she and Arthur had been happy but also that her husband's alleged killer – whom she'd known for eighteen years – had been a 'frequent visitor' to their home over the past six months.

At trial, Laurence's counsel claimed his statement was inadmissible because it hadn't been made voluntarily. It was the age-old question of whom to believe. The judge ordered the jury to retire while evidence was heard from McRae and a Berry local constable. They said the usual: the statement was made without any threat or promise. From the dock, Laurence made a statement – which was unsworn and not subject to cross-examination – in which he claimed he'd only made his confession to protect Martha, because the Berry copper had said one of them was going down for the murder. The judge rejected the allegation and admitted the statement, which effectively scuttled Laurence's defence before the jury. Found guilty, he was sentenced to death.

Laurence maintained his innocence and intimated that he was protecting 'someone'. Martha publicly denied she was that someone, or that she'd been intimate with him or had anything to do with her husband's murder. She said she wanted Laurence to hang. But the last time someone went to the gallows in New South Wales had been in 1924. Laurence's death sentence was commuted to life imprisonment.

McRae didn't do all his major investigations outside Sydney – and not every suspicious death resulted in him hunting for a killer. Late in 1930, he was on the case of elderly wool broker Frank Bell, found dead at Taylor Bay, near Mosman, with a bullet in his head and a revolver near the body. Everything pointed to suicide. At a time when this was shameful, and thought to ensure eternal damnation, Bell's family wouldn't accept that their loved one had killed himself. McRae's enquiries found no evidence of foul play, and that the man had a recent history of depression. But with his efforts to trace the revolver's ownership unsuccessful, coroner Mr May returned an open verdict. How the detective felt about his efforts amounting to nought can be guessed. But despite the varying outcomes in these cases, through his investigations into the deaths of Frank Bell, Arthur Wornes, Thomas O'Brien and Vera Stirling, McRae had gained valuable experience that would soon be useful when he was confronted with similar but far more sensational cases.

~

William Moxley was finally released in August 1929. Two months later, Wall Street crashed. The carpentry skills Moxley had honed in prison wouldn't be much protection against the economic woes to come. But while Moxley had been inside, MacKay's star had risen even higher. Moxley was soon snitching for him again.

The relationship wasn't always smooth. The inspector suspected his informer was taking payment but feeding him 'hooey'. So he asked

Frank Fahy – aka The Shadow – what he knew.

'Moxley's scared stiff just now,' the undercover man told his boss. 'He knows the boys suspect he's been fizgigging, and he's frightened of what might happen to him.'

MacKay ordered Fahy to tail Moxley, who was supposed to be keeping tabs on safecrackers hiding in Manly. The Shadow watched unseen as the fizgig spent police money at a wine bar, then stumbled into a brothel for a happy ending to his night.

The next day MacKay hauled Moxley into his office and demanded an update. Moxley lied his head off, saying he'd been at Manly keeping an eye on the crooks.

'Get out of here, Moxley,' MacKay thundered, 'and don't ever let me see you coming in here again unless you're under arrest!' He rattled off Moxley's every mendacious movement. 'I had you followed, and you never went near Manly. And don't look to me for any protection from the crooks you knock about with after this. They'll be after you, and I've finished with you. Get out!'

Despite the ultimatum, Moxley continued informing – likely still for MacKay directly, but at the very least for his subordinates. Such snitching paid off on the night of Saturday 20 September 1930 in Sutherland, when a dramatic road chase ended with Detective-Sergeant Lionel Bowie and his patrol car crew arresting men suspected of being about to break into a bank. The quartet of crooks – Ernest Devine, Albert Kellow, Richard Pearce and Raymond Skelly – were charged with having a gun, explosives and housebreaking tools in their possession. Each was allowed free on bail, to appear in court the following month.

For these villains, the pressing question was this: how had Bowie and his men known what they were up to? There was only one answer – a rat in their criminal ranks.

Three weeks later, on another Saturday night, Moxley was found shot in the head on Parramatta Road in Auburn. 'Man Dying in Hospital,' read

The Daily Pictorial's headline. But Moxley didn't die. He'd been blasted in the right ear and undergone an operation to remove fragments of lead in his head. By Monday, his long face framed by bandages, Moxley was propped up in his hospital bed and giving his story to *The Evening News*.

He said he'd gone for a drive with three men and they'd been having a beer in his car at Auburn when one had shot him point blank. The other two grabbed him and the gunman had stuck the revolver in Moxley's mouth, but it had misfired. He'd kicked his way free. 'I managed to struggle out of the car in which we were sitting, and ran on to Parramatta Road, where I was picked up by a motorist.'

Moxley was lucky to be alive. '[Doctors] told me that the bullet struck a bone and went down my neck. If the bullet had gone into my brain, I wouldn't be here now.' Moxley's occupation was given as carpenter, though it was noted he was known to police. Whatever he was, he wasn't a snitch. 'I haven't told the police anything, and I don't intend to do so,' he said. 'There were three of them. I know them all, and I'll get them!'

Moxley's bravado surely masked huge trauma. He'd nearly been murdered and would suffer a great deal. He remained in hospital for eleven days, enduring oozing wounds and painful swelling in his neck. On several occasions, Moxley was 'very abusive' to his carers. An X-ray confirmed that lead fragments remained in his head – including a quarter-inch piece above the mandible. Given his father's fate from a bullet in the belly, Moxley likely wondered whether the metal inside him would cause his own slow death. Nevertheless, he refused a further operation and checked himself out, against doctor's orders. In the wake of the shooting, he would suffer headaches and exhibit a 'stuttery' way of speaking.

As for Moxley not telling the police anything – this was an utter nonsense that few crims would've believed. He sang like a bird. On the day after the attempted murder, MacKay led raids on Redfern houses, narrowly missing the men who'd tried to blow off his fizgig's head. But Ernest Devine, a notoriously violent criminal, was caught soon enough, along with another thug named Robert Duncan. The third man, Albert Kellow, however, evaded capture.

At the November committal hearing for Devine and Duncan, Moxley said he'd been driving the car, with the accused and Kellow as his passengers. Moxley claimed he had refused to participate in a hold-up the trio were planning. Devine had pulled a revolver and was playing around with it. Addressing Moxley by a nickname, he said: 'Well, Snowy, I am going to shoot you.' Moxley thought he was joking. But a few minutes later, Devine said, 'You are a friend of Bowie!' Moxley had denied this vehemently.

Devine got out of the car, walked around to the driver's side and in a flash shot Moxley in the ear, knocking him across the seat. Kellow had asked: 'Did you get him?' Moxley heard Devine say: 'Yes, I think I got him all right.'

Stunned, but thinking he wasn't badly hurt, Moxley sat up and asked why he'd been shot. Devine repeated the Bowie accusation. Kellow said: 'You told the police that we were going to Sutherland to rob the bank that night.' Moxley denied it. Kellow said: 'You did, and you are a friend of Bowie's.'

Moxley told the court: 'Devine then leaned over the seat, while the others grabbed him, and said, "I'm going to put this bullet right down your neck!"' Moxley recounted the moment he thought he was going to die: 'Devine aimed the revolver at my head a few inches off. Then he pulled the trigger, but the gun misfired.' Moxley kicked Duncan, struggled free, threw open the car door and made his escape.

Devine and Duncan went to trial in December, charged with having maliciously wounded Moxley with intent to cause grievous bodily harm. Their defence was that Moxley had been struggling for a revolver with another man – they didn't name the still-missing Kellow – when the gun had gone off. Under cross-examination, Moxley admitted he'd been declared a habitual criminal in New South Wales and he lied to say he'd been innocent of his trouble in Queensland, before claiming, 'I am now a reformed man.' The judge directed the jury to acquit Duncan – and they then found Devine not guilty. Kellow wouldn't be charged when he resurfaced shortly afterwards. Both Devine and Kellow would get twelve months with hard labour for the original charge of planning to break into the Sutherland bank – these convictions made possible in the first place by Moxley's work as a fizgig.

For his trouble, Moxley came out of the ordeal with nothing but trauma, bullet fragments in his head and a new widespread reputation as a police informant. Just because he was a habitual criminal, was it right for the judge and jury to disbelieve what he'd said about Devine, Duncan and Kellow trying to murder him? Given the ripple effects of such decisions, several lives might have been saved if Moxley's evidence had been accepted, if Devine and Duncan had been given harsh sentences, and if Kellow had faced the same punishment when he was caught. Sadly, Devine and Kellow each followed a trajectory to tragedy that saw them take innocents with them during the very type of vengeful rages described by Moxley.

In March 1952 Devine's de facto wife Joyce Vining fled with her children to her parents' flat in Kings Cross. He came after her. In a fury, in front of everyone, he said, 'This is your finish,' pulled a gun from his pocket and shot her in the head, and then pumped a bullet into his own skull. She died within an hour of reaching St Vincent's Hospital; Devine expired there two days later.

In August 1954, in a similarly maniacal rampage, Kellow chased his wife, Lavina, into the yard of their Darlington house, bashed her with a brick and then bounced her head off a path until their twenty-year-old daughter pushed him away and cradled her mother. Kellow stalked away, returned with a rifle, killed his wife with a bullet through the face and then went upstairs to shoot himself dead.

Yet twenty years *before* these bloodbaths, Devine, Duncan and Kellow's attempted assassination of MacKay's fizgig Moxley was directly and inextricably linked to three even more horrifying deaths in Sydney.

~

In June 1930 the Bank of England's emissary Sir Otto Niemeyer was sent to Australia to offer an austerity cure for Australia's economic woes. The bitter medicine – cut spending on public works and welfare, accept a lower standard of living and prioritise the repayment of loan interest owed to Britain – split the nation. In New South Wales, it also galvanised support for Jack Lang, who gave thundering speeches in front of crowds of up to 100,000 people.

The Big Fella would campaign in the upcoming state election on increasing spending on public works to put people in jobs, reversing salary cuts for public servants and restoring the forty-four-hour week. Lang also wasn't letting anyone forget what Bavin had done at Rothbury. But in the days before voters went to the polls, there was another curious hint at a forthcoming rapprochement between former enemies.

At the tenth annual CIB night to entertain prominent citizens, Billy MacKay, just promoted from Inspector to Superintendent Third Class, made a point of speaking about Rothbury. The law of the CIB, he said, was not to reason why but to obey the orders of the government. *Truth* hit the nail on the head: 'As the dinner was held almost on the eve of the election battle, his references were far from "in apropos".' Lang won in a landslide on 25 October 1930.

In the wake of Labor's victory, *The Workers' Weekly* said miners wanted MacKay and other senior police who'd orchestrated the coalfields terror campaigns to be sacked. 'W.W. readers echo their wishes,' the paper wrote, 'but will Lang & Co. do the job and kick them out? We are doubtful.' It had also hit the nail on the head. MacKay – who'd led the charge on unionists – would now obey Lang and take the fight to the premier's enemies, who would quickly grow in number until chaos and crisis had many citizens worried about civil war.

On the day of Lang's election, Moxley, just a few days out of hospital, bullet fragments in his head thanks to his work for Big Bill, had no idea that his life would ultimately depend on the political fate of the Big Fella.

5

In the Execution of Their Duty

In early January 1930, when the coalfields were battlefields, *The Sydney Morning Herald* had reported on the esprit de corps among MacKay's men: 'Everyone in Rothbury camp was well prepared for a strenuous fight, and the police, especially the volunteer men, were literally on their toes with expectancy.' Among the hundreds of officers deployed to Rothbury were two young constables who'd become firm friends and whose names would go down in New South Wales police history a year later.

Ernest Andrews was born in 1908 on the Isle of Wight and migrated to Australia in November 1928, joining the New South Wales police force the following April. An unmarried man, he had only one relative in Australia – a sister in Newcastle. In the short time Andrews had been in the police force, he'd not only served at Rothbury but shown his bravery by chasing down and peacefully disarming a deranged man carrying a loaded revolver on Macquarie Street.

Adam 'Scotty' Denholm was also an immigrant. Born in Scotland in 1906, he'd come with his family to Australia when he was four and grown up in Goodna, Queensland. Like his father, he was an expert dog trainer. Scotty had also been middleweight boxing champion of Queensland in 1926, and soon after had moved to Sydney to join the police. At Rothbury, to entertain himself when he wasn't on duty, he bought an Alsatian pup, which he trained and later gave to his dad.

Since Rothbury, the two constables, both stationed at George Street North, had taken a house together in Woollahra. Andrews was amused that Denholm couldn't help himself, training a neighbour's dog to do amazing tricks. When the weather was good and the young cops were on a later shift, they'd hit the beach before starting work.

Saturday 3 January 1931 brought one of these mornings. The mates were at a tram stop near Bondi Junction, wearing civvies and carrying their towels, when they heard a series of bangs from farther down busy Oxford Street.

'A shot or just a backfire?' Denholm asked.

'A shot!' Andrews said. 'Look – there's a crowd down the road. Must be a hold-up. Come on!'

Andrews was off like a rocket, Denholm struggling to keep up at first, until he kicked off the uncomfortable shoes he'd been trying to break in and raced barefoot after his mate. Neither knew they were running headlong at a hulking man haunted by his experience of *not* serving in the Great War.

John Kennedy's battle had been long and painful – and fought mostly inside the confines of his own skull. Born in Sydney around 1889, he'd grown to stand six-foot-two and weigh sixteen stone. In 1914, though dedicated to his mother and earning a small fortune as one of the city's few colour printers, Kennedy was prepared to sacrifice everything to fight for King and country. But when he tried to enlist in the AIF, he was rejected on account of his varicose veins. He subjected himself to the painful and expensive process of having them stripped, but Kennedy was again knocked back. Sometime afterwards, someone concluded that this big, fit-looking young man was a coward, and sent him white feathers day after day. Like other men treated in this disgraceful manner, Kennedy was ashamed and frustrated; unlike other victims, he couldn't forget it and move on.

After a brief farewell to his family, Kennedy went overseas without saying where he was going or what he was doing. It turned out he went to Canada, where he joined the North-West Mounted Police and trained as a marksman. Back in Australia, his siblings hired private detectives to try to find some trace of him, and one gumshoe's investigations led them to believe their brother had been killed in an anarchist's bomb explosion in San Francisco.

Then, in mid-1928, Kennedy showed up in Sydney at his sister's workplace. She fainted from the surprise. But he was in for a bigger shock when he learned that their mum had been dead eight years. With grief adding to his mental woes, Kennedy became increasingly reclusive – and still brooded over those white feathers.

Around March 1930, again working as a printer, Kennedy moved into a cottage a few blocks south of Bondi Junction. He bought a .22-calibre repeater rifle and stockpiled huge amounts of ammunition. Isolated and having lost his job over his odd behaviour, Kennedy sank deeper into mental illness. He obsessed over cigarettes, imagined poisoning plots against him, and acted out militaristic fantasies, marching around his backyard, rifle on his shoulder, re-enacting Zulu War battles and obeying drill orders only he could hear.

Neighbours worried about ricochets from the hundred rounds a day Kennedy would fire on the little shooting range he'd set up. Although frightened, they thought it none of their business and didn't report him to the police. If they had, he might've been arrested on an insanity charge and held at Darlinghurst Reception House until a doctor could make a recommendation to a magistrate about release or further detention in an asylum.

Instead, through December 1930, Kennedy's strange behaviour escalated. Every day for weeks, he'd enter Oxford Street shops, demand cigarettes or other goods and then refuse to hand over money, shouting things like 'I won't pay – I'm a communist!' and 'Charge them to the Supreme Court!'

On the summer morning of 3 January 1931, Kennedy, gun in hand and bowie knife on his belt, stalked to the Mick Simmons store in Bondi Junction, where he demanded cigars and cigarettes and tried to leave without paying. When the manager blocked the exit, he laughed maniacally, hurled the smokes on the counter and threatened: 'You be careful or you'll face the firing squad.' Kenncdy ran off, and the manager sent his salesgirl to find the nearest police officer.

This turned out to be Constable Norman Allen. Born in Goulburn in 1901, he'd been educated at Brisbane Grammar School and worked in a bank and on his father's property before moving to Sydney in 1926, where he joined the police and briefly served as a mounted constable. Yet he changed his mind and resigned to train as an Anglican minister. Deciding that being a man of the cloth wasn't his calling after all, he went back to the police in September 1928, and was stationed at Waverley. It was around this time he and his wife had their first child.

Now Constable Allen heard about the big bloke with a rifle. He seemingly knew the oddball the salesgirl was talking about. 'Don't you worry,' Allen said, 'it won't take long to deal with him.' Stepping onto the footboard of a bus heading west along Oxford Street, Allen saw Kennedy loping along the footpath and waving his gun at bewildered pedestrians.

The constable jumped from the bus, caught up to him and put his hand on Kennedy's shoulder. 'Just a minute, old man,' he said. 'You can't carry a rifle round the streets like this, you know.'

Kennedy turned, lifted the .22 and fired three times. The young policeman crumpled in a pool of his own blood. As the Saturday-morning shoppers reeled and screamed, Kennedy looked down at Allen, then quietly walked away.

Detective-Constable Andrew McGill of Paddington saw what happened from a passing bus, jumped off and chased after Kennedy, who whirled and raised the rifle. Unarmed, McGill could only ask why he'd just shot his colleague. His eyes mad, Kennedy growled: 'I have passed sentence on him according to the law. You had better leave me alone. I am only exercising the law.'

Kennedy walked south along Newland Street, pedestrians scattering before him and McGill following at a distance. A young Bondi bloke named Steve Robinson, who'd witnessed the shooting and, hoping he could help, had taken Allen's revolver, had also joined the chase. By now, off-duty constables Andrews and Denholm had shouldered through the crowd and found Allen bleeding out on the footpath. A young witness said: 'A man shot him. A loony – but I'll show you where he lives, where he's gone.' With nothing they could do for their wounded comrade and an ambulance on the way, the two constables followed this youth south of Oxford Street.

John Kennedy arrived at his Lawson Street cottage, whirled to aim his rifle at McGill again, then with a laugh ran inside and bolted his heavy front door. Catching up, Steve Robinson gave Allen's revolver to McGill. Meanwhile, Andrews and Denholm were racing through the rear of neighbouring properties. A woman shouted a warning: 'Look out. He's raving mad. He has been running about the yard naked lately.' At this time, Constable Thomas Johnson, one of Allen's best mates, was racing on a motorbike from Waverley station with Sergeant James Seery.

Reaching the fence bordering Kennedy's backyard, Andrews was met by another uniformed officer, Constable Henry Rolfe, and saw a narrow flight of steps up to the back door of the gunman's house. 'We will go in and get him,' Andrews said.

Rolfe replied: 'No, wait a minute. He's got it on us. He can see us and we can't see him.'

Andrews said: 'Give me your gun. I will go.' Rolfe refused, telling him not to rush a madman. But Andrews wasn't listening. He went through a gap in the fence, despite Denholm catching up and calling out: 'Go easy.' But with Andrews running up the stairs, Denholm scrambled after his mate.

Andrews reached the landing. Kennedy roared from inside: 'Don't come in here!'

The constable opened the door, the gunman fired twice at Andrews and then aimed the rifle at Denholm, who jumped clear before he could shoot again. At the front of the house, Johnson and Seery, who were trying to break in the door, heard shots and the chaos of a wild fight inside. Then there was an ominous silence.

Denholm rushed along the side of the house, grabbed the service pistol from McGill, raced back and charged up the back stairs. But Kennedy was then storming up the hallway, raising his rifle at Johnson, who'd smashed the leadlight to try to unlock the front door. The madman pulled the trigger. Nothing happened – his gun was jammed. Johnson fired his automatic through the leadlight and hit Kennedy in the chest. The gunman screamed, staggered deeper into the house and disappeared from view.

Coming in from the back, Denholm saw what Kennedy had done to his friend. Andrews had taken two bullets in the chest and then been all but decapitated with the bowie knife. Johnson and Seery, having broken in, found Kennedy on his bed, alive but bleeding heavily. Though seriously wounded, he fought ferociously as he was taken from the house to the ambulance.

Unlike Constable Norman Allen, who had died as he was being carried into St Vincent's, Kennedy survived long enough to give a dying deposition from his hospital bed. He declared he was Lord Judge John Kennedy and he'd gone to the Mick Simmons store to retrieve cigarettes stolen from him in 1888 and 1893, taking the rifle because he'd been targeted for assassination by the Canadian police. Kennedy said he'd shot Allen in self-defence and then executed Andrews in accordance with the death sentence he'd passed on the officer.

Before he died, Kennedy raved to his brother-in-law: 'How many Germans have you killed, Jack? Not enough! Go and do your duty like me! Get some more!'

On Monday 5 January 1931, the state paid tribute to the slain policemen, with thousands of people lining George Street as hearses took the coffins to the mortuary station at Central for their final journey to Rookwood Cemetery, where they were laid to rest side by side.

'They saw their duty and the fear of death could not deter them,' the reverend told hundreds of mourners at this graveside. 'These two young men, Norman Thomas Allen and Ernest Andrews, died in the execution of their duty. There is no higher glory to which a man can aspire.'

But there were reasonable questions as to whether Andrews and Denholm had been foolhardy. If so, perhaps it was understandable. Andrews had just four months earlier peacefully disarmed a deranged fellow with a revolver, while Denholm was a boxing champion who had his mate's back, in the spirit of comradeship forged at Rothbury. Following the tragedy, Denholm called himself 'the luckiest man alive' but was otherwise too traumatised to speak to the newspapers.

Coroner Edwin May tried to draw a line under murmurings about the constables when concluding the inquest:

> I can hardly find words to express appreciation of their great bravery in facing the madman as they did. Some people might say that they were a little too brave, but there is no doubt that they took their lives into their hands in trying to arrest this madman without having to take his life.

Mr May was sorry to hear that Denholm had been criticised, saying he'd done everything he could; if he had rushed the maniac unarmed, then New South Wales would probably have buried three police officers instead of two. It's very likely Denholm suffered trauma and felt immense survivor's guilt, and endured sideways glances from some colleagues. But CIB chief Billy MacKay – who always played favourites, particularly with fellow Scots – had the young constable's back. The inspector would take him under his wing and give him the chance to play a prominent role in New South Wales police history, not once but twice.

6

Old Bill's Porridge, Silent Bill's Patience and the Rise of the Right

In the same week New South Wales buried the victims of the first double murder of police since 1877, Tom McRae was ordered to Yadboro, twenty-five miles inland from the little South Coast village of Milton, to investigate a poisoning that could've killed dairy farmer John Rixon, his teenage daughter and two of his workers. Eating their morning porridge, they found it tasted bitter and threw it away. All four became violently ill from the little they'd swallowed. They soon recovered, but a dog that ate the discarded scraps died in spasms.

McRae learned that the porridge, which the government analyst found contained strychnine, had been made from oatmeal delivered as usual with other groceries to the family's roadside box. Was there a tainted batch or had the family been targeted? Recalling his days as a Cooma constable, the detective-sergeant from Sydney's CIB saddled up a packhorse and rode through hilly cow country for several days to question farmers living in remote homesteads. Some had oatmeal from the same consignment. None had been sick. Someone had tried to murder the Rixons.

Questioning John about any enemies he might have, McRae learned of bitter Rixon family disputes that dated to 1928. The previous

September, John had argued with his uncle William, who was also his landlord. 'Old Bill', as he was known, had said he'd get his nephew off the farm. Under questioning, Old Bill told McRae his side of the dispute and denied any wrongdoing. But his brother Albert Rixon wasn't as staunch. He said when Old Bill knew he was going to be interrogated, he'd asked him to hide a bottle of pure strychnine. Assisted by the CIB's Detective-Sergeant Len Allmond, McRae searched the suspect's property and found the poison stashed in a tree. When McRae showed it to Old Bill, and revealed he'd been ratted out by Albert, the codger said: 'Well, if he has told you that, I had better tell the truth.'

Old Bill said his no-good nephew had stolen his cattle and guns, hadn't repaid money he'd borrowed and was generally ungrateful for all the help he'd given. So when Old Bill had been going along the road and had seen the groceries, he'd made a spur of the moment decision to sprinkle some strychnine in the sack of oats. Why did he have a bottle of poison in his pocket? To kill wild dogs. But he told McRae he hadn't meant to kill John: 'I thought that I was only putting in enough to frighten them and to make them sick.'

At the committal hearing in Milton Court in mid-February, Old Bill was represented by fiery barrister William Dovey – soon to be a King's Counsel, later a Supreme Court judge and father-in-law to Gough Whitlam. In his questioning, Dovey flirted with the theory that McRae had fitted up his client and that John Rixon had poisoned himself and the others to frame his uncle. But that was never going to stick. Old Bill was committed to stand trial for attempted murder – and he would have to face court up in Sydney.

McRae had bested Dovey in this round. When they squared off again nearly a decade down the track, the results would be far more bruising for the detective.

Old Bill went to trial at the end of March. His defence was that he hadn't used enough poison to endanger anyone's life. But it was shown there had been enough strychnine in the oats to kill John Rixon. Old Bill was sentenced to six years. But the appeals court accepted that no evidence had been given about *how* the poison was distributed through the oats, and thus it hadn't been established that any *one* serving of porridge would be fatal. In an unusual move, this appeals court acted as it believed the jury should have, finding Old Bill guilty on a lesser charge of poisoning with intent to injure, aggrieve or annoy. His sentence was cut in half.

How McRae felt about this hair-splitting might again be guessed. In any event, he'd done his job, putting his second poisoner in prison and gaining further experience he would soon call on in a case far removed from cow country.

~

In February 1931, at the same time journalists were chuckling about handcuffed hillbilly Old Bill taking his first-ever train trip to stand his trial in the big smoke of Sydney, a new threat was stirring away from the prying eyes of these pressmen. At a secret meeting at the Imperial Service Club, thirty-seven-year-old Great War veteran and city solicitor Colonel Eric Campbell and a small band of ex-AIF officers founded the New Guard; it was so named because it sought to supplant an existing right-wing paramilitary called the Old Guard, whose offer of auxillary policing support MacKay had privately accepted.

In the month or so that followed, this shadowy outfit was the stuff of rumours and jokes. But the Labor Party wasn't laughing. It called a rally in the Domain on Sunday 29 March, where 6000 people turned up to vote into existence the Australian Labor Army, which would 'meet with force and smash a Fascist attempt to install a dictator'. Federal member of parliament and ardent Lang supporter Jack Beasley warned that the New Guard was 'recruited from non-commissioned officers and officers of the

AIF, to attack, at the psychological time, the present Labor government and those behind it'.

That day's resolution said the present Depression was being intensified by the capitalists of Great Britain and Australia, who, in retaliation for rejecting the Niemeyer policy, were fostering 'seditious organisations' such as the New Guard to 'overthrow the Labor movement and, by force, the Lang Government'. Senator Jack Dunn – another Lang loyalist – promised that 'if the working classes are forced to the barricades, then, so far as I am concerned, it is going to be shot for shot'. Donald Grant – who had been convicted on MacKay's evidence at the IWW trial in 1916 – thundered: 'If there is going to be civil war, we are going to win.'

Two weeks later, the New Guard's structure and statement of purpose was made public. Trades Hall Council heard from a unionist who'd gained entry to a meeting at Collaroy. His report was detailed by *Labor Daily*, although, for unknown reasons, it only identified the leader as 'a military colonel'. Readers learned the New Guard was organised on strictly military lines, with the state divided into four districts, each under a commandant who reported to a controlling council of ten men. The colonel predicted that the imminent collapse of the dole system would be followed by societal disorganisation, discontent and disturbance. This was when the New Guard would restore order. Its rank-and-file members would serve as mobile troops, home troops for carrying on industry, troops for guarding and supplying those workers, and 'another section for a variety of purely military duties'. Naturally, faced with chaos, Lang's Labor government would try to appoint special constables who would be loyal to them, so the New Guard would have to step in to help carry out police duties. The colonel told his audience he had already been in 'close communication' with Superintendent MacKay.

The New Guard sounded ominously like a private right-wing army intent on a coup, and Trades Hall voted to alert the government to its aims and objectives. Having seen his name taken in vain, MacKay acted fast to set the record straight in the next day's *Labor Daily*:

> The gentleman who approached me, and who spoke at a supposed secret meeting of an organisation, termed the 'New Guard' at Collaroy ... did not give the whole of the conversation that transpired between us. I warned him not to have anything to do with such an organisation. The suggestion that the police would need assistance, I emphasised, was without foundation and absolutely unnecessary. Any organisation that advocated the doctrine of force, which is not organised by authority and acknowledged by the government, is illegal and its organisers may lay themselves open to a charge of sedition. I say definitely that I have given no encouragement to this or any similar secret organisation which seeks to break the laws of the land.

Colonel Campbell risked making a powerful enemy in Big Bill.

~

The day after Anzac Day in 1931, McRae found himself looking at a dead woman who recalled poor Vera Stirling. Emma Philbrook, a fifty-year-old widow, had been found in the bedroom of her run-down Surry Hills terrace. 'Old Kate', as she was known, had a gash on her head and was fully clothed except for one silk stocking tight around her neck. Inspector Prior, who had charge of Area C, took charge, assisted by McRae and Detective-Sergeant Matthew Sedgwick.

Alerted by a neighbour, who'd seen the dead woman through a window, detectives and the witness had to break in because the back and front doors were locked. This pointed to suicide. So did the fact there were no signs of a struggle or any blood-encrusted weapon. Newspapermen's interviews with locals painted Old Kate as a violent-tempered, drunken manic-depressive living in squalor who'd once attempted to poison herself, and had talked of getting it right next time. Yet if she'd strangled herself, how and where had she sustained the head wound? Falling against furniture or fittings would have left bloodstains. One theory was that she'd drunkenly toppled in the streets before coming home, and in her delirium had done herself in. But had Old Kate known how to tie a reef knot like the one around her neck?

If not, and she was murdered, what was the motive? She hadn't been robbed. Maybe it had been the result of a drunken row with, as *The Sun* put it, 'one of the many men with whom she was associated'. Maybe her killer had jumped from her small balcony to make his escape. But he would've been conspicuous, and no neighbour reported anything like that. Nor were there chips out of the rusty railing to suggest a man had climbed over it.

As usual, the newspapers floated all theories and opinions in the early days of the investigation. But gradually mistakes were corrected and the depiction of Old Kate as a suicidal harridan receded. While she had been an alcoholic and an insomniac, she'd been well-groomed and well-dressed and regarded as benevolent and good-natured. The outside of her house was shabby, but she'd kept the inside in pristine condition, and her front door was fitted with a Yale lock, which would click behind anyone leaving.

Police told *The Sydney Morning Herald* they believed that, late on 24 April, Old Kate had been sitting at her settee, having removed one stocking, when she was struck on the head with a heavy blow. Once she was unconscious, her killer strangled her.

Inspector Prior was nicknamed 'Silent Bill' or 'William the Silent' for his habit of telling reporters 'I could answer that question but I'm not saying anything.' Now he was holding back a crucial clue. A partly consumed bottle of port wine had been found on Old Kate's bedroom mantelpiece, and it bore fingerprints belonging to a thirty-five-year-old Swede named Gustav Reichardt. Further, the inspector had learned that in Stanmore, on the afternoon of 24 April, this creep had violently assaulted Gwenholme Latham, a fourteen-year-old girl he'd been 'seeing' with her mother's consent.

In the hours between that attack and Old Kate's murder, a man fitting Reichardt's description bought a bottle of port wine at a pub in nearby Enmore. Following the mother's complaint against Reichardt, a warrant for his arrest for assault had already been issued, and his details and description circulated to police in all states. But procedure at this time didn't include divulging the names of murder suspects to the press. So there was nothing to spook Reichardt in the papers, and the story soon went cold. But for Silent Bill, the case remained a priority as he waited for his quarry to let down his guard and make a mistake.

~

While Prior was patiently stalking Reichardt, the Great Depression was getting ever worse and Jack Lang's reactions were becoming ever more infuriating, not only to the New Guard and the braying Nationalist state opposition, but also to Scullin's federal Labor government, Australia's conservative elite and the newspapers they controlled.

Back in February, the premier had announced the 'Lang Plan', which included temporary cessation of his state's interest repayments to London, with this revenue instead earmarked for social welfare. Not paying debts due to Mother England risked shame to Australia, so Scullin coughed up what was due from the federal treasury and added the bill to New South Wales' growing tab. Now, in June, seeking compromise, the prime minister and the state premiers met in Melbourne.

With Lang's reluctant agreement, they adopted the 'Premiers' Plan', which endorsed loan repayments and cut wages and pensions. But when

Lang proposed that, in the spirit of purse tightening, public service salaries should not exceed £500, the reaction showed the depth of opposition he faced. *The Sydney Morning Herald* said the premier:

> intended to sharpen the already raw edge of class consciousness to a razor keenness. It is Mr Lang at his worst ... Are we to be driven to absolute desperation by his exactions and threatenings before the Governor dismisses him and his Ministers, and gives the electors a chance of dealing with him?

Of course, those electors had just eight months earlier 'dealt with' Lang by giving him an overwhelming electoral victory and a clear mandate. Cognisant of this, New South Wales's newish governor, Sir Philip Game, was deeply reluctant to interfere.

Lang didn't only have enemies on the right. To his left were those who believed him a capitalist puppet – as he'd supposedly shown by retaining and relying on MacKay, whose cops were now turfing Depression victims out of their homes on behalf of landlords. The Unemployed Workers' Movement organised anti-eviction committees, who resisted by barricading themselves inside houses whose residents had been ordered out.

On 17 June, at Bankstown, forty police fought their way through barbed wire to smash their way into a house the leftists had dubbed 'The Eureka Stockade'. Stones were pelted at the police, who responded with batons. One officer fired two shots, hitting a man in the leg. Eighteen UWM resisters were arrested, and sixteen of them wounded, nine seriously, while nine police were hurt, including an inspector whose skull was fractured. On its breathless front page that afternoon, *The Sun* called it the 'fiercest fight between police and Communists in the history of Sydney'. If that was true, the record lasted only two days.

At eleven o'clock on the morning of Friday 19 June, nineteen activists were barricaded inside a two-storey terrace in Union Street, Newtown, giving speeches from the balcony to a sympathetic crowd of thousands. Just before noon, sixty police summoned from stations across Sydney arrived to enforce the eviction order. Officers suddenly opened fire with revolvers, either in response to stones thrown at them or as cover for officers storming the rear of the house; as with Rothbury, accounts varied widely.

After a twenty-minute battle inside the house, the activists were battered into submission and 'dragged almost insensible to waiting paddy wagons', which then ran a quarter-mile gauntlet of hostile Newtown people, with more squads of cops holding these incensed locals back and throwing cordons across roads. Two of the UWM men arrested suffered gunshot wounds, while nine had head injuries – this time only two police required hospital treatment. One of the arrested men, John Stace, would later say that, inside the house, the cops 'batonned us unmercifully, whether we showed fight or not, calling us communist b's, and saying "I'll give you red Russia, you bastards" ... They said that Lang should pass a bill to shoot the lot of us at sight.' Those arrested claimed they were beaten further while in custody at police stations.

A *Workers' Weekly* headline read: 'Lang's Police Shoot Pickets'. It seemed like Rothbury all over again – only this time organised by its fiercest critic.

~

The following month, Prior got the tip he'd been waiting for in the murder mystery the newspapers had forgotten. A man fitting Gustav Reichardt's description, calling himself 'Jones', had applied for dole rations to Townsville police. But this fellow's accent had aroused suspicion, and local detectives alerted Sydney and then kept tabs on him. Silent Bill grabbed Detective-Sergeant Sedgwick and they rushed to Townsville – without a word to Commissioner Childs or Superintendent MacKay. Working with the local CIB, Prior and Sedgwick arrested the suspect, who admitted he was Reichardt. After he was told his fingerprints had been found at the crime scene, he was charged with the murder of Old Kate, extradited to Sydney and held at Long Bay Gaol.

Meanwhile, the New Guard held its first public rally, with 2000 supporters packing into Sydney Town Hall. Eric Campbell declared the organisation wasn't a secret society or even a political party that would seek election. Instead, it was a body of loyalists grimly determined to prevent the socialisation of the state. Campbell explained the New Guard's structure and aims – which were as had been reported by *Labor Daily* – along with an economic policy to gladden the heart of any fiscal conservative. But the part of Campbell's speech that really fired up the crowd was when he demanded:

> that Communism be declared illegal and that proper legislative authorities be obtained for the deportation of all Communists, imported or indigenous, and all unworthy and disruptive individuals. Who will doubt that with these things accomplished, confidence will in a measure be restored and conditions begin to improve? It is our boast that we act. And if no heed is given to this our declaration, act we will, lawfully of course, but nevertheless swiftly and surely.

Campbell declared that if Lang disagreed with the New Guard's goals and believed it to be an illegal organisation, then he was a 'traitor'.

~

In August 1931 – as New South Wales public-service salaries went unpaid and Lang was forced to rejoin the Loan Council and borrow half a million pounds to keep the state from going under – Gustav Reichardt faced Mr May's inquest into Old Kate's murder. Detective-Sergeant Sedgwick claimed the accused had confessed and made a signed statement. In it, Reichardt said he'd been depressed because he'd had a row with his young girlfriend, Gwenholme Latham, and so he bought Lysol from a chemist's shop with the intention of killing himself. Even though he hated wine, he purchased a bottle because he thought it'd mix better with the poison. Reichardt had been walking in Surry Hills and asked a woman where he could get some beer – which was the drink he really liked. This had been Old Kate. He gave her money and she invited him into her place. But then she wouldn't give him any beer or give him his money back. They argued, she screamed, he punched her in the head and then he strangled her to shut her up.

At his September murder trial, Reichardt denied the critical parts of his signed statement. He said that after buying the Lysol and wine, he'd asked Old Kate about beer and briefly gone into her house. He had given her wine and told her of his plan to commit suicide. She'd said she was sorry for his woes and had farewelled him from her gate. That was the last he'd seen of her. Rather than end it all, Reichardt had sobered up and over a period of weeks drifted north in search of work. When Prior and Sedgwick collared him in Townsville, he thought he was being arrested for hitting his little girlfriend in Stanmore.

Reichardt claimed he had been manipulated into writing a statement; the detectives had asked him to refer to Gwenholme as 'Emma', and he'd gone along with it to get along. When they charged him with the murder of Emma Philbrook, aka Old Kate, Reichardt realised he had been stitched up. All he was guilty of, he told the jury, was hitting the Stanmore girl. 'She had a habit of screaming out, gentlemen,' he explained, 'even if you were only playing with her.' Reichardt hadn't even belted her that hard. The reason he'd fled was she fell over and hit her head. He'd thought, 'I've done it now,' and set off on his despondent mission to end it all with Lysol and wine. That was what put him on course for his entirely innocent encounter with Old Kate – who, as his bad luck would have it, just happened to get herself murdered that night.

Sedgwick and Prior denied they'd tricked a confession out of Reichardt. The defence told the jury of Old Kate's bad character, and produced witnesses testifying to Reichardt's good character – even Gwenholme Latham's mother, who'd been the one to take out the warrant for his assault on her daughter. Sedgwick admitted under oath that his investigations had revealed people believed Reichardt a decent man and a good worker. The jury found him guilty of manslaughter, with a recommendation of mercy, and the judge sentenced him to a mere eight years. Chances were he'd be out in six.

The Old Kate case was portrayed as stellar police work by Silent Bill – and it inherently served as a rebuttal to the theory that a repeat slayer was preying on women of the underclass while also refuting the argument that Sydney cops didn't go the extra mile for such victims. Prior was lionised. *Truth* wrote that that he'd burned the case into his brain when everyone else had forgotten:

> It became the single dominating thought in his life … He could be seen often quietly walking around the locality of the tragedy, and the picture of the man he wanted to see was always in his pocket. Bustle and noise are not part of his investigation make-up. So week after week for months he sought the man tirelessly.

Prior was on track for a promotion to CIB chief – just as soon as MacKay took his next step up the ladder. Under his new master, Jack Lang, that seemed assured.

7

Red Rallies, Fascist Fury and Another Dead Cop

Premier Lang's reputation as the people's champion was redeemed somewhat when his government passed a law to postpone evictions in response to 'the Siege of Union Street'. But the nineteen men charged with 'common law riot' still went to trial in September at Darlinghurst Court. The defence argued that there was no such charge in Australia. Besides, riots by definition happened in public, and this affray occurred inside a house stormed by the police. The jury acquitted all the defendants.

Two moments in the trial pointed to a police force acting as a law unto themselves, with a judiciary willing to give them cover. Asked by barrister Clive Evatt about alleged custodial bashings, one sergeant replied: 'If it was done and the accused were batonned or beaten at the station after the arrest, I would not admit it.' After the court heard from a dozen police who denied even hearing gunshots, two officers claimed Rothbury-style justifications for using their revolvers – one saying he fired only in the air; the other saying he shot in self-defence. Evatt lamented that officers were generally too willing to use their guns. His Honour Mr Justice Coyle disagreed: 'After all the things you read in the newspapers, it's a pity more people weren't shot at by the police.'

During the trial, a surging mob of nearly a thousand communist supporters gathered outside the court, the sort of scene that made the New Guard believe its mission was all the more crucial. During the same week, Campbell held another rally at Bondi, telling the crowd that membership would soon reach 100,000. Even before then, he said, the New Guard stood ready to take over if the police couldn't maintain law and order. It was a fiery speech that edged towards sedition, particularly when Campbell proposed that the state be ruled by a commission of ten men because Lang's government was infected by foreign communists. 'We are in the same position as if we were harbouring spies and enemies in our ranks in time of war,' he thundered.

This rally was a modest affair, attended by around 600. But the next one, on 16 September, saw some 3000 supporters pack into Sydney Town Hall. Campbell ran through his usual dark materials, but he folded the police further into his argument. They were underfunded, he said, and the rank-and-file constables and sergeants who overwhelmingly supported the New Guard were being muzzled by a few men at the top. This was a shot fired at Lang's Chief Secretary Mark Gosling, Commissioner Childs and Superintendent MacKay. 'It is the weeds in the garden,' Campbell said, to laughter, 'that must be pulled out, to give the decent plants an opportunity to grow ...'. He continued:

> I openly defy the socialistic government of this state to interfere in any way with the New Guard ... The New Guard will not be bullied; it will not be diverted or deflected ... If the government wishes to become our greatest recruiting agent, let it attempt to interfere. Then would our members increase to half a million.

This rally was front-page news, with photos of the leader and his massed faithful. *The Sun* – which had a daily circulation of 200,000 in a city of 1.25 million – painted a glowing picture of a patriotic crowd from all strata of society, comparing the scene to the glorious rush to enlist in the first years of Anzac.

A month later, the New Guard went into 'battle' in Bondi to break up a communist gathering, the 'shock troops' under the command of its 'eastern zone' commander, Captain Francis de Groot, an Irish-born former British Army officer turned suburban antiques dealer. Only the swift intervention of police, who told the Red leaders to leave and formed a protective cordon around them, prevented the clash from turning violent.

Days after the Bondi showdown, Campbell saw an opportunity for the New Guard to insert itself into the paralysing seamen's strike. He promised his troops would organise volunteer workers or volunteer themselves, and would 'deal with' any union basher gangs. Insinuating that the government and senior police were colluding against him – and that he had spies in these high places – he challenged the chief secretary to publish the secret report the CIB had prepared on the New Guard. 'It is in his possession now,' he said, 'and I know what it contains.'

From this time on, Campbell said, his men had to intervene in all industrial disputes; the police could not defend against communism as a doctrine 'any more than an undertaker could stamp out a virulent disease'. Beyond that, the New Guard stood ready when the crisis came to preserve law and order, carry on all essential services and feed the population. It wouldn't do so while 'duly constituted forces of law and order were able to handle the situation'. 'But,' Campbell added, 'if called upon, our battalions are ready at a moment's notice.'

Campbell's provocations were met with fury from unionists. Jock Garden said: 'I think Mr Campbell has lit a fire, with his bravado … which will be difficult to extinguish.' But the New Guard had support in Rothbury antagonist Reginald Weaver. The member of state parliament bellowed:

> Although I must say that they have been somewhat flamboyant in their methods, I say, 'Thank God for the New Guard. The New

> Guard is an expression of the state's better-minded citizens against
> the inroads being made by red-raggers, and the only way to treat
> these rebellious ruffians is to march them out of New South Wales
> or into gaol.

There would be more clashes as these 'better-minded citizens' intimidated Red gatherings. The police ran interference and three officers were wounded in a De Groot–led New Guard attack on communists in Kings Cross on 11 December. MacKay's force was criticised by the New Guard for protecting the footsoldiers of Lang's socialist dictatorship – and by the far-left for being tools of Lang's secretly capitalist, secretly pro–New Guard basher government.

Tensions heightened further when Lang renounced the Premiers' Plan. The Lang Plan was now to stop paying interest to British bondholders, reduce interest rates to 3 per cent on domestic borrowing, and abandon the gold standard. Lang refused to reduce wages, pensions or social benefits. The premier's persona and politics saw him acclaimed at huge rallies where crowds chanted, 'Lang is right!' and bought plaster busts inscribed 'JT Lang – the people's champion'.

Five federal ALP Lang supporters – including Beasley and Dunn – pressed Prime Minister Scullin to adopt their hero's plan. He refused and they moved to the crossbench. Scullin now led a minority government that depended on their support. Meanwhile, on the other side of the chamber, the Nationalists, the Australian Party and a few Labor renegades merged to form the United Australia Party. The UAP was led by Joe Lyons, a former member of Scullin's cabinet who'd resigned in protest at the prime minister's response to the Depression. When the UAP held a no-confidence vote in the Scullin government, Lang's crossbench supporters joined them. At the federal election in December 1931, Lyons led his party into government.

Lang's stance had reshaped federal politics. But, like Dr Frankenstein, he'd created a monster who was bent on breaking him. In Lang's case, this was Prime Minister Joe Lyons.

~

Against the backdrop of these rising tensions, McRae was given a sensitive mission: investigate the suspicious death of one of the police's own. On 7 October 1931, Constable Trevlyn Nowland was found drowned in a shallow part of the Macdonald River at Bendemeer, where he was stationed, twenty-five miles north of Tamworth. Some district coppers were sure he'd been murdered; he was lured out the previous night by a mystery call. Nowland's wife had overheard him talking on the phone, and he'd told her he had to go out because a madman was running amok at the river. But other district police thought that Nowland may just have fallen over, hit his head and toppled unconscious into the water.

McRae knew the professional and personal hardships of a country copper. In the decade he'd been in the force, Nowland had been bounced around remote postings. McRae was likely sympathetic to another tragedy: the officer had endured the death of his baby son, and his wife's health had subsequently suffered. Interviewing swagmen who frequented the riverbanks, McRae would have wanted to find some shifty character who couldn't account for his movements. But he cleared them all. Reading the post-mortem report, he would've wanted to see evidence of an attack or an accident. But there were no external injuries to suggest Nowland had been hit or had a fall, and Kamilaroi tracker William Dennison said prints showed that one man had gone into the river and did not come out.

McRae's enquiries revealed that Nowland had been, at best, unstable, and, at worst, malicious. He heard the constable had spread rumours about citizens. Nowland had told a local man he'd received fifty or sixty anonymous letters about townspeople. But the constable hadn't entered anything about this volume of sinister letters in his duty book. Further, he'd falsified entries in this log to show he'd been working when he was actually playing tennis or going to the pictures.

McRae heard from a witness that, in the month before Nowland died, the constable had undergone tremendous mood swings. Even more significant was that in tiny Bendemeer no one had reported any 'madman' running amok at the river – other than the constable to his wife, before he went out to his death. To McRae, it looked like Nowland had concocted the story, likely to spare her knowing he was going to suicide, and to ensure she got the pension by making his death seem to have been in the line of duty. This wasn't going to be a popular conclusion – with the constable's wife or with the detective's own bosses.

McRae testified at the inquest in Tamworth in early November. Tracker Dennison gave his evidence. Nowland's superior officer, Inspector JP McDonald, said he'd believed the constable had been sane and capable right up to the day he died. But what McRae had uncovered had changed his opinion. A leading psychiatrist said the evidence, when taken with a family medical history of mental illness, pointed to Nowland having committed suicide while insane. But he couldn't say for sure – and this led the coroner to deliver an open verdict. The silver lining in this cloud of doubt was that the widow might have peace of mind and she would receive her husband's pension.

Less than a fortnight later, McRae faced another country case that made Constable Nowland's demise seem straightforward. How did you solve the mystery of a man's death when there was barely anything left of him?

8

The Bungendore Bones, the Razor Murder and the Slashed Ribbon

On Friday 20 November 1931, seven miles from Bungendore, near Goulburn, squatter Bernard Cunningham was on horseback mustering sheep when he came across the ashes of a huge bonfire. Amid the charcoal were the barrel of a rifle, a trigger guard, part of a charred human skull, a section of spine, bits of thigh and pelvis, and other bone fragments.

McRae and Detective-Sergeant Len Allmond were partnered again and at the crime scene by the next morning. They were met by the local GMO and Inspector Matheson from McRae's old beat of Cooma, who'd come with a talented Ngarigo tracker named Alexander Brindle. Goulburn police records showed no one from the district had been reported missing in the past year. So the victim was likely passing through, looking for work or prospecting for gold. Had swaggies camped here and had a fatal fight like the one McRae had investigated at Barraba? Did the killer build an inferno and tend it long enough for his victim's almost total cremation? Working against this theory was the fact there were no signs of any camp; swaggies usually left empty tins and bottles in their wake.

Before the CIB men arrived, Goulburn cops had probed the charcoal and found a locker key and a strap buckle. Now McRae and his colleagues kept searching and sifting. Their finds included coins to the value of just over eight shillings, a small gold wristwatch, a brass tiepin and two more trouser buckles.

The pitiful pieces were enough to tell McRae something about the victim. The buckles and tiepin pointed to a man who'd been well-dressed, rather than an unemployed tramp. That he'd burned with his coins and watch didn't suggest robbery. As for the bones being mostly gone – it could've been the killer raking the coals, but it might also have been the work of scavenging crows and foxes.

A cartridge shell in the rifle breech indicated that the victim had been shot, but there was no trace of the bullet. That made sense because it was made of lead and would've melted. But the barrel and trigger guard were steel – they wouldn't melt. Any killer would likely have known that. So why throw the rifle into the fire, where it wouldn't be destroyed? He could easily hurl it into any gully and it'd never have been found.

McRae had to consider the possibility that this was another suicide: a man builds a pyre, lights it, steps into the centre and shoots himself. As bizarre as it sounded, it had happened at least twice in the past few years of Depression despair, but in those cases the corpses hadn't been fully cremated. Maybe this fellow had made a better job of it. And perhaps, like Constable Nowland, he'd wanted to spare his family's feelings, in this case by removing all trace of his existence.

Yet McRae saw other puzzling evidence. Large logs had been dragged from a hilltop two hundred yards away to make the fire. Could one man have done that? There were also the remains of six smaller fires encircling the main bonfire. McRae thought they were set at the same time. Was it part of some insane ritual? Or did it indicate a killer who knew a single blaze might lead a nearby bushman to investigate, while numerous fires would merely look like a burn-off? Of course, a suicidal man could've used the same ploy so his self-immolation wasn't interrupted before he was reduced to ash. With the remains in such a state, the detectives couldn't even say when the victim died. It might've been last week. Or last year.

McRae and Allmond had far more questions than answers. But Brindle's examination of the grass regrowth in the ruts left by the dragged logs told him the fire had been made three or four weeks ago. This gave the detectives a crucial time frame.

As McRae had been stationed at Queanbeyan briefly back in the day, locals would've remembered him handling the sad case of the little drowned boy and been more likely to think harder about what they could remember. He and Allmond crisscrossed the district and people told the detectives what little they knew. These witnesses said that about a month ago a pair of prospectors had been working in the Bungendore area. One looked like a well-dressed city lad, while the other was a rougher country character. A few locals told McRae they'd seen the glow of a big fire on 26 or 27 October.

A coronial inquest was opened in Queanbeyan, with the local GMO reckoning the victim had been a man aged about thirty-five. But McRae wanted a second opinion. He took the bone fragments to Dr Anthony Burkitt, professor of anatomy at Sydney University, who said the man was definitely younger – twenty-one – and that he'd stood around six-foot-one.

'The Bungendore Bones' was a big story all over Australia. Headlines like one in *The Sun* – 'Ghastly Midnight Mystery Blaze – World's Coolest Murderer – Bungendore Horror: Inside Story' – were irresistible. Such articles carried a police appeal for people to make contact if they'd gone four weeks without hearing from any friend or family member who'd been in the Goulburn area. Articles described the items from the ashes in the hope someone might recognise the watch or the locker key numbered 784MV 12774 and stamped with the British trademark 'Vaun'.

Metallurgical tests on the watch revealed part of a serial number. As for the key, McRae asked Childs and MacKay to authorise assistance from Scotland Yard. They liaised with the makers, the Yale Manufacturing Company, and learned that 784MV 12774 had been part of a large consignment sent to Wormald Bros of Waterloo in February 1929.

Wormald had since supplied lockers to hundreds of clubs, factories, warehouses, businesses and other organisations. McRae requested their customer list, and then got the cops under his command to start wearing out their boot leather. The meticulous strategy paid off. Just before Christmas, they'd matched the key to a locker at a YMCA gymnasium in Pitt Street. McRae now had the dead man's name.

Sidney Morrison had, as Dr Burkitt said, been twenty-one and had stood six feet and half an inch, and the watch's serial numbers matched one he'd owned. He'd lived with his parents in Bondi and was an active surf lifesaver. Morrison had worked as a lift driver until he lost his job at the end of September. Despondent, a week later he'd told his sister he was leaving, and his family said they hadn't heard from him since. McRae questioned Morrison's loved ones but they were adamant the lad was not the type to commit suicide. They were sure he'd been murdered.

To McRae's ears that was a familiar refrain. But this was the job. So, as 1932 got underway, he and Allmond went back to the Goulburn area, driving 1200 miles in a week as they spoke to everyone within fifty miles of where the bones were found. They learned nothing new.

McRae returned to Sydney, sure the answer lay in the dead man's history. Sure enough, he found Morrison had been seeing a Macquarie Street psychiatrist. Interviews with this psychiatrist strongly suggested suicide. McRae reported his conclusion to Superintendent MacKay, which angered the grieving family.

When the inquest resumed in Sydney near the end of January, the psychiatrist testified that he'd seen Morrison several times in the months before his death; the lad was struggling with depression, suffering feelings of worthlessness and unable to shake his bitter outlook on life. Morrison's sister told the court her brother's personality had darkened after a head injury in the surf in the middle of 1931, and his mental outlook worsened when he lost his job. She testified he'd once said, 'I feel that useless that I wouldn't care if I died tomorrow.' Morrison's father related conversations he'd had with his maudlin son, while the mother revealed she'd found the boy's stashed .22 rifle. They admitted that, after he left their home, Sidney had stayed for a week with his brother, but, suffering from nerves, had then departed abruptly. When he'd disappeared, the family's search had included Darlinghurst Reception House, where the city's mentally ill were assessed.

Despite their own testimony, much of it reluctant, the Morrisons had retained a lawyer to argue that Sidney had not committed suicide, and he produced witnesses who said the young man hadn't seemed depressed and elicited from a Goulburn sergeant his belief murder was 'possible'. McRae, no doubt wearied by this refusal to accept reality, testified about his intensive investigations and said he would continue his enquiries. Proceedings were adjourned.

Before they resumed, in late April, a Glen Innes grazier killed himself in exactly the way McRae believed Morrison had: he built a pyre, sat atop it, set it alight and shot himself, the fire reducing him to a few bones. But there was no doubt in his case: the farmer left a suicide note. When the Morrison inquest continued one month later, the coroner congratulated McRae on his detective work and criticised the family for not being more forthcoming. But he also acknowledged that there were suspicious circumstances. Everything said, the coroner had to return an open verdict. Officially, at least, the death remained a mystery. The family's determination to get this result – even if it wasn't true – was captured by *The Daily Telegraph* headline: 'Stigma of Suicide Removed Now – Dead Man's Name Cleared'.

Even so, unofficially – and in the press – McRae's work in putting a name, face, state of mind and method of death to a few burned bones found in a remote paddock was the making of his reputation as Sydney's super sleuth. From now on, whenever he was assigned a new case, reporters would remind readers that he'd solved the 'Bungendore Bones Mystery'.

~

While McRae was making his name, Eric Campbell was sullying Lang's. In a speech at Lane Cove, broadcast on radio station 2GB, he revealed the New Guard would petition the King for the premier's removal. If His Majesty refused, he warned, 'we have plans for other action – constitutional and lawful – but not peaceful'. Campbell insulted Lang as a 'buffoon' and 'nasty tyrant', alluded to him being full of bullshit, referenced the premier's death and vowed he wouldn't open the Sydney Harbour Bridge. In an echo of the IWW case, MacKay had a shorthand writer taking notes, and Campbell was charged with using insulting words and faced Central Summons Court on 15 January 1932.

Thousands crowded the streets around the court. Inside, Campbell clicked his heels before emphatically pleading not guilty, while his New Guardsmen filled the gallery standing at attention, leading *The Barrier Miner* to observe that 'the scene was more like that of a Nazi-German Fascist demonstration than a Sydney court. There, when a member is charged, the Nazi[s] stand stiffly throughout the hearing of the case.' Campbell went to trial the next week, amid further crowd scenes. With the proceedings lasting four days, he had the city's attention, and claimed his remarks about Lang were entirely justified. A £2 fine bought him far more publicity than the New Guard had previously enjoyed.

Campbell would appeal the conviction, but in the meantime, on 19 February, he held another Town Hall rally. Timed to the first anniversary of the New Guard's formation, it was reportedly attended by 5000 supporters, with many more of the loyal and curious tuning in to the broadcast of speeches on 2UW. Campbell's recent prosecution provided new grist for his mill: Lang, a 'rank communist', had surrounded himself with Red ministers who were leaning on the weak police commissioner to turn the force into a political body like those of Soviet Russia. On stage, Campbell led everyone present in an oath to continue the New Guard's mission 'until communism has been completely crushed, and until sane and honourable government has been re-established'. He did this while wearing a dark armband, with his head slightly bowed and his right arm raised – a stance mirrored by his army of followers. Glancing at the photo of Campbell on the front page of *The Daily Telegraph* the next day, readers might've been forgiven for assuming it was a story about Herr Hitler and his Nazis over in Germany.

~

Love them or hate them, the New Guard couldn't be ignored. But they weren't the only striking new figures commanding Sydney's attention amid divisive fanfare. Everywhere you looked around the city these past few weeks, on massive posters plastered on walls and on even bigger billboards, Dracula loomed over a sleeping woman, Bela Lugosi's vampire in the vanguard of a controversial new vogue in cinema: the horror movie. The film was already a sensation in America and Sydneysiders proved to have the same morbid taste for the monstrous.

When *Dracula* opened at the 3000-seat Capitol Theatre on 19 February – the same day Campbell threw his Nazi-like salute at Town Hall – the police had to be called to control a surging crowd that spilled into the street. Demand didn't let up, and two weeks later Sydney was also thrilling to the next horror sensation, *Dr Jekyll and Mr Hyde*, with one opinion writer reckoning this was a form of catharsis for audiences frightened by the Depression.

Whatever their movie-going motives, as autumn got underway, people flocked to cinemas to see a supernatural fiend with an unquenchable bloodlust and an urbane gent who courted his evil other self and went on a killing spree. Fright fans could hardly wait for the next horror on the horizon: *Frankenstein*, about a man-made creature, cursed with a murderer's defective brain, who was hounded by a mob through the countryside until his sacrificial destruction.

~

MacKay kept constant tabs on the New Guard. In early March, McRae got a turn when he and two other detectives took seats at a meeting in Gordon and refused to leave when asked. Flummoxed, the New Guardsmen left, thinking the cops would follow them. McRae and co. stayed where they were, having the right under law to be in any public hall at any time, forcing the men to take their mutterings elsewhere. But while Lang was scoring minor points against the New Guard, he risked being routed by Prime Minister Lyons's *Financial Agreements Enforcement Act*, which would give the federal government the power to remove all revenue due to the Commonwealth from New South Wales banks. In response, Lang ordered all of these funds – well over £1 million – to be withdrawn as cash and stashed in the Treasury.

New South Wales was moving closer to the brink right as the Sydney Harbour Bridge was set to open. Campbell, with a dozen of his men, all wearing New Guard armbands denoting their rank, presented to Sir Philip Game the petition to be forwarded to the King, demanding the dissolution of state parliament on account of Lang's alliance with 'revolutionary socialists'. In a speech at Manly, again broadcast on radio, Campbell blasted Commissioner Childs as a liar and claimed the New Guard enjoyed the support of 90 per cent of rank-and-file policemen and had the 'greatest liaison' with the force – leaving aside the top echelon, who were doing the bidding of the 'communist' state government. Campbell even took aim at the very top – Prime Minister Lyons – claiming the New Guard had put him in power and it would put him out if he didn't crack down on the Reds as he'd promised. Turning to the upcoming opening of the bridge, he railed against Lang for having the audacity to want the honour of opening it for himself, when this was clearly the duty of the King's representative. But Campbell said the New Guard council had voted against trying to prevent Lang from cutting the ribbon. Being a good democrat, he would abide by that decision.

On the night of 15 March, the bridge's roadway lights were turned on for the first time, forming a ribbon of light from shore to shore. The next morning, 56,000 school students from all over Sydney poured out of trains and trams for their big day out, walking across the bridge ahead of its opening in three days' time.

In a spirit of merriment, in Union Street, Erskineville, a stone's throw from the eviction battle of the previous year, children danced on the footpath as an organist played music. When the tune stopped, a woman who'd been watching heard a deep groan from the neighbouring house of Katherine Sims. She alerted the woman's niece, Mary Thomas, who lived a few houses along. Referring to Katherine's de facto, Alfred Ball, the neighbour said: 'Ball just went in. The cow might have bashed her again.'

Mary found the door half open, then Ball appeared, covered in blood. 'What have you been doing?' she asked. He didn't answer. She pushed the door open and saw her aunt inside in a big pool of blood and gasping for breath. Ball ran out the back and went over the fence. Mary ran screaming for help. A local nurse did what she could and an ambulance was summoned. But Ball's attack had been frenzied. He'd tried to cut out Katherine's heart, stopping only when his razor's handle shattered, the blade and pieces of the weapon scattered around the room. Katherine Sims died on the way to hospital.

This was in Area C, and Inspector Prior rushed to the scene with three detectives and a squad of uniforms. Detective-Sergeant James Comans would be lead investigator. They fanned out to interview witnesses and search for the fugitive. Ball had been seen running towards Erskineville railway station. A quarter of a mile from the crime scene, he'd rushed into a shop and asked to wash his bloodstained shirt. In tune with the turbulent times, he claimed he'd been set upon by a mob. When he couldn't clean his shirt, he asked to borrow one and disappeared.

Prior learned that Ball had become jealous because days earlier he'd found another man's letter to Katherine. Yet the suggestion it'd been a crime of passion was at odds with his stewing on this letter and calmly going to a pub for a whisky before committing the murder. Mary told the detectives Ball was a basher, but they could see that for themselves: Katherine's face was covered in bruises he'd inflicted recently. Prior's police radiated out, searching Redfern, Newtown and Waterloo, and investigating leads farther afield in the south-western suburbs. Following procedure, the suspect wasn't named in the newspapers, and neither was his description circulated publicly.

Where was Alfred Ball? Police learned he'd once been in the habit of sleeping in parks and empty buildings. The chances were he'd simply melted into the growing army of Sydney's dispossessed.

~

On Saturday 19 March 1932 nearly one million people packed into the city for the opening of the Sydney Harbour Bridge. One hundred thousand or more lined the southern approach to the bridge and its roadway, where, on a dais, were perched Lang and his antagonist, Prime Minister Lyons; the Governor-General, Sir Isaac Isaacs; state governor Sir Philip Game; and dozens more VIPs. Also in the exalted spot: Childs and MacKay, who had 100 men on the bridge for security, and another 1300 on opening-day duty, comprising much of the city's police force.

Queued through the Sydney streets was the biggest procession of pageantry Australia had ever seen. There were dozens of floral floats, accompanied by white men and women in colonial garb and Indigenous people in tribal costume and ceremonial paint, these colourful displays ranging from Captain Cook and the *Endeavour* to the glory of the different districts that had grown from his discovery. Students, nurses, firemen, coalminers, lifesavers, boy scouts, young soldiers and old veterans massed. Onlookers smiled at old modes of transportation – a Cobb & Co. coach, a boneshaker penny farthing, a horse-drawn bus – juxtaposed with the motorcars in the procession. Little Lennie Gwyther – a nine-year-old boy who'd ridden his horse alone from Melbourne to be here – got his own special place. The harbour below the bridge held every conceivable craft, from liners and warships to ketches and dinghies, while the skies above buzzed with biplanes and Charles Kingsford Smith's circling *Southern Cross*.

Amid the excited crowd, Francis de Groot, wearing his 15th Hussars uniform and Campbell's AIF tunic, complete with ceremonial sword on his belt, rode a retired racehorse and surreptitiously tagged along with a cavalry formation making for the bridge. Although Campbell had spoken about taking no action to stop Lang, he'd changed his mind and declared to his inner circle that he wanted to arrest the premier during the bridge opening for corruption. How he thought that was remotely possible wasn't clear. In any case, De Groot had a better idea – one that was directly inspired by a *Smith's Weekly* cartoon from just days earlier titled 'The Man Who Beat Lang to the Tape', showing a gleeful bloke cutting the bridge ribbon ahead of the shocked premier.

When Sir Philip Game had finished speaking and Lang was yet to commence, De Groot rode up in front of the dais. He appeared to be trying to get his horse to ride through the ribbon, but the beast shied, so he raised his sword, as the photographers clicked, the newsreel cameras whirred and a radio announcer described what he was seeing to listeners across the state. Billy MacKay, Inspector Robson and other senior police finally woke up to what was happening. De Groot slashed at the ribbon once, only partly cutting it. Then he tried twice more, finishing the job and saying loudly: 'I declare this bridge open on behalf of the respectable citizens of New South Wales.'

A detective grabbed the reins of De Groot's horse. The New Guardsman said: 'I am a King's officer, don't interfere with me!' MacKay did more than that. Big Bill unceremoniously yanked De Groot from his saddle. His boot caught in a stirrup, the protestor was briefly suspended upside down, before falling onto the roadway. MacKay hauled him up, helped by two constables, including Adam 'Scotty' Denholm, whose favoured status was shown by his being so close to the action on this historic day.

De Groot was taken to the little police office in the southern pylon of the Harbour Bridge and interrogated by Childs, MacKay, Prior and others. Rather than take him to the George Street North police station and charge him with what would only be minor offences for which he'd make bail quickly, MacKay inflicted a calculated insult on the man who'd just shown up him and his force: he charged De Groot with being insane and had him removed to the Darlinghurst Reception House. That way he'd be held over the weekend until doctors could assess him and advise a magistrate on Monday as to whether he was fit to be released.

Meanwhile, a reporter for *The Sun* was on the phone to Campbell, who hadn't attended the bridge opening. He was mighty pleased with what De Groot had done. 'Although we had 100,000 men we knew that one British officer was sufficient to deal with Lang and the Bridge situation, in spite of the precautions of 1400 policemen,' he crowed.

Despite De Groot's stunt, the ceremony had within minutes resumed and proceeded as planned. The ribbon was retied, Lang officially cut it and declared the Sydney Harbour Bridge open. Streamers cascaded down, cheers went up, planes flew over and the procession began its thirty-minute crossing. It's thought that 300,000 people that weekend made bridge journeys on foot, on bicycles and motorbikes, and in cars and trucks, trams and trains. That night the city marvelled at a twenty-minute fireworks display that showered the bridge in light and colour and rendered the harbour waters a brilliant kaleidoscope. Yet for everything – two decades of planning, a decade of construction, enormous expenditure, the loss of sixteen lives – it was De Groot and his stunt that dominated *The Sun*'s front page that afternoon, and the headlines of the Sunday papers and many published nationwide on Monday.

Within hours of his ribbon-slashing, newsreels of the uproar were being shown in a few city theatres; by the start of the next week they would be in around 100 cinemas. Big newspaper advertising – 'Every electrical moment of the startling incident that set the world aflame with excitement was captured in Sensational Cinesound Scoop' – didn't even mention the pageantry of the day. Audiences hooted with laughter at seeing De Groot's larrikin take-down of Lang, not least because Campbell had reportedly ordered that each screening be attended by a dozen or more Guardsmen to get the chuckles going. The premier looked even more humourless and dictatorial when he moved swiftly to suppress the film. MacKay's police briefly had a new duty: ensuring the footage was cut from newsreels.

Campbell visited De Groot in the Reception House, telling the press that his confinement there was 'the most unforgivable insult to a well-known and level-headed businessman, and a very gallant cavalry officer. If the people of New South Wales will stand the Lang government for 48 hours after this act, I will be very surprised.' The entire state, Campbell added, owed De Groot a debt of gratitude for 'preventing the political inebriate at the head of affairs from formally opening the historic Harbour Bridge'.

Buried amid the bridge coverage were short reports noting that the murderer of Katherine Sims hadn't been caught. Detectives had been told Ball had hacked his wrist with the razor before fleeing, and relatives reckoned he'd commit suicide in a brick pit. Even so, *The Sun* dutifully reported that Prior's men were still on the job: 'They were out all night and while the city celebrated today they were still hot on the scent.' Yet, just a few days later, *Labor Daily* had a very different take:

> The CIB would not be surprised if his body was found with self-inflicted injuries – or floating in the sea or a river. There is none of the feverish excitement and tenseness of the man hunt associated with murders in this case. The men who were assigned to the case are now engaged on other duties.

The paper added that 'just in case' the wanted man was still alive, it was printing his full description, which had, in a 'rare occurrence', been issued by the CIB. Had Prior really given up so soon? Perhaps. It seemed as likely that Silent Bill wanted Ball to think so.

On Monday 21 March, as Australia thrilled to the overnight news that Phar Lap had won the Agua Caliente handicap in Mexico, and was being acclaimed as one of the greatest racehorses in history, De Groot appeared before a magistrate at the Lunacy Court, which was surrounded by a tremendous crowd. MacKay recounted the events on the bridge and tried to justify laying the insanity charge by recounting previous occasions on which he'd met the accused. On the night police were injured when New Guardsmen had attacked communists in Kings Cross, De Groot had been 'in an extremely nervous and excited condition'. Later, the superintendent met De Groot again when he came to the CIB to complain about police harassment, and they had an argument about who'd win if there was a showdown between 500 police and 5000 New Guardsman occupying parliament. 'I say, as the result of my observations and his manner and actions on Saturday last, I deemed him insane,' the CIB chief testified.

It was as thin as it sounded. Doctors who'd seen De Groot over the weekend testified that he was 'perfectly sane'. The magistrate discharged him. De Groot left the court to cheers and hoots from the crowd – and was immediately rearrested by MacKay and charged with 'maliciously damaging a ribbon valued at £2', with offensive behaviour and with using threatening language to a police inspector on the bridge. Freed on £10 bail, paid by Campbell, De Groot would face a trial – which would give the New Guard yet another public platform.

Despite MacKay's failure to prevent the bridge embarrassment, Lang gave him an unprecedented promotion, skipping him from Superintendent Third Class to Superintendent First Class. MacKay had leapfrogged older men of higher rank to become Metropolitan

Superintendent of Police. The premier supposedly gave his former enemy a simple order: 'Sort out those New Guard bastards.'

~

The Sydney Harbour Bridge was the realisation of an idea that went back almost as far as the First Fleet's arrival. But this symbol of progress and achievement didn't make an immediate difference to those without jobs, food or hope. Unemployment was approaching one in three men; in Redfern it was to reach 48 per cent. And a week after De Groot's stunt, McRae again gazed on a direct outcome of the Depression. William Henry Potter, a twenty-six-year-old English immigrant, had lain down in Centennial Park after swallowing cyanide. The bottle was in his pocket and he'd recently sent a friend a letter saying he couldn't face the 'degradation of the dole'. At least this time it was a clear-cut suicide.

A week after he attended that sad scene, McRae spent a happier day in Centennial Park when he married divorcee Janet 'Jean' Harrison. He was forty-five; she was thirty-nine. They would take a house at Kingsford, with Tom able to indulge his love for golf at the nearby links. There would be no children, and no repeat of the tragedy that had ended his first marriage a decade earlier. But Jean was to endure a different type of hell as Tom McRae's wife.

For the moment, though, it seems the McRaes enjoyed a honeymoon, as Tom wasn't on hand to help out in the blood-spattered month to come.

Inspector Prior would need all the assistance he could get. In a remarkable piece of timing, he succeeded MacKay as CIB chief – now overseeing all divisional areas – just days before a double murder that was even more savage and senseless than the previous year's attack in Bondi. This new slaughter would be closely followed by so many other grisly killings that people would ask: what was behind this 'murder wave'?

9

The Moorebank Murders: Terror Reigns

At around 8pm on Tuesday 5 April 1932, Frank Wilkinson and Dorothy Denzel went for a drive in his red Alvis sports car. This handsome couple were doing all right despite the Depression. Frank, twenty-six, lived with his parents in Homebush, and worked as a compositor for *The Sun*. Dorothy, twenty-one, previously a teenage beauty queen, had in 1931 lost her job as a GPO telephonist, but had since become a live-in nursemaid to a Burwood family. After picking her up from this residence, Frank drove them towards a quiet spot near a Strathfield park that was popular with young couples.

There was plenty to talk about. Just days before, Frank had been at the wheel of the Wilkinson family car when they all drove across the Sydney Harbour Bridge together for the first time. Everyone was still in awe of Phar Lap, and excited to know when he'd race for the first time in the United States. And Francis de Groot's trial had opened the past Friday with wild scenes. Three thousand people – many of them New Guard members or supporters – had filled the streets around the Central Police Court until MacKay sent 200 police to clear them. Fists had flown and there had been injuries and arrests.

While the unrest around De Groot's trial had simmered down, there'd been even wilder scenes the night before, when Frank and Dorothy had originally planned to have their romantic drive. An electrical storm of hurricane intensity had shattered windows and smashed roofs across Sydney. At Wirth's Circus in Redfern, two elephants had been so terrified they'd snapped their chains, crashed through iron gates and rampaged through the streets for an hour. Frank and Dorothy had understandably rescheduled.

The lovers in the Alvis on Tuesday night were both sensible and hardworking young people. They were close to their families. That made it immediately concerning that, by the next morning – as radio broadcasts announced the sudden shock death of Phar Lap – they hadn't returned from their drive or slept in their respective beds. Dorothy and Frank's people called the police. A search of the hospitals turned up nothing. The Denzels and Wilkinsons quickly feared the worst.

That day a man dropped off a red Alvis sports car at a garage he'd rented in Ashfield. This fellow took the licence plate and some car parts with him and came back the next day with another chap to remove more components. When news of Frank and Dorothy's disappearance made the newspapers, the garage owner – who was likely in on the stolen-car racket but not wanting to get mixed up in something far worse – reported the man's activities. Police staged a stakeout but he didn't return to the Alvis. The cops had made chilling discoveries in the car: a picnic rug missing strips torn from it and a rough mask made from a hessian bag with slits cut for the eyes. Inspector Prior kept the latter discovery out of the newspapers for the moment.

As Australia wondered whether Phar Lap had been murdered by the Yanks, police received more reports that seemed to confirm Frank and Dorothy had met with foul play. A Liverpool winemaker said that, at 1am on the night in question, the driver of a red Alvis called at his house saying he was out of petrol. The witness sold him a quarter-gallon of fuel.

The man had been alone but there'd been something bulky wedged beneath the partly folded down 'dicky seat' at the rear. Another witness had seen the same car hours later parked half a mile from Rookwood Cemetery.

These witnesses gave matching descriptions of the distinctive-looking man and, when shown photos of criminals from the area, both identified the same suspect: William Cyril Moxley. Later, Superintendent MacKay would say that when he heard this news, he thought the minor crook he'd known for years must've gone mad.

A witness told detectives that the man he'd seen had a bandaged right hand and torn clothes, which strengthened the police's theory that Frank and Dorothy had been killed in a robbery gone wrong. Frank, they thought, had fought back and injured his assailant. Everything pointed to murder, with Moxley perhaps using the torn strips of rug to bind and strangle Frank and Dorothy. A search of the Burwood residence he shared with his son, Douglas, and girlfriend, Linda Fletcher, turned up hessian bags in which he'd deliver wood. One had a piece cut from it that perfectly fitted the mask. Police also impounded Moxley's truck, which was found to have bloodstains on one running board. As had been the case with Alfred Ball, Moxley's identity and description weren't yet revealed to the press; reports simply said police were looking for a 'well-known criminal'.

Prior was assisted by Detective-Inspector John Walsh, who had recent form as a murder investigator, having nabbed a stick-up artist who'd shot a man dead. The inspectors commanded a party of some 200 police searching both for Moxley and for the bodies of his presumed victims.

Their efforts became more focused after a truck driver came forward with a black beret, inside which had been wrapped a nickel-plated cowl from a car's dashboard. He'd found these on a lonely road near Bankstown golf course around the time the couple were presumed to have been killed. The beret was identified as Dorothy's; the cowl came from Frank's car. After making these finds, the truckie told police, he'd gone to a petrol station at Milperra. When he apologised for calling so early, the owner told him he wasn't the first customer of the day: an hour earlier, an agitated Alvis driver had tried to shield his face as he got his tank topped up, and had appeared unsure how to work the vehicle before finally driving off.

Lost amid major news stories of the grim search for Frank and Dorothy was a new report confirming that Alfred Ball – still not identified by name – hadn't committed suicide in the wake of murdering Katherine Sims. A young woman who knew him previously said she'd been assaulted by him on the night of Wednesday 6 April. He'd encountered her in an Erskineville street and threatened to cut her throat unless she went with him to a vacant lot. Detectives were reportedly renewing their search of the Depression landscape: empty houses, vacant factories, disused sheds.

But Moxley and his victims remained the main game. Various witnesses told of dealings with the suspect, including the Milperra garage owner, and several men who'd bought Alvis parts from him. The search now concentrated on a vast tract of bush south of Moorebank. On Monday 11 April, a constable following a faint car track on a dirt road spotted blood on a tree near a pile of branches. Moving them aside, he saw three fingers protruding from freshly turned soil. Frank's body was facedown in a shallow grave; both his hands were tied behind his back with one of Dorothy's stockings and strips of rug. He'd been battered and his jaw was broken; he had been killed by a shotgun blast to the left side of his head.

That late morning, Moxley showed up at the Bankstown house of his former neighbour and workmate Frank Corbett. Corbett and his wife invited the man they knew as 'Hudson' in for a cup of tea and scones. Moxley didn't appear nervous, and left after making an arrangement to deliver four tons of firewood a few days hence. With the fugitive's name and description not in the newspapers, the Corbetts had no idea they'd just hosted a suspected double murderer.

On Tuesday 12 April, Lang instructed his public servants to pay any revenues directly into the Treasury, which potentially contravened

Commonwealth law. The increasingly worried state governor, Sir Philip Game, sent a telegram to London asking for the King's advice. Moxley couldn't have known how the arcane bureaucratic politicking that followed would factor into his fate just as surely as the police posse on his trail.

Late that afternoon, a search volunteer found Dorothy's shallow grave, half a mile from where Frank had been buried. She was facedown, her hands tied behind her back with a strip of rug. Dorothy's face was battered and she'd been killed by a shotgun blast to the back of her head. She wore a blue dress and a blue coat and the top part of her undergarments. Her bloomers were around her neck, though not tightly, and she had bruising on her throat. There was evidence she'd had sexual relations – possibly forced – just prior to her death, although the police's suspicion of rape wasn't immediately disclosed. *The Sun*'s headline the next day captured Sydney's feeling of shock, anger and urgency: 'Amazing Callousness of Girl-Murderer – Almost Naked Body Recovered – Cold Blood; Features Obliterated – Not Outraged – Efforts Redoubled in Man Hunt'.

Frank Corbett, presumably having heard through the grapevine that Moxley was wanted, told police of his recent encounter, including the fugitive's promise to return. If that happened, Corbett said, he'd shoot him on sight. But Prior and Walsh thought this so unlikely they didn't assign officers to stake out the house. Instead, heavily armed police and an increasing number of civilians drove out of Liverpool to search the thick bush beyond the rifle range.

Although hundreds of police were trying to catch a maniac, Lang and MacKay seemed more concerned about other menaces. Sydneysiders awoke on 13 April to a huge army of uniformed sergeants and constables drilling in the city's parks. *The Sun* reported that, contrary to what some thought, this was merely prescribed annual practice and 'not a display of force on Mr Lang's behalf'. Which was precisely what it was: the premier and his police superintendent were showing the New Guard what they'd face if they didn't pull their heads in.

By the next morning, Childs and MacKay had taken the unusual step of releasing a photo of Moxley. It appeared full-length on the front-page of *The Daily Telegraph* beside an article headlined: 'On the Track of the Wanted Man'. This report included a detailed description, although his name and various aliases still weren't printed, and it also related his visit to the Corbett house, noting the police had conducted a fruitless search of its immediate surrounds. In making these details public, the CIB was now opening 'out a man hunt on a scale never attempted before in Australia ... [and they] will flood NSW with crime circulars and photographs concerning his appearance and habits.' Remarkably, Moxley did return to see Frank Corbett that morning. For the past couple of days, Corbett and a mate had waited in concealment with their rifles. They'd just given up on their ambush and gone into the house when Moxley came crunching up the path.

Corbett grabbed his gun. 'Put your hands up, Bill,' he said. 'Don't move. I know what you have done.'

Moxley bolted as Corbett fired a warning shot, which didn't slow his escape into the scrub. Corbett phoned Bankstown police. The station didn't have a car and a constable had to catch a bus to the house. He didn't arrive until 10am. Only after he heard the story in person did he call the CIB. By the time Prior and his men arrived, Moxley had a two-hour head start.

More than 100 plainclothesmen scoured a large area of scrub from Bankstown to Chullora. But the manhunt was hindered. The force still didn't have enough wireless cars, making coordination difficult, nor did it have a dog squad, which might have tracked Moxley to where he was actually hiding. MacKay resolved to fix both problems. The former was a question of resources, ever scarcer when costs were being cut to the bone. But the latter might be solved cheaply and simply, as MacKay knew just the dog-loving constable for the job: Adam 'Scotty' Denholm.

After fleeing Corbett, Moxley knocked on the door of a nearby

Bankstown home. When mother-of-two Marie Harding answered the door, the man she also knew as 'Hudson' forced his way inside and she became more terrified when she saw he had a shotgun under a blanket. Moxley said he needed to hide because he'd gone to see a mate about money and this fellow had shot at him. He ordered Marie to draw the blinds and to not answer the door to the butcher and baker when they called. Moxley also reassured her, saying he wasn't one to hurt women and children. He took a pair of socks, a hat and some old trousers from Marie. What he really wanted was that morning's newspaper; presumably, Corbett had said something about it – or Moxley simply suspected he'd been named in the press. But Marie didn't have one. Moxley said: 'You make sure'. She was sure, repeating she didn't get the paper delivered.

Marie didn't know his identity – or that he was wanted. She cooked him some chops, and cleverly put her clock forward an hour to make him think it was later. Moxley paid her a shilling for the meal and gave her children a penny each. Then, thinking it had reached four in the afternoon, he left them unharmed to continue his fugitive existence.

At one o'clock the next morning, Moxley approached a dairyman who was milking a cow and asked for a drink. The man saw that he fit the description of the suspect and threatened to unleash his dogs on Moxley, who melted back into the gloom.

Just after dawn, locals began their search, not waiting for police to arrive from the city. By now hundreds or even thousands of unemployed men and boys had joined the manhunt. Later that day, Childs and MacKay finally issued an arrest warrant and released the suspect's name: 'William Fletcher – aka Moxley'. His photo was published on the front page of *The Sun*, and 10,000 wanted posters were plastered up, not only in police stations, as was usual, but also in Sydney's hotels and billiard halls, which Moxley was known to frequent.

Prior made police history in New South Wales by making an appeal via the 'talkie' newsreels. Like Frankenstein's monster – now on dozens of massive billboards ringing the city and in thrilling coming-attraction cinema trailers – Moxley's face was everywhere. The public response was also akin to something from the upcoming film sensation. Civilians armed themselves with revolvers and rifles, clubs and other weapons, both to join the hunt and to protect themselves and their people. *The Sydney Morning Herald* reported: 'Residents of the district are in a state of terror, men walking around with firearms being a common sight.' Under the headline 'Terror Reigns', *The Sun* told its readers: 'Milkmen have told the police that, in scores of places, they are greeted early in the morning by fear-stricken householders with guns.' The paper worried that 'the reckless use of firearms might be responsible for serious consequences', especially now that even 'children are participating in the grave adventure'. *The Daily Telegraph* chimed in: 'Bankstown is in a state of panic, and anyone who goes prowling about houses is risking death.'

Truth wrapped it all up in its headline: 'Lynch Law Parties Are on the Trail – Grim Man Hunt Stirs Residents of Bankstown – Public Posses Are Out to Get Their Man'. The article flirted with endorsing vigilantism: '*Truth* has been informed that they will hang the man and then throw his lifeless body into a bonfire – vengeance!' When one Alexandria councilman demanded drastic reforms to the justice system to ensure murderers were hanged, a Redfern alderman went one better by saying such monsters should be flogged and boiled in oil.

Police were inundated with more than fifty reports from people who reckoned they'd seen or heard Moxley near their homes, which sent officers rushing from one location to the next. But when it counted most, a local again let the suspect slip away. On the afternoon of Friday 15 April, in Lakemba, with police searching bush just fifty yards away, a resident disturbed a fellow in the scrub who jumped up and ran away from his camp. Thinking the bloke was just a drifter who didn't want to be rousted by the cops, the man didn't bother to alert the search party. Then, on the Saturday afternoon, curious because the hobo hadn't returned, the man went to see if he'd left anything behind. The witness found a shotgun, with cartridges jammed in its barrels, and its wooden stock split. Only then did he call the police.

Days went by without another confirmed sighting. *Smith's Weekly* ran a front-page article exposing Moxley's criminal history, including that this 'Pariah of the Underworld' was a suspected police informer who'd once taken a bullet to the head for his betrayals. In its details of his crimes, including all those daring cat burglaries in different suburbs, the article depicted a cunning character who knew both the city and the bush. Their profile was accompanied by a ghastly illustration imagining Moxley hiding somewhere in the scrub inside the vast search area. The effect on potential jury members can be imagined – as was true of much of the sensational coverage.

But *Smith's Weekly* and the police didn't have a clue that for the past week the search had been entirely in the wrong location. After Moxley fled his scrub hiding spot, he used an escape route never before available to fugitives. Traipsing through the bush to Earlwood, he stole a bicycle and rode it into the city. Plucking up his courage, he pedalled onto the Sydney Harbour Bridge, paid the threepenny toll to the collector, almost under the watch of constables, and continued his ride north. Moxley set up beneath a rock overhang near a stream in rugged bush at Balgowlah.

But he didn't just hide out. He used grease from the bicycle's chain to darken his eyebrows, his hair and the beard and moustache he was growing. At night he rode into Mosman or Spit Junction to buy food and newspapers so he could read about the manhunt. Moxley even went to the pictures and saw the talkie newsreel about him, ducking down in his seat as the audience discussed the monster in their midst.

The police's publicity blitz eventually paid off. On the afternoon of Thursday 21 April, as Moxley was riding back into the bush off Frenchs Forest Road, he was seen by a young man who recognised him and called Manly police. Shown where the fugitive had gone along a scrub track,

Detective-Constable Walter Tassell, Detective-Constable Norman Newton and Constable Kenneth Gill followed the bike's tyre marks for half a mile. Up ahead, they saw shirts and singlets hung on trees as if to dry. This was the sort of duty that had gotten two of their comrades killed at the beginning of the previous year.

Creeping through the undergrowth, they spotted a man lying on his back on grass in the shadow of huge rock.

Newton pulled his revolver and shouted: 'You're Moxley! Stop or I'll shoot!'

The fugitive raced into the bush, disappearing before the officer could fire. The trio of policemen charged after Moxley, taking divergent paths, but he'd vanished. Then Newton and Gill converged at the edge of a small cliff: Moxley was crouching about a dozen feet beneath them. Both men took the plunge. Gill landed on Moxley and sent him sprawling. Newton dropped nearby and helped overpower and handcuff the fugitive.

After fifteen days, one of Australia's most intense manhunts was at an end.

Hauled to the police car, Moxley was driven to Manly station. 'I am the man,' Moxley allegedly told Newton. 'I have read all the newspapers, and I know what I am wanted for. I did not kill those people, but I know who did, and if you take me to Superintendent MacKay, I will tell him all I know about it.'

Moxley was allowed to call MacKay. 'They have got me at last,' he supposedly said. 'I am glad it is all over. I would like to see you and would like to speak with you.' He got his wish at CIB headquarters. The superintendent later related that when he arrived, Moxley said to him: 'Good day, Mr MacKay. I am sorry I let you down.'

MacKay replied: 'This is a serious thing you have been retained on.'

Later that afternoon, Moxley accompanied MacKay, Prior and other detectives to his house in Burwood, and then to a bush cottage and the murder scenes. When they returned to the CIB offices, Moxley was interrogated for about eight hours. Across this period, he allegedly made a statement confessing he had abducted, robbed and tied up Frank and Dorothy. Yet he maintained that he *hadn't* killed them – the murders, he said, were committed by another man.

While Moxley had dinner, MacKay left the CIB to check in on a huge rally Lang was holding outside Sydney Town Hall. The premier thundered to a crowd of 50,000, saying he would prevail in the looming showdown with the prime minister. Somewhere in this vast audience was Jack Saywell, a twenty-year-old law student who'd stopped to listen to Lang on his way home from tuition. Most in the crowd had a vested working-class interest in the premier's fate, but the Saywell family had a different stake in Lang's political fight. Just hours earlier, Jack's immensely wealthy father, Victor Claude Saywell, had concluded a controversial company takeover that had for months been brewing as a scandal for Lang. That it was now a done deal wasn't going to make the premier's lot any easier.

Lang's rally went off without incident and MacKay returned to the CIB. At 1.45am on Friday 22 April 1932, he charged his long-time informant William Cyril Moxley with murdering Frank Wilkinson and Dorothy Denzel. The accused was led to a cell, where he immediately fell into an exhausted sleep. With Moxley's arrest written up in the evening papers, the citizenry could also slumber peacefully, safe in the knowledge that the monster was in chains.

But right at that moment, another creature was creeping towards his sleeping victims.

10

The Hammer Horror

At six-thirty the next morning, Jack Saywell got out of bed in his upstairs room at Medway, the two-storey house in Fairfax Road, Bellevue Hill, that he shared with his father, known as Claude, his mother, Adeline, and his younger brother, Tom. Downstairs in the kitchen, Jack read the day's newspapers. The big front-page stories concerned the capture and charging of Moxley, and Lang's defiant rally at Town Hall. Of course, his father's dealings were there too. *The Daily Telegraph*'s headline read: 'Tin Hares: Mascot Sells Out! £83,000 Co. Goes for £21,000: Trouble Expected.'

At about five minutes past seven, with Jack in the lounge listening to the wireless, the family's live-in maid, Hilda Champion, took tea upstairs to Claude and Adeline. After knocking on their bedroom door and getting no response, she pushed it open and beheld a nightmare. Hilda rushed to tell Jack his parents were 'smothered in blood'. He raced upstairs. Their room was ransacked. Claude and Adeline Saywell were in their bed, blankets up to their chins, foreheads caved in, blood soaking the pillows and sheets and splashed right up one wall to the ceiling.

Incredibly, his mother and father were both still breathing.

~

Claude's father, Thomas Saywell, had been an English immigrant who made his fortune as Sydney's dominant importer, manufacturer and retailer of tobacco from the mid-19th century. He'd used his wealth to buy the Zig Zag colliery at Lithgow, and amassed still greater riches with other mines, a finance company, an ironmongering business and property developments, which included constructing a private tramway to the seaside resort suburb he built and named 'Brighton Le Sands'.

Claude was one of Thomas's thirteen children, and while other sons became managers of family businesses, he and his brother Thomas Jr became solicitors and formed Saywell & Saywell. But as major family shareholders, they also served on Saywell company boards. Claude married Adeline Herald in 1910 and they had son Jack in 1911, with Tom following in 1916. When Thomas Sr died in 1928 at the ripe old age of ninety-one, he left each of his sons an inheritance valued around £27,000 – equivalent to about $2.7 million today.

Four years later, on 17 February 1932, Claude Saywell and his four wealthy business partners formed the Greyhound Racing Club (GRC), whose only asset was a ten-shilling *option* to lease the government-owned racecourse at Kensington. That same day, the GRC was awarded Sydney's second licence to run mechanical 'tin hare' greyhound races at that venue. This was a scandal because Lang had publicly promised it would go to the Australian Coursing Club (ACC). But the premier had abruptly changed his mind – reportedly on learning that Eric Campbell was a major ACC shareholder – and made his decision without consulting cabinet.

Once so favoured, the GRC immediately registered as having £25,000 in capital in £1 shares. Large holdings went to the five directors, with Saywell receiving 1201. The public would be able to buy 10,000 shares at £2 each, with 5000 more shares reserved. Overnight, the directors made a paper fortune. They had also ensured a monopoly because four of them – Saywell included – already controlled the Greyhound Coursing Association company (GCA), which operated the original Sydney tin hare racecourse license. The ACC had spent £58,000 on operations, and was ruined.

The opposition called for a royal commission, but it wasn't the Campbell angle they wanted investigated. Instead, it was alleged that Premier Lang been swayed by infamous tin-hare identity Frederick Swindell, who was linked as a director of the GCA and who'd donated thousands of pounds to Labor. Without referencing his ACC holdings, Eric Campbell called the 'Tin Hares scandal' evidence of government corruption; new state UAP opposition leader Bertram Stevens met with MacKay to demand a police investigation rather than a royal commission.

Then, on Thursday 21 April, came the final play when Claude Saywell negotiated the fire sale of the ACC to the GRC. The company he partly owned acquired its previous rival's track, equipment and other assets for shillings on the pound. With the deal done, and back home that night, Claude, Adeline and Tom entertained their next-door neighbours Mr and Mrs Pitt. It was the maid Hilda's day off, and she returned to the house at 9.30pm. The visitors left about half an hour later, and the Saywells and their maid had retired to their respective upstairs bedrooms.

Jack told police he'd been studying with his tutor until ten o'clock, and then they'd gone to Town Hall to listen to Lang. After that, Jack took a tram to Double Bay and visited his girlfriend, Jean Comerford, whose family also lived in Fairfax Road, Bellevue Hill. Jean was asleep when he got there after eleven. He'd been due earlier and so, to avoid getting into trouble, he wound her clock back forty-five minutes. This, he said, was just a little joke that she was wise to when she woke up.

Jack said he changed the clock back to the right time when he left Jean's around 1.45am. Arriving home, he took the front door key from its place under the welcome mat. Jack crept upstairs quietly, because his late nights were the cause of many arguments with his parents. On the landing, he saw three things that were a little unusual. First, his parents' bedroom door was closed, and they usually kept it open. Second, his damp towel was on the hallway floor, and third, a little farther along lay his dad's dressing gown – both of these were at odds with his mother's tidiness. But none of it was worth waking his parents about, so Jack scooped up his towel and went to bed. Before going to sleep, he heard the family's clock chime 2.15am. Less than five hours later, in the moments after the terrible discovery of his battered parents, Jack called the telephone exchange and asked for a doctor to be sent. Then he raced to get the family car from its garage nearby and drove to the police station at Double Bay. There he saw Constable John Carey, who came back with him to the house. 'I don't know what has happened,' Jack told the policeman. 'Go up those steps and you will see.'

Jack arrived at Denholm, the private hospital at Darling Point, ahead of the ambulance transporting his parents, both of whom were in comas after suffering multiple skull fractures. They'd need to be stabilised before surgeries that weren't expected to save their lives. Jack told doctors to do whatever was possible and that no expense should be spared.

Inspector Jacob Miller – his career long since back on track after the IWW case – had charge of Area B and would lead the investigation. His officers swarmed over the mansion crime scene. While the ransacked bedroom made it look like the Saywells had been attacked by a panicking burglar, none of the couple's valuables – including jewellery worth thousands of pounds, some of it out in the open – would be found to have been stolen. Detectives interviewed Tom, who said he'd woken up around 1am. He couldn't say what, if anything, had disturbed him, and he hadn't heard any noise in the fifteen minutes it had taken him to fall back to sleep. Likewise, Hilda told police she hadn't heard anything even though her bedroom shared a wall with that of her employers.

Jack said he hadn't heard any noise after he came home, and that the front and back doors were both locked when he arrived. Given it had been Hilda's day off, and the house was empty for about an hour in the late afternoon, he theorised to police that the attacker must've come in then and hidden in his mother and father's bedroom. As for how this assailant got in – he might've used the key under the mat, or reached through a window by the back door to unlock it. Jack also offered that the intruder could have climbed from a bay window ledge onto the balcony connecting the parental quarters with Tom's bedroom. But to do so, the assailant would have to have stood in the garden, and there were no footprints to suggest this, just as there were no marks on the ledge to indicate anyone had stood there. Hand marks were found on the drainpipe that went up by the upper-floor lavatory window, but Jack explained that he'd made those about a week ago, when he'd climbed up to get into the house after arriving home late and finding himself locked out.

Detective-Constable Arthur Burns discovered two fresh footprints in a garden at the front of the property. He believed these hadn't been made by a shoe but by a size-seven slipper. Burns searched a vacant lot opposite the house. One hundred and sixteen feet from the footprints, he recovered a claw hammer. This tool had been washed clean of fingerprints, but it still bore traces of blood. The scenario suggested by his discoveries? After smashing the skulls of the sleeping couple, the attacker had rinsed the hammer, gone into the front garden, put his weight on his slipper-shod foot and hurled the weapon as far as possible into the darkness of the vacant lot. This posed obvious questions. Why had he been wearing slippers? Why not dispose of the hammer far from the house while making his escape?

Suspicion fell on Jack. Detectives searched his clothes, with Hilda's assistance. She said none were missing, and nothing they inspected was bloodstained. Further, Hilda told detectives that Jack had acted normally the morning she made her terrible discovery – and that he had seemed genuinely shocked by everything. Hilda stated that while Jack had arguments with his parents, he had loved them – as did younger brother Tom.

Jack was questioned for hours. He admitted his relationship with his parents hadn't been perfect. They'd had ongoing arguments about him staying out too late. His staunchly Protestant mum and dad also made it clear they wouldn't allow him to marry Jean Comerford because she was a Catholic. Jack said he'd laughed this off, saying he was young and not thinking of marrying anyone. But his mother warned that they were serious: defy them and he'd be cut out of their will. In the Saywell family, this wasn't an idle threat. When Claude's brother Bruce had died in 1925, his will stipulated that his children would get nothing if they were married to Catholics. Jack also told police that his mother had believed his £2 weekly allowance was too much, and his father had agreed to suspend it until he passed his law exam. Shown the hammer, which his brother had identified as belonging to the family, Jack said it looked like one they owned but he couldn't be sure. As for who could've attacked his mother and father, he reckoned his father had no enemies.

But perhaps Adeline had made one. The Pitts told detectives that, hours before the attack, she'd been concerned about a foreigner who'd come to the door that morning looking for work. He'd become abusive when she turned him away, and stuck his foot in the door before she finally slammed it on him. Detectives would follow up on this. But there were other potential attackers and motives. Could Claude's law work have made him enemies? He was involved in conveyancing, rather than criminal work, so a violent crook with a grudge didn't seem likely. But the Tin Hares scandal might prove a tantalising angle. Except, according to the *Sydney Morning Herald*, the police had all but ruled out such a motive: 'To this theory the police have not paid serious attention. Enmity strong enough to lead to a carefully planned murder is rare, and most of the objections to the theory of robbery apply also to this conjecture.'

Late on the night of Saturday 23 April 1932, Claude Saywell died in hospital, never having regained consciousness.

The Saywell newspaper coverage rivalled that from just weeks earlier. *The Sun* updated readers with the development-packed headline: 'Saywell Dead: Assault Is Now Brutal Murder. Can Wife Tell Attacker? Her Life Despaired of: Doctors' Views. Police Guard Home.' Could the public help? The paper ran a photo of the murder weapon, asking: 'Do

You Recognise This Hammer?' *Truth* was to come up with the most memorable catchphrase for the crime: the 'Hammer Horror'.

~

The day after Claude died, hundreds of Sydneysiders witnessed a new type of horror that would plague the city during the worst years of the Depression. Just as the bridge had given Moxley a novel method of escape, it now offered a new way for people to exit lives of desperation.

That Sunday, amid a throng of pedestrians enjoying a stroll over the monumental marvel, a middle-aged man calmly climbed the walkway railing and hurled himself into the waters nearly two hundred feet below. There was another suicide the next day – Anzac Day – and forty-four would follow before a barrier fence was finished in February 1934.

~

The day after Anzac Day there was another sensational and senseless murder. Albert Chaffey, cousin to former chief secretary Frank Chaffey, was early that morning shot dead in his yard two miles outside of Glen Innes, in the Northern Tablelands of New South Wales. The forty-year-old husband and father of a young son had a milk run and was well known in the district. Albert had risen at 4.45am, said goodbye to his wife and then gone to get the carts ready. Before she'd gone back to sleep, she'd drowsily heard what sounded like a stone hitting a fence and a horse galloping off.

At six o'clock, a lad that Albert employed as a driver came to start work and found his boss lying facedown. He'd been shot in the head, the bullet from a .22 'pea gun' fired into the back of his neck, reportedly at close range. Albert still had horse winkers grasped in one hand, which meant he'd been killed within minutes of stepping from his house. A small leather bag containing around £10 was missing. It wasn't much, but more than he'd usually carry as he'd been unable to bank payments he'd received over the Anzac Day long weekend. That night in Sydney there was another murder. Police were called to a humpy at a Sutherland unemployment camp. It'd been the scene of a 'drunken orgy' earlier that evening. The hangover was horrific. Officers found Michael Desmond, aged about fifty, dead of a head wound in his crude bunk, blood splashed on the tent walls. Curled up on the floor a few feet away was a woman. She was blood-spattered but alive and unhurt – just passed out from the booze she'd drunk. Another woman and a man named Thomas Jenkins were also the worse for wear outside the humpy.

The Sun reported: 'Eight men and two women [were] found in the camp and all in a drunken condition were detained by the police. They were in no condition to be questioned. One hurled the typewriter in the police charge-room to the floor and threw an inkwell at a constable.'

The culprit was soon clear. When he sobered up, Jenkins, thirty-four, admitted he'd struck the fatal blow with a tomahawk. But he'd done so in self-defence, he said, after drunken Desmond – known to police as an erratic and abusive character – had attacked him with a lump of wood. Jenkins was charged with murder.

As *Truth* would have it, this was 'another bloody link in the grim and ever-growing chain of this State's gruesome murders for the year'. *The Sun* kept tally: eleven in just four months. While it was actually about the same as in previous years, it seemed worse because there'd been five in the past few weeks. What's more, they'd all been of a savage nature and three killers were yet to be caught. Mr GFK Taylor, of the Chamber of Commerce's Institute of Psychology, reckoned 'suggestivity' could be blamed:

> Murders come under three headings – where a person commits the crime out of sheer fear; where anger or rage overcomes someone; or when a person deliberately plans the crime, possibly because he or she had no sense of responsibility. Where police have difficulty

in tracing suspects, this probably gives a murderer an idea of security – the idea that he can get away with it. Probably we will have more crimes of a violent nature.

Unsolved murders, Taylor was claiming, would embolden new murderers.

With the Glen Innes police stumped in the Albert Chaffey case, McRae was sent to investigate. He was teamed again with Detective-Sergeant Len Allmond. *The Glen Innes Examiner* reported that even McRae – 'whose work in connection with the Bungendore mystery ranks him as one of the leading criminal detectives in the Commonwealth' – might not be up to solving 'one of the most baffling crimes on record in the State'.

McRae quickly dispensed with the idea that Albert had been shot by a stranger; the killer had clearly known his routine. Perhaps he'd also been aware that Albert would have more money than usual. Even so, was robbery the primary motive? Was it worth risking your neck in a noose for ten quid? McRae interviewed locals, who could all account for their movements, even if they just claimed to have been asleep, which wasn't unreasonable given the time Albert had been shot. But McRae asked each the same question: 'Do you own a .22-calibre rifle?'

The science of 'forensic ballistics' was very new, another of the methods MacKay had studied abroad in 1929. In September 1931, Jim Devine had gone to trial for the murder of a taxi driver. (Despite sharing a surname, he apparently wasn't related to Moxley's earlier assailant.) The victim had been found shot dead in his car outside the Maroubra house that 'Big Jim' shared with his crime queenpin wife, Tilly Devine. Big Jim's defence – conducted by barrister Bob Sproule – was that he'd been firing his rifle in an attempt to lawfully apprehend Frank Green, his erstwhile gangster comrade, who'd robbed him and was blazing away with a revolver as he made for the taxi. It had been night-time, the bullets had been flying, and one of Big Jim's shots had hit and killed the taxi driver by accident – for which Jim was very sorry.

At trial, MacKay, who'd taken the accused's long statement in private at the CIB, testified that Frank Green was indeed a 'bad man', and anyone expecting 'to arrest him might expect to be shot'. The jury took five minutes to acquit Big Jim. This case was notable not only for MacKay's very direct involvement and influence but also as the first time in New South Wales that forensic ballistics were used: cartridges found on the lawn had been shown to bear distinctive marks from Big Jim's rifle. The bullet in the dead man, though, couldn't be subjected to comparative tests because the CIB didn't have the right equipment. That had changed by the time Albert Chaffey was shot. McRae confiscated .22 rifles from any possible suspects for testing in Sydney. He would also send the experts the bullet from the dead man. While newspaper headlines about the Chaffey case used phrases like 'No Headway', 'Not Slightest Clue' and 'Detectives at Dead End', McRae kept his cards close to his chest and waited for the ballistics reports.

~

MacKay wasn't keeping his cards hidden: he was showing his hand to the New Guard. Lang later recalled that, with a 'quizzical grin on his face', his superintendent had said: 'We are going to let them see what they will be up against if they start any trouble'. On Friday 29 April, some 1500 police officers of all ranks marched, drove and rode through the city, their route taking them by the banks, clubs and restaurants where New Guard members worked and socialised. Campbell and De Groot witnessed a show of police force never before seen in the state.

Their ally Reginald Weaver had asked in parliament: 'What was the object of the parade, and was there any significance to it?' Lang's chief secretary, Mark Gosling, replied: 'A parade of policemen holds no terrors for any law abiding citizen.' MacKay had put on a spectacle. But his next moves against the New Guard were to be far more shadowy – and far more devastating.

11

The Strange Case of Snowy Mumby

The inquest into the murders of Frank Wilkinson and Dorothy Denzel was scheduled to start on 3 May. Under normal circumstances, it would be held at the Liverpool Coroner's Court, near the scene of the crimes. But Moxley's safety couldn't be guaranteed in Sydney's enraged south-west, so he'd face the Sydney Coroner's Court instead.

The newspapers promised that the inquest would reveal startling details about the crime. But *Truth* readers didn't have to wait, because the paper printed Moxley's version of events – as set down in a statement he'd made to MacKay. This was a genuine scoop, outlining Moxley's defence as it would be presented at the inquest, delivered to the newspaper by MacKay, who carefully cultivated the press as a policing tool and to burnish his professional and personal reputation. Despite the risks to due process, *Truth* often had the skinny on serious cases – from the superintendent himself or from his senior detectives.

Moxley claimed that on the night of the murders he'd left his house to go to his Liverpool bushland camp, because he'd been offered a lot of firewood. On approach, he found the previous night's big storm had made the tracks impassable, so he turned around and headed for home. But he had minor motor trouble and stopped near Strathfield Golf Course. That was when he saw a car parked beside the road and a couple sitting on the grass.

Moxley claimed he'd had the sudden impulse to rob the man and woman. Taking the shotgun he carried in his lorry for shooting rabbits, he'd threatened them and demanded money. Frank said he only had seven shillings, and Dorothy had taken this money from his pocket and handed it over. Moxley said Frank then rushed him and they fought. 'We came to grips, but I must have hit the man first,' he said. 'I had nothing in my hand when I hit him. The girl never squealed. She seemed more terrified. I then told the girl if she sang out I would hurt her.'

Moxley claimed to have been empty-handed but it's likely he used the shotgun to smash Frank, given it had been found with a shattered stock. His statement continued: 'I tied the man's hands and placed him in the back of the car and told the girl to sit in beside me.' Moxley had to ask her how to start the Alvis. Nonsensically, he also claimed he hadn't intended to steal the car, merely to drive it far away from his own vehicle, which he'd then return to in order to make his getaway. But it ran out of petrol, so Moxley walked Frank and Dorothy to an empty cottage in the bush, leaving them tied up while he went to get fuel. Having gotten some petrol from a householder, Moxley returned to the cottage.

> The man said, 'Will you untie us?' I never had the gun with me. The gun was in the car. I untied the girl's feet and we undone the man's hands and feet and when I did so the man came at me again. We had another fight. We came to blows and I don't really remember just what really happened. We had a good fight. I can't recall anything being said or done. All I know is we were both fighting and struggling on the ground. From then on my memory is a blank.

Moxley said the next thing he remembered was driving the Alvis across the bridge at Milperra. After going to the garage for more petrol, he left the car at Strathfield – near where he'd abducted Frank and Dorothy –

and retrieved his truck and drove home, arriving about half-past seven. 'I stayed home a little while and then went out again,' he said. 'I went up the road and thought that I would put the car that I had been riding in out of the road. I put it in the garage and left it there and went home.'

Moxley claimed his hand had been injured before that night but he'd hurt it further during his fights with Frank. He agreed the hessian mask was his and that he'd been wearing it during the attack. Moxley admitted to tearing up the rug to tie his victims, and to having sold the Alvis's generator, carburettor and magneto. While he identified the shotgun as his, he said he had no recollection of shooting the couple or of burying the victims:

> I had no intention of doing those people any harm. Anything that happened was beyond my control. I have never seen those people before in my life. I don't know them. I had never met their parents. They have never done me any harm and, as far as I know, I had no reason to do them any and I regret having done these people any harm. I am very sorry for what I have done now that I can see what has happened. My only explanation to offer is that my own father was shot and died with a gun. When I was a boy ten years of age, through no fault of my own, my brother was killed in front of my eyes by me with a gun.

He continued:

> I firmly believe that what has happened was fated to happen and nothing could stop it. Some two years ago I was shot through the head. I nearly lost my life for doing a service to the public and the police. The bullet nearly took my life and since then I have never been the same man. I am unable to control my temper. The only thing I can put it down to is that I unconsciously done this thing

and that is the only explanation I can make. I suffer from pains in the head continuously and the only relief I could get was from Aspros, of which I am in the habit of consuming boxes. Some time ago I was ordered to have another operation by the doctor but I never went under it. There is still parts of the bullet in my head and whether that has anything to do with it I don't know. I went to the war, and was discharged with a clean discharge, after having about two years' active service.

Moxley went on:

I would like to say that I had been working that day and had work to go to and I don't know why I done this thing. I have been working hard from morning to night in the Bankstown and Liverpool area cutting wood for the past eighteen months and can produce evidence to this effect. I have never previously, except as stated herein, at any time used violence against any person.

Moxley's statement had included his response to this question from Detective-Inspector John Walsh: 'Was there any other person with you on the night these people were taken to that house?' Moxley answered no – though he would also contradict that.

MacKay had almost certainly – at the very least – coached Moxley on what to say and how to say it in his statement. Talking about their arrangement explicitly was *verboten*. As for the statement's contents, and MacKay leaking it, the cop's motives can be guessed. Likely he wanted Sydney's people to know the police had the right man in Moxley. It would also prime potential jurors with the 'facts' before they were tested in court. But MacKay might also have been giving his informant – for whom he felt some sympathy – the beginnings of an insanity defence that might save him from hanging.

When the inquest began, the Sydney Coroner's Court was besieged by hundreds of people desperate to get a look at Moxley. The accused's statement was read. Detective Newton testified that, after his arrest, Moxley had told him: 'I did not kill those people, but I know who did.' Dr Palmer gave evidence about Frank and Dorothy's facial injuries, and that they'd been killed with shotgun blasts to the head. Asked if Dorothy had been raped, he gave a qualified yes:

> There had been relations not long before she died, and perhaps forcible or unusual. There was evidence of force. The fact that she had been nearly choked made it seem so. She had a garment around her neck, and that it had been drawn tightly at some time seemed to be borne out by the bruise on her neck, which might have been caused, however, by a hand.

The court heard about the discoveries of the bodies, the discovery of the rough mask and matching hessian bag at Moxley's house, and about the injury to the accused's hand and the previous bullet wound to his head.

Detective-Sergeant Hill testified that MacKay, in the defendant's presence in the detectives' office, had said: 'I have had a talk with Moxley and he says that he knows all about the holding up of Wilkinson and Miss Denzel and that there was another man with him. He wants to show us the places.' Hill told of the car trip they made and what Moxley said at the cottage:

> The last I saw of them was when the man was in the shed, and the girl was in a room on the back verandah. The man who was with them was sitting down close to the girl. I then went to Liverpool, and got some petrol, and when I got back, the man and the woman and the man I had left with them were all gone.

115

Hill said Moxley clammed up when taken to the shallow gravesites. Only on their way back to the CIB did he resume talking: 'I will tell you all I know about the murder. I know the man who has done it and I will tell you his name. I know where he lives.'

Now, in court, it emerged that Moxley had identified the killer as 'Snowy' Mumby. He described the man as being about thirty-four, standing five-foot-eight or five-foot-nine, with fair hair brushed back. He had a fair complexion, and blue or grey eyes. Moxley had claimed to MacKay that he'd known Mumby in the army – they'd served in the same unit, and later knocked around together in pool halls. This fellow – also called 'Bill' – had a speech impediment, was in the habit of robbing drunks and was always 'knuckling around' with women. But right down to age, height and colouring, way of speaking, army service, the names 'Bill' and the nickname 'Snowy', Moxley had described himself. The coroner was told that police were still looking for this man. If, of course, he existed.

On the second day of the inquest, witnesses testified to seeing Moxley with the Alvis as he drove around, and how he'd sold parts of the car a few days later. The garage owner said Moxley told him he owned the Alvis. Men told the court they'd been hired by Moxley to drive his lorry, and one had seen the truck's side-irons splashed with blood the day after the murders. Marie Harding related how the fugitive had invaded her home – which was the first time her harrowing experience was made public. In total, about three dozen police, medical experts and civilians testified, and much physical evidence was produced, including a shovel believed to have been used to dig the graves, pieces of rug, the shotgun and pellets retrieved from Frank's shattered head. Acting on the advice of his solicitor, the accused did not testify and reserved his defence.

The Liverpool coroner, who presided despite the change of venue to Sydney for Moxley's safety, said he was satisfied that the accused had left his home with a gun and a mask, which showed criminal intent.

His story about the fight in the house I cannot believe, and I don't think he ever untied those two people in the house. Moxley says he does not remember anything until crossing the bridge, which is only a small distance from the house, and he said a bullet wound in the head may have caused him to forget his memory. The doctor, however, examined him, and he did not seem to notice that fact very much.

The coroner noted that Moxley was seen by numerous witnesses between 12.30am and 1am – and then again around dawn. What had he done between these sightings? As for his claim that 'Snowy Mumby' committed the murders, the coroner said: 'That I cannot believe.' He committed Moxley to stand trial for both murders.

If found guilty, Moxley would be sentenced to death. Yet, with Lang in power and Labor staunchly against capital punishment, even Moxley wouldn't hang if convicted of these most diabolical of crimes.

12

The Grim Riddle of the Murder Wave

Adeline Saywell remained in hospital, comatose and in critical condition. Even so, the newspapers reported that she had briefly surfaced from her limbo and been able to speak – and that an arrest was imminent. These details weren't true; Inspector Miller had likely fed them to reporters in the hope of spooking the killer into making a mistake.

As days passed without any developments, the newspapers kept the story alive with increasingly exploitative angles. On 28 April, *Smith's Weekly*'s front page was devoted to photos of the grief-stricken sons at their father's funeral, and the accompanying article detailed how the family had a deeply anti-Catholic streak that readers might link to Jack's forbidden love for papist gal-pal Jean. *Truth* leaned into the suspicion about Jack in convoluted fashion. In an article headlined 'Planned Murder with Devilish Cunning – Scheme to Implicate Dead Man's Household – Fiendish Murderer Left No Useful Clue', it claimed detectives thought Jack's hider-in-the-house theory was absurd:

> It is difficult to see how anybody from outside could have committed the blood-chilling deed and left without detection.

So, ask the police, did some fiend with super cunning deliberately attempt to make it appear an 'inside job'; deliberately try to direct a finger of suspicion at someone in the house?

The police weren't really asking this question; the logical answer to it was no – it had to have been Jack. His desire to marry Jean was a possible trigger. But money might be a stronger motive.

Claude Saywell had been worth £110,000 – about $12 million in modern terms. After probate, £40,000 would go on duties, leaving £70,000. Adeline was to get £1000 annually for the rest of her life and £40,000 had been set aside for this. So Jack and Tom were each to get about £15,000, which might seem a less compelling motive for murder, though, of course, people had been slaughtered recently for far less. Further, whoever had killed Claude had also meant to kill Adeline, which meant Jack and Tom would've inherited £35,000 each.

Jack would counter this by saying that although he'd recently had to borrow £2 from his girlfriend Jean, he hadn't been worried about money because it was his understanding that he was, on his twenty-first birthday in October, to get about £8000 from his grandfather's estate. Why murder for money when he'd soon be rolling in cash?

With the Saywell slayer no closer to being identified, Katherine Sims's razor murderer still on the run and McRae seemingly stumped on the Chaffey case at Glen Innes, the newspapers worried about the fiends roaming free. *The Sun* went with the headline 'Three Killers – Murder Mysteries Unsolved', while *The Sydney Morning Herald* opted for 'Unsolved Crimes. Police Investigations'. Variations on the theme appeared in regional publications. *The Sun* wondered what was behind the 'Grim Riddle of the Murder Wave' and asked: 'What Brings Cycle of Killings?' Its report considered a scientist's sunspot theory, perhaps because the usual earthbound triggers didn't seem to be to blame:

> In Australia there now exists ... a period of financial depression, with concomitant unemployment, starvation and misery. It is only natural that there should be a series of crimes against property ... But murder is another matter: especially as, in the recent horrifying murders, robbery has not been a direct motive ... One characteristic of them, in any case, is a total disregard for human life.

The pressure was on, particularly for Prior, who since taking over as CIB chief just a month before had faced five of the most cold-blooded murders in recent memory.

Within days of this flurry of articles, the tide began to turn in favour of the police. In the early morning of Thursday 5 May 1932, five detectives were prowling the dark streets and parks of Kensington in a patrol car. Over the past seven weeks, Alfred Ball had eluded them by living rough, with the police missing their man by just minutes on numerous occasions. Detective-Sergeants Keogh and Comans, and Detective-Constables O'Neill, Bushell and Crimston were following their latest lead that the razor-killer was in the area.

When it started raining, they stopped the car to confer, agreeing that if their man was here he'd be looking for shelter. They split up to search any place he might try to stay dry. As Detective O'Neill stalked through a field near Kensington Golf Course, he saw a shadowy figure up ahead making for a little cottage. The officer sped after the man and got the drop on him.

Like tens of thousands of unemployed men, the bloke was bearded, unkempt and shabbily dressed. But he was in his forties, standing five-foot-six or so, with a stout build, rounded shoulders, dark eyes and dark bristly hair going grey. A perfect fit for Alfred Ball. O'Neill told him: 'You answer the description of the man wanted on a charge of murdering Katherine Sims.' The suspect – cold, wet, starving and exhausted – made no denial and didn't resist as he was arrested and handcuffed.

That night Sydney went to sleep knowing a monster was off the streets. It awoke to another one lumbering around the city. Newsboys did double-takes as they saw this seven-foot-tall creature stalking Sydney's streets: towering forehead, big dead eyes, flesh like a corpse, bolts in his neck. Their surprise turned to amusement when they realised this was a stunt to promote the movie *Frankenstein*, set to open in a week's time. But newsboys that day were soon shouting about real monsters in the city.

Overnight, eight men had beaten union leader and Lang supporter Jock Garden in his Maroubra home. Seven of the attackers had escaped, but Garden and his son had caught one, William Scott, and handed him over directly to MacKay. This creep admitted he and his seven fellow thugs were all members of the Fascist Legion, a deranged inner circle of the New Guard, who wore black Ku Klux Klan–style hooded robes. MacKay and Prior swung into action, directing police in raids that rounded up these cowardly bully boys.

On the same day Garden was bashed, the Lyons government unleashed its latest tactic to bring Lang to heel, ordering that all monies from the sales, lease, disposal, et cetera, of any Crown or state land in New South Wales must not be paid into the state Treasury, as per Lang's orders, but into the Commonwealth Bank. The showdown Lang had thundered about at his Town Hall rally was imminent.

That same day there was also good, if grim, news out of Glen Innes. McRae had received the ballistics reports in the Chaffey investigation. A week earlier he'd interviewed nineteen-year-old local Maurice George O'Hara. The lad stood out as a potential suspect: he'd recently worked for the victim, and the widow claimed they had argued about money. When McRae had asked if he owned a rifle, Maurice said he owned a .44 – not a .22, as used in the shooting – although his brothers owned two such guns. McRae took those into evidence. The Sydney expert's conclusion was that the death bullet had been fired from one of them: a Remington repeater. McRae went to the family home and arrested Maurice. While the forensic ballistics evidence wouldn't be needed in the case against him, this was the first time in New South Wales police history that such work had pointed a detective to a killer.

Maurice O'Hara allegedly cracked under McRae's questioning. The suspect claimed Chaffey had owed him money. O'Hara had asked for payment repeatedly, but each time been rudely rebuffed. He told McRae he'd gone out that early morning with his brother's rifle to confront the man once again. 'How about that money you owe me?' he demanded. Chaffey said: 'You can go to hell and get out of here.' There had been further words. 'I lost control of myself,' O'Hara confessed, 'and pulled the trigger.'

O'Hara told McRae he'd snatched the cash on the spur of the moment. Some he'd given to his mother, and the rest he'd handed over to the police when arrested. O'Hara told McRae where he'd dumped the leather cash bag – in a reedy section of river near Chaffey's house – and constables soon found it there in three feet of water. The accused claimed: 'When I pulled the trigger of the rifle, I had no intention of killing him, but only of wounding him, and I am very sorry that this happened.'

But O'Hara's claim that it had all been a terrible accident and he was very upset about it seemed at odds with how he'd acted in the immediate aftermath of Albert's death. The lad had almost immediately gone to the widow and said he'd be happy to perform his former work by taking over the milk run. In the week since, right up to the morning he was arrested by McRae, he'd been driving the dead man's cart. With Maurice O'Hara and Alfred Ball now joining William Moxley and Thomas Jenkins in Long Bay Gaol, Sydney's CIB were getting on top of the recent 'murder wave'.

MacKay had cracked the New Guard too. On Monday 9 May, the eight Fascist Legion men pleaded guilty in Central Court to attacking Jock Garden. William Scott testified the secret society comprised fifty-two members, who had been issued robes and were only known to each other by code numbers. They had driven in two cars to Garden's home, where they had posed as plainclothes police to get access and had then assaulted him in the backyard. Garden's two sons let the family dog loose as they came to his aid. They were assaulted too, before the canine chased the attackers off – all except Scott, who was bitten by the dog and then grabbed by the Gardens. The union leader had suffered a slight concussion and abrasions.

Detective-Sergeant Watkins said that when he'd searched Scott's flat, he had found secret reports and a black gown and hood. When Scott testified, he said he'd been directed to meet the other seven by an anonymous note he assumed was from the New Guard. He didn't know Garden – or that Garden was even the target. As for the hood, he wouldn't say which member of the New Guard gave it to him, just that he knew there were fifty-two or so other members like him. 'Our job,' he said, 'was to do special jobs at different times for the intelligence branch and put our reports into headquarters.'

One of the other accused men testified that their mission had not been to hurt Garden but more along the lines of 'horseplay', with the worst that would happen was his being dumped in a pond. Statements from each of the others were read: all admitted to being New Guardsmen, although only one confessed that he and another member were part of the Fascist Legion. Each man was sentenced to three months' gaol.

In the meantime, MacKay had delivered his knockout punch. In the immediate wake of the Garden outrage, his cops had cause to raid the New Guard's headquarters. The seized files were damning, showing preparations to secure weapons and take over state infrastructure. They also recorded that members had been shadowing Lang. It was believed they'd plotted to kidnap the premier, along with other Labor cabinet ministers and union leaders, and detain them all in the Old Berrima Gaol. In other words: a *coup d'état*.

Eric Campbell was suddenly on the backfoot. He denied authorising the bashing of Garden, and said there was no such thing as the Fascist Legion. He tried to deflect attention to what should really be concerning the people of New South Wales:

> Murderers wander at large in Sydney, yet at the present time a large number of the leading detectives are employed in harassing the only organisation that is a bulwark against Sovietism, and which treasures the British tradition. In the meantime, the state is going fast to destruction, while Mr Lyons seeks by acts of Parliament to cast out the profligate manager of the bankrupt state.

Reginald Weaver took up the fight in the New South Wales parliament. He said that the creation and direction of the Fascist Legion had been orchestrated by an agent provocateur. This was Walter Warneford, until recently a captain in the New Guard, but also a special constable for the police, which meant he'd been sworn in by a magistrate and could be called to help guard public buildings in an emergency.

Weaver said Warneford was in the pay of Lang's 'criminal government', and that Garden had been in on his own bashing. He alleged that, days before the attack, the police had already known the names and addresses of the eight men who were going to be set up. Warneford, their inside agent, had been hanging around the New Guard headquarters of late. He – or other infiltrators – must've placed the files for the cops to find as a plot to discredit and incriminate the organisation. Weaver demanded an immediate inquiry.

Responding to this conspiracy theory, one Labor member shouted that the UAP member should be locked up in Callan Park asylum. Weaver, who'd worked with MacKay when he was suppressing Rothbury, knew the superintendent had employed these sorts of tactics against timber workers and coal workers. Now the jackboot was on the other foot. Not that Weaver could prove it.

If Francis de Groot's stunt on the Sydney Harbour Bridge had appealed to the larrikin spirit, many Australians were now appalled to read that the New Guard were hood-wearing extremist cowards who bashed men in their homes and who were planning a coup. In the federal parliament, Lang supporter Jack Beasley accused the Department of Defence of conspiring with these right-wing rabble-rousers; Prime Minister Lyons denied any such link but promised a royal commission into the New Guard. At the state level, Lang also announced a royal commission into the organisation, and, wanting to appear even-handed, said the commission would also investigate Weaver's claims of a frame-up. For it to go ahead, though, Lang would have to still be in power.

New South Wales was plunging deeper into crisis, with both the conservative and leftist press saying the situation could lead to civil war. On 10 May, the federal government ordered that, from the following day, all state revenue had to be paid directly to the Commonwealth Bank. This would render New South Wales penniless and powerless. In response, Lang's government reaffirmed its 12 April memo, which directed that all state taxes, licence fees and other payments had to be received in cash – or as cheques made out to cash – and physically delivered directly to the heads of departments or to the Treasury.

The next day, as a last desperate measure to raise funds, Lang introduced the Mortgages Taxation Bill, which would charge 10 per cent on every mortgage in the state. The mortgage-holder would need to pay within two weeks, and defaulters were liable to have the mortgage revert to the state. This was met with absolute outrage, and Lang's critics called him a robber. Although the bill really didn't seem workable – in particular, its sudden and draconian enforcement – Lang knew it would be rubber-stamped by the Legislative Assembly, and he might even get it through the Legislative Council.

In Canberra, the federal parliament voted not to go into recess, so that Lyons could rush through the Financial Emergency (State Legislation)

Bill, meant to counter any *Mortgage Taxation Act*. If both bills were passed, the laws would be contradictory and the stand-off between Lang and Lyons would become a showdown. Chaos was almost guaranteed.

One man changed that course. Robert Beardsmore was a former AIF officer and a deeply conservative veteran public servant. He'd been the man who set up the 'volunteer' camp at Rothbury and stood with Reginald Weaver inside the compound as battle raged outside the colliery. Beardsmore was now chief accountant in the New South Wales Department of Lands. In one hand he had Lang's new circular, ordering him to pay all revenues in cash to the state Treasury; in his other hand he had the recent federal government *Gazette*, directing him to pay those same monies into the Commonwealth Bank. Which should he obey?

On 11 May 1932, Beardsmore followed the directive from Prime Minister Lyons. When he did so, his department head told him to take leave. Beardsmore refused. His boss ordered him to take leave. This veteran public servant was shamed and punished for trying to follow the law of the land. Beardsmore or his conservative friends briefed reporters on what had happened and it blew up overnight and forced Sir Philip Game's hand. Although the governor was reluctant to intervene in state affairs, he told Lang to retract his memo. The Premier would not.

That evening, with New South Wales on the brink, twenty newspaper boys went shouting into the streets, holding up copies of the first free issue of new Sydney tabloid *The Daily Mirror*. The headline screamed bloody murder: 'Thousands Comb Countryside for Human Fiend'. The front page showed police and citizens with weapons and torches and portraits of yet another young couple who'd fallen victim to a bloodthirsty murderer. How could another maniac like Moxley be upon the city again so soon? Opening the paper, readers saw a headline screaming 'The Monster's Loose!' – and a photo of actor Boris Karloff under creepy make-up, alongside blurbs offering £1000 life insurance to anyone who died of fright watching this latest horror film.

An actual newspaper called *The Daily Mirror* wasn't to come into existence in Sydney for almost a decade. This tasteless promotion for *Frankenstein* had cashed in on the public's very real fears – and movie trade paper *Everyones* thought the stunt was boffo:

> The newspaper was produced in tabloid style and headlines and photographs graphically portrayed a man-hunt for a criminal, similar to that conducted in Sydney suburbs recently when police and civilians frenziedly searched for the murderer of Dorothy Denzel and Wilkinson.
>
> Those who received the paper at key centres thought that another double murder had been committed ... The boys could not cope with the demand.

The next day – Black Friday, 13 May 1932 – as the first sessions of *Frankenstein* unspooled in Sydney cinemas, Sir Philip Game sacked Jack Lang and his government, installing the UAP opposition leader Bertram Stevens as caretaker premier, who'd call an election on 11 June. Lang went quietly, saying he'd done so because if he'd fought back, it risked state cops and federal soldiers clashing in Sydney. Such a scenario would also have seen battles between the New Guard, the Labor Army and the Communist Workers Defence Corps. Civil War had been averted.

Even though political tensions had been escalating for more than a year, Lang's dismissal was still shocking and unprecedented in Australian history. His sacking was felt keenly everywhere, being greeted with relief by the right and dismay by the left. But it was possible it would be an actual matter of life or death for William Moxley, Alfred Ball, Thomas Jenkins and Maurice O'Hara. If they were found guilty of murder, a newly-elected conservative government might hang one or even all of them.

13

I Did Not Do It!

In the week that Lang put the New Guard in check – and was then checkmated himself – Jack Saywell was roaring all over the Eastern Suburbs in his dead dad's powerful Studebaker, receiving cautions from some of the same cops who were investigating his father's murder. On the night of 11 May, Constable Carey – the policeman Jack had summoned after the discovery of his parents – saw him on New South Head Road at Darling Point hurtling at sixty miles an hour past a stationary tram. Carey arrested Jack for dangerous driving. Ten days later, going even faster, again on New South Head Road, Jack slammed into a car that had stopped to turn, and his Studebaker had ricocheted into a third vehicle. The driver who'd been turning was thrown onto the road and knocked unconscious, and was taken to hospital with facial lacerations.

A few weeks later, Jack faced court twice. His defence included the plea that these offences occurred when he was upset by his family tragedy. But he didn't admit fault, and arrogantly disputed police and witness evidence that he'd been speeding. More cold-bloodedly, he tried to blame the second incident on the injured man – a doctor who'd been driving longer than Jack had been alive. In fining the young man £8 and suspending his licence, the magistrate said his dangerous actions could easily have killed someone. Whether he was acting out of grief, anger, guilt or some combination of these, his behaviour had done him no favours.

So many people believed Jack Saywell had wielded the hammer that he felt compelled to defend himself to *Smith's Weekly*. In a front-page exclusive headlined 'I Did Not Do It', he put forward his theories and tried to explain every circumstance and refute every allegation. Jack said the murderer could've used the key from under the mat to enter the house. Numerous people – such as the milkman – knew it was kept there. Or the intruder could've climbed up to the balcony – he'd shown the police how it was possible without leaving footprints in the garden. 'I have often got in by climbing over the balcony,' he said. 'Often I must admit to slipping in without being heard, it being fairly late.' Jack offered his opinion on one motive:

> If you ask me for an opinion as to who did the awful business, I would say some small shareholder in the Tin Hare Co., who lost £100 or so and became deranged. Such a person would not know that my father had little to do with the business except as a solicitor and has satiated his insane fury on Dad and Mother. I can think of no other motive.

That might have been Jack's impression of his father's business, but in fact Claude was a director of the GRC, had been present when major decisions were made and owned shares worth £1500 in the two companies that profited from the shady deal that destroyed a rival company. If someone was aggrieved, they might have been more than just a small shareholder.

Speaking with *Smith's Weekly*, Jack addressed rumours of insanity in the Saywell clan. Of course, he said, in such a large family there were inevitably some cases of mental disorders, though he took care to note they didn't come from his paternal bloodline. Even so, he cast his own recent road rampages as being in the spirit of the daredevilry he'd shared with his father. 'We have been called the "Mad" Saywells,' he admitted with what seemed a touch of pride.

> Perhaps some people may be excused for saying we are 'mad'. Both
> Dad and I had a fondness for fast driving and we vied with one
> another to see who could put up the best time between Sydney
> and Bowral, and Sydney and Katoomba. That's about the only
> time we were mad.

Why had Jack got up earlier than usual on the morning he found
his parents? For a very 'natural reason' – that is, he had to go to the
bathroom. Why drive to Double Bay police station instead of phoning?
The police wouldn't be ready for an urgent call at that time of morning,
and a constable would've had to walk or maybe get a bus. As for Jack's
arguments with his parents over his girlfriend's Catholicism and their
forbidding marriage to her, Jack said the relationship hadn't been that
serious. He admitted that his keeping late hours drove his father 'wild',
but, despite repeated patriarchal dressings-down, 'I bore him no animosity
as I deserved his censure'.

Jack spoke directly about the night in question:

> It has been suggested to me that I got home earlier than I state and
> that my father was very annoyed and we had words; that I lost my
> temper and went to my room; that after father and mother had
> gone to sleep, I crept downstairs, got the hammer and then went
> to their room and committed the crime. I say this is absolutely
> absurd. What an inhuman brute a boy would be to do such a thing
> after a petty telling off by his father?

Jack was wrong if he thought his interview would end speculation. On 22
May, *The Sunday Sun* ran a provocative article headlined 'Know Saywell
Slayer? Police Sure They Can Secure Committal. Have They Found True

Clues? Startling Facts. Search For Clothing'. The paper claimed to know police had completed their chain of evidence – save for one bloodstained garment and Mrs Saywell's being able to confirm what they already knew. The article didn't specifically point the finger at Jack, but it said police could pick up the suspect at their convenience.

Jack went to *Smith's Weekly* again, telling them:

> It looks to me as if the article published in *The Sunday Sun* is designed to make me confess. If so it fails miserably for I repeat what I said before and with emphasis – I did not do it. If you go through that article you will find that questions are asked; and the statement is made by *The Sunday Sun* that police are sure they can secure a committal. There is no doubt in my mind that the police are convinced that I committed the crime.

Sensationally, and perhaps self-incriminatingly, Jack revealed that a subsequent police search of his room *had* turned up one of his singlets with bloodstains. This had been found in a pigeonhole in his desk by Detective-Sergeant Frank Matthews. But Jack told *Smith's* what he told the officer – he'd cut himself shaving:

> There is nothing very unusual in the finding of a blood-stained singlet. I only wear a singlet when I am in evening clothes, and it is usual for one to shave before going out in evening clothes. I wore the singlet they have about a month before the crime was committed.

Surely, if he was guilty, Jack argued, more of his clothes would be bloody: 'Perhaps they have an idea that I committed the crime in the nude, and then had a bath to wash any stains off.' Detectives perhaps hadn't entertained that theory, but they had asked the Saywells' maid, Hilda, if it looked like the bathroom had been used for a bath overnight or in the morning. She'd told them no.

Jack couldn't help theorising yet again to *Smith's*. Maybe the killer had washed his hands and then dried them with Jack's towel – which was the most easily available in the bathroom – and then dropped it on the floor. As for another angle, Jack's remarks didn't help his image:

> I noticed that *The Sun* asks, 'Did he wear gloves?' when discussing the intruder. Perhaps the police have passed this on to the paper following a remark of mine to a lady acquaintance. I said: 'If I were doing a crime like that, they would not find any fingerprints, for I would wear gloves.'

Jack reiterated the police's theory – that he had a violent quarrel with his parents upon coming home, waited until they were asleep to creep out and get the hammer, and then bludgeoned them both before going back to bed and waking up and acting unflustered – before dismissing it as 'ludicrous in the extreme'. But his detailed imagining of himself in this moment also didn't make him sound innocent:

> Can you credit the story that any boy who was fond of his parents as I was, could do such a thing? Why, even if such a thing came into a boy's head when he was smarting from a telling off, he would surely cool down and realise what an awful fool he was to even think of such a thing long before he could go downstairs and hunt about for the hammer. In any case, any telling offs I ever got from Father were not of such a nature that they would breed any such feeling.

Jack, the young law student, predicted he'd face trial because detectives were desperate:

... I fully expect that they will secure a committal if they try, for,
after all, the Coroner and police are public servants, and it will suit
the police better to secure my committal than to leave the crime
unsolved. However, I can tell you this: that if I am committed,
that is all that will happen to me. No jury would ever convict on
the evidence that the police may bring against me.

Jack had a point. Bloodstains on the singlet were of no evidentiary
value – the police could at most determine that they were from a human
and identify the blood type, and Jack had a reasonable explanation
that Detective-Sergeant Matthews had accepted. Everything else was
conjecture upon circumstantial evidence. But when *Smith's Weekly* went
with a front-page screamer, 'No Jury Will Ever Convict', it just made Jack
seem arrogant and guiltier.

The newspaper war of words wasn't over. *The Sunday Sun* went front-
page to claim that Jack had made a 'dramatic outburst' to them. He said
he'd made his statements to *Smith's* off the record and nothing was meant
for publication. Their articles had created public prejudice against him.
The Sun reported Jack saying he could sue, but all that mattered to him
was solving the crime. Then *Smith's* hit back by saying *The Sun* had made
up their interview. It reaffirmed that what Jack had told them had been
intended for print.

With no other denials published, *Smith's* appeared vindicated. But
it would soon commit a far worse crime against an innocent man – and
against journalism itself.

14

An Automatic Slayer

Moxley was insane with a bullet in the brain. While *Smith's Weekly* and *The Sunday Sun* fought over Jack Saywell, *Truth* scooped them on Moxley's defence in its 29 May edition. X-rays had shown the accused had three metallic bodies embedded in his head; two were 'in the tissues outside the skull' and the third was 'more deeply placed, perhaps intercranial'. *Truth* explained:

> The point in Moxley's defence to be raised will be that, assuming
> he perpetrated the terrible crime, it is conceivable that he did it
> at a time of complete blankness of mind, brought about by the
> effects of a shot from which he himself once suffered. Either that –
> or that he acted in a moment of temporary insanity.

Did *Truth*'s scoop give Alfred Ball's barrister Bob Sproule – who had repped Tilly and Big Jim Devine so successfully – a last-minute brainwave that might save his client from hanging for the murder of Katherine Sims? Although Ball had been in Long Bay for over three weeks, he hadn't seen a psychiatrist. But the morning after *Truth*'s exclusive, an hour before Ball's murder trial was to begin, Sproule hastily organised for his client to be seen by a Macquarie Street psychiatrist. It was the first time this specialist had met the accused. Ball told the psychiatrist his mother was an epileptic, his father was a drunk and he'd fallen and hit his head a number of times. The doctor took him at his word. Their consultation lasted just thirty minutes.

Ball's trial opened on Monday 30 May. It would be the first of four back-to-back murder cases at Central Criminal Court, with Justice Percival Halse Rogers presiding and Leslie McKean acting as senior Crown prosecutor. McKean told the jury that the accused had killed Katherine Sims – with whom he'd lived for eleven years – because he'd found a letter written to her by another man. Ball had slashed her throat with a razor and been seen fleeing, covered in blood. That he had taken evasive action – claiming mob attack and getting fresh clothes – was indicative of a sound, if guilty, mind. So was his eluding police for the next seven weeks.

The court heard that Ball had made a statement to Detective-Sergeant Comans. But it only took him up to the point of arguing with Katherine over the letter. After that? The accused didn't remember. Sproule called his psychiatrist, who told the court the accused's mind might have been blank when he wielded the razor. On account of being the offspring of an epileptic and a drunkard, Ball, at the time of the killing, may have been an automaton – an 'automatic slayer' – and thus couldn't be held accountable. The doctor added that the accused was of low intelligence, and while perhaps temporarily insane when he killed Katherine, he was now sane. In court, Ball was perfectly pathetic, pleading from the dock: 'No one ever loved like I loved her. I would not have harmed a hair on her head.'

What the jury couldn't be told included that Ball's 'love' had died with a black eye from a vicious beating three weeks earlier, in which he had also smashed her false teeth. They deliberated for two hours before returning the verdict that Ball was guilty – 'but with unsound mind'.

Justice Rogers sought clarification: 'Do you mean that he did not know what he was doing?'

The foreman said yes.

The judge replied: 'That amounts to a verdict of not guilty on the ground of insanity.'

The foreman said: 'Yes, that is what we mean.'

Everyone in the court was stunned, not least His Honour, who thought it 'very dangerous for a jury, on such evidence as in this case, to give a verdict of automatism'. Yet he had no choice but to abide by their decision. Alfred Ball would be detained at the governor's pleasure until he was deemed sane enough to be returned to society – which would happen by the early 1940s.

Ball's acquittal would do Moxley no favours, as the verdict created a backlash with newspapers questioning 'automatism' defences. *Truth* commented bitterly: 'So according to this theory, Ball was just a robot. He was like Frankenstein; a monster in spite of himself. Certainly, it was most unfortunate for Katherine Johanna Sims.'

The next day, in Central Court, McKean seemed to have yesterday's outcome on his mind when he told the new jury they'd be relieved they didn't need to consider insanity in the trial of Thomas Jenkins for murdering Michael Desmond during the drunken orgy at the Sutherland camp. The defence here – conducted by James Kinkead – was simple and based on the statement Jenkins had voluntarily made to the Sutherland police. The accused had been drinking less than his companions – two women and the deceased – and left them to make a fire for some stew, splitting the necessary wood with a small axe. Desmond had started arguing with him. Jenkins's efforts to calm him down were useless. Desmond had then belted Jenkins on the face and shoulder. Jenkins had tried to get away but the drunken attack got more serious.

He told the jury from the witness box: 'It all happened very quickly – a matter of seconds. Desmond hit me with a piece of wood. When he came at me again, I jumped backwards and went into a tent. Desmond followed me in, and I hit him in self-defence.' Desmond had lain down on his bunk.

Jenkins said he did what he could to help the man, bathing his head wound, and he thought he'd be all right. His statement continued: 'I am sorry that I was placed in the position to have to defend myself, but if I had not done so he would probably have killed me.' Several witnesses – including a local police sergeant – testified that the dead man had been very abusive.

McKean told the jury that, on these facts, they might return a verdict of manslaughter. But they took just ten minutes to acquit Jenkins – a verdict with which Justice Halse Rogers agreed entirely.

Maurice George O'Hara was next, on trial for murdering Albert Chaffey. The widow testified that her husband had suspected the accused of stealing from him when he'd worked on the milk run, and they'd subsequently argued over money. O'Hara maintained he'd gone to confront Albert about commissions owed to him. He'd taken the rifle to 'frighten' him because his former boss was a 'coward'. They'd argued, and Albert had insulted him and thrown a stone. Retreating, O'Hara had climbed through a fence, bumping the rifle against a post, and it had gone off and killed Albert.

But that wasn't what he'd said in his statement. Police alleged that O'Hara told them he'd pulled the trigger in a moment of anger. So how had this admission been made? O'Hara now claimed that, during his interview with detectives, Allmond had said to McRae: 'Leave the kid alone and take a walk. I will have a word with him.' It sounded like a classic 'good cop, bad cop' routine.

After McRae left, Allmond sat beside O'Hara. 'Look, son,' he said, 'I have handled hundreds of these cases before, and if you come my way, I'll come yours.' O'Hara should tell him then and there if he had not shot Albert. Offering him a cigarette, the detective continued: 'Now, if you did this thing, tell me, and instead of your getting fifteen years, you will only get two or three.' O'Hara had thought it over, and when McRae returned he wrote his statement. But with their 'help', he now claimed, he had misrepresented what he'd meant:

> When I said I lost control of myself and pulled the trigger, I thought that was the same as saying that the gun hit the fence and accidentally went off, and I also say that the following part is not true: that when I said I only intended to wound him, I thought that that was no worse than saying I only intended to frighten him ...

Allmond and McRae denied making any inducements or promises, or that they misled O'Hara into making admissions. Concluding his lengthy unsworn statement from the dock, the accused said he'd been on the best of terms with the Chaffey family, and that while he felt very sorry for Mrs Chaffey and her baby, he was innocent of the charges because he'd gone out to the farm with no intention of hurting or killing her husband.

Had the detectives coaxed O'Hara into equating bumping a fence with losing his temper and pulling the trigger? It was difficult to believe, especially as the accused had written his own confession – and when taken with his theft of Albert's money, and his attempt to cover up the crime while cold-bloodedly taking over the milk run. Then there was the very inconvenient fact that Albert had been shot in the back of the neck, which was hard to reconcile either with what the police said O'Hara had told them or with the revised version he'd just told.

The jury found O'Hara guilty of murder. But they recommended mercy on account of his youth. While the judge sentenced O'Hara to death, it was with the expectation that the Executive Council of New South Wales – the cabinet – would commute this to life in prison. But that wasn't guaranteed, particularly after the election results were tallied on Sunday 12 June. Lang had suffered a huge defeat. Bertram Stevens was now premier and, under UAP rule, hangings might resume in New South Wales.

Moxley's trial began the next day.

15

In the Grip of the Demon Madness

On Monday 13 June 1932, a throng – including many chicly attired women – gathered outside Sydney's Central Criminal Court from eight o'clock in the hope of securing a seat for the first day of the Moxley trial. When the doors opened at 10am there was a rush, and police had to break up the queue. Another stampede ensued when some 200 people ran to the rear of the building, hoping to get a glimpse of the accused arriving.

Moxley entered the dock just after 11am and pleaded not guilty in a loud, clear voice. For much of the rest of the proceedings, he'd sit with arms folded, chewing gum incessantly, and occasionally wipe his hands with a handkerchief.

Opening the prosecution's case, McKean said:

> The Crown takes the view that this is a case of plain murder and that no self-respecting jury can, in accordance with the facts, possibly return a verdict on the ground of insanity ... He is charged with murdering two innocent and inoffensive persons with gross brutality and callousness that beggars description.

Failure to convict for murder might see Moxley set free to 'be a further menace and prey on society'. McKean outlined what the accused admitted doing to

139

Frank and Dorothy: he had ambushed, robbed, beaten, bound and kidnapped his victims to the bush cottage, where, after leaving them to get petrol, he'd had a second brutal fight with Frank. 'From then on Moxley's memory is a convenient blank,' McKean said. 'About this time two unfortunate persons were taken into wild country and were shot at close range.'

Despite Moxley's memory being a 'blank', the Crown would show he'd had his wits about him sufficiently to do a lot of driving at night on very bad roads and to steal a shovel that he'd use to dig their graves. Soon after, Moxley had sold parts of the Alvis and disposed of its licence plate to obscure the car's ownership. 'Taking everything into consideration, the Crown says that the accused showed deliberation in the extreme and his actions were those only of a person who had a thorough knowledge of everything he was doing.'

The Sun covered Moxley's trial in detail that afternoon – and provided the latest on the election fallout. While Lang was out of office, his actions as premier remained under scrutiny. The royal commission into the Tin Hares scandal had opened that day, and promised to be a labyrinthine affair. Also that day: the New Guardsmen who'd bashed Jock Garden began appeals against the severity of their sentences. But only William Scott's would be reduced to one month, for telling the 'truth' about the fascists' plans for an armed takeover of NSW. This result fuelled suspicion he'd been a police infiltrator, and Walter Warneford's admissions that he'd been undercover with the New Guard for MacKay suggested a frame-up.

By hook or by crook, the 'Fascist Legion' thugs were behind bars but, the bigger picture was to be a defeat for MacKay. The superintendent would urge his new boss, Premier Stevens, to prosecute the New Guard for sedition. But he'd be ignored. One reason for this inaction was obvious: with Lang gone, Eric Campbell's organisation no longer posed a threat to the new government. But it also seemed likely that any investigation – even a royal commission – might reveal uncomfortable truths about how much support the New Guard had enjoyed in mainstream conservative circles.

The second day of the Moxley trial saw the rough mask he'd worn when allegedly robbing and killing his victims tendered in evidence. The hessian bag found at the accused's house was also produced. McKean asked Detective-Sergeant Thomas Hill: 'Does the mask fit into the other piece?' Hill didn't reply out loud. The court was silent as everyone leaned forward, a couple of people rising to their feet, to watch the detective reunite the two pieces. The jury also heard about the discovery of the bodies and examined evidence that included bottles containing dirt clotted with blood, one of Dorothy's stocking, strips of rug still knotted as they'd been to bind the victims, and the shotgun and pieces of shot.

Francis Corbett testified about shooting at Moxley. Marie Harding told of the home invasion. The jury heard from men who'd sold him petrol, and from the owner of the shotgun the accused had allegedly stolen and used to commit the murders. A witness who'd worked for Moxley said he was very excitable, would fly into rages for no reason and had once threatened to blow a bloke's head off. Men who'd paid bonds to Moxley to drive his truck said he'd called himself 'Swan', while those he'd dealt with when selling Alvis parts testified that he'd called himself 'Heath'. The wife of a bootmaker Moxley engaged for repairs just after the murders said he gave his name as 'Heane'.

Another witness said that Moxley, on 8 April, had rented a room from him, saying he'd be staying a week. The accused had stayed a few days before leaving abruptly. But during his time in the house, Moxley had mused about Frank and Dorothy, whose disappearance had just made the papers: 'People don't know what they get when they leave the main roads these days.' This witness stated that Moxley had said his name was 'Bill'.

Thomas Cahill – the owner of a Moorebank sawmill – testified that the accused had, for the two months before the murders, been hauling timber from a nearby reserve. He'd known him as 'Hudson'. Given Moxley was claiming to be a simple cutter and carter of wood, he sure had a lot of aliases – as he had throughout his criminal career.

On the night of 5 April, Cahill said he left four gallons of petrol in an engine in his mill. The next morning there were footprints all around the engine and the petrol tank had been drained. A shovel and a kerosene tin had been stolen. This tin had later been retrieved from Moxley's bush camp. The shovel was found on a road, seemingly thrown from the car, like the cowl and beret. William Burns, who delivered wood for Moxley, said he'd gone to the accused's house seeking work on the day after the murders and seen that his hand was injured. Moxley's girlfriend, Linda Fletcher, said he'd told her he had been at his bush camp all night. A doctor detailed how he'd treated Moxley's right hand that night at Western Suburbs Hospital: his ring, middle and little fingers were crushed, and there were small cuts on the little finger. Moxley claimed the injuries had been caused by cranking a car, and the doctor testified that they were consistent with that.

On the third day of the trial, Detective-Sergeant Hill said he'd been with the police party at the murder scene, and had later heard Moxley say his accomplice had been 'Snowy Mumby'. Moxley had described this man and said they'd known each other since they'd gone to war together. He said Snowy lived in either Pelican Street or Brisbane Street in the city, and that he was in the habit of 'knocking around' Oxford Street. Constable Charles Godwin had taken shorthand notes of what Moxley said of this man: 'He is a great bloke with the sheilas and I think his job is robbing drunken men. But I have never known him to break and enter. I know he is always hanging around sheilas.'

Neither the Crown or the defence would raise that Moxley had been known by the nickname 'Snowy' – and that he'd testified as such during the 1930 trial of the men who'd shot him. It wasn't clear why. Perhaps neither side wanted Moxley to admit he was a habitual criminal who'd been shot because thugs suspected he was a police informant. For the defence, it'd make his testimony less trustworthy. For the prosecution, it'd raise the question of what Superintendent MacKay had been doing regularly giving money to this crook.

The last prosecution witness was MacKay himself. He had to tread a fine line, testifying in both a personal and professional capacity, unable to deny he'd known Moxley but unable to admit the man was his long-time fizgig. The bullet fragments in the accused's head – the ones the defence were going to argue had contributed to his being unaccountable for his actions – were there because of their relationship. MacKay, rather like Dr Frankenstein, had helped make this monster and, like the mad movie scientist, he appeared to pity and revile his creation.

'I have known Moxley for some years,' MacKay began in a quiet voice, setting the scene for his description of the accused's phone call after his arrest and their meeting at the Central Police Station. After Moxley had eaten, MacKay said, he'd asked detectives to leave the room because the accused would only talk to him. 'I was not in this alone,' Moxley had allegedly said. 'I admit I held them up along with another man and that I took them to Liverpool and left them in a house there but I don't know what happened after that.'

Moxley said he could show MacKay this site. While arrangements to do this were being made, he drew plans of the house and a map that showed where 'they' had taken the couple and the places Moxley had later gone for petrol. 'Who is the other man?' MacKay asked. He testified that Moxley had replied: 'I will tell you later. I will think that over.'

MacKay and other police had driven Moxley to the cottage, where they found threads from the picnic rug strips he'd used to tie up his victims. At the bush gravesites, Moxley wouldn't say anything other than he'd never been there before. But in the car on the way back, he'd scribbled something on a scrap of paper and handed it to MacKay. The superintendent couldn't make out what it said. 'What's that?' he asked. Moxley replied: 'The other man's name – Snowy Mumby.'

Back at Central Police Station, MacKay testified, Moxley, referring to his girlfriend, had said: 'I wonder what Lin is thinking of the matter. She won't want to see me again.'

MacKay told him: 'If I am any judge of a woman, she will come to see you, if you want to see her.'

Moxley had then asked him: 'Mr MacKay, what did you think of me when you heard about this crime?'

He replied: 'Well, I discussed it with Detective-Sergeant Bowie and he will tell you what I thought about it.' The superintendent called Bowie – the officer Moxley had been shot for knowing – into the room and had him repeat MacKay's comment: 'When you discussed the matter, you said, "Moxley must have been off his head."'

Moxley replied to them both: 'I must have been.'

While Moxley had dinner, MacKay told the court, he'd gone to Lang's rally at Town Hall. Back at the CIB, Moxley said he wanted to see Linda. Despite the late hour, MacKay offered to go and pick her up in his car. 'A sad scene ensued,' he said. 'I sat in another corner of the room and did not hear what was said.'

By giving Moxley unsupervised access to Linda, Sydney's top cop had just given the accused the chance to tell his girlfriend what to say in further police questioning or as a court witness. But, in MacKay's account to the jury, his soft touch produced stellar results. After Linda left, Moxley said: 'Well, Mr MacKay, I told you lies about Mumby. I am not going to waste your time and the time of the police on a false trail.' MacKay said Moxley then gave his official statement – which didn't mention Snowy Mumby – and he was then charged with the murders.

MacKay's reputation wasn't trifled with publicly. When Eric Campbell and Reginald Weaver had accused Lang's 'criminal government' of framing the New Guard, they had kept MacKay's name out of it, even though it'd been his police who'd made the arrests, carried out the raids and interrogated suspects. The lowly Moxley was hardly about to dispute what MacKay had said under oath – even about him recanting the Mumby story *before* he was charged. Yet if that had been the case, why had the Mumby claim been included at the inquest? Why had Bowie then said he was still following this angle – even going so far as to say, 'There is no doubt that I will eventually trace this man Mumby'? Why do that if Moxley had already admitted to MacKay that it was a lie?

The discrepancy was likely MacKay putting words into Moxley's mouth to deny him this avenue of defence, which, if he were about to argue it in court, might've had the public wondering if the real killer was still out there. MacKay's testimony put an end to Snowy Mumby as a viable alternative suspect. To raise him in this context in defence would be tantamount to saying the top cop had committed perjury, though Moxley's barrister Mr Hungerford had another role planned for the elusive figure.

But MacKay also threw Moxley a lifeline, testifying that the accused was a changed man after he took a bullet in the head in 1930. 'Before that shooting Moxley was a bright, alert, cheerful man. After that he had a morose and suspicious disposition. He used to make a confidant of me.' *Confidant:* it was the closest MacKay could get to admitting the truth, that Moxley was a paid informant.

Moxley didn't admit it either, when he made an unsworn statement from the dock, which was not on oath and not subject to cross-examination. He spoke for thirty-five minutes, and he played the pity card, just as he had early in his criminal career when he pleaded leniency because it'd been 'steal or starve' for him and his family. Moxley told the jury he'd contracted syphilis before the war and it hadn't been treated. Moxley recounted how he'd been shot in 1930, targeted for assassination because he'd warned a bank manager he was going to be robbed and perhaps murdered. This was putting a heroic spin on his nearly being rubbed out because some crooks got wise to his being a rat who set them up in a police trap.

Moxley said the doctors had wanted to operate to remove the bullet fragments from his head, but he couldn't afford this and checked himself out. He'd returned later but baulked at going under the knife – which he regretted. Around this time, he said, 'Superintendent MacKay assisted me with a couple of pounds.' Moxley said that, despite being partially paralysed after the shooting, he'd had no choice but to work on the roads for a few months. Then his guardian angel had come to the rescue again with money in late 1930 or early 1931. 'Through the kindness of Mr MacKay I was able to purchase a horse,' he said. 'I borrowed a set of harnesses and a cart.'

Moxley told the court he'd got on with the hard work of cutting wood, but his bad luck continued. His car's chassis collapsed while he was driving in mid-1931, and he was flung to the road, knocked out and suffered a double fracture of his collarbone. Even so, he went back to work with his arm in a sling. Not long afterwards, it'd been a car wheel that collapsed, and he was again thrown out and injured. Nevertheless, Moxley had soldiered on. For the past year and a half, he said, he'd been working seven days a week and up to twenty hours a day. As for the bonds he'd charged multiple men, he said he'd had to take them to ensure honesty, though he didn't explain why he'd given these blokes and so many other people so many different aliases. What Moxley did say was that his hard work meant he had lots of money and therefore didn't need to rob anyone. What he'd said in his statement about needing money had been wrong.

Moxley tugged on heartstrings: 'Gentlemen of the jury, I wish to state that on no occasion have I injured to my knowledge any person in my life. I have a mother and sisters.' Moxley broke down crying. When he recovered, he continued: 'I have always respected them. Up to the day of my mother's death, I supported her.' Moxley wept again before denying he'd hurt Frank and Dorothy. 'I state that from the heart,' he said. 'I don't say that because I am charged with doing them harm. I state it because I know it is the truth. Whether you believe it or not is another thing. I say it is the truth.'

Moxley returned to his head injury:

Ever since I have been shot I have suffered from severe headaches. I have been told by friends that I have done things that afterward I couldn't account for – I had no knowledge of it at all ... Before [the shooting] nothing seemed to worry me but since [then] everything seems to have upset me. Had I been able to get a bit of good treatment, such as a convalescent home or something like that, I don't think I would be standing here today.

With that in the jury's mind, he made his concluding plea:

I say that on the night of this tragedy I had no control over my actions whatever. Perhaps these things can be explained. I cannot. You only have my word for it, gentlemen. The night of this tragedy I had no control over my actions and I went out on legitimate business ... I know nothing about the shooting of these people. That is the last word I wish to say, and I still maintain I am innocent.

What the court couldn't know was that Moxley had, in Brisbane in 1921, also pleaded mercy in an 'impulsive' violent theft, claiming he hadn't realised what he was doing. Next, Linda Fletcher testified that she'd known Moxley for two years, lived with him and looked after his son. But she hotly denied McKean's suggestion they were lovers or shared a bedroom. When the prosecutor openly doubted her claim, Moxley leapt to his feet and shouted: 'This woman would not tell a lie to save my life!' Linda told the court the accused had suffered terrible headaches and fits since the shooting. But when she admitted he hadn't seen a doctor about his supposedly serious condition, Moxley interjected from the dock to shout: 'We couldn't afford it!' Which, given he'd just testified he had plenty of money, seemed a strange claim.

Continuing, Linda testified that, during his fits, Moxley couldn't do anything – certainly not drive a car, tie knots or dig a grave. These seizures, which lasted anywhere from twenty minutes to two hours, would see him collapse, froth at the mouth and flail uncontrollably. Moxley, she said, only came good after sleeping for about three hours – and he wouldn't remember what had happened. Linda said he endured these fits, on average, twice a week. McKean wondered how that was possible, given Moxley had just said for the past year and half he'd worked seven days a week and up to twenty hours a day.

George Lawrence, who'd worked cutting timber with the accused, said he'd only known him three weeks but dubbed him 'Dopey' for his stuttering way of speaking and his tendency to forget where he was supposed to deliver wood. 'Once when I was with him in the bush chopping down a tree, he fell straight over in a fit, and stretched out stiff on the ground,' Lawrence said. 'When he came round he was drowsy. After fits like this he could not work as well as before them.' But, Lawrence said, within half an hour he was back at the heavy labour of chopping, sawing and stacking.

The defence's next scheduled witness, Moxley's sister Ivy Bradley, couldn't be called because she'd taken ill, her nerves so shattered that she'd earlier been close to collapse outside the court. Justice Rogers adjourned proceedings.

When the court reconvened the next morning, Thursday 16 June, Ivy was still too unwell to appear. Dr Edward Spencer Holloway, a physician who'd been attending Moxley in Long Bay Gaol regularly since his arrest, testified for the Crown that, in all that time, the accused hadn't suffered a single fit – although he allowed that seizures were less likely when a man wasn't working long hours to the detriment of sleep. He agreed that the fits could be caused by epilepsy, and that epileptics sometimes had bouts of insanity after which they were unable to remember anything.

Dr Holloway also confirmed that Moxley had syphilis, and that this disease could affect the brain. He said he'd seen the first set of X-rays showing foreign matter in the accused's head, but not a more recent set of images the prosecution hadn't put into evidence. Dr Holloway had not seen anything abnormal in Moxley's behaviour, nor had he seen any indication of mental deterioration or evidence of epilepsy.

This was the point in the trial where it was expected the defence would call psychiatrists to testify about Moxley's mental state. But not a single expert was summoned on his behalf. Later, it would be reported that the defence had approached ten Macquarie Street specialists, but, in the wake of the Albert Ball backlash, all had declined to be involved.

In his closing argument for the defence, barrister Hungerford said McKean had misled the jury by claiming that acquitting Moxley could lead to him being released immediately. In reality, he said, if they decided the accused was insane at the time of the murders, he would be detained at the pleasure of the governor. Hungerford said all the evidence was circumstantial, but he leaned most heavily on the argument that had spared Alfred Ball: 'The defence is that if these two people lost their lives at Moxley's hands, then he knows nothing about it.' He reminded the jury that a person wasn't guilty unless he knew what he doing and that it was wrong.

Then he offered a circular argument: whoever committed these crimes had to be insane, because the crimes themselves were insane:

> Cold-blooded and murderous were the actions of the person who did this terrible deed and in the criminal history of this state probably no more horrible crime has been committed. On that ground I ask you whether it was possible that a person in his right senses could perpetrate this terrible deed.

Hungerford reminded the jurors of the bullet fragments in Moxley's head, of his syphilis, of his fits and headaches, of Superintendent MacKay's testimony about the accused's change in character. But Linda's testimony – the corroborative backbone of the defence – had depicted her boyfriend's fits as being so overpowering he couldn't have been in the grip of one when he committed the crimes. So Hungerford argued that whatever caused the fits might *also* have caused a 'malady which subjected him to periods of madness. He was a lunatic at the time, suffering from a mental aberration which obsessed and dominated him for the time being.'

Hungerford then enlisted Snowy Mumby to Moxley's defence, not as a murderous accomplice but as mental aberration:

> Isn't that an extraordinary thing? Did he believe that there was
> another person there, seeing his own picture? We don't know too
> much of the workings of the human mind. Certainly, we don't know
> the working of a deranged human mind. The fact is that he gave an
> amazing description of himself as being that of the man with him.

Hungerford implored: 'I ask you in all earnestness to say that at the time he took the lives of these young people Moxley was in the grip of the demon madness and that he is not guilty on the grounds of insanity.'

McKean ripped this defence apart, starting with the circular argument: 'It will be a very sorry day when any jury says that a man is insane because his particular crime has such horrible features and is performed under such awful conditions.' McKean defended the use of circumstantial evidence, saying it was often all prosecutors had in murder cases where the victims could no longer speak and a sane killer had made efforts to cover his tracks. As for the argument that Moxley was insane, McKean asked: where was the proof? 'There are any amount of doctors in Macquarie Street who would be available if they could give evidence. But such evidence has not been put before you.' On the question of fits: 'Do you believe a single word of the evidence? The only person called in relation to it is Mrs Fletcher, and you can guess her relations with the accused.' Regarding testimony that Moxley had been 'excitable', McKean asked: 'Is that insanity? If so, we are all insane.' Everything Moxley had done that night and afterward showed he was mentally in control. Why else the mask and the gun? 'Because he had a criminal intent. The accused went on a criminal expedition that particular night. Review his actions and see whether he didn't know what he was doing.'

Moxley had admitted he demanded money. 'Did he know what he was doing then? Did he know what he was doing when he fought Wilkinson and was victorious?' From shooting the couple onwards, McKean argued, Moxley had known what he was doing at all times. While Hungerford had seized on the government doctor's reluctance to definitively say who'd had sexual relations with Dorothy, McKean had no such doubts. The dead girl was found nearly naked. Her boyfriend was fully clothed. It was clear Moxley had interfered with Dorothy. As for 'Snowy Mumby'? He pointed at Moxley: 'Mumby sits there – undoubtedly and without a shadow of a doubt.' He concluded: 'I said at the opening that no self-respecting jury could say that this man was not guilty and I repeat it.'

The jury retired at 12.55pm. They returned at 3.45pm. Moxley stood, pale and trembling, chewing gum still. The foreman read the verdicts: guilty of both charges of murder. Moxley stopped chewing. Justice Rogers asked him if he had anything to say. Moxley didn't. 'Nothing!' he replied. The judge sentenced Moxley to hang. But he'd soon be making an appeal. If he failed, his fate would rest with Premier Stevens and the cabinet he was selecting even as the condemned man was being returned to Long Bay.

The newspapers bayed for Moxley to be the first man to go to the gallows since 1924. *The Sun* ran a cold-blooded editorial:

> For an abnormality which ends in such a crime as Moxley's, there is no place in the world of human beings. Even those who on some general principle do not believe in capital punishment are silent before a case such as this. Moxley is far better out of the world. We may pity him that he was born into it, but still see his exit as the only solution of the problem he has set. We feel no anger against the tiger as it falls before the hunter's rifle, but we recognise that it is necessary that it should die.

But *Truth* outdid itself with the lurid headline: 'Sacrificed on Altar of a Murderer's Lust – Victims of Callous Cur – Who Killed and Ravished – Moxley, the Monster, Must Hang'.

16

I Won't Hang!

Moxley had no intention of hanging. Having visited him in Long Bay, Linda Fletcher related their conversation to *The Daily Telegraph*: 'The tears were streaming down his face when he told me that he didn't do it, and if they hanged him it would be for stealing the car, and not for murder.' Linda said Moxley was under immense strain, barely eating, sleeping badly and suffering headaches. Despite this distress, he was planning his appeal, which would not only focus on the Crown's case – including that they hadn't tendered the most recent X-rays of his head – but also raise the fact that Moxley's defender, Hungerford, hadn't called any psychiatrists.

Linda's visit was a good story for *The Daily Telegraph* but *Smith's Weekly* scored the real scoop. One of its journalists went to see his sister Ivy. According to his article, he didn't tell her he was a reporter and she didn't ask. He found her in tears, unhappy she'd been unable to testify for her brother, and worried she was still too much of a nervous wreck to see him in Long Bay. Helpfully, the journalist offered to organise a visit, giving her a sedative and taking her to the sheriff's office, where Ivy and her 'friend' received permission to see Moxley. Before the *Smith's* man drove them to Long Bay, she gave him a lengthy interview, telling him everything she would've said if she'd testified.

According to Ivy, Moxley had behaved oddly from an early age. He'd been a sleepwalker, and was prone to strange behaviour, such as getting dressed for school and then lying under his bed. 'There's that boy again,' their mother would say. 'He must be mentally deficient.'

Ivy recounted how Moxley had accidentally shot their brother dead, and how their father had died from the effects of a bullet wound. These incidents had been recounted at trial via Moxley's police statement, but what the jury hadn't heard was how affected Moxley had been by their mother's death. Ivy said Julia Moxley got very sick while her son was in prison under indefinite sentence as a habitual criminal. He was refused permission to visit her, which had nearly driven him crazy. Then, after Julia died in 1928, Moxley was only allowed to attend her funeral under the guard of armed detectives, who threatened to shoot him if he tried to escape. Standing over his mother's grave, Moxley had made a solemn promise to go straight. But her death had haunted him, as Ivy explained:

> He seemed to change completely. His happy nature disappeared and he would sit brooding with a far-away look, taking not the slightest notice of anything that was said to him. Then after some minutes, he would remark, 'What was that you said?' or he would make a different observation about something that no one had been discussing ... Life seemed to hold nothing for him. Nothing mattered.

Ivy described what she'd learned from Linda about Moxley's actions the day after the murders. He'd blamed his injured hand on motor trouble, made claims about spending the previous night in an empty house, and had been moody and complained of headaches. Then Moxley disappeared again that night without explanation. Returning the following day, he went for a walk with Linda, saying his head felt crook, and had suddenly blurted: 'I feel sick.' Moxley dashed off – Linda thought he'd gone into a lane to vomit, but he had disappeared again. The next morning Moxley turned up at his son's school, gave the boy seven shillings and told him to go home and give it to Linda. Then he'd vanished. The next time Linda saw him, he was under arrest at the CIB headquarters.

Ivy's story, as told to *Smith's Weekly*, might not have helped her brother had she given it in court. Her description of Moxley's devastated reaction to their mother's death undermined his testimony that it had been the gunshot wound to the head that had darkened his disposition – a claim that MacKay had sympathetically corroborated. Further, her hearsay account of Moxley's behaviour after the murder seemed the picture of a man with a guilty mind, sick at what he'd done and realising he needed to run. But Ivy didn't see it that way. 'No one knows better than I that Bill is not right in his head,' she said. 'If they hang Bill, they hang a madman.'

Yet the Moxley that *Smith's Weekly*'s undercover reporter met in Long Bay Gaol's reception room didn't seem at all like a madman. 'He dominated the proceedings,' the journalist wrote, 'like the chairman at a board meeting.' When they met – in the presence of a warder so uninterested he might've been 'deaf, dumb and blind' – Moxley shook his fists and declared: 'I won't be slaughtered like a string of sausages; they won't hang me!' Moxley was bursting with confidence when weepy Ivy asked if he had a chance on appeal. 'Chance! Got a chance? I should say I did have a chance – and a good one!' Ivy asked: 'On what grounds?' Moxley replied: 'New evidence. There is lots of medical evidence regarding the bullet in my head and we'll have to bring it out.' He went on:

> The Crown called only one doctor. Why did they not call all the others they had? They were afraid because the only one they called gave evidence in my favour. We have to get those medical witnesses. The Crown had X-ray photographs taken of my head, showing where the bullet was. If they are not available, I shall have

to get some taken. They never gave me a chance in the medical evidence.

Moxley told Ivy he needed an affidavit from her and even enlisted the undercover journalist to find out from a doctor what tests could be run to help his cause.

This scoop appeared under the page-one headline '"I Won't Hang" – Moxley – Condemned Man Amazingly Confident. Smith's Takes Convict's Sister to Long Bay Gaol'. The paper modestly called it 'the most sensational story of the year'. But *Smith's Weekly* was getting ahead of itself there.

Moxley appeared in the Court of Criminal Appeals on 1 July 1932. The Crown again assigned him Hungerford but, against the advice of Chief Justice Sir Philip Street, Moxley insisted on representing himself. He argued passionately, at one point crying out, 'I appeal for justice!' Moxley presented four grounds for appeal: he was not guilty; he wanted the court to examine new medical evidence; he believed Justice Halse Rogers had misdirected the jury; and he believed the jury verdict had been against the weight of evidence. Moxley named the doctors he wanted to call, including Dr Holloway, who'd already testified inconclusively regarding his mental state, and Dr Gordon Bray, a physician from his youth who'd also examined him at Long Bay but had not been called at trial. Moxley believed the Crown hadn't called Dr Bray and others because of a wish to hide their conclusions. As for Ivy's affidavit, despite everything she'd told *Smith's Weekly*, one wasn't presented to the court.

What Moxley didn't understand was that it hadn't been the Crown's obligation to prove he was sane. It had been up to his counsel to convince the jury of his insanity defence, yet Hungerford hadn't produced any medical experts to say his client was mad at the time of the murders. The chief justice asked Moxley if he'd be willing to have a three-week adjournment to give him time to amass this evidence. The appellant didn't agree. He wanted to be granted an appeal now. Moxley didn't understand that the court could only do that if he could show right there and then new evidence that would justify a retrial. But Moxley didn't know what the witnesses he wanted to testify would say, or what any new X-ray images would show.

The chief justice had no option but to refuse the appeal. Moxley repeated several times that he was destitute and couldn't pay for new evidence to be collected. Risking cutting off his own legal avenues, he blindly argued that he must be granted an appeal immediately. Finally, Moxley settled down and accepted the chief justice's offer of an adjournment.

Moxley was taken back to his cell at Long Bay. At eight o'clock that evening, while much of the nation was enjoying the inaugural program of the new Australian Broadcasting Commission, the clock was ticking for the condemned man. Moxley had three weeks to establish the character of the evidence that would justify a retrial and maybe save his neck.

17

The Poisoned Thorne

During the week around Moxley's appeal, Sydney newspapers waged one of their regular bombastic battles. *The Sunday Sun* had a scoop under the front-page headline 'Mrs Saywell Speaks Again at Last! Leaving Hospital: Inquest Soon? Only Simple Words Yet; Gradual Cure'. The article claimed she'd soon 'testify against her husband's slayer'. It wasn't close to true. *Smith's Weekly* devoted its next front page – and an entire inside page – to blasting its rival, quoting Saywell family friends and even getting MacKay and Miller to refute the claims.

Truth weighed in, taking aim at both *The Sunday Sun* and *Smith's Weekly*, its headline bellowing: 'Those Cruel Catchpenny Canards – Sydney Newspapers Lost to All Sense of Common Decency – Sensationalism Lust Leads to Distorted Facts'. This was pretty rich coming from the same paper that, two weeks earlier, had assaulted the senses with the screamer 'When Dorothy Denzel Prayed for Death – Tortured Hours of a Night of Horror – Nightmare Drive – Monster at Wheel – Haunted by Huddled Figure of Boy Who Was Her Friend'.

Why all the fake news and the newspaper war of words? Saywell stories and the controversies around them sold copies in lieu of any real developments in the case. Nor had there been any shocking new murders to scream about in the streets. But reporters, editors and newsboys had only a few days to wait.

~

On Tuesday 5 July 1932, with the sun yet to rise over midwinter Sydney, Dorothy Thorne, a thirty-three-year-old wife and mother, was already up. Her husband, Reginald, ten years her senior, was under the blankets in his separate bedroom in their comfortable brick bungalow in leafy Mosman. Dorothy took their infant daughter, Joan, in to see him.

Leaving the child there, she went to wake Alfred Lockyer, their thirty-nine-year-old boarder, because she hadn't heard his alarm go off. He was still in bed. With a laugh, Dorothy said: 'I have beaten you to it this morning.'

Alfred replied: 'Good oh – there's no need for me to get up so early.'

Dorothy went to the kitchen, where she reached into a cupboard for a Seidlitz powder, a popular over-the-counter preparation to assist digestion. Each dose was delivered by mixing powders from two paper sachets. Dorothy tipped them into a glass of water and stirred the concoction with a spoon. Despite noticing that the Seidlitz wasn't effervescing as much as usual, she gulped it down – only to be left with a bitter taste in her mouth. Just as unusual: there were dregs left in the glass.

Dorothy sought advice, not from her husband but from Alfred in his bedroom. She told him what'd happened. Alfred sampled a spot of the dregs and spat it out because it was bitter like quinine. Seemingly unconcerned, Dorothy left him to get dressed.

Coming into the kitchen a few minutes later, he found her making breakfast and lunches. A good boarder, Alfred took tea and toast to Reg in bed. Returning to the kitchen, he found Dorothy reeling and struggling to stand. 'I'm losing the use of my legs,' she cried. This wasn't some sudden swoon. Dorothy was soon twitching and screaming in agony.

~

Dorothy Cropley was the only daughter of a wealthy Sydney family. Her grandfather had been a successful bootmaker, getting his start in the 1840s. Dorothy's father had expanded the business to four city stores by the time she came of age. In 1922 she married Reginald Thorne, an English immigrant, and soon afterwards he and a countryman named George Burrows set up a motor garage in Cremorne. Tragedy struck in 1925 when George died suddenly, aged just thirty-eight. Despite this setback, Reginald kept the garage going.

In 1927 Dorothy gave birth to a son; the boy lived only fourteen months. Their daughter, Joan, came into the world in December 1929. The difficult birth nearly killed Dorothy, and she and Reginald decided there'd be no more children.

But they did make an addition to their household in the form of boarder Alfred Lockyer. Born in England around 1893, he arrived in Sydney in 1914, having worked his passage as a seaman. He established himself as a commercial artist until the Great Depression forced him to make ends meet as a gardener. Alfred had met the Thornes around 1927, and become friendlier with them in 1931. At Reginald's invitation, he had moved into their house in February 1932. No explanation would be published as to why he was living with a married couple who had a small child. Perhaps they were just helping out a friend in need. But times were getting tougher for the middle class too. Reginald's garage wasn't thriving as car ownership and usage declined, with many motorists electing to make their own repairs or leave them undone. He and Dorothy may have been able to use a little extra cash.

~

Five months later, on 4 July, the Mosman household appeared to be ticking over pleasantly. After going to work that day, Reginald went to watch a big boxing match at Sydney Stadium. Meanwhile, Dorothy and

Alfred had taken baby Joan out that morning. That evening, after dinner, the landlady and the boarder sat by the fire, her reading, him sketching. When Reginald got home just after eleven o'clock, Dorothy and Alfred were still by the hearth, laughing about a picture he'd drawn. Hubby said he had a headache and was turning in; Dorothy fixed him a Vincent's headache powder and said goodnight.

Eight hours later, Reginald was in bed having the tea and toast Alfred had brought him when he heard Dorothy scream from the kitchen: 'I'm losing the use of my legs!' He raced to her. His wife was standing but shaking violently. Alfred explained Dorothy had taken a Seidlitz powder, and that he'd just given her a glass of mustard mixed with water in the hope she'd vomit up whatever she'd swallowed. But the emetic wasn't working. Reginald carried his wife to her bed. He frantically telephoned Dr Thomas Pawlett, who lived nearby and who'd been her physician for twenty years. Alfred tried to put his finger down Dorothy's throat to induce vomiting. But her jaw was clenched too tightly as she spasmed in agony.

When Dr Pawlett arrived, one look at Dorothy told him she had to be rushed to hospital. Reginald was too distressed to be of any assistance, but Alfred helped him carry the patient to his car. Dr Pawlett sped for the Mater Misericordiae Hospital, just three miles away in North Sydney. But he'd only gone a few hundred yards when he realised Dorothy had died. Dr Pawlett drove her back to her house, from where he called the police, saying he believed she'd been killed by a fast-acting poison.

Detectives descended on the Mosman home. As this was Area A, Inspector Lynch would have charge, with McRae brought in as lead investigator, assisted by a trio of CIB detectives. They interviewed Reginald and Arthur, and collected evidence, including the glass, spoon, Seidlitz box and sachet papers. Government medical officer Dr Sheldon examined Dorothy's body and concluded that the rapid onset of symptoms, the severity of her spasms and her contorted corpse were consistent with her having consumed strychnine. This would be confirmed by an autopsy, which found enough of the poison in her stomach to kill two people. Strychnine crystals were also found on the glass, spoon and wrappers. But fingerprints taken from these were of no help as they'd been touched by all three adults in the house.

Given McRae had investigated several mysterious suicides and solved two recent poisoning cases, he was in familiar tragic territory. Had Dorothy killed herself, accidentally or deliberately? Or had she been murdered? On 6 July, when Reginald buried his wife beside their infant son at Northern Suburbs General Cemetery, detectives watched the husband, the boarder and other mourners for any flickers of guilt.

In the past few weeks, Dorothy had consumed four doses from the Seidlitz box without incident. The other powders remaining didn't contain strychnine. Poison crystals were found on only one used wrapper. As when he'd investigated the poisoned oatmeal in the Southern Highlands, McRae and colleagues would need to establish where the Seidlitz had come from and how it'd come to contain Strychnine.

They began by quizzing Dorothy's pharmacist in Cremorne. He'd sold her the Seidlitz in mid-June in a sealed box, just like dozens of others from the consignment that had been bought by his customers, none of whom had become sick. Nevertheless, detectives confiscated what remained of the batch for testing. No poison would be found.

Dorothy's pharmacist said he hadn't sold her strychnine. While the poison was legally available from chemists to poison rats, cats, dogs and other pests, any purchaser had to sign a register after producing a witness to its legitimate use. McRae's men enquired with other nearby pharmacists, and none had sold strychnine to Dorothy. Discreet inquiries with the Cremorne chemist and his local colleagues didn't reveal Reginald or Albert as having bought the poison either. The problem was: strychnine could be purchased in bulk from wholesalers without regulation or identification.

But even if Dorothy had used such means to get the poison, no one believed she'd commit suicide. Relatives, friends and acquaintances said she had everything to live for; she doted on her daughter and was happy with her husband. But McRae had heard such protestations from grieving loved ones many times. He had to consider the possibility that Dorothy had been suffering in silence.

But the evidence argued against suicide. Why mix strychnine into the Seidlitz powder in its wrapping paper? Why not mix it directly into the glass? It was possible that she'd blended them first, in the hope they'd dissolve more fully and be easier to swallow. Yet if that was so, then why come to Alfred saying the drink tasted strange and point out the dregs? Why not just lie down and wait to die? Why no note? Why no dying confession to her husband, her boarder or her doctor? Perhaps Dorothy's plan was to make it look like an accident and spare their feelings. But surely she'd know that dying this way would only throw suspicion on Reginald and Alfred. For all these reasons, Lynch and McRae did not believe Dorothy had committed suicide.

This didn't rule out the chance she had killed herself accidentally with an accidentally adulterated dose. McRae visited the company that manufactured Seidlitz to observe the process. Bulk quantities of the powders, untouched by human hands, were fed through three machines, which wrapped them in their respective papers and sealed them into boxes ready for sale. It appeared impossible for strychnine to have been introduced into a single sachet during this process.

Murder looked most likely. But had Dorothy actually been the target? The poison could have been meant for someone else in the household. But Reginald didn't take Seidlitz and Alfred took it only very occasionally. Dorothy consumed it more regularly. That indicated she'd been the intended victim. But who would want her dead? And why? Everyone said Dorothy had no enemies.

McRae had to consider the most obvious motives. Had Reginald killed his wife for being unfaithful with Alfred? Or had Alfred sought revenge on Dorothy after being rejected? Questioned, Reginald claimed it'd been a happy marriage and Alfred was nothing more than a friend to Dorothy. Alfred told the same story.

Beyond the husband and boarder, could someone else have snuck into the house and poisoned the sachet? If so, they would have to get past the household's Irish terrier, which was said to take 'savage exception' to strangers. But that might be possible, given that anyone who knew Dorothy regularly took Seidlitz and where it was kept might also be acquainted with the family dog.

Dorothy's death was so impenetrable that *Truth*'s reporting on 17 July echoed its convoluted theorising about Jack Saywell: 'Was the devilish cunning on somebody's part intended to convey an impression that the hideous deed was an "inside job" perpetrated by a person coming in frequent contact with Mrs Thorne?'

Three days later, there came another awful echo of a recent horror. While the sick *Frankenstein* stunt had posited another Moxley-like monster on the loose, now there really was another such ghastly double murder. It wasn't in Moorebank but in McRae's old beat in the Snowy Mountains. And it hadn't been committed by a notorious character like Moxley, but was almost certainly the work of a fellow who'd once made the papers as a spoiled teenage runaway.

18

Slaughter in the Snowies

Late on the wintry afternoon of Wednesday 20 July, eighteen-year-old Moya Hain returned from a horse ride to The Willows, her family's homestead three miles out of Cooma. She called out to her mother but got no response. Going into the house, Moya saw blood splattered across the kitchen, up the hallway and onto the verandah. Terrified, she followed drag marks 100 yards, through a gate to the feed shed.

Frantically calling for her mother, Moya tried to open the door but it wouldn't budge. With all her strength, she shouldered and shoved until it gave way. In the dim shed, Moya found what had been used to block the door – the bodies of her forty-year-old mother, Eileen, and the family's twenty-two-year-old maid, Geraldine Tucker. Both had suffered severely destructive shotgun wounds. Another blood trail showed where the killer had gone out the window after barricading the shed. Though he'd tried to cut the telephone wires, he'd slashed the wrong cables so Moya was able to call for help.

When the Cooma police arrived, they took the distraught girl to hospital. Her father, Harry, was located, given the terrible news and brought to her bedside. The whole Monaro district knew what had happened almost immediately because a switchboard operator called everyone with a telephone to tell them there was a maniac on the loose.

While it'd taken a few days for Moxley to be identified, police knew who they were looking for almost immediately.

Robert Audley had made headlines in Sydney in 1926 as the spoiled teenage runaway who'd been lured back to his father by the promise of riches – and who the following year had been charged with car theft. Now twenty-five, he had worked as a farmhand for the Hains for the past three months, staying in a cottage on their property. When the Cooma police searched his quarters, they found all his belongings were gone – as was the Hain family car. A description of him and the vehicle was circulated and a manhunt began.

Local cops quickly learned Audley had filled the Hains' car with petrol at Cooma soon after the murders and charged the family's account. When he ran into a bloke he knew, he offered this fellow a lift home, saying he'd been allowed to borrow the car. As they drove, the men chatted about horseracing and Audley hummed as though he didn't have a care in the world. After dropping off the mate, Audley drove towards Nimmitabel, where his wife and children lived. This tiny village lay some twenty miles to the south-east, across the icy high country. But on the road he encountered a swaggie, who'd already heard via the bush telegraph that the coppers were after a murderer. Audley understood that his attempts to hide the bodies and cut the phone lines had been for nothing.

In Sydney, MacKay toyed with sending Constable Adam 'Scotty' Denholm and his canines south. The superintendent had asked the young policeman and another officer to start a dog squad, and they'd officially started training a couple of weeks earlier. But they were using borrowed mutts and were far from ready. MacKay decided this wouldn't be their first case. In any event, he had at his disposal something of a human bloodhound, a man who knew not only the Cooma district but also of Robert Audley from his troubled juvenile capers. Tom McRae was ordered temporarily off the Thorne case, and he and the tracker Alexander Brindle, with whom he'd worked the

Bungendore Bones, were told to board the night mail train.

They weren't the only men racing south. *The Sun* chartered a plane to fly a photographer to the crime scene at dawn. But before any of them arrived, the Cooma police found the Hains' car on the side of the road to Nimmitabel. Audley had left two suitcases packed with his clothes in the vehicle. Knowing the police were on his trail, he'd fled into the high country. Local cops believed he'd be hard to find if he was holed up in one of the area's many caves.

On Thursday morning, McRae inspected the bodies and the Hain farmhouse. The killer had crept up on Mrs Hain while she was making a cake in the kitchen. He'd shot her at close range, first in the back and then in the back of the head. Hearing the gunshots, the maid had come in, seen the horror and run down the hallway towards the phone. She'd been killed with a single close-range shotgun blast before she reached it.

Brindle led the police search, focusing first on the area where the car was found. There were echoes of the Moxley manhunt as 150 heavily armed men fanned out in search parties, leaving behind their gun-toting wives and daughters, who were ready to shoot to kill in order to defend themselves and their homes.

When a shot rang out, search party members scrambled to a hilltop. A Cooma man had fired his gun as a signal that he'd found Robert Audley. The suspected murderer was dead by his own hand.

McRae had seen many suicides, but seldom anything as desperate and pathetic as this man's last moments, which he'd written into the landscape. Audley's clothes were soaked, and there was a sodden sack of potatoes nearby. He'd first tied it to his neck and gone into a nearby lagoon. But the water had been too shallow for him to drown himself. Audley had then looped his braces around his neck, tied them to a tree branch and let himself drop, only for his makeshift noose to snap and for him to hit the dirt, alive and unhurt. Next, he put fencing wire around his neck, fixed it to another tree limb and tried again. But this branch was too low and Audley's feet reached the ground. Now wanting to live, he pulled at the wire, but it was tight around his neck and he fractured a finger in his frantic but doomed effort to stop his strangulation.

The Sun's man had departed by plane before this final desperate act was revealed. His story – along with photos of The Willows, its kitchen and wall phone, a portrait of the dead maid and a shot of McRae with a cigarette clenched between his teeth – were all in Thursday's afternoon edition, the paper celebrating its reporter's derring-do. They even managed a front-page stop-press item: 'Suspect Found Hanged'.

Robert Audley was in the morgue but McRae's work wasn't done. He needed to establish why he'd murdered Eileen Hain and Geraldine Tucker. Rumour said the farmhand had been in love with the housemaid and, when she rejected him, he shot her – with Mrs Hain killed because she got in the way. But the evidence didn't bear this out: Mrs Hain had clearly died first. Further, Mr Hain told McRae that his wife and maid hadn't complained about Audley. Nor had he been aware of any tensions on the property.

Audley's stunned widow offered a more dismal motive. A few days earlier, her husband had said: 'I have a good mind to take the car where I am working and I will very likely go down over the mountain.' McRae would tell the inquest that, as far as he could establish, this senseless double murder had been committed because a young man wanted to steal a car. It was another awful echo of Moxley.

Harry Hain, distraught husband of the murdered Eileen Hain, soon received a letter from a woman he didn't know. 'I have to tell you that my heart bleeds for you,' she wrote. 'I know your anguish. I have felt it all ...'

The letter was from Dorothy Denzel's mother.

~

The day after Robert Audley was found dead, Moxley stood in Sydney's Court of Criminal Appeal before Chief Justice Sir Philip Street and two other judges to present the evidence he'd assembled during the three-week adjournment.

A week ago, he'd seen Dr Gordon Bray at Long Bay. This physician had known him since 1914, when Moxley saw him to be treated for gonorrhoea. Four years later, before he'd gone overseas with the AIF, the doctor had diagnosed him with syphilis. Having now re-examined Moxley, Dr Bray found that his patient was 'egotistic, easily disturbed, emotional, extremely suspicious and distrustful'. Moxley claimed anger made him lose control. Even so, Dr Bray reported, he found no evidence of mental aberration – let alone automatism. He did want to do a spinal tap, to see if syphilis was in his brain. But this was deemed too expensive. Needless to say, Moxley chose not to present Dr Bray's evidence to the court.

But he did now present Ivy's affidavit. She said that when her brother was two years old, he had an inflammation of the brain that left him hovering between life and death for eight weeks. The little boy's doctor had said he needed an operation – which he didn't get. When Moxley was four, Ivy said, he'd fallen down forty stone steps and suffered a serious concussion – with a doctor predicting he'd be mentally dull for the rest of his life. Four years after that, he had more head injuries after falling from a roof. Ivy's statement reiterated how Moxley had accidentally shot dead their little brother, but she added the previously unknown information that, in the wake of the tragedy, he had tried several times to commit suicide and had to be taken out of school.

Ivy's presentation of this early history of head traumas made her argument clear: Moxley hadn't been right in the brain nearly since birth. But these new claims raised questions. Why had Moxley not included any of these stories in his long statement from the dock at the trial? For that matter, why hadn't Ivy shared any of these illnesses and injuries with

Smith's Weekly's reporter during their long heart-to-heart interview? Next, Moxley directed the judges' attention to an affidavit by a Detective-Sergeant Smith in support of his contention that one of the witnesses at his trial gave contradictory evidence. But the chief justice wasn't interested: 'There may have been small discrepancies in the evidence, but these are matters to which attention should have been directed at the trial.' He pressed Moxley to continue with his other claims.

Moxley told the court that X-rays of his head had been taken by a Dr Tillett at the Royal Prince Alfred Hospital. 'I would like his evidence to be placed before the court,' he said. 'His report says that one piece of the bullet is left an inch and a half from the surface of the skin and that there are other fragments of the bullet in my head.'

'I have Dr Tillett's report before me,' the chief justice replied. 'Your suggestion is that particles of metal are embedded in your head and affect your brain. Dr Tillett says there is no evidence to suggest that part of a foreign body is now in the brain.'

Moxley asked the chief justice to read the report made by the medical man who had testified at his trial: 'Dr Holloway says that the dizziness I complained of was due to the gunshot wound.'

His Honour read aloud a line from Dr Holloway's report: 'During my examinations there was nothing to suggest abnormality of mental condition.'

Moxley had nothing else. The chief justice's judgement, which also dismissed the suggestion the trial jury had been misdirected, told Moxley that the 'evidence' he'd just presented wouldn't have had the slightest chance of changing the verdict. There would be no new trial. The condemned man staggered under this realisation, mumbling 'All right' as he was led away. But outside the court, Moxley recovered his moxie and shouted: 'All right – I will make application on Monday to make the Crown carry out its sentence!'

Moxley now wanted to be hanged. He didn't want the sentence

commuted. It might have seemed he had said this out of shock and anger. But Moxley was as good as his word. Back in his observation section cell at Long Bay, where he was watched around the clock, he wrote to the Minister for Justice asking to be sent to the gallows. But detectives who knew him – MacKay likely among them – briefed reporters that this might actually be Moxley's last throw of the dice to *save* his life. He knew his letter would be read by the members of the state cabinet.

Maybe, just maybe, they'd ask themselves if any sane man would request to be executed, and so they would then commute his sentence.

19

Nailed to a Cross of Shame

Inspector Miller's investigation of the Hammer Horror had stalled. In mid-July, after ten weeks in hospital, and still unable to speak, Adeline Saywell was discharged to a private residence in Rose Bay. While she settled into nursing care in her fugue state, her dead husband's name was daily in print as the royal commission into the utterly labyrinthine Tin Hares scandal continued.

The commission had established that the directors of GRC – Saywell, Anthony Hordern, Felix Booth, A.W.M. Seaward and Harry Wiles – had supposedly secretly 'given' 5000 shares in their proposed company to Frederick Swindell, the American huckster who'd pioneered tin-hare greyhound racing Down Under. Swindell then made a public-spirited *donation* of £4000 to Jack Lang's Labor Party. In a striking but supposedly unrelated development, the premier had abruptly awarded the city's second tin-hare licence to the newly formed GRC – despite having promised it to the ACC. Justice Halse Rogers headed the royal commission, assisted by William Monahan, KC, who asked Swindell about this donation.

Mr Monahan: 'You realised perfectly well that you would be making application for a licence under the new act?'

Swindell: 'Yes.'

Mr Monahan: 'Do you say the realisation of that fact had no bearing in any way on your giving £4000?'

Swindell: 'Not in the slightest.'

Even more gobsmacking was Tony Hordern's wall of obfuscation, which caused Justice Halse Rogers to interpose during questioning: 'I do not know whether you realise that practically every answer you have given this afternoon has been that you "do not know"?'

To which Tony Hordern replied: 'I do not know.'

Against the backdrop of this ongoing royal commission, *Smith's Weekly* had a front-page screamer on 23 July: 'Saywell Murderer Is Now KNOWN!'. The accompanying article claimed police were watching a man around the clock. The man – styled by the paper as the 'MAN' – had no idea he was being shadowed. *Smith's* was choosing not to identify him, and instead offered tantalising details: he was a materially comfortable fellow with a number of aliases; he'd tried to leave Australia on a false passport after the murder; and he now lived a fugitive existence, going from lodging to lodging.

> Wherever he goes, the detectives go also. Whatever roof covers his head, they sleep under the same roof. These vigilantes of the law will mark his slightest gesture and note every minutest change in his nervous condition. The detectives have sat beside this man at meals, and in the smoking rooms and lounges of guest houses. He does not conceal the fact of his acquaintance with the Saywell family; and these, his affable fellow guests, have allowed and encouraged him to chatter about the Saywell murder, concerning which he betrays perpetual curiosity and speculation.

The *Smith's* piece contained other balderdash about a blood-curdling scream in the night in the Saywell house, which Claude and Adeline had somehow ignored to their peril. The nonsense built to a dizzying crescendo like something from sci-fi magazine *Amazing Stories*:

> Not only are the detective police trailing the <u>MAN</u> whose voice
> when once it begins to speak freely and truly will unveil every
> secret. Unknown to him they live by his side. By day or by night,
> whatever this <u>MAN</u> reveals, whether consciously or unconsciously,
> comes within the perception, the knowledge and the judgement
> of the police. Murder will out. The Eye is watchful. The Eye is
> sleepless. The Eye is all discerning.

If MacKay's undercover man Frank Fahy, aka The Shadow, had been on
this case, it would've come out decades later. But when his story was
told – including the beatings he copped and his shadowing of Moxley –
there was no reference to the Saywell case. Yet while *Smith's Weekly*'s story
was fiction, the CIB didn't deny it. Perhaps this was because it painted a
favourably omniscient impression of the detectives, and might even spook
whoever had killed Claude Saywell. But to the *Smith's* editors, the police
silence might have been interpreted as a green light for even wilder stories
to boost circulation in the cut-throat Sydney market.

A week later, the newspaper outdid itself. The edition dated 30 July –
though it hit the streets a couple of days earlier – featured a trifecta of
true-crime scoops that made its front page among the most sensational
ever printed in Australia. *Smith's* had shocking exclusives about the
Dorothy Thorne murder *and* about how Claude Saywell had been killed
over the Tin Hares scandal. Yet both of these paled beside the biggest
story to share that front page.

'Moxley: Astounding Turn in Events!' screamed the headline. The
paper could now reveal that Frank Wilkinson hadn't been an innocent
young man murdered at random by a deranged maniac. Instead, he'd been
an associate of gangsters and was assassinated by Moxley on the orders
of the city's crime bosses. A sub-headline made a worse allegation: 'Gang

Sentence of Death – Underworld Got Wilkinson – Sacrifice of the Girl Victim'. Among the lurid claims: 'The worst horror of the whole ghastly story is that Dorothy Denzel was innocently dragged into the company of this vile fraternity, by the double-dealing Wilkinson. He suffered death; he also brought a light-hearted and unsuspecting girl into the terror of unspeakable outrage, followed by death itself.'

Smith's went into huge detail to rewrite the recent criminal history of the city, explaining how the Moxley murders were the outcome of the underworld wars waged between Tilly Devine and Kate Leigh. The accepted version went like this. In July 1929, in Woolloomooloo, one of Kate's henchmen, Frank Gaffney, shot Frank Green, then a gunman with Tilly's mob, but failed to kill him. Green holed up with Tilly and her husband, 'Big Jim' Devine, at their house in Maroubra. Later that month, three of Kate's men – Barney Dalton, George Gaffney and Walter Tomlinson – came to the house intending to kill Tilly. Things went badly wrong when Big Jim came out shooting, leaving Gaffney fatally wounded and Tomlinson injured. Big Jim was acquitted for acting in self-defence.

But he wasn't done yet – and neither was Frank Green. On 9 November 1929, Barney Dalton, Walter Tomlinson and Edward Brady were leaving the Strand Hotel in East Sydney when they were ambushed by Big Jim and Green. Bullets flew, Dalton fell to the footpath dying, Tomlinson was shot through the arm, and Brady was hit in the hand. Big Jim and Green were acquitted because none of the horrified witnesses would testify. By 1932 this was a well-told part of Sydney's bloodthirsty gangster lore.

Smith's Weekly's scoop exposed what had *really* happened that night in November, and its cast of characters was very different. Supposedly innocent citizen Frank Wilkinson had not only been good mates with Dalton, but had also been with him and another man at the Strand. The trio had been drinking and decided to hunt down and shoot dead Frank Green. When they found Green, he'd been with crook mates William

Moxley and Roy 'Dud' Prendergast. Bullets flew in this version, too, with Frank Green killing Dalton and sending Moxley and Dud into hiding. Later, Dud was shot dead by Kate Leigh when he broke into her place. But the truth about Green and Moxley made them vulnerable to blackmail – and Wilkinson had since played a dangerous game by demanding money for silence about what he'd seen. At the same time, Wilkinson was working as a police informant. When unidentified underworld bosses – *Smith's* might be foolhardy, but it wasn't about to openly name Tilly and Big Jim – learned all of this about Wilkinson, they commissioned Moxley to assassinate him.

Using Wilkinson's latest demand for money as pretext, Moxley arranged to meet the blackmailing fizgig at his Liverpool scrub camp. 'I cannot raise the money,' Moxley told him. Wilkinson renewed his threat to go to the police. *Smith's Weekly* told readers: 'Then Moxley walked into his tent: picked up his gun; and without a word of warning shot Wilkinson, who fell. Moxley fired a second barrel point-blank in the head of the fallen man.' That left Dorothy, who, *Smith's* believed, was likely there because her boyfriend believed Moxley would be 'restrained from violence' in her presence. It didn't work out that way, and he killed her next.

Stunningly, Moxley had *confessed* to the newspaper: 'Miss Denzel saw me shoot Wilkinson and if she were alive I would not have stood a chance with a jury. With Miss Denzel out of the way, I could make a good alibi that would clear my name."

Smith's Weekly's sensational claims about Frank Wilkinson as criminal blackmailer and Moxley as cold-blooded hitman were slammed from every side. For *The Sun* and *The Daily Telegraph*, this wasn't just a professional rivalry, it was personal, because Frank had worked as a compositor at both papers for many years. His former colleagues issued an angry statement of regret and disgust at the slander in *Smith's Weekly*. Frank's grieving family was even more hurt and bewildered.

Their son had been brutally slain and now his good character had been posthumously assassinated.

In an unusual move, the CIB weighed in. Inspector Lynch, who'd investigated the Dalton murder, told *The Sun*: 'Wilkinson, who was murdered by Moxley, was not an associate of gangsters. He was officially and unofficially unknown to the police. He was not connected with the Dalton matter.' Inspector Walsh, who'd investigated the Moxley murders, said all enquiries led him to believe 'young Wilkinson was a man of unimpeachable character'. CIB chief Prior thundered: 'Wilkinson had nothing to do with any gangs. He was as good a man as one could wish to find.' The CIB also issued a statement about Moxley that all but confirmed he had been a fizgig:

> He was a dingo. The established underworld would not tolerate him. They actually avoided him, and he, them. He was suspected of being a pimp. We believe that is why he was attacked and shot in the head two years ago. Wilkinson never knew him, and Moxley had never seen him before the night he murdered him. This Moxley confessed in sworn statements at his trials when he was trying to save his life.

Truth used Linda Fletcher to quiz Moxley about the quote he'd supposedly supplied to *Smith's*. A reporter took her sworn statement, in which she quoted her boyfriend as saying: 'I say definitely now that I had never set eyes on Wilkinson. As far I know he was a member of a very good family and I know that he was absolutely unknown among criminals.' Moxley also denied having known Dalton or Green.

Truth surveyed their criminal contacts and reported: 'Wilkinson was unknown – not even heard of. Hardened creatures of the underworld, men and women, spoke freely for once.' The paper made a mockery of the *Smith's* article by sitting down with one crook, Dud Prendergast, who 'stoutly denied that he had ever been shot dead in Kate Leigh's or anybody else's house!'. The man Kate Leigh shot and killed had been his brother, John Prendergast. Anyway, Dud said, when Dalton was shot, John had been behind bars. *Truth* sniped: 'They don't allow people out of gaol, even to attend the killing of underworld celebrities!' Big Jim also told the paper he'd never heard of Moxley until the man was shot in the head in 1930:

> *Smith's* story is the hottest lot of lies I have ever read. Wilkinson was certainly not present when Dalton was shot. Neither was Moxley. I have known Frank Green since 1919. When Dalton was shot, Green was actually living with me. I can positively say that Green never knew Wilkinson or Moxley.

The Sunday Sun also proudly displayed its underworld contacts. Walter Tomlinson said he never knew or saw Wilkinson or Moxley. Kate Leigh commented: '*Smith's* story is a vicious pack of lies. Wilkinson was never known to any of the people in these districts or the underworld. I know that Green never knew Moxley or Wilkinson. Barney Dalton never knew them either. Nor did Tomlinson.' Tilly Devine agreed: 'Wilkinson has never been near these districts, nor was ever know to the inhabitants.'

While Sydney's cops, crooks and citizens enjoyed a rare moment of unity in their disgust at *Smith's Weekly*, Moxley's fate was considered by the state government on Wednesday 3 August 1932. As much as they cared to, cabinet members reviewed the trial and the appeal evidence, along with Moxley's letter asking to be hanged and more recent correspondence in which he'd cleared Frank Wilkinson's name. Their decision was unanimous: the death sentence would be carried out. Moxley would be hanged in a fortnight.

Despite the backlash against *Smith's*, the paper doubled down with another incendiary front page. They demanded the government investigate Moxley's assassination of gangster Wilkinson, and that it enquire into *The Sunday Sun* and *The Daily Telegraph*'s legitimising of 'Sydney's Criminal Colony' by publishing interviews with these 'social outlaws', which served only to 'decorate the criminality of the city with a glamorous romance'.

Smith's revealed that last week's scoop had been based on revelations by former Sydney cop Harold Roach, who stood by his claims and had volunteered the sworn statement the paper now reproduced verbatim. In it, Roach said he'd spent four years as a police constable and had known Wilkinson most of that time, having been introduced to him by Dalton. He'd used Wilkinson as a paid fizgig and said the young man boasted it was 'a lot of fun mixing with criminals'. Roach said that Wilkinson, via his friendship with Dalton, saw and heard much and, for two years, 'constantly supplied me with information regarding crime and criminals and upon that information offenders were arrested'. After Dalton was shot, Roach said, he had advised his informant to quit and live a decent life. But Wilkinson said he was having too much fun, and making too much money, living the double life of paper compositor and police informer. It was around this time, Roach said, that Wilkinson told him Moxley had been present when Dalton was killed. A month before Wilkinson was murdered, he'd said to Roach that he was going to see Moxley and 'hand him over to the police'. Complicating matters, Moxley had then told Roach that he was afraid Wilkinson was going to kill him, for reasons he didn't disclose.

As to the credibility of the man telling this tangled tale, *Smith's Weekly* said Roach had been upfront about the fact he'd been dismissed from the New South Wales police after his superiors overreacted to him improperly disposing of stolen hats. In Roach's sworn statement, he said he'd welcome the fullest investigation into his claims: 'I am prepared to face any inquiry or tribunal and be examined on these facts, which I will substantiate from my own knowledge.'

Truth went hardest at its rival under the 7 August headline 'Wilkinson's Memory Nailed to a Cross of Shame – Smith's Weekly Returns to Dastardly Attack – Steeps Reputation Deeper in Vile Abuse of Murdered Youth'. *Truth* made some excellent points, among them that Roach hadn't sworn to anything about Wilkinson blackmailing anyone, about Moxley saying he intended to kill him or about having any information of such an admission. Moreover, *Smith's* hadn't explained how it had obtained Moxley's 'confession', which he'd emphatically denied and would hardly have made around the time he was hoping to be granted an appeal that would save his life.

This was now more than a war of words between newspapers. *Smith's Weekly's* editor was summoned to see Frank Chaffey, once again New South Wales chief secretary. Chaffey read him the riot act and showed him Roach's police record, which disproved several of his allegations. *Smith's* had no choice but to recant. But in doing so, it tripled down. Under the front-page headline, '*Smith's* Clears Wilkinson', the paper claimed *it* had vindicated the murder victim, whose goodness had been smeared by the sworn testimony of an ex-police officer whose bona fides they had checked assiduously. Noble and gallant, 'misled into doing a wrong', they had not sinned but had been sinned against.

Smith's said it would immediately prosecute Roach for making a false sworn declaration. But it didn't. No doubt any legal action would have revealed, at best, that they'd neglected simple fact-checking, hoping to get away with publishing horrible but circulation-boosting slanders.

Truth was beside itself with glee. 'Can S*mith's Weekly* say anything that ever again will commend for it the respect of an outraged community?' it wondered. Apologies would only go so far, because *Smith's* would 'stand condemned for all time as being guilty of creating the foulest blot in newspaper history'.

Truth was right. In the book *Remember Smith's Weekly?*, George Blaikie wrote: 'Normally the public is quick to forget a newspaper gaffe but it never did forgive *Smith's* in this matter. From 1932 onwards *Smith's* reporters seeking interviews were looked upon often with suspicion and distaste by many who had previously been ardent admirers of the paper.' Although the paper closed in 1950, Blaikie dated its death to the moment it nailed a murder victim to a cross of shame.

20

The MAN – and the Man Who Thought of Suicide

What was forgotten in the *Smith's Weekly* furore were the two other stories that had shared the infamous front page of 30 July 1932. The one about Claude Saywell read: 'Wires Flashed Warning! Smith's Has Facts in the Saywell Case. Tin Hare Holders Went in Fear.' This continued their previous story about the <u>MAN</u>, which, despite its breathless fictions, had actually contained a piece of evidence that did call for further investigation:

Very many persons looking for an interest in Tin Hares dealt directly or indirectly with Claude Saywell. Disputes were probably frequent enough. One incident may be quoted. An acquaintance of Mr Saywell's wanted to buy a fairly solid holding in a Tin Hare float. A substantial sum of money was involved; and the buyer, though he was a man with certain 'incidents' in his past, had money enough to keep him buoyant in making this plunge. The money was paid over to the proper quarter: but because of certain difficulties, the shares were not promptly delivered to the buyer. This purchaser, therefore, was parted from his cash, and had not yet received his commodity. He did not invoke the courts in a law suit because there were reasons in his past which made him shrink from the witness box. He preferred to adopt a threatening attitude to Claude Saywell. On one occasion this disappointed man was in the Saywell home: and when he made demands on Claude Saywell for money, Mr Saywell refused and the argument rose to a hot temperature.

This hearsay was vague, and the paper's claim 'Tin Hare Holders Went in Fear' seemed sensationalist. Yet Harry Wiles, a partner in the GRC, had told the royal commission that after the group got the tin hare licence, they gave Frederick Swindell another 2500 company shares. As this wasn't a sale, it was off the books – and, further, the shares weren't physically transferred to Swindell until later.

Mr Monahan, assisting the commissioner, asked Wiles: 'Will you detail the circumstances in which you handed those shares to Mr Swindell?'

Wiles: 'He rang me up and asked for the scrip. I took it to his office, and handed it over to him as his property.'

Monahan: 'Why didn't you hand them over straight away?'

Wiles: 'I handed them over when he asked for them.'

Monahan: 'As a rule do you hold people's property till they ask for it?'

Wiles: 'I was holding them and when Mr Saywell met his death, I realised it was a rather dangerous thing to do, so I saw my solicitor and he advised me to put them in trust.'

What had Wiles meant by 'dangerous'? This was certainly intriguing and worthy of a follow-up. *Smith's Weekly* claimed that it had:

Mr Wiles told *Smith's* that the 2500 shares which he held for F.S. Swindell were 'a mystery'. The late Mr Saywell made a deal with someone, selling the shares to him, but held them back. Mr

Wiles knew that this buyer of the shares had been 'kicking up a fuss about them' ... But Mr Saywell kept the man quiet as he held some information which the other man did not want to be made known.

The paper quoted Wiles:

> I never saw this man, nor do I know who he is. None of the directors knew him; and I have not heard of his whereabouts since Mr Saywell's death. He is the only person who we cannot account for as holding shares. Since Mr Saywell is dead, there seems no hope of tracing him. His evidence might throw light on the Saywell tragedy.

Despite the hammering that the reputation of *Smith's Weekly* was about to take over its smearing of Frank Wilkinson, Harry Wiles did not recant his interview or claim he'd been misquoted. If what he'd said was true, it might offer a big-money motive for Claude Saywell's murder – beyond the deranged-small-shareholder theory Jack Saywell had floated. Yet if more light was going to be shone on this, it wouldn't be until the inquest – and no date for that had been set.

The third exclusive on *Smith's Weekly*'s infamous front page contained more sensational allegations that wouldn't be refuted. A photo of a man staring plaintively was captioned: 'The Man Who Thought of Suicide – Alfred George Lockyer'. He had – at the suggestion of a 'friend' – given *Smith's* a lengthy statement just before he was due to testify at the inquest into Dorothy Thorne's death. Alfred maintained he'd had nothing to do with the poisoning – and that he and his landlady had only been friends. But he said the police hadn't believed him, and that their accusations and threats had nearly driven him to kill himself.

Lockyer said he'd first been questioned on the day Dorothy had died.

But a week later, at 7.30am on Tuesday 12 July, detectives had come to the Mosman house he was still sharing with Reginald Thorne. They took him to the CIB and interrogated him for fifteen hours. *Smith's* reported: 'One detective was particularly aggressive and told him bluntly that he believed he killed Mrs Thorne.' Lockyer told *Smith's*: 'They bullied me, they cajoled me …' The paper didn't dare name the detective when quoting Alfred: '—— told me that I had been taken there for a certain purpose, but they had decided to defer it till a later date.' This 'certain purpose' was presumably charging Alfred with murder. But the unidentified detective or detectives had another way out for their suspect. Lockyer told *Smith's*:

> It was suggested to me that I should commit suicide but leave a written statement behind me exonerating Reg Thorne. If it were possible to do this, I would do it. I know things look very black against me – the way that the detectives put it – but all I can say is that I am absolutely innocent in the matter, and it looks as though the police are making me the scapegoat, as they can see no motive for the murder.

After being released from custody, Lockyer was so anxious he feared he'd take his own life. But Lynch called him into the CIB again and said something to ease his mind. Lockyer said he learned he was no longer under suspicion from another source, not specifying whether it was a detective, a lower-ranked cop or a civilian. If this serious abuse had happened, who was responsible? Given Lynch seemed to have taken the role of 'good cop', suspicion had to fall on McRae as the other senior CIB man on the case.

While Sydney cops had lined up to defend Frank Wilkinson's memory against the *Smith's* slanders, they didn't bother to deny allegations about their own brutal conduct made in the very same issue. Perhaps it was because the paper hadn't named any names. Or maybe they were simply used to such claims, and would have refuted them if Alfred Lockyer repeated the allegations at the inquest – which he wouldn't. Nor would he repeat something else he made a point of telling *Smith's*:

> I know I did not put poison in the Seidlitz powder. I cannot say, but it could have happened accidentally. Thorne and I are still living at the house. He has been quite friendly, except on one night, about a week ago, when he did not speak to me throughout the evening. When I was going to bed, I asked: 'What's the matter, Reg?' 'Plenty,' he said. 'Well, tell me what the trouble is,' I said. 'Nothing that will bear talking about,' was his reply.

The coroner, Edwin May, opened the Dorothy Thorne inquest on the morning of 27 July. He spent a lot of time listening to evidence from those involved with the manufacture of the Seidlitz powders. When May heard from Dr Pawlett, who'd tried to save Dorothy, one of his questions was beyond the witness's knowledge: 'Was the manner of Mr Thorne consistent with innocence?' Dr Pawlett replied: 'Mr Thorne's distress was quite genuine. I know him very well.'

Reginald Thorne told May that Dorothy had been cheerful, they'd been happy and never fought, that she had no reason to kill herself and no one had any reason to kill her. Reginald said neither he nor his wife ever had any strychnine in their possession. May asked another odd question: 'Did Mr Lockyer have any in his possession?' How Reginald could have known this one way or the other wasn't clear. In any case, he answered no.

Coroner May asked Reginald: 'Was there any undue familiarity between your wife and Lockyer?'

He answered: 'No. I noticed nothing.'

The witness was about to leave the box when May reluctantly asked: 'When you got home that Monday night and found your wife with Mr

Locker, was there any difference between you and others of the party then?'

'Oh, no,' Reginald replied. 'They were discussing the picture and laughing about it. When I arrived I complained of a slight headache.'

May: 'Although you and your wife occupied different rooms—' But he stopped himself: 'I won't ask that question.'

Reginald, alert to the insinuation, answered anyway: 'The reason why we occupied different rooms was because I was interested in the wireless and the baby used to sleep with her.'

The coroner had Alfred detail his and Dorothy's movements the day before she died. This established the house had been empty for a little while. But the coroner also accepted their Irish terrier would've prevented anyone sneaking in.

For the police, Inspector Lynch asked: 'During the time you have known Mr and Mrs Thorne have you ever known them to quarrel?'

Alfred replied, 'Never' – and he said he hadn't argued with either of them. Lynch asked him why he didn't call Reginald before giving Dorothy mustard and water as an emetic. Alfred answered: 'I did not think it was anything serious.' Lynch asked if he'd ever had strychnine in his possession. Alfred said he hadn't and he didn't even know what it looked like.

The inquest was over in three hours. Coroner May said in his finding: 'I have never seen a case more mysterious than this.' He didn't believe Reginald or Alfred had killed Dorothy. But his stated reasons were somewhat subjective. 'I have watched them carefully. Their whole attitude from the time before the doctor was sent for and since seemed to point to nothing else but innocence.' Nor did May believe Dorothy had committed suicide; rather, she had accidentally administered herself the poison, believing it was Seidlitz. Yet he did not think there had been any adulteration of the powders during manufacture or at the pharmacy. The coroner was leaving the verdict open: 'The extraordinary thing is: how did this poison get there as it did? ... The whole thing is a mystery and we would be very pleased if that mystery could be solved.'

If it all seemed rushed, it was because the coroner had to hurry away to attend to another matter. This only added to the sense that the inquest was far from satisfactory. Sydney newspaper *The Arrow* provided a rigorous critique. Too much of the little time that was available had been devoted to formal evidence about the manufacture of Seidlitz powder. This, it argued, could have been established by police testifying that they were satisfied the poison hadn't been introduced in the factory or pharmacy. *The Arrow* reckoned all the production detail – which had included having drug company executives testify – was more about protecting business reputations than penetrating further into the mystery of Dorothy's death.

The paper was similarly displeased that testimony from detectives, the autopsy results and the analyst's report on Dorothy's stomach contents were submitted as written statements and hurried through. *The Arrow* criticised May for seeking Dr Pawlett's opinion about Reginald Thorne's apparent innocence. It also slated the coroner's interpretation of the evidence about the dog, arguing that the mutt may have been familiar enough with any killer to not bark. The paper further criticised May and Inspector Lynch for not asking Reginald or Alfred if they'd discussed Dorothy's death during the past three weeks, in which they'd continued to live under the same roof. 'Surely this was a pertinent question,' the paper said, claiming it had information that the two men had in fact not once discussed the tragedy. Indeed, Alfred's curious statement about Reg to *Smith's Weekly* – which could be read as casting suspicion on him – would have justified such a line of enquiry.

Who had killed Dorothy Thorne? McRae and his colleagues had any number of theories but only two real suspects. To *Smith's Weekly*, Alfred said the police had 'put certain things to him'. One would've been the accusation of an affair. He denied it. Admitting an affair would've given police the motive they were looking for. Perhaps Alfred and Dorothy had been involved and she'd broken it off. Or he'd made advances that she rejected. In either scenario, he might have taken his revenge by handing her a glass of poison. While detectives hadn't found any records of him buying strychnine, he would likely have encountered the stuff in his work as a gardener. And the world only had his word that Dorothy had mixed the powders herself.

Yet an extramarital affair also gave Reginald a motive. He might have discovered the adultery and poisoned his wife, expecting that blame would fall on their boarder. If this was the case, it was in his interest to say he knew of no affair or ill will. Reginald also had his wife's assets as a possible motive. When she died, his garage business claimed assets of £12,195 but had debts of £9166. Reginald was above water on paper but his listed cash on hand was just £7/11/10. It wasn't much of a buffer and business wasn't about to bounce back any time soon. Dorothy's will left everything to Reginald: the Mosman house, which she had owned, valued at £1650; £2800 in shares, one-fifth of them in his business, the rest in her father's company; her £500 bank balance and all the household effects, which were also in her name. All up Dorothy was worth £5109/18/7 – about $560,000 today. Had Alfred Lockyer been charged and gone to trial for Dorothy's murder, his defence would likely have pointed to this windfall as motive in establishing her husband as an alternative suspect.

It was also possible that Dorothy had an outside lover – or unknown enemy – familiar with her use of Seidlitz and able get past the dog. Another theory that no one even dared hint at publicly: Reginald and Alfred had been lovers. Discovering this, Dorothy had threatened divorce and exposure. So one or both of them decided she had to die, and they subsequently covered for each other to protect their secret. Yet there was another possibility: Alfred – despondent for whatever reason – had that morning mixed himself a suicide concoction, and Dorothy drank it by accident.

Below: Big Bill MacKay, who enjoyed a meteoric rise in the New South Wales Police Force, reshaping it for better and for worse. *(The Sydney Mail)*

Above: Fresh from arresting and charging the Park Demon murderer in Sydney in January 1933, Detective-Sergeant Thomas McRae (centre) and his men (left to right): Detective-Sergeant James Comans, Detective-Constable Arthur Burns and Detective-Constable William Payne. *(National Library of Australia (NLA))*

Despite individual senior officers being well-known enough to merit caricature in *The Sydney Mail* (above), many people in Depression-era Australia couldn't shake the image of cops bashing and shooting miners at Rothbury in 1929 (left). *(NLA)*

In 1929–1931, McRae investigated increasingly high-profile cases. He made his name with brilliant detective work that solved the mystery of the Bungendore Bones. *(NLA)*

While NSW police had been tainted as bashers, there was still a massive outpouring of grief when two young constables were murdered by a madman in Bondi. A third officer, Adam 'Scotty' Denholm, would escape with his life and go on to establish the police dog squad – and later train Skippy for television. *(NLA)*

Populist New South Wales Labor Premier Jack Lang often addressed tens of thousands of supporters, delivering firebrand speeches critical of the federal government's response to the Depression – and pillorying his New Guard opponents as anti-democratic bully-boy fascists. *(NSW State Archives Collection)*

Above: Member of the New Guard, Francis de Groot, during his infamous 'opening' of the Sydney Harbour Bridge in March 1932. *(NSW State Archives Collection)*

Right: New Guard leader Colonel Eric Campbell denied this was a fascist salute, but it certainly looked like one on newspaper front pages. *(NSW State Archives Collection)*

OPENING THE BRIDGE.—The Premier of N.S.W. (Mr. Lang) cutting the ribbon stretched across Sydney Harbor Bridge on Saturday. The ribbon was cut previously by Captain F. E. de Groot, of the New Guard.

CAPTAIN DE GROOT'S EXPLOIT in forestalling Mr. Lang by severing the ribbon with his sword formed a sensational incident in official opening of Sydney Harbor Bridge on Saturday. Captain Groot is shown being arrested by police officers after he had been dragged from horseback immediately after his unexpected coup. Right: A portrait of the officer, who made several ineffectual slashes at ribbon before he cut it through.

Francis de Groot's stunt captured newspaper front pages and newsreels everywhere – such as the above clipping from Melbourne's *Sun News-Pictorial* – and is still remembered today as a spirited larrikin moment. Less remembered: the New Guard's alleged plot against an elected state government and the political bashing carried out by its hood-wearing inner circle, the 'Fascist Legion'. *(NLA)*

NET WEEKLY SALES LARGER THAN THOSE OF ANY OTHER NEWSPAPER IN AUSTRALIA

FINAL EXTRA

THE ☆ABOVE ALL☆ SUN
FOR AUSTRALIA

FINE AND COOL
City Forecast; Fine, with clouds, and cool during day; fresh to usually W. to S.W. winds; cold night and frosts on Wednesday morning.

No. 6976   (Registered at the General Post Office, Syd-) for transmission by post as a newspaper.   SYDNEY: TUESDAY, MAY 10, 1932   PRICE 1½d   'Phone: B. O. 333

Alleged New Guard Plot to Kidnap Lang

MINISTERS AND POLICE EXECUTIVES

Plan of Berrima Gaol
Found at
Intelligence Branch

CHILDS TAKES ACTION

AN extraordinary plot to kidnap the Premier, Cabinet, and police chiefs before the opening of the Harbor Bridge, was revealed to-day, according to the Commissioner of Police (Mr. Childs), during an examination of papers connected with the New Guard.

The Commissioner of Police (Mr. Childs) made the following statement this afternoon:—

"The Police Department yesterday received information concerning a plot formed prior to the opening of the Sydney Harbor Bridge to seize certain Ministers of the Crown and high police officials, and

Mr. Childs

to incarcerate them in the disused Berrima gaol, which is alleged to have been prepared for the purpose.

"To-day, by virtue of a special warrant, detectives acting under the supervision of Mr. Mackay (Metropolitan Superintendent) searched the intelligence section premises of the New Guard and seized certain papers among them being a plan of the Berrima Gaol.

"The police," added Mr. Childs, "are moving very swiftly in the matter, and later developments may be expected."

Captain Jones, talking to the airliner and betsman of the "Flying Scotsman," which he defeated in an air versus train race between London and Edinburgh. (See air thrill story on Page 7.)

NOBBLING A FAVORITE

Spectators' Tricks

FLUID SQUIRTED

("Sun" Special)

LONDON, Monday.

HOW spectators may cripple a favorite's chances by spraying his mouth with fluid from the Paddock may shortly be revealed by a special inquiry by the Jockey Club.

For 10 years vague allegations of nobbling have occasionally been made on various racecourses, and now the

Two More Raids

DEVELOPMENTS in police activity against the New Guard followed in quick succession early this afternoon when detectives raided the intelligence headquarters of the organisation in Hunter-street, seized a number of documents, and detained an official.

Later he was allowed to go ..... asked by Detectives Wilkes and

BLACKMAIL — MURDER?

The lonely area near the Rookwood Cemetery, where the missing couple are feared to have met with violence. The car was seen early Wednesday morning being driven down the road indicated by the arrow.

VANISHED COUPLE FEARED SLAIN

Lonely Pool May Hold Secret Of Their Grim Fate

ARREST IS EXPECTED

Now ranked as the deepest mystery for years is the complete disappearance together from their homes last Tuesday night, of Frank Bardsley Wilkinson, aged 26, compositor, of 11 Beresford Road, Homebush, and Miss Dorothy Denzel, 21, of 12 Clifton Avenue, Burwood.

Police engaged in the day and night search have been forced to the dramatic conclusion that the young couple were brutally murdered and their bodies done away with.

THAT seems the only logical conclusion. But if this is so, what can have been the motive for the crime.

From their intensive inquiries, detectives believe only one answer is possible. They suspect that two men.

The last studio portrait of Miss Dorothy Denzel, the beautiful young brunette who has mysteriously disappeared with Frank Bardsley Wilkinson.

their parents, Mr. and Mrs. Denzel operate rival taxi businesses.

The domestic position can have no influence on the present tragedy.

Dorothy Denzel, once a fortnight, made a habit of visiting both her father and mother at Windsor.

Interviewed last night, they could not account for the disappearance or offer any motive for violence against the couple. Mr. Denzel has spent two days in his car scouring the Gosford district, tracking down false clues, but last night he felt convinced that the couple had met a violent end. Mrs. Denzel, brokenhearted and prostrated, now imagines the worst.

REWARD OFFERED

Wilkinson's father, Mr. Alexander Wilkinson, auctioneer and valuator, of Wyong and Gosford, acting on the advice of the police, last night offered "a substantial reward to any person who supplies such information as will lead to the discovery (dead or alive) of his son and Miss Denzel." His telephone number is UM679.

All the parents and police feel that, owing to the publicity given to the mystery, the affectionate children would have long ago sent word that they were safe, IF THEY WERE ALIVE.

They were last seen alive together on Tuesday night, when they left on one of their usual rides, dressed in informal clothes and taking no luggage or anything else which might suggest an elopement with them. The Alvis car, an unusual type, was next seen by a resident in Newtown Road, Strathfield.

strangers to the couple, approached them, probably for the purpose of bluffing them to the handing over of money.

When the couple, though alone, and without defence, resisted, they were attacked and slain, according to this theory.

Frank Bardsley Wilkinson, the missing man.

Walking Ticket!

Big Dole Squad Sacked

Forty men and six women dole inspectors were given a week's notice by the Labor Department on Friday.

NO reasons were put in the dismissal notices, but it is understood that the financial position and prospects of the

In Good Taste

It is a greater beauty and distinction in a fortnight's time.

BECAUSE faces to-day that it is impossible to be attractive with imperfectly formed hair. Fashion on arrest women come to the salons where their hair is waved in a manner which best suits their features and tones.

The mysterious disappearance of young couple Dorothy Denzel and Frank Wilkinson came just weeks after the Sydney Harbour Bridge was opened – and on the same day that the news of Phar Lap's death was announced. *(NLA)*

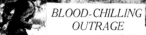

The Moxley manhunt, inquest, trial and appeal were accompanied by sensational newspaper coverage – some of the stories and images potentially prejudicial. *(NLA)*

No sooner had Moxley been caught than Sydney and New South Wales were gripped by a succession of savage crimes. It wasn't unusual to see multiple murder stories covered on the same newspaper page. The Saywell Hammer Horror case would be one of 1932's many headline-grabbing homicides – and a mystery worthy of Agatha Christie. *(NLA)*

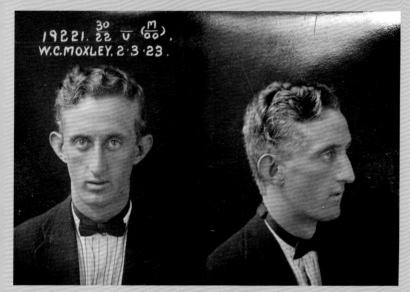

When Dorothy Denzel and Frank Wilkinson were found murdered, a massive manhunt was launched for suspected killer William Moxley, previously a small-time crook who'd also been working as a police informer for CIB chief MacKay.

Left, below: A constable has a well-earned smoko after catching Moxley.

Right, below: Moxley emerges in handcuffs from a police van to attend his life-or-death court appeal. *(NSW State Archives Collection, State Library of New South Wales, SLNSW)*

Left: In the wake of the Moxley manhunt, conducted without a dog squad, CIB chief MacKay decided the NSW force needed canine constables – and Adam 'Scotty' Denholm would be the one to train them.

THE GRISLY TRAIL OF A KILLER

CLUES THAT MAY SEAL PARK DEMON'S DOOM

"Truth" Reconstructs
INCIDENTS OF
Dread Death Drive

WHAT is the evidence against Sydney's spectral Park Demon and who will bravely come forward to testify against him? "Truth" will reveal for the first time the main witnesses for the Crown and the main evidence against the

Bessie O'Connor's Murderer May Be Unmasked!

KNOWN SUSPECT TO BE CHARGED WITHIN FEW DAYS

Police Finalising Plans For Startling Sequel To Monstrous Crime

THE police feel certain they know the murderer of Bessie O'Connor. WITHIN THE NEXT FEW DAYS THERE WILL BE SENSATIONAL DEVELOPMENTS, AND A CHARGE OF WILFUL AND FELONIOUS MURDER IS EXPECTED TO BE LAID AGAINST A YOUNG, GOOD-LOOKING MAN.

SLOWLY, a web of circumstantial evidence is being woven around the suspect. As cold and impassive as a scientist injecting a new specimen, Detective-Inspector Miller is preparing for the big move he will make this week.

CRAIG'S AGONY OF SUSPENSE

"CANNOT AGREE"
Jury's Dramatic Declaration

BESSIE O'CONNOR CRIME UNSOLVED

TERRIFIC ORDEAL
Craig May Face Second Trial

COURT SPELLBOUND AT FINAL TABLEAU

763.L.B.

As 1932 came to a close, Sydney was shocked by the murders of three women. The Park Demon case would be in the headlines for months.

Above and above right: police mugshot photos of Iris Marriott, aka May Miller, the second victim. *(NLA, NSW State Archives Collection)*

On the Saturday in January 1933 that Tom McRae laid a murder charge in the Park Demon case, he and his men were photographed walking from the CIB, and a newspaper caption said they were going home for a well-earned rest. But it'd seem the pub was the first stop, as this picture was taken the same day. *(SLNSW)*

HOCKING BONDI TRAGEDY

TWO MEN ON CHARGE OF MURDER

UNIQUE POLICE EVIDENCE AT INQUEST

Alleged Statements Of Accused Men Read In Court

LAST WORDS OF JOHN ROWLAND

HENRY BARCHAM, seated at the wheel of the car which he said ... from outside his home at Eastwood on the night of May 15.

...lice story of the killing of John Albert Rowland—a crime without an apparent clue, ...laying that shocked this State—was told to the City Coroner, Mr. Farrington, last ... It was a blood chilling story, a narrative of clever police work and ... c deduction.

...young unemployed men were charged with the terrible offence ...r alleged statements were submitted to the Coroner, who committed ...hem for trial, on a charge of murder. The police alleged that William Wallace, aged 24, and Eric Newlyn, aged 26, stole a car on ...t of May 15 and embarked upon a desperate adventure as armed

HE alleged state-
ments were
amongst the
most remark-
able documents
ever submitted
in the historic
Coroner's Court
at Circular
Quay, Sydney.

...bait witness against the
...new stand charged with
...his story, one of absorb-
...interest, told how a gun
...such information given to
...las arrest on a mind-
...stealing was the weapon

he did not think he could identify
the men as it was dark, and also
declared he had never seen them
before.

"I could not see the colour of the revolver," the deposition went on, "but
I got the impression it was a square
shaped one and small."

Witness said that when Rowland
was ordered to turn his statement he
had, "I want to go to sleep and shut
his eyes."

Hale was cross-examined at length
by Mr Sproule, who wanted to know
just what questions were put to Row-
lands before he made the deposition,
by either Hale or the magistrate.

To another question, Hale replied
that Rowland said two men got out
of the car, while he said deceased had
volunteered the main part of the deposition without questioning.

Dr. Henry George Pierce, of St. Vincent's Hospital, told of Rowland's in-

LEFT: The car that was alleged to have been stolen by Wallace and Newlyn, snapped
outside the Coroner's Court.
ABOVE: John Albert Row-
land, the young indent agent,
whose tragic death shocked the
State.

Manslaughter, Said Jury

STATE WIDE ASTONISHMENT

At Verdict On Callous KILLING OF JOHN ROWLAND

Highway Robbers Gaoled For Life

GUILTY of manslaughter—and the crime of Eric Newlyn and Claude William Wallace was the cold-blooded killing of an unarmed, respected
Sydney citizen, together with an act of highway robbery.

The entire State was dumbfounded and amazed at the
jury's verdict in the case of the conscienceless slaughter of
John Rowland at Bondi on May 18. A hushed, crowded
court gasped audibly when the decision was announced, and a quickly passing shadow
flitted across the stern features of his Honor, Mr. Justice Kenneth Street, son of the ex-
Chief Justice, who presided at the hearing of the atrocious crime.

The two ruthless slayers were sentenced by Mr. Justice Street to penal servitude for life, the
greatest punishment he could impose, but a punishment that does not meet the dastardly killing
of a good man, the wrecking of a good home, the sorrow of a widow, and the pangs of a little
orphaned baby boy; a baby boy who once kissed his daddy good-night, but who now says
prayers for him.

The two cowardly killers may get out in 20 years.

They must never be released; they must be closely caged forever!

David Joseph Deeye,
man, who told of being
robbed on the night
... shooting. (At right)
... thompson also told of
... ded by two desperados

HE crime, the
clever detective
hunt, the mes-
sage to the C.I.B
and the arrest
and then the
incredible ver-
dict, provide a
startling story.
The arrest was
most sensational
... has remained on
... to-day. Truth
... exclusive disclosure.

Rowland, prominent city
... out spending Mlandh, had
... when eight of his
... by William Pryor, then
... his men into opera-

...Mr Liddell, who grate-
... placed in charge of
... mentioned each prominent
... no Detective-sergeants
... Mann, Alleroad and Deter-

...d not be shaken from his
... he also would be found
... dead district, from whence
... car had been stolen on
... May 15. He was cold.

...considered the unprovoked killing of
John Rowland was merely a panoram?... incident.

Briefly, the law is that murder is the crime of malicious
killing, while manslaughter is
the crime of accidental—
though culpable—killing.

Alexandak on the night of June 3
when he saw the younger of two
... the another motor vehicle towards the

The police took up the chase and
crowded Wallace's car into the curb,
but although Detective Allsoped drew
his revolver and levelled it at the fugitive's head, Wallace sprang from his
own car, rolled over in the street and
then ran away

...for a moment there there was a bullet
in the breech at all.

"I knew in my own mind there was
no bullet in it. As far what the police
... about that safety-catch, it mean't
nothing because I didn't know the law
as it was there

"I said, 'Put your hands up.'
but he started to yell. I said.
'Don't be silly. I've got a gun'

Then he
heard a shot
and saw
I did not
Shandler

The cross-examination of
this witness concluded the
Crown Prosecutor then
called the first of the "two

The court
... shortly ...
... and did not reach ...
... 2.20 p.m., when the whole
... proved that the twelve
... were baffled by the facts
and Newlyn had reached a
verdict.

Officials took up their
... around the various points of
... mass and Mr. Justice Street
... and grim, having taken h?
... the bench, the peers of Wm.
Newlyn once again returned h?
... in the jury box after they re-
... tabled.

As the doors trooped of
... distance which lay befo?
... court-door and the jury may
Wallace and Newlyn waited
... faces closely. At every-
...seemed the more composed
... ter. At every stage as the ju?
... slowly, it seemed, took u?
positions amid the deaths?
of the court, Newlyn was
... a shaking palm aer?
month. He averted his eye
the jurors and seemed t?
what might have been a pr?
hind his sheltering hand.

The Judges Associate, wr?

While the Park Demon was enduring his numerous court trials, McRae headed up
another murder squad to solve Sydney's latest cold-blooded killing – but the verdict
was to cause outrage. (NLA)

Last Drinks Before Deat[h]

THE SUN

HUMAN GLOVE CLUE K[EY] TO RIVER MURDER

MOVEMENTS OF CHAFF-BAG VICT[IM] TRACED

SENSATIONAL REVELATION[S] ARE ANTICIPATED

(FROM 'TRUTH'S' SPECIAL REPRESENTATIVE)

WAGGA, Saturday.

A GRIM and tragic real life story that is more thrilling and absorbing than most detective shockers is being unfolded in the courthouse at Wagga the story of the murder of Percy Smith, Riverina wanderer and vagabond.

It is a narrative pulsing with mystery, and to explain and solve the crime the police have woven a fabric of circumstantial evidence. In no case in recent criminal history have detectives so completely relied upon tiny fragments of circumstance and points of probability to formulate a capital charge.

THIRTY-NINE witnesses comprise the police case of alleged wilful murder against Edward Henry Morey, a tall, angular, weather-beaten man, who was brought into the court under police escort. Morey listened with unwavering attention as the police unfolded their case against him.

EDWARD HENRY MOREY (at left), who was at the moment in custody. (Below) The waggonette a prominent exhibit at the hearing.

DOLE TICKETS FOUND IN BLOODSTAINED WAGGON

STORY OF POLICE INTERVIEW WITH MAN HELD IN CUSTODY

MARRIED WOMAN'S LOVE LETTERS TO MURDERER MOREY

Charged Now With Husband's Death

WAGGA WAGGA, Saturda[y]

Murrumbidgee Mystery Murder— **THE SUN** *—First Pictures In Sydney*

The Human Glove mystery, which began in Wagga Wagga on Christmas Day in 1933, was marked by astounding forensic work and intensive investigation by McRae and his colleagues in Depression-era unemployment bush communities. Just when the murder trial was nearly completed, a second bizarre murder was committed – and McRae would also lead this investigation. *(NLA)*

A Unique Web of Circumstantial Evidence
has Convicted Edward Morey of a Brutal

MURDER

DECLARED HIS INNOCENCE IN WHISPERED TONES

CONDEMNED to death and rushed straight to Sydney, Edward Henry Morey, brutal Wagga murderer, arrived at the Central Railway Station yesterday morning and was transferred immediately to the observation block at Long Bay Penitentiary. Inexorably the police had woven a fine mesh of evidence around him. The death of Percy Smith, saving trapper, was avenged by the verdict of "Guilty"...

McRae put Edward Morey behind bars in the Human Glove case – along with Lillian Anderson, the woman who murdered because of her deranged 'love' for Morey. But before her trial had even concluded, Australia was gripped by the most infamous of 1930s murder cases: the Pyjama Girl. *(NLA)*

NET WEEKLY SALES LARGER THAN THOSE OF ANY OTHER NEWSPAPER IN AUSTRALIA

FOOTBALL RESULTS

THE SUN

ABOVE ALL FOR AUSTRALIA

UNSETTLED AND COLD
City Forecast: Unsettled and cold, with more rain; heavy rain squalls probable; strong S.E. winds to gales

No. 7697 (Registered at the General Post Office, Syd.) SYDNEY: SATURDAY, SEPTEMBER 1, 1934 PRICE 1½d 'Phone: BO 333

CHARRED AND BATTERED BODY IN SACK

MAKE PEACE

COTTON DISPUTE
NEW MOVES
POLITICIANS ACT
("Sun" Special)

LONDON, Friday.
PUBLIC men are bestirring themselves in England to discourage Lancashire's agitation for a boycott of Australian produce in retaliation for the new cotton duties.

The ex-Premier of South Australia (Mr. Hill) tells "The Sun" that he strongly deprecates South Australian and Queensland talk of a retaliatory

Girl In White Pyjamas

Taking It Up

CULVERT HORROR

On Albury Road

TOWEL AROUND NECK

THE partly-charred body of a girl, about 20, clad only in pyjamas, was found in an old wheat sack under a culvert on the Howlong-road, four miles from Albury, about 1 p.m. to-day.

The body was found by Mr. Thomas Hunter Griffiths, a well-known farmer of Albury. It had evidently

MOVE EMPIRE PEOPLES

Visiting Australia

NEW PLAN
MEN, MARKETS
PAST REVIEWED
SETTLER TYPE
("Sun" Special)

LONDON, Friday.
AN important report dealing with the re-distribution of the Empire's people will be issued next week, "The Sun" learns, from the Overseas Settle-

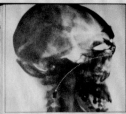

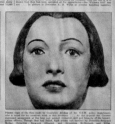

In 1938, *Pix* magazine ran a large feature about the police's ongoing efforts to solve the Pyjama Girl case. *(NLA)*

While the Pyjama Girl is well remembered today, the Lady in Grey case has been forgotten – but it had a far more disastrous impact on Tom McRae. *(NLA)*

•Ex-policeman's "new evidence"
I DEMAND JUSTICE!

Mr. McRae, as he is today, 17 years after his dismissal from the Police Force.

A former detective-sergeant claims he has uncovered "sensational evidence" to prove he was wrongly dismissed from the Police Force 17 years ago.

He says the Premier, Mr. Cahill, has refused him a Royal Commission.

The former detective is Mr. Thomas Walter McRae, now aged 70.

He was dismissed from the Police Force in November, 1940, when a Divorce Court jury found him guilty of adultery with Mrs. Freda Agnes Caesar, aged 25.

Once the chief of the C.I.B. Homicide Squad, top "glamour" detective of the force, Detective-Sergeant McRae figured in practically every murder investigation in N.S.W. in the wild 1930s.

He once estimated that his photograph appeared in 32 out of 52 weekly editions of a Sunday newspaper.

The Pyjama Girl, the "Human Gloves" case, and the Craig park murders were some of the famous cases on which he worked.

For 17 years since his dismissal, Mr. McRae has said that he was innocent.

He has worked non-stop to prove it.

Last October his solici-

Divorce is recalled

Mr. McRae (left) as he was when he headed investigations into the famous "Pyjama Girl" mystery.

tor sent his file, together with what was claimed to be "vital fresh evidence" to the Attorney-General, Mr. Downing, with an application for a special judicial inquiry into the dismissal and divorce.

The solicitor wrote: "The information now to hand in the light of all the past circumstances is of such a nature as to call for a full and urgent investigation so that a grave miscarriage of justice should not occur."

"I will not stop fighting"

A Queen's Counsel has undertaken the brief, free of charge, to prepare the case for hearing.

This is the appeal that Mr. Cahill last week refused.

Tall, stooped, and a semi-invalid, Mr. McRae told "The Sun-Herald" at his

home in Gardeners Road, Kingsford, yesterday:

"I will not stop fighting until I get justice.

"I have been an innocent victim and I mean to clear my name before I die.

"I am not interested in money. All I want is a re-hearing of my case in the light of this fresh evidence I've uncovered.

"It is sensational.

"I want the facts brought up in Parliament.

"I've been fighting for it for 17 years, and I'll leave no stone unturned until I get an inquiry before a Supreme Court Judge."

Letter from Mr. Cahill

Mr. McRae held out the letter of refusal he had received from Mr. Cahill.

In part of the letter Mr. Cahill had written:

"The representations made in this case have been carefully considered and I have been advised that the type of inquiry contemplated seems to be a Royal Commission committed by a Supreme Court Judge and having the special powers conferred by Section 17 of the Royal Commission Act.

"The Government's legal advisers who have examined the matter have expressed the opinion that the appointment of a Royal Commission with the very drastic powers conferred by Section 17 would not be justified.

"In the circumstances, it is regretted that your request cannot be granted."

Unknown man made offer

Mr. McRae said: "What do they mean by 'drastic powers'?

"It seems that the only alternative is that I am to be denied justice.

"Yet I have six unsolicited declarations from unconnected people, supporting my innocence and telling the story of what happened.

"The last declaration was supplied a little over a year ago by a man who voluntarily came to see me. He was unknown when the case was heard—now he is vitally linked to it.

"I believe I put sufficient evidence before the Govern-

MR. CAHILL

(the name of Mrs. Caesar's father) on only three occasions. I took no disciplinary action against him on the thing having him paraded.

"When I made my appeal Cabinet knocked back in two hours a recommendation for reinstatement than had taken the Police Board 10 days to prepare.

"If I had been the guilty party I would not draw attention to myself—would have crawled into obscurity by now.

"I've been fighting since the day they wrongfully convicted me and I'll keep on fighting till the end."

His wife, slim Mrs. Jane McRae, said:

"If I believed my husband had been guilty I would not be with him today.

"But I know he is a good and an innocent man. I know what was done to him.

"It has meant pain, humiliation and suffering for us, and loss of money. My husband had a bad breakdown in health three years ago—I thought he would die.

"I am fighting back with him."

Caesar, 32, an electrical mechanic, of Doncaster Avenue, Kingsford, cited McRae as co-respondent in a divorce action against his wife, Freda Agnes Caesar, and claimed £2,000 damages from him.

Mrs. Caesar, a striking blonde, failed to defend the suit, and gave evidence that McRae had been her lover for some time.

She said she submitted to McRae because she feared that her father, a police sergeant, would suffer in the department otherwise.

Evidence was given that Caesar and private detectives had found Mrs. Caesar and McRae in a city hotel room in circumstances which suggested a guilty association.

McRae denied the allegations.

He said the only time he had met Mrs. Caesar was in the course of his police duties to receive information from her about an alleged fight between her husband and her father, the policeman.

Jury found him guilty

The jury, before Mr. Justice Street, found McRae guilty and he was dismissed from the force. Caesar settled for £400 in damages and costs.

McRae appealed for reinstatement, which was recommended by the Police Appeals Board, but reinstatement was rejected by Cabinet.

McRae appealed to the Chief Secretary in 1941 and to Premier McKell, on the basis of fresh evidence, in 1943—both without result.

His application for an inquiry was also put to Parliament by Mr. Athol Rich-

ardson, M.L.A., and refused.

Mr. McRae told "The Sun-Herald": "I repeat today what I told the jury then."

"I went to Smith's house"—

HERE ARE

ESSENTIAL Facts on Prudent Investment

Three essential facts:—

SAFETY
AVAILABILITY
RETURN

Here is an investment that offers absolute security — the "Bricks and Mortar" of Australia's Housing Program!

This is the only investment available offering such individual facilities. You may withdraw in full or part at any time—with full interest paid right up!

Australia's highest return for GILT-EDGED investment of this kind—

5½% NET PER ANNUM

NO BROKERAGE or "extra expense" to eat into your capital and interest.

NO STOCK EXCHANGE LISTING — no fluctuation — Your money grows steadily and always remains full par value whatever economic conditions may happen to be.

Post this coupon today — or call or 'phone for full particulars

N.S.W. CO-OPERATIVE PERMANENT BUILDING AND INVESTMENT SOCIETY LTD.

Co-operation House, 129 Bathurst Street, Sydney. Phone MA9546.

Please send me full details without obligation.

NAME ....

ADDRESS .... S.H.

MR. R. R. DOWNING

Sir William McKell

ment is 1943 to justify a Royal Commission, which was refused.

"Now Mr. Cahill refuses me. Why?"

The divorce suit brought against McRae aroused intense public interest.

He had a record of 29 years' first-class service in the Police Force and was close to receiving his commission.

In November, 1940, Thomas Walter James

THE SUN-HERALD, September 15, 1957   **5**

McRae's last case would be his own – and he'd investigate it for 17 years. *(Nine/Fairfax newspapers. Used with permission.)*

In December 1934, Reginald, who had reportedly visited his wife and son's grave every Sunday, had one last visit with Inspector Prior at the CIB. It was a 'friendly chat' in which they 'earnestly discussed' the case. Reginald had by now sold all his assets for a reasonable sum and was returning to England with his little daughter. As *Truth* reported: 'By his departure Mr. Thorne leaves his broken heart behind. The other man in the case, Alfred George Lockyer, has long since been lost to public attention.'

But there was a startling postscript. In 1939, Alfred, now in his midforties, and still working as a gardener, was living in North Sydney when he started seeing a woman named Patricia O'Keefe. But the relationship was rocky and he was temperamental, and sometimes, when they fought, he'd say life wasn't worth living. Around February 1941, the day after yet another argument, Alfred confessed to Patricia that he'd almost committed suicide. 'It was a near thing last night,' he said. 'I was going to take poison, but the lid would not come off.'

In June 1941 they split up. Alfred wasn't happy, but at least he didn't threaten to kill himself. Yet on 28 July he swallowed cyanide and was found dead in his room. By then the Thorne case had been forgotten and wasn't mentioned in the brief newspaper coverage of his death. Had Alfred Lockyer simply been suffering from depression, exacerbated by his relationship woes? Was he tortured by what he'd done to Dorothy Thorne, whether accidentally or intentionally? Had he been deeply traumatised by how he'd been treated by the police? Was his life ruined by suspicion that rightly should have rested on Reginald? Was it some combination of these?

Dorothy Thorne's death would remain a mystery.

Back on 27 July 1932 – nine years almost to the day before Alfred's suicide – when Coroner May hurried away from the Dorothy Thorne inquest, he really had been on urgent business. At seven that morning, the body of another murder victim had been found in Centennial Park. A new reign of terror was starting.

21

A Carnival of Killing

Hilda White was born in June 1900 in Auckland, New Zealand, one of seven children to Annie and Francis. The girl knew heartbreak growing up: when she was eleven, her infant brother died; at sixteen, her parents divorced; two years after that, her teenage sister passed away. Annie White brought her surviving children to Australia in 1928 and they settled in Liverpool Street, in East Sydney. But heartache haunted the family, and Hilda's older sister died of tuberculosis in April 1932.

Hilda was dark-complexioned and attractive. Slightly mentally impaired, unable to read or write, she earned a few shillings by working as a cleaner and liked going alone to the movies on Oxford Street. On the night of Tuesday 26 July, Hilda told her mother she was going out – though she didn't say where. Annie objected because it was chilly out, and her daughter had but a thin coat and was already suffering from a cold and sore throat. But Hilda said she'd only be a few hours. Leaving, she said: 'Cheerio, Mum.'

When Hilda didn't return on time, her family was immediately worried. She wasn't in the habit of staying out late. Her brother George and one of his mates went out looking for her, combing her usual haunts without success. It was around two in the morning when they notified police she was missing.

Five hours later, a council ranger found Hilda's body behind a bench in Centennial Park. She was on her back, naked from the waist down, her left stocking pulled down over her ankle, her clothing and face bloodied. Hilda had been strangled with her underwear.

Detective-Sergeants Keogh and Matthews would lead the investigation. After Coroner Edwin May arrived to inspect the scene, Dr Palmer examined the body. Hilda's upper lip was cut, she had a large bruise over her left jaw, there was evidence of concussion and a small bone in her throat had been fractured by the strangulation. Dr Palmer believed Hilda had been killed late Tuesday night or early Wednesday morning.

The detectives theorised that this trusting soul had been lured into the darkness by a man who'd tried to rape her. From the injuries, marks on the ground, soil on her hands and clothing, and blood on the nearby roadway, they believed Hilda had fought her attacker. He'd punched her on the jaw, stunning her, and then carried her to where she was found. But Hilda had come around and struggled so fiercely that she'd repeatedly bitten her tongue before succumbing to strangulation.

The detectives fanned out, interviewing people who lived and worked in the area, wanting to know if anyone had seen Hilda enter the park or heard anything. While no one admitted to having seen anything the previous night, locals knew she'd worked as a prostitute. As *Truth* put it, detectives 'were able to discover that the girl's magnetic personality had attracted the friendship and affection of many men'. These customers seemed to include soldiers. The paper reported: 'She was a great favourite with some of the members of the Permanent Military Forces. And on some mornings when she would stride past Victoria Barracks, she would flash a winning smile on the young artillerymen and exchange a merry jest with them. She was often seen in the company of soldiers.' Any such 'friends' as the police could trace, the paper reported, had been able to prove they'd not been with her on the night she was murdered.

This latest cold-blooded slaughter saw *Truth* run the headline

'Carnival of Killing Horrifies Whole State – Appalling List of Monstrous Murders Growing Daily in New South Wales'. It was the 24th slaying since the start of the year.

But the state would soon be rid of one monster, with Moxley scheduled to hang at 8.30am on Wednesday 17 August. Yet he still had a chance to dodge the noose if a deputation to Premier Stevens was successful in pleading that the sentence be commuted. This bid was being organised by the Howard Prison Reform League, but when they met on Friday 5 August to call for a public protest against the execution, their own president, theatre producer Sir Benjamin Fuller, caused an uproar when he spoke vehemently *against* the condemned man, saying he hadn't heard a single convincing argument for sparing Moxley. Similarly, while the Labor Party was against the death penalty on principle, the women's central organising committee voted against protesting his hanging.

At least *Labor Daily* remained staunch, arguing against false Christian piety and against capital punishment, and saying that 'if the law hangs Moxley, it will hang a madman'. They blamed conservative rivals *The Sun* and *The Daily Telegraph* for convicting the man before his trial, their 'newspaper terrorism' cowing cabinet into carrying out the death sentence. Yet Lang's leftist paper also used Moxley to hit some other sore points:

> Is it to be the hangman's rope for the Moxleys who commit murder in frenzied passion, and have no influential friends and no money to fight for them, and the patronage of the Government for the New Guards and their ilk when they plan mass murder on a wholesale scale? If this stage is reached, justice can be obtained only at the point of a gun.

Labor Daily didn't specify who'd be wielding the gun. Certainly, after the bruising political battles of the past few years, the people of New South Wales weren't about to rise up in revolution when so many were having so much trouble just living day to day.

~

On Friday 5 August, as Moxley supporters were fighting among themselves, the state government offered a £250 reward for information leading to the conviction of Hilda White's killer. Newspapers ran her photo and description again. Now Oxford Street cinema doorman and Special Constable Matthew Kennedy remembered seeing Hilda on her last night on Earth: she'd been with a man in a yellow coat. On Saturday afternoon, this witness stood with Detective-Sergeant Matthews and Detective-Constable Burns and watched the world walk by on Oxford Street. Remarkably, this long shot paid off when Kennedy pointed out the man he'd seen with Hilda.

Matthews and Burns took Victor Lamerto into custody. Born Victor Januschevsky in Russia in 1896, he'd run away to sea as a teenager, and deserted from his ship in Western Australia in 1913. In the past decade, he'd been in a bit of trouble: in Victoria in 1922 he'd been sentenced to eighteen months for counterfeiting; in 1925 in Sydney he was charged with breaking, entering and stealing from a woman's house, but got twelve months for receiving; in 1927 he scored another two years for counterfeiting. Now he was on the dole and earning a little money watching parked cars. What really cemented him as a strong suspect – and Kennedy as a strong witness – was that Lamerto lived in the same building as the murder victim and her family. What were the chances? Taken back to the CIB, he denied being with Hilda on the night of the tragedy and said he wasn't friendly with her. Lamerto's denials didn't cut it with the detectives, who charged him with murder.

On Monday, Lamerto appeared in the Central Police Court. His barrister appealed to the magistrate for bail, saying his client had been nowhere near the scene of the crime, and had been held and charged on purely circumstantial evidence. Lamerto needed bail so he could assist in finding foreign friends who could vouch for his whereabouts on the night in question. But the police prosecutor vigorously opposed bail, and claimed detectives would be presenting more than just witness testimony, though he was unable to disclose the nature of this evidence.

The magistrate remanded Lamerto to Long Bay's observation section until the inquest. Behind bars, Lamerto was all too aware that Moxley was in a nearby cell, awaiting his date with the hangman. Other prisoners wouldn't let this new man forget he might share this fate. Murderers again got the noose in New South Wales.

While Lamerto trembled, Moxley was reportedly resigned to his fate, spending his last days smoking and reading the Bible. His sister Ivy had visited once or twice since his death sentence was confirmed. Linda Fletcher came every day around noon. But Moxley's most faithful companion was Colonel Pennell, the Salvation Army's gaol chaplain, who saw him from six to seven o'clock each morning and then for several hours each evening after dinner. This man of the cloth had arranged it so the condemned man could summon him whenever he needed it. The colonel had made some visits in the earlier hours, including one where they gazed on what Moxley called 'my star' through his tiny cell window.

Despite his religion and resignation, Moxley maintained his innocence and hoped science could prove it. After he was hanged, he wanted his brain to go to Sydney University, where he'd worked as a boy all those years ago. Maybe expert examination would show that his grey matter had been damaged and he'd had no control over his actions. With Australian audiences having just flocked to *Frankenstein*, which had added the 'murderer's brain' angle to Mary Shelley's novel, Moxley's timing was ghastly. Sydney University's registrar was quick to say he knew nothing about it, and that any such offer would be rejected 'in view of the notorious circumstances'. Meanwhile, Colonel Pennell told his congregation that Moxley wanted the world to know he'd embraced God:

The next three days are going to be harrowing days but there is no
spirit of boasting about Moxley, no evidence of anger or of hatred,
but every indication of the spirit of the Lord ... When I bid him
good-bye on Wednesday morning as he goes to his death, I know
that I will meet him on the day of Judgment.

On his last Sunday, Moxley asked to see Superintendent MacKay. Big Bill
spent four hours with him at Long Bay, and returned the following day
because the condemned man had something more to say. This wasn't a
last-minute confession. Instead, MacKay claimed, Moxley had wanted to
say: 'I believe firmly that there is a God and that there is a hereafter, and
I hope that I meet you when you follow me over the Great Divide.' *The
Sun*'s star police reporter, Bill Carrick, tried to get more, but MacKay
would only tell this trusted newsman: 'We spoke about a heap of things,
but they were confidential – just between him ... and me.'

On Tuesday, Ivy and Linda made their last visit. This time they
brought Moxley's twelve-year-old son, Douglas. Over the past four
months, Linda had done her best to keep the boy in the dark. Now she
told Douglas that his dad was about to have a brain operation from which
he might not recover. The prison authorities kindly decorated a reception
area to look like a hospital room. In soft light, Moxley lay in a raised bed,
told Douglas to be brave and gave him a Bible to remember him by.

There were last-ditch attempts to save Moxley. Norman Sachisthal,
secretary of the Howard Prison Reform League, led a final deputation to
Premier Stevens. They asked that the hanging be postponed so Moxley
could be examined by three medical experts in the presence of three
Crown lawyers. A passionate woman in the deputation told the premier:

Your government is going to allow one man to murder another
man – two wrongs never make a right. If this execution is carried
out, every person becomes a murderer and I appeal to you as a

citizen of this state to stop this execution, as I do not want to be a murderer.

Premier Stevens that afternoon announced there would be no reprieve. 'This is such a ghastly case,' he said, 'that it has not a single redeeming feature.' New South Wales was to stage its first execution in eight years.

Moxley spent Tuesday night and the early hours of Wednesday morning with his spiritual adviser. After dawn, he set pen to paper:

Colonel Pennell and I have spent a happy night together. We looked for my star. It appeared at 5.25. We gazed at it together. It is my guiding light. I feel quite calm. I shall leave here at 7.45 to go to B Hall. It doesn't worry me, as death is sweet to me. I have said good-bye to my friends and relatives for this earth. I know I shall be with my mother by 9 o'clock today. I shall know the great secret. My mind is at rest. I have put my trust in God. He has led me for twelve days. This morning I shall have no breakfast, but Holy Communion: If I cannot get help from that, then nothing will help me. My last words are these: 'I would not change my peace of mind for all the money in the world.' This little book I leave to Colonel Pennell. He has the right to make known anything in it to the world, as it is with the hope that it will do some good that I have recorded the happenings as they came to me. Good-bye, Colonel. May you be spared to carry on for some time yet to help the poor unfortunates that are in this place. William Cyril Moxley, 17/8/32. OBS. Long Bay, Sydney.

Soon after he wrote these words, Moxley was moved to the condemned cell. Five paces away was the trapdoor, beneath a stout beam to which the hangman attached his rope. A small crowd gathered, including the sheriff, selected gentlemen of the press and Dr Holloway, whose examinations of Moxley in life would now be followed by an examination in death.

At 8.35am Moxley was led to the little scaffold, where he stood, heels together, silhouetted against a beam of morning light streaming through a high window. The hangman dropped a white cap over Moxley's face, knotted its flap in place and fastened the hemp noose around his neck. The executioner stepped back, pulled the lever and Moxley dropped to his death. From cell to hanging, it had taken ten seconds. Moxley didn't say a word.

~

Did Moxley kill Frank Wilkinson and Dorothy Denzel? It has been argued that only the statement taken by MacKay connected him with anything more than the theft of the Alvis, which he could have found by the side of the road after someone else abducted and killed the couple. Yet there was other evidence: the hessian mask found in the car, and the piece of material it fitted at Moxley's residence; his armed invasion of Marie Harding's residence; the shotgun murder weapon with the shattered stock found in his bush camp; and so on. Despite the influence MacKay had over his informant, and the fact that he took the key statement, even if it was reworded by police, there would seem too much else to conclude it was an elaborate frame-up.

One troubling question – why did the usually non-violent Moxley suddenly became a double murderer? – might be answered with reference to the fate he faced if caught for armed robbery. If his hold-up of Frank and Dorothy had spiralled out of control, as he claimed, then it's likely that Moxley's mask came off during his fight wth Frank. He was a distinctive-looking man, so any description would have been enough for the police to know who they were after.

Moxley had then had a second fight with Frank – and it's probable Dorothy also resisted. Both had been badly beaten. Having inflicted serious injuries on his victims, Moxley was looking at a long gaol term –

especially as a habitual criminal. He might not see freedom for a decade. But *any* prison term might be a death sentence for a known fizgig whose betrayals had been widely reported in the papers in 1930. Frank and Dorothy couldn't be allowed to talk. So, in a rage, a fugue or cold blood, Moxley had shot them both.

Another puzzling angle was the rape. Moxley had not been charged with or convicted of sexual assault in his criminal career. But GMO Dr Palmer hadn't been certain Dorothy had been 'outraged', only that she'd had sex shortly before death – although the bloomers around her neck were suggestive of rape. It was possible Frank and Dorothy had been having sex on the rug just before – or even when – Moxley came upon them. That would explain how he got the drop on them. The bloomers she'd taken off might then have been used as an additional restraint as he led her and her boyfriend around.

Even if this scenario was correct, was Moxley legally guilty of murder? Had he been in his right mind? He had suffered at least one verified major head trauma, said that he had endured numerous others, and had been psychologically scarred by experiences stretching back into childhood. Then there was his syphilis, his alleged fits and blackouts, his odd behaviours and the dark shift in personality said to have come after his 1930 shooting.

As for 'Snowy Mumby' – maybe Moxley really didn't remember killing Frank and Dorothy because the horror of what he'd done exacerbated a pre-existing dissociative disorder. Such states and their accompanying amnesia, it would later be found, didn't preclude the performance of complex tasks, such as going for petrol, driving on dark roads and burying victims. It's conceivable that Moxley's guilty behaviours afterwards could have been because he remembered beating and robbing and stealing from Frank and Dorothy, and because he knew they had been murdered, even if he put that down to his alter ego, to whom he attached his previous underworld nickname, 'Snowy'.

If Moxley genuinely didn't remember his actions, arguably he couldn't be fairly tried for them, as he would have failed to meet the *mens rea* requirement, and his amnesia would also have negated his ability to mount a proper defence. It wouldn't be until 1968 that the second edition of the *Diagnostic and Statistical Manual of Mental Disorders* would recognise what was then called 'Hysterical Neurosis, Dissociative Type', the symptoms of which included 'amnesia, somnambulism, fugue, and multiple personality'. The Mayo Clinic would later describe the condition as follows:

> Dissociative disorders usually develop as a reaction to trauma and help keep difficult memories at bay. Symptoms – ranging from amnesia to alternate identities – depend in part on the type of dissociative disorder you have. Times of stress can temporarily worsen symptoms, making them more obvious.

Much work has since been done on these conditions. We can't fault the New South Wales legal system for not knowing this in 1932. But, given the gravity of the crimes and the irrevocability of the death sentence, it's hard to argue there was anything but a miscarriage of justice in how little effort was put into definitively establishing Moxley's mental state – during the inquest, the trial and the appeal, by the prosecution, the defence, the judiciary and the executive.

What's more, this issue doesn't have to be judged by contemporary standards, because other cases from that same year serve as a comparison. Alfred Ball was found insane in far less compelling circumstances. Moxley was unfortunate to be tried during the backlash. But before the year was out, in the wake of his hanging, three other killers would enjoy the same benefit of the doubt or have their death sentences commuted.

William Cyril Moxley seemed to have been sacrificed to satiate a people who had been whipped into bloodlust by their newspapers.

22

Did You Have the Hammer in Your Hand?

Edwin May had transferred to the water police but was still acting city coroner until his successor took over. His final days in the job would be busier than ever.

On 25 August 1932, Victor Lamerto faced the City Coroner's Court inquest into Hilda White's death. Annie White testified about her daughter's mental impairment, holding back a sob as she told of how she'd tried to get her to stay home the night she died. Lamerto's solicitor probed gently, eliciting that Hilda had 'lots of men friends' – the inference being that she was a prostitute who could've gone into Centennial Park with any number of blokes willing to take advantage of her. Questioned by the Crown prosecutor, Annie testified that a man whose name she hadn't known lived downstairs in her building and would sometimes enquire after Hilda's health. Asked if he was in the court, she became agitated as she looked at Lamerto and said: 'You're the gentleman!'

Lamerto remained composed, half-rising from his seat to reply: 'Yes, that's me, Mrs White.'

George White testified that he didn't know if his sister had a boyfriend. He said she used to go to the movies almost every night but come home straight afterwards. At least, that's what she said she was doing. Centennial Park ranger David Frame described finding Hilda's body, and GMO Dr Palmer testified as to how Hilda had died, noting the evidence of sexual assault and the signs that she'd previously 'associated with men'.

The most compelling testimony came from cinema doorman and special constable Matthew Kennedy. He said Hilda was a regular customer at his theatre, and usually saw movies by herself. Kennedy had seen her with a man on Oxford Street at 8.15pm on 26 July. They'd been just a few feet away, under strong light, and her companion had worn a 'yellowish gabardine overcoat'. They had walked towards Dowling Street. It'd been on Saturday 6 August when, in the company of the police, he next saw the man: Victor Lamerto.

Detective-Sergeant Matthews said Lamerto had been living in the same building as the Whites for the past nine months. Under questioning, the accused had denied knowing anything about Hilda's murder. Shown her photo, he said: 'I have never spoken to her, and I have never been out with her in my life.' From 7.30pm until 11pm on the night in question, Lamerto claimed, he'd been watching over parked cars outside St Andrew's Cathedral. Matthews had searched his rooms and found three overcoats; none was yellowish or made of gabardine. One was marked with a few spots of blood. Lamerto said the spots must've been there when he bought it two years earlier.

The defence called taxi driver Roy Billion, who knew Lamerto and corroborated his alibi, saying the accused was working within his sight on 26 July until nearly midnight. He also said Lamerto hadn't been wearing a yellowish gabardine overcoat, and he'd never seen him sporting such a garment.

Coroner May said the case gave him a 'certain amount of concern', because credible witness Kennedy was so sure of having seen Lamerto with Hilda. Yet the man had also been sure about that yellow coat – and there was no evidence of its existence. Because of these contradictions, May didn't think any jury would convict. He returned an open verdict:

Hilda had been murdered 'by some person or persons unknown'.

Truth's report on the inquest bore the lurid headline 'Does Foul Park Killer Hide Behind Yellow Overcoat?' A relieved Lamerto spoke to *The Sun* and said he had feared he'd end up like Moxley. 'I was in the Obs section, and the prisoners related how innocent men had been hanged,' he said. He had suffered a lot, as the paper put it: 'nights of mental torture, the terrible strain of the inquest, listening to sworn evidence against himself – the agony of cross-examination in a police superintendent's office and finally the joy and satisfaction of freedom again'.

Lamerto's future held periods without freedom – he'd be sentenced twice in 1933 for stealing, pay various fines for indecent language charges over the few years following and get a twelve-month bond for assault occasioning actual bodily harm in 1938. But now, in August 1932, he faded from the newspapers. As did Hilda White – for the time being.

~

There was no rest for Coroner May. On 31 August he conducted the long-awaited inquest into the death of Claude Saywell. The court was packed and all eyes were on Jack Saywell and the gruesome exhibits carried in by police.

Dr Walter McCullum testified about being summoned to the Saywell house by Jack and arriving to find the Saywells under the blood-spattered sheets produced in evidence. Indicating the claw hammer found in the vacant lot, the Crown prosecutor asked if it could have been the weapon used to cave in Claude and Adeline's heads. The doctor believed it was. The witness testified that Jack had told him to spare no expense to try to save his parents, and had seemed very distressed when told his father had died. Dr McCullum also told the court that Adeline had made some progress, was able to answer 'yes' and 'no' to questions, but that 'no complete reliance could be placed upon statements made by her'.

Neighbour Amy Pitt testified about visiting the Saywells with her husband on the night before the tragedy. Adeline had told her about arguing with a foreign stranger who'd come looking for work, but she said Mrs Saywell hadn't expressed undue concern about this man returning. Mrs Pitt also testified about the tensions between Adeline and Jack about his late hours and him wanting to marry Jean Comerford. But none of this, Mrs Pitt said, went beyond ordinary family quarrels. 'She seemed very fond of the boys, and they of her,' she testified.

Constable Cecil Jardine of the CIB produced plans of the house, saying a fit man could climb the fourteen feet onto the verandah that adjoined the upper-floor bedrooms used by Mr and Mrs Saywell and their younger son Tom. But he reckoned such a climb would be difficult – and impossible to do without disturbing the garden. The Saywell family barrister disputed this conclusion, saying any athletic young man could jump across the garden and not leave footprints as he got a foothold.

Fifteen-year-old Tom Saywell testified that two men had actually called at the house in the daytime before the murder: one was a hawker and the other that foreigner looking for work. But Tom didn't remember any disturbance related to these visitors. He said he and his parents had retired around 10pm, shortly after Mr and Mrs Pitt left. He'd gone to sleep in his room and remembered stirring at about one o'clock. This was unusual as he was a heavy sleeper. Tom didn't know what woke him up. He'd remained awake for fifteen minutes before drifting off again.

At around 7.30am Jack had rushed into his room and said: 'Where is your dressing gown? Hurry up and get it on.' His brother had ushered him downstairs, sat him on the lounge and said he was going away in the car. Jack didn't say why – and the maid didn't tell him anything either. Tom said he didn't know his parents were hurt until later, when he overheard a constable say over the phone, 'Crook case, head injuries.'

Tom told the court Jack often argued with his parents about staying out late, and they'd threatened to lock him out. He didn't think they'd actually gone through with it, though he knew Jack had once climbed up a drainpipe to get into the house. Despite such quarrels, they'd been a happy family, Tom said, and Jack had been on great terms with their parents. As for the claw hammer, Tom told the Crown solicitor: 'It's not ours, though we have one like it.' This wasn't the definitive 'yes' he'd offered when previously asked if it was the family's tool.

The Saywell lawyer Mr MacMahon's questioning elicited from Tom that Jack hadn't acted unusually with regard to what he found when he got home in the early hours of 22 April. The closed bedroom door? Tom would also have assumed his parents were just cold. A towel and gown on the floor? It was odd because their mother was so tidy, but it wouldn't have led him to check on his parents by opening their door.

Hilda Champion testified that Jack had appeared to be on very good terms with his parents, though he did argue with his father about staying out late and not studying. Hilda also said that Jack had argued with his mother on the Wednesday night before she died because Mrs Saywell had snubbed his girlfriend, Jean, in the street. Hilda testified that she hadn't heard any noise overnight. She said Mrs Saywell left the key under the mat for Jack – and she believed only the iceman knew it was kept there. She told the court that neither Tom nor Jack had bathed early that morning, suggesting there was no way for them to have washed blood off themselves. Hilda said she'd checked Jack's clothes with the police and nothing had been missing. Nor were any towels unaccounted for.

Since the attack, Hilda had been to see Mrs Saywell in Jack's company. Adeline had seemed pleased to see her son, but she also didn't appear to have any idea what had happened to her and her husband.

On the second day of the inquest, Coroner May and the police visited the Saywell house. Back in court, fingerprint expert Inspector Chaseling testified that he'd dusted the crime scene but found nothing of significance. But on the morning of the crime, like Hilda, he'd observed that the back window was open about two inches. Chaseling said someone could have reached in to open the kitchen door, but it would have been difficult. The

Saywell lawyer disagreed: 'As a matter of fact, the Coroner did it himself this morning.' Constable John Carey said he'd been driven to the house on the morning of 22 April by Jack Saywell, and testified that Jack had seemed very distressed and was later bordering on collapse. The officer said he'd observed nothing to suggest Jack was anything but a son in deep shock and sorrow.

Detective-Sergeant Matthews – whose case against Lamerto had recently failed – told of his interviews with Jack. The lad had told him he'd left Jean Comerford at 1.45am, arrived home around 2am, used the key from under the mat and taken off his shoes. Jack had crept quietly upstairs, where he'd seen that his parents' door was closed and spotted the towel and dressing gown on the landing. As it was his towel, he took it into his room. Jack told Matthews he thought he must've dropped it there before going out, and that his mother had left it there for him to find wet in the morning as a lesson. Jack agreed that his mother had complained about him not studying enough and going out too often. She also believed his father gave him too much money. Jack said his dad had cut off his allowance two weeks earlier, saying it wouldn't resume until after he passed his exams. As for his girlfriend Jean and his apparent belief that he was soon to receive a large sum of money, Matthews read aloud from Jack's statement:

> They both said, 'We will not let you marry a Roman Catholic' …
> I saw mother in her bedroom, and told her not to be silly, as I
> was only a kid, and was not likely to marry anyone or everyone
> I took out, and she said, 'If ever you do, I shall cut you out of my
> will, and your father would, too.' They used to tease me about Jean
> Comerford. When discussing matters with my dad once he told
> me that I would be paying income tax when I was 21 years of age,
> which conveyed to me that I would have a sum of money settled
> on me by him when I was 21. I have no recollection of my dad
> ever saying he would cut me out of his will. Dad and I were never

enemies. Mother and I used to argue a little about different things.
Dad and mother did not like me stopping out late at nights.

Matthews had searched Jack's room and found two singlets and some soiled
handkerchiefs tucked in a pigeonhole in a desk he'd reluctantly unlocked.
One singlet bore blood spots. But the detective said he'd been satisfied
that the lad's explanation about the stains resulting from shaving was true.
Jack, Matthews said, had been interviewed for one full day, and on another
occasion for three hours. At all times he'd answered every question frankly.

The court heard about the numerous pieces of valuable jewellery that
had not been stolen. But at first many of these valuables – as itemised in
the Saywells' insurance policies – were believed missing. Oddly, some had
been found in a secret compartment in a trunk in Tom's room. Then, on
the Saturday after the crime, Jack had been certain the rest would turn
up, telling Matthews: 'I feel sure there is none stolen.' And, sure enough,
the balance of his mother's jewellery, worth £1000, was discovered on a
shelf in the centre of a wardrobe in his father's room. Evidence was also
given that Mr Saywell had, a few days before the attack, cashed a cheque
to the value of £79, though this money wasn't accounted for in the police
search of his clothing and wallets. Yet Jack had been found to have only
£15 – £10 of which was saved in an envelope for a new suit.

Jean Comerford testified about Jack's visit to her home. As her parents
didn't approve of him, he'd climbed to her balcony and come in around
11.15pm. She was angry he was late. Jack said her clock was wrong and
put it back to 10.30. Jean said she wasn't fooled and treated it as a little
joke. But while Jack had said he'd not been serious about marrying Jean,
she told the court they had discussed it that very night, even talking about
a wedding in about eighteen months. He'd left around one o'clock in the
morning – by her altered clock.

Jean's testimony concluded the police evidence. Now MacMahon
dramatically announced that Jack wouldn't testify, because he couldn't

add anything to the statements he'd already made to police. In response, the Crown asked for a two-week adjournment in the hope that Mrs Saywell might recover further and be able to give evidence. MacMahon didn't object, but said he didn't want any further delays because his client deserved to be fully exonerated as soon as possible.

Granting the adjournment, Coroner May said he'd actually been ready to give his verdict. But he would now have to withhold it until the inquest resumed. MacMahon requested that the coroner say something regarding his client's position. Jack stood and May said that, given the evidence so far, 'I don't think that he need lose any sleep.'

Jack sagged back to his seat as the public gallery burst into cheers and applause. Two weeks later, on 16 September, the inquest resumed. Mrs Saywell's condition was unchanged but Jack had had a change of heart. Perhaps emboldened by the coroner's premature commentary, he now elected to give evidence.

Jack recounted his story – of going to law tuition in the city, then to Lang's rally, then to Jean's place. He made it clear he'd stayed with her until the real 1.45am, before coming home and letting himself in. Crown prosecutor Mr Hayes fired question after question at him. Why had he set Jean's clock back? Because he was late, Jack said. Was there any other reason? No. Had he gone into the shed and taken the hammer? Jack said no.

The prosecutor put it every other way: 'Did you have a hammer in your hand between leaving to go for your studies and hearing the maid say something when she came downstairs the following morning?'; 'Did you throw a hammer on to a vacant piece of ground?'; 'Before you went to bed, did you go into your parents' room?'

'No,' Jack answered each time.

Jack said he'd gone to bed at 2.15am – marked by the family clock chiming – and the first thing he knew about the attack was when Hilda had called to him around 7.15am. Then he had phoned the doctor and gone for the police. While his father was wealthy, Jack didn't know who'd want to kill him, and he didn't know anything about his father's legal practice or clients. Jack had no idea who had attacked his father and mother.

As 21 April had been Hilda's day off, and the Saywell house empty between five and six in the evening, Coroner May had a question: 'On the assumption that somebody may have come in and done your father to death, have you formed any opinion as to whether that person may have hidden himself in the house?'

Jack said that because his mother was such a light sleeper, he reckoned the killer had been hiding in their bedroom all that time. But he didn't mention the Tin Hares theory he'd floated in the newspapers months earlier.

Coroner May then delivered his finding. The crime had been committed with the Saywell hammer, which had been taken from their toolshed and later thrown onto the vacant lot. But there was no evidence Jack or Tom had committed the terrible deed. Despite what Tom and Mrs Pitt had said to downplay the foreigner angle, May focused on Adeline supposedly slamming the door on the man's leg and him hurling abuse as he left:

> There is evidence that the place was left unattended for an hour on the night of the tragedy. I am not going to say there is a probability, but there is a possibility of a man – a foreigner – having had a row with the unfortunate woman who was later so badly injured, getting into the house some time during the night and committing the crime.

Yet he also said the murder and attack seemed the work of a clever criminal, who had left no clue behind. Thus, May had to return yet another verdict of murder committed by a person or persons unknown. After so much intrigue, suspicion and speculation, it was a disappointing denouement, not least for the newspapers. *Truth* would in November 1933 revive the notion that the mystery might *still* be solved when it ran yet another front-page story headlined 'Mrs Saywell May Give Name of Husband's Murderer!'

~

Adeline Saywell, who was a partly paralysed invalid requiring around-the-clock care, would live until 1953, but she would never be able to shed light on who had killed her husband. Claude Saywell's murder, like that of Dorothy Thorne, seemed to have been the perfect crime.

Was it the foreigner? Cold-blooded planning followed by frenzied savagery seemed hard to credit, and out of all proportion for the supposed offence given. How would he have known the house would be unoccupied in that crucial hour? Had he taken the hammer from the shed and then got lucky with the open kitchen window? After remaining hidden for hours, had he got lucky again when he battered his victims and ransacked the room without waking Tom or Hilda? And even luckier when he left without leaving a blood trail, or, if he went off the balcony, footprints in the garden? Yet for all this luck, why not realise his other good fortune by stealing jewellery worth more than he might make in a lifetime from the bedroom he'd just torn apart and from the couple whose battering he might hang for?

The detectives were reasonable to suspect Jack Saywell. He was inside the house and had hours to commit the crime and cover it up. After bludgeoning his parents, he could've quietly staged the ransacking in the hope it'd look like someone had wanted his father's legal documents, perhaps even in relation to the Tin Hares scandal. Stealing jewellery wouldn't serve the same purpose; he would've had to leave the property to hide it, and in doing so risk being seen or heard and leaving a trail. Yet it was strange the jewellery wasn't at first discovered, that some had been in Tom's trunk, and that Jack was so sure it'd turn up. And, of course, the physical evidence suggested the killer had put weight on a slippered foot in the garden and thrown the hammer from the property. Not that he'd left it.

But why would Jack murder his parents? Over his cut allowance, his desire to stay out late and to perhaps marry a Roman Catholic girl? It seemed out of all proportion. Perhaps, if he really feared being disinherited, Jack had a greater motive, but he also supposedly believed he'd be getting a substantial sum of money soon. If Jack had done it, how had he disposed of clothes almost certainly soaked with blood? Could he have gotten lucky with just those spots of blood on his singlet? It really was a mystery worthy of Agatha Christie.

As in the Dorothy Thorne case, there was a tragic postscript that seemed like a ripple effect. Jack continued to speed. In 1935 he was convicted on three separate counts of dangerous driving, incurring heavy fines and the loss of his licence. After that, Jack finally pulled his head in. In 1936, working as a law clerk, he married Eileen Fay – a Protestant, as it happened – of Bellevue Hill, the couple taking a long honeymoon in America. After they returned to Sydney, Jack was soon speeding again – this time legally, as a racing car driver. His imported Alfa Romeo could hit 160 miles per hour and was the fastest car in the country. From 1937 Jack would compete in Australian Grand Prix and smash land speed records.

Tom Saywell took after his brother and his father in putting the pedal to the metal. He also liked a drink. On the evening of 23 December 1937, Tom was driving drunk with three mates in his open-topped car. He was going so fast one man's hat blew off. When this bloke shouted for Tom to stop, he braked so hard that the fellow and another passenger were thrown from the vehicle. Unhurt, they dusted themselves off but refused to get back into the car. Tom sped off and was roaring along Darley Road, Randwick, when he lost control on a corner. The car skidded for twenty-five yards, hit a gutter, spun and flipped. Tom's passenger was critically injured but would recover. Tom himself suffered massive head injuries and died later that night in hospital. His estate – by then worth some £100,000, equal to $9 million today – was divided equally between his brother and mother.

Jack went on to serve in the Australian Tank Corps in World War II. He continued racing cars until the mid-1950s and lived a long life as chairman and managing director of his family's companies.

Questions lingered about the Tin Hares scandal. The royal commission continued into the spring of 1932, with tens of thousands of questions asked of dozens and dozens of witnesses. Jack Lang invoked his right not to testify, maintaining that the whole affair was a beat-up and smear campaign. But of those who did give evidence, Justice Halse Rogers said he'd never before seen 'such an amount of false swearing'. He was scathing when he handed down his findings in November. *The Sydney Morning Herald* reported:

> He had been driven to the conclusion, he said, that in the granting of permits for tin hare racing, Swindell's wishes were followed in almost every case, and that Swindell was in close touch with the Labor cabinet, although the means of communication were not disclosed. The Commissioner found that unaccounted funds received by Swindell, for obtaining permits, went either to party funds or to persons having some means of control.

His Honour said it was 'beyond belief' to think that there hadn't been cash for licences:

> He also held that the directors of both metropolitan tin hare companies made available with corrupt motives the 17,000 shares given to Swindell and that the basis of the transaction was bribery, though the evidence did not show that Swindell used any part of the funds to influence the passage of legislation.

Was it merely a coincidence that a key player in this scandal linked to the state's premier was bashed to death in a ransacked bedroom from which nothing of value was stolen? This angle hadn't been explored at the murder inquest. Yet if Jack had gone to trial, his legal team would surely have made this part of his defence, arguing that Claude's involvement with the Tin Hares had provided plenty of people with motive. As it was, that can of worms was never opened.

While Mr May had been frustrated in the city by presiding over murder inquests with open verdicts, Detective-Sergeant Tom McRae was in the country investigating mysteries that also offered few certainties.

In August, Commissioner Childs sent him to Forbes to re-investigate the death of Christopher Hepburn, a wealthy blind man who'd succumbed to cyanide in the house he shared with his mother. Just before her son had called out in pain, she'd heard fleeing footsteps. But Hepburn hadn't confessed what had happened before he died. The local coroner's inquest had already concluded the man had perished from poisoning, though it wasn't possible to say whether it was self-administered.

Yet there seemed little doubt it had been suicide; Hepburn had lost his sight two years earlier after shooting himself in the head and had so often talked of finishing the job his mother kept all sharp implements out of his reach. He'd also tried to bribe people with as much as £400 to obtain poison for him. But no one had admitted assisting him and local chemists said they'd not sold him cyanide.

McRae's investigations added little new, other than that Hepburn had likely convinced – and possibly paid – someone to get the cyanide from a nearby gold mine and had put it into his hands before running from the house. This accomplice wasn't found, and the coroner's verdict stood.

In September, McRae was off to Tamworth, investigating the discovery of a partial and headless skeleton on a small river island. It was thought these were the remains of a bootmaker named William Appleton, who had been missing for more than a year. His wife said the last time she'd seen him he'd been heading towards the river, that he was a poor swimmer, and that she thought a sock found with the bones may have been her husband's. She'd also reveal that Appleton had been sacked the day he'd vanished. McRae could only say the bones might have been Appleton's, and he probably met with an accident or committed suicide.

A coroner's inquest would later conclude nothing more than that the bones were from a human who'd died of unknown causes.

If there was a silver lining for Commissioner Childs, it was that neither case added to the list of unsolved homicides.

~

But through the rest of 1932, the state's murder toll continued to rise. A grisly round-up would appear in *The Sun*:

August 28 – James Oswald Smith, 20, shot dead in a flat in Bondi Road, Bondi, by Richard Bond, 40, who shot himself dead.

August 28 – Frederick Hogansen, 30, of Cullen Bullen, was shot dead with a gun by his brother John, who was convicted of manslaughter and sentenced to four years.

November 11 – Phillip Herbert Govett, 18, battered to death by his aged father at their home in Old South Head Road, Bellevue Hill. The father was declared insane.

November 13 – Isabella Golden, 25, was murdered by Lyla Samule Withers at Narrabri. Withers committed suicide.

November 18 – Lily Bent, 39, fatally attacked with a razor at Hurstville by her husband, John Henry Bent, who was declared insane.

These crimes were horrific but didn't generate newspaper hysteria because they were open-and-shut cases, with the culprits either dead by their own hands or quickly captured. The insane were given the benefit of the doubt that had been denied Moxley, while this period also saw the death sentence that had been given to convicted murderer Maurice O'Hara commuted to life in prison.

Then, days into summer, Sydney was again stalked by a monster.

23

The Park Demon

On Saturday 10 December, 1932, Sydney was licking its wounds and nursing a grudge. That week, the Australian cricket team had been thrashed by the English side in the first Test at the Sydney Cricket Ground in front of a record crowd of 70,000. What really rankled about the defeat was that visiting captain Douglas Jardine had instructed some of his fast bowlers to deliver balls short so they rose at Australian batsmen. Defending themselves risked being caught out by five or more fielders standing close on the leg side. Everyone was debating: 'Is this cricket?' The question was soon be settled when this aggressive tactic continued through the Ashes and became known as bodyline.

On that morning, around ten o'clock, fourteen-year-old Bondi boy Bernard Green was walking through Queens Park in Waverley when he stopped, startled and scared. Through a tangle of lantana, he could see a woman's head and shoulders, a bloody dress hanging from one of the bushes like a grisly Christmas ornament. Terrified, Bernard ran to summon the Waverley police. First on the scene were Detective-Sergeant Patrick Power and uniformed men. They knew to preserve the scene by not touching the body. Yet, while awaiting the arrival of senior CIB men, after making careful measurements of the distances between items of clothing and of the drag marks, Power collected these bloodied items and some bloodstained leaves. Inspectors Prior and Miller arrived with other detectives and Dr Palmer. The body lay facedown about fifty yards from the park fence, between two lantana bushes and beneath a coral tree. The woman's head had been caved in, nearly split in half by eight separate wounds inflicted with a blunt instrument. Apart from her threadbare dress hanging on the bush, near the body Power had found a pair of patched leather shoes, a pair of garters, a pair of stockings and a bloodstained blue beret. From this evidence it seemed she'd been killed and then stripped. But there was clothing missing – most obviously her underwear, if she'd been wearing any – while a scrap of pink material suggested another garment unaccounted for. Pools of blood, drag marks and a blood trail indicated she'd been battered and dragged to where she'd been stripped and dumped.

Fingerprints returned her name: Iris Marriott, aka May Miller, thirty years old and known to work as a prostitute. Her age, her occupation and the way she'd been attacked and dumped in Queens Park – the eastern extension of Centennial Park – all pointed to the horrific possibility that she'd been a victim of the same man who'd murdered Hilda White in late July.

~

Iris Marriott was born in August 1902 in Fremantle, Western Australia, to unwed parents. Her father, Henry Marriott, claimed to work as a wharf porter, while her mother, Elizabeth Currie, was supposedly busy with home duties and looking after her nine children. In reality, Henry was regularly before the courts on charges of theft, larceny, robbery and assault. Elizabeth was twice convicted of drunkenness and once of being a disorderly person. The Marriot family 'home' was, as the Perth *Daily News* reported in March 1906, a 'disorderly house frequented by reputed thieves and prostitutes'. A detective in this case gave evidence that '[t]here were children about the premises in a shockingly dirty and neglected state … A naked baby was lying on a dirty stretcher. The flies were worrying it, and it was on a blanket not fit for a pig.' Two years later, Elizabeth again made shocking news when it was revealed she'd been pimping out her sixteen-year-old daughter, Nellie.

Iris was sent to an orphanage in 1908. Ten years later, after having her own brush with the law for theft, she was working as a domestic servant when she fell pregnant to her employer's son. Iris took herself and her newborn baby across the country to the east coast, placing it in a convent and selling herself for sex in Sydney from 1922 or 1923.

In April 1929, on a city street near Hyde Park, perhaps on alert in the wake of Vera Stirling's murder, Iris got into an altercation with a client and punched him to the ground. A police car stopped, and a constable placed both of them under arrest, sticking the man in the front seat and Iris in the back. Leaning forward, she whispered, 'I'm sorry,' grabbed the man by the neck and bit a piece out of his ear. Iris was charged with assault and grievous bodily harm. Her crime, her good looks and her nonchalant air resulted in amused coverage of a trial that saw this femme fatale sentenced to twelve months' gaol.

Iris served six months and would be in trouble regularly after her release. In October 1929, she was convicted of soliciting, and she'd get strikes against her for the same offence in May 1930 and March 1931. Around this time, Iris took up with a twenty-one-year-old unemployed labourer named Stanley McGroder; after living here and there, by December 1932 they'd shacked up in Dowling Street, Paddington.

~

McGroder – who'd recently beaten a break-and-enter charge – told detectives Iris went out every night but never told him where. This was a lie: he was her pimp. On Friday 9 December, she'd left as usual around

7.45pm with, as a memo from Miller stated, 'the expressed intention of going to Park Road to carry on her nefarious practices'.

That was the last time McGroder saw her until he identified Iris's corpse. Though he had lived with her – and off her – he didn't claim her body from the morgue, so she was buried as a pauper.

The Sun latched onto the Hilda White connection, its front-page headline reading: 'Park Pest Believed Slayer of Two Women. Grim Coincidence of Nude Bodies. Both Battered and Dragged into Thick Scrub. In the Same Death Zone.' But there was dissent among the detectives that this was the work of a repeat murderer. *The Sydney Morning Herald* reported:

> The police are of the opinion that the crime was not premeditated but that a violent quarrel preceded the murder, and that the assailant picked up a piece of stone, and while the woman was lying on the grass, struck her unconscious, and battered her brutally about the head with his improvised weapon.

Detectives weren't going to publicly link the murders of Hilda and Iris, aka May Miller – and they most certainly weren't going to connect them to the years-old suspicious death of Vera Stirling and the slaying of Selina Stanley. But investigators faced the same problems they had in each of these previous cases in trying to establish Iris's movements. *The Sun*'s report of the demimonde read like a reprint of Prior and McRae's investigation of Vera's life in 1929.

> Drifting from park to park, from suburb to suburb, are about 200 lost souls who would do anything for a drink of methylated spirits. Det-Inspector Miller and his assistants investigating the murder on Friday night of May Miller, who was battered to death in Queens Park, have questioned many of these human derelicts.

Some were found to be so crazed from the effect of the terrible drink that they could not fully understand the police queries.

Detectives didn't turn up any clues – including the murder weapon – or valuable witnesses in four intensive days of searches and interviews. But on Wednesday 14 December, a Waverley man found bloodstained clothes wrapped in newspapers on a nature strip. Miller took possession of an old coat, underskirt and pair of bloomers, and McGroder confirmed they belonged to Iris.

Police established that the bundle hadn't been on the street earlier that day. They believed the killer had only just dumped the items, for fear they'd be found in his possession. That he hadn't gone further afield suggested he lived close by. This was a big development. A worse one came the next morning.

~

George McNamara was walking on a lonely bush road through the Royal National Park near Loftus railway station in Sydney's south-east. Another economic victim, he was out of work, camping in the scrub and trudging the track with his eyes peeled in the hope he'd find a smokable cigarette butt or two. What George saw around nine o'clock was a half-empty bottle of beer. Picking it up, he took a few more steps before nearly treading in what looked like a pool of oil. Except it wasn't black. It was dark red.

Dread mounting, George followed drag marks and a scarlet trail off the road to a culvert. What he saw in the undergrowth was horrific. 'I almost stepped on her,' he'd say. 'The naked body of a beautiful girl.' Her face was turned to the blazing sun, and her hair was caked with blood and black with flies and ants. She wore only fashionable beads around her neck and new-looking patent-leather shoes on her feet.

George ran, hailed a passing car on the Princes Highway and summoned the police. Three Sutherland detectives, along with a doctor and ambulancemen, rushed to the scene with the witness. Despite horrific injuries, the girl was still alive and was rushed to St George District Hospital. This victim of a terrible crime had six distinct head wounds – they suggested she'd been battered with a tyre lever – and her condition, exacerbated by shock and exposure, was so grave that surgeons couldn't operate. It wasn't clear whether she'd been raped. A detective was left with her in the hope she'd regain consciousness and be able to say who had attacked her.

It was clear the girl had been driven to this remote spot. A vehicle with odd tyres had left mismatched prints in the dirt. Indigenous trackers said the car had come from the direction of Sydney – and had returned that way. The pool of blood was very close to where the driver had stopped and detectives believed the car would've been considerably spattered. Drag marks told the rest of the story. The girl had been brought here by a man who'd attacked her savagely before hauling her to the culvert, tossing her into the bush and leaving her for dead.

That the CIB chief, Prior, would attend this Area C scene was a given. But the presence of Inspector Miller – who had charge of Area B – was unofficial confirmation that the CIB believed this case was linked to Iris Marriott, and thus possibly also to Hilda White. Two dozen other police and trackers scoured the snake-infested crime scene. They found a road-toll ticket from St George's Bridge – number 196112 – near where the girl had been dumped. Her clothing was discovered 200 yards away: her dress, slip, bloomers and brassiere had all been torn to shreds and hidden in a bundle in the undergrowth. There were also old underpants, not the victim's, smeared with blood.

While the attacker had tried to destroy and hide the girl's clothing, he'd made the mistake of leaving her shoes. They bore the name of a shop in Redfern, which Miller visited. A salesgirl didn't have a record of the sale. But she did remember it had been on Tuesday, because the girl who'd bought them had been with a friend – and this girl had put another pair on lay-by. With the details from this receipt, Miller visited the girl, who gave him the name of her friend: Bessie O'Connor.

Miller took the bad news to the O'Connor house in Redfern. Bessie's mother, Patience, rushed to her daughter's bedside and prayed for a miracle. In contrast to social outcasts Hilda White and Iris Marriott, the newspapers depicted this latest victim as a good girl from a good home – and cast the attack as worse for an innocent being preyed upon so diabolically.

~

Bessie – whose birth name was Elizabeth – was born in September 1916 in Pyrmont, to Patience and Arthur O'Connor. But in 1924 Arthur separated from Patience on the grounds of her desertion, and won custody of their four children: Bessie, her older brother, Arthur Jr, and her younger brothers Stanley and Albert. He and the kids lived with a woman named Eileen. Arthur senior ran a hairdressing shop in Waterloo and was devoted to his children, who were popular, academic and sporty. His greatest pride was coaching them to become champion swimmers and high-divers. The daredevil antics of the diminutive Arthur, Bessie and Stanley saw newspapers run photos of these tykes plunging from tall towers. In March 1927, *The Evening News* reported:

> Bessie is a member of the Randwick and Coogee Women's Club and not only is she showing that she may be a future diving champion, but she also demonstrated remarkable form as a swimmer. She can swim any distance and recently was placed in a club 220-yard handicap event. She is the club's tiny tot champion.

When Bessie was interviewed in *The Sun* in April 1928, she proudly told the reporter how well behaved she was to earn little rewards under her father's honour system, and that she'd been able to swim for as long as she could remember. A photo showed a bright little girl with a big life ahead of her.

But times got tougher as the new decade began. Bessie moved back with her mother around the time her father finally married Eileen in April 1930. While her name no longer appeared in reports about races, Bessie remained an active member of the Randwick and Coogee Ladies' Swimming Club and was said to be training for the Australasian Swimming Championships. Then, in late September 1932, around the time she turned sixteen, Bessie's father died.

~

As Bessie fought for her life in hospital, detectives tried to piece together her movements in the days before the attack. On Wednesday evening, her mother had given her a shilling that she'd borrowed from the woman who owned the corner shop. This was enough to cover Bessie's entrance fee to Coogee Baths, a packet of chewing gum and a return tram fare. But her daughter's money-saving habit was to catch a tram most of the way there and walk the rest of the distance. Coming home, she'd do the same.

Bessie had arrived at the Coogee Baths and taken part in a swimming event. She'd left alone. Bessie was back home around 9.30pm. She tossed her wet costume and towel on the bed, changed into a dress and rushed out again, telling her mother that she wouldn't be long. But Bessie hadn't walked the last part of the journey home. She'd been picked up by someone in a car – and he was waiting for her outside.

Prior and Miller got a break with a report that an Essex car had been stolen near Centennial Park early on Wednesday night, and was then found around 3am the following day not far from where it'd been taken. When the owner, Lionel Downey, of Cook Street, had retrieved his vehicle, he found there were bloodstains inside and out. Items were missing, including a new tomahawk, which fit with the sort of weapon used in the attack, and old underpants, which he'd used as cleaning cloths.

It was clear that detectives had the car that the maniac had used to drive his victim to the national park. They'd found those bloodstained underpants, and the Essex's odd tyres were a match for the tracks on the dirt road. Unfortunately, police investigating the original stolen car report hadn't known it would be valuable evidence, and had done only perfunctory fingerprint work, deciding the vehicle was too smeared to yield anything. Downey had washed it as clean as he could of blood after getting it back.

But there were other clues. Downey had found an oil can in the vehicle that didn't belong to him. He'd tossed it away but was able to retrieve it and hand it to detectives. The fanbelt had also been repaired, rubber stripped from it discarded in the car. This led detectives to think the killer had had engine trouble on the way back from the national park, and that he may have stopped at a garage. That he'd left the Essex near where he'd stolen it suggested he lived in the area and had walked home. Detectives now started checking reports of stolen vehicles near Centennial Park around the time that Iris Marriott was murdered.

On 16 December, about 7am, Bessie O'Connor died in hospital, having never regained consciousness. A post-mortem concluded she hadn't been 'outraged'. What didn't make the newspapers, though, was that Dr Palmer had taken vaginal swabs that revealed semen, though government microbiologist Dr Stanley King couldn't determine how old the samples were.

By now police had a valuable witness in Elizabeth Hamilton Watts, proprietor of the kiosk at Tom Ugly's Point, who'd seen Bessie around 10.15 on the night she died. She'd bought sandwiches. A man had got out of the car but remained in shadows. Bessie had paid a shilling for the food – detectives presumed this money was given to her by the man – and they'd driven south. Mrs Hamilton Watts had positively identified the dead girl in person as she lay in the funeral home. As for the murderer, her description would prove to be problematic. For the moment, the existence of this witness was also kept quiet.

With three dead women – all found battered, naked and discarded in parks – *Truth* dubbed the culprit 'The Park Demon' and compared him with Peter Kürten, the blood-drinking 'Vampire of Düsseldorf', who earlier in the year had been found guilty of nine murders and was executed via beheading. Yet senior police were still divided as to whether one man was responsible. Those who believed there were multiple killers pointed to the differences. Hilda had been hit, yes, but she'd been strangled, whereas Iris had been battered, seemingly after a quarrel. These women were streetwalkers, thirty-two and thirty respectively, while Bessie was an innocent half their age, who'd most likely got into a car with someone she knew. Further, she'd been killed in the south of the city. Even so, as *Truth* noted, 'perhaps the park demon knew that city parks were being watched for his re-appearance'.

Truth struck up a relationship with the dead girl's mother, who gave them her story exclusively. Patience recounted how she had awoken on Thursday 15 December to find her daughter's bed hadn't been slept in. She was immediately alarmed, but was repeatedly given the brush off by Redfern police. Then Inspector Miller had come to confirm her worst fears. Patience told *Truth* she'd always used what little money she had – even if it meant going hungry herself – so Bessie could continue swimming practice and 'develop into the world champion her father had tried to make her before his death left them in poverty'. That had continued right up to the fateful Wednesday night when she borrowed one shilling to send her daughter off to Coogee Baths. When Bessie came back that night, Patience said, she was:

... sparkling and full of life, bubbling with youth. And she hung her wet 'cossy' and towel over the line and then said, 'I am going out for a while, mum; I won't be long.' She fairly danced from the house and I thought that she was probably going out the front to have a chat to some of her swimming friends. It appears now that she must have met the maniac in the car as he cruised about looking for a fresh victim.

Patience felt Bessie had gone with a stranger, even though she'd been cautioned about such dangers since she was a baby:

Anyway, when I would reiterate my warning, the girl would simply give me a hug and a kiss and say, 'Don't be silly, you old dear.' ... I think she must have been walking round to her girl pal's place when the man picked her up and drove her away. Why did she go! Why didn't she heed her mother's ceaseless warning?

After Iris's murder, Perth's *Mirror* had interviewed her parents, who cast their daughter as an innocent preyed upon by the world – and themselves as blameless, hardworking and supportive folk. Patience's story to *Truth* also left out much: that Bessie's father had divorced her for desertion, that she'd lost custody of the children and that her daughter hadn't lived with her again until relatively recently. These were understandable face-saving omissions.

But Patience wasn't saying anything about the suspicions she had that Bessie was living a secret life, one that might explain why she'd get into a stranger's car.

24

The Red Year

At dawn on Saturday 17 December, acting on information from Bessie's girlfriends, who seemingly at this point were sticking with the line that she would only have gone in a car with someone she knew, Detectives Keogh and Allmond raided the Paddington and Redfern homes of several young men who'd been acquainted with the dead girl. While dramatic, these searches and the interviews that followed didn't yield anything, except fellows of good character who could prove they were innocent and wanted to join the hunt.

Later that day, hundreds of people crowded into Eveleigh Street, Redfern, to farewell Bessie, who lay in an open white coffin, beneath a cross and surrounded by flowers. Dressed in black, Patience was so close to collapse that she had to be practically lifted into the mourning coach that took close family and friends out to the Botany cemetery.

That day, Commissioner Childs called a CIB conference of detectives so they could compare notes on the three park murders. Those present included Prior, Miller, Matthews, Keogh, Power, Allmond and Comans, who'd each worked one or more of the cases. *The Sun* was sure justice would be delivered, printing that afternoon glowing mini-profiles of the lead investigators.

Miller, nicknamed 'Bull' because he was a 'sleuth of tireless energy', had 'successfully handled thousands of crimes, including some of the most mysterious major ones in the last ten years'. Keogh 'revels in a fight against heavy odds' and, like Miller, was a 'homicide specialist, although he has elucidated some of the most intricate robberies and swindles'. Allmond, once attached to the London police and widely read on criminal science, had won his recent promotion to detective by 'sheer merit', which included his work with McRae at Bungendore and Glen Innes.

Beyond such boosterism, what resulted from the meeting depended on which newspaper you read – and what they reported depended on which detectives had briefed which reporters. Broadly, some police, including Childs, wouldn't entertain the theory of a single killer, while others, notably Prior and Miller, thought the same man was responsible.

The Sun's front page the following day was headlined 'CIB Decides on Triple-Murder Theory'. It pointed to the similar *modus operandi*. While it was true Hilda had been strangled, she'd first been beaten and dragged, like Iris and Bessie. All victims had been stripped, their clothes taken away and torn, and none had been raped. Without sex as a motive, stablemate *The Daily Telegraph* agreed, detectives were hunting a monster like the Vampire of Düsseldorf, their task possibly more difficult because such maniacs could be superficially sane and charming.

Yet *The Sydney Morning Herald* had the opposite take on the conference, saying detectives believed they were hunting three different killers. Its report highlighted the differences in the cases: streetwalker Hilda was strangled, but no car had been used; Iris, also a prostitute who might have enemies, was likely battered after a quarrel; Bessie was an innocent who had seemingly accepted a ride from a friend or acquaintance. The paper reported that detectives didn't believe Bessie's killer had planned to murder her, otherwise he wouldn't have driven her home first, which ran the risk of him being recognised. At the national park, he might have forced his attentions on her and lost his temper when she threatened to tell the police.

As for the similarities, the detectives believed this was the phenomenon that would later be dubbed 'copycat' killing, combined with the prevalent theory that such tragedies came in clusters:

> Detectives ... consider that in the later crimes the murderers may have been influenced to strip the clothes from their victims by the publicity given to the first crime. They point out that crimes of a particular nature occur in cycles, and that at present there appears to be a wave of this description of crime. The recent frequency of Harbour Bridge suicides is an illustration of the theory.

On Monday 19 December, Childs recommended the state government offer £250 rewards in the Bessie O'Connor and Iris Marriott cases – as it had for Hilda White. From the condition of her body, detectives believed Bessie had fought her attacker, and that he may have been scratched. They asked keepers and residents of hotels and boarding and lodging houses to make contact if they knew of anyone with such injuries – or anyone acting suspiciously.

By now detectives had visited garages in the Eastern Suburbs and all the way south to Tom Ugly's Bridge, trying unsuccessfully to find who'd fixed the fanbelt in the stolen Essex. Childs appealed for whoever had unwittingly helped the killer between midnight and 4am on Thursday 15 December to come forward.

The Sun drew a link to the crowded year's most infamous case: 'Will criminal history repeat itself in the investigations now being made into the three park horrors? A mishap which Moxley had with the Alvis car he stole from Frank Wilkinson, one of his victims, helped towards his ultimate capture.'

Childs also issued a warning that women and girls shouldn't ride with strangers – particularly at night. This might have seemed like common sense, but, as *The Sun* reported:

> Detectives who move about the city and suburbs all the year
> round declare that the willingness of some girls to accept offers of
> car rides from men who casually pull up by the road or sidewalk
> is amazing, and they wonder that the daily crime-sheets do not
> contain more cases of assaults upon girls attracted by a motor car.

This practice was known as 'pirating' girls, and it was widespread.

Now detectives announced another significant new lead: an Essex
stolen from the city on 9 December, the night Iris was murdered, had
been found abandoned near where her body was found in Queens Park
the following day. That it was the same sort of car, dumped in the same
area, seemed further evidence that Iris and Bessie had been killed by the
same person. Not long afterwards, a witness came forward to say that
on the night Iris was murdered, he'd seen an Essex parked in a dead end
near Queens Park. It seemed she might have been picked up in the car
and brought to this spot, which was frequently used by prostitutes and
their clients.

Childs released a long list of items the owner had reported
missing from the Essex. Along with a pocketbook, flashlight, scarf
and handkerchief, a lot of tools had been stolen. Prior speculated that
one might've been used to batter Iris. The tools also suggested another
possible connection between the murders of Iris and Bessie. As exhaustive
investigations had failed to turn up a garage owner who'd worked on the
Essex's fanbelt between Sydney and the national park, it was thought
that the murderer may have been something of a mechanic and had used
the tools to effect his own dead-of-night repair. Of course, by releasing
such a list, Childs might also have given the killer a list of what to get rid
of, including 'a light fawn cardigan jacket with ribbed collar and ribbed
around bottom, three buttons on front'.

As was regularly the case, newspaper sensationalism also contained
genuine revelations. *Truth* ran a Christmas front page whose headline

asked: 'Desperate Attempt to Kidnap Girls – Park Killer's Frenzied Effort to Cover Tracks?' One of Bessie's friends, Daisy Moffatt, told the paper she'd been chased all the way home in the dark of Sunday night by a man. Another of Bessie's pals, Jessie Dawson, reported a similarly narrow escape.

These were unlikely to have been abduction attempts by the killer. More likely was that Daisy and Jessie – already on edge after Bessie's murder – panicked after being approached by random creeps. More revelatory – and credible and corroborated – were admissions to *Truth* from Daisy and another friend, Dot O'Dell, that they and Bessie had often let themselves be 'pirated' by strangers. Since their friend's slaying, these two girls had been driving around with detectives, 'trying to catch a glimpse of the men with whom they went riding in an innocent search for fun'. *Truth* collectively quoted Daisy and Dot:

> We had been told hundreds of times by our mothers never to go for car rides ... but we thought it was all right as long as the three of us were always together. Several times we three inseparables were 'pirated' or 'mashed' by men in cars – there are always a lot driving about the streets – and we went for short rides with them.

The girls had kept these adventures secret from their mothers for fear of getting into trouble. But now they revealed they'd even gone for a ride to near where Bessie was murdered: 'Once, we were taken out just past National Park by a very well-dressed man. He was exceptionally gentlemanly and spoke in a cultured voice.'

Detectives wanted to interview men who had pirated Daisy, Dot and Jessie. *Truth* reported that police believed these jaunts had been innocent but foolish reactions to troubled times: 'The girls are from poor families, families which have been sorely stricken by the Depression and a car ride provided that adventure which other girls get at dances and parties and pictures.'

Surely detectives were now intensely questioning Daisy, Dot, Jessie and Patience O'Connor about Bessie's night-time activities. Yet if the police pursued this line, they kept it quiet – perhaps to help preserve the victim's reputation.

It was only eight months later that Patience would publicly reveal what she'd known. She hadn't previously offered the information, she was to claim, because detectives hadn't asked – which was difficult to credit. Bessie's mother would admit she knew her daughter lied about where she went at night, that she knew she went driving with men, and that she'd once gone to Sutherland, near the national park.

Patience had also known Bessie was getting money from some unknown source. By her own account, Patience owed £49 in rent and had to borrow a paltry shilling for her daughter's entry to Coogee Baths and for her tram ticket. Yet, despite this poverty, Bessie was paying off brand-new shoes and had recently been able to afford 12/6 – close to a day's wages – to have her hair set in a permanent wave. Given these circumstances, Patience's lack of curiosity was hard to understand. Bessie's mother would also eventually lash out at Daisy Moffatt, saying her daughter would be alive if not for the lies Daisy had told.

These then unreported angles – along with Bessie's vaginal swabs containing semen – suggested she and her friends were selling sex to men in cars. But in mid-December 1932, all that was publicly known was that Bessie had been in the habit of getting into cars with strangers – which made the suspect pool far bigger than her male friends and acquaintances. The Christmas newspapers said police were no closer to catching the murderer.

But behind the scenes, detectives had found other witnesses and were reconstructing Bessie's last night. Their best lead came from Thomas Brown, a twenty-three-year-old travelling bootmaker who worked for Willis Bros of Newtown. He said that on the night in question, he'd been driving from Kiama to Sydney. Having stopped at Sutherland for a late supper, he'd continued north around midnight, but pulled over after just a mile when he saw an Essex on the side of the road, its driver standing by the open bonnet.

> I sang out, 'What's the trouble?' He replied, 'My fan-belt's almost broken.' As I couldn't see the engine, I turned my car so that my headlight shone on the engine. The fan-belt was almost broken, and I gave him wire. He didn't know how to go about it, so I fixed it for him with the wire. He had a couple of scratches on his face, and there was blood on his shirt. He said he had hit some ruts along the road and bumped his nose on the steering-wheel.

Brown had continued to Sydney, thinking nothing more of it. The next day he'd gone to Armidale, 300 miles north. This witness had only learned of Bessie's fate upon his return to Sydney on 27 December. Then he'd come forward with what he knew – and was now helping detectives.

Brown wasn't identified publicly – his identity was 'jealously guarded' by Prior, Miller and their murder squad – but his description of the suspect was printed in newspapers and on posters and delivered to talkie audiences in another newsreel appearance by Prior. The incredibly detailed portrait of the suspect read:

> ... 25 to 28 years of age, about 5 feet 9 inches high, thin build, broad shoulders, walks erect, dark complexion, black hair parted down the centre, broad high forehead, prominent cheek bones, eyes deeply set in head, sunken cheeks with pointed narrow chin, had two fresh scratches on face extending from the cheekbone down towards the mouth, probably on left side; soft hands, nails well-manicured, dressed in a navy blue serge suit with what appeared to be a cream-coloured silk shirt with collar to match; no hat; tan shoes, almost new; sized about 8, broad square toe, white stitching around the welt of the boot; well spoken, could be taken for a clerk or business man.

When *The Daily Telegraph* printed this, it appended Prior's instruction: 'Try to impress the description upon your mind; carry a copy of it wherever you go – it is your duty.'

The day following his appeal, some 200 citizens made contact. This sort of publicity might put a murderer behind bars on the way to the gallows, just as the ubiquity of Moxley's description had done.

But there was a huge problem. Thomas Brown hadn't seen *anything*. He was a part-time factory worker for Willis Bros. He hadn't been driving that night. He didn't own a car, have a licence or even know how to drive. Brown hadn't eaten for a few days and hoped he'd get a little money for helping the police – which proved to be the case. All up, he'd be paid £6/5.

The description he provided was wholly fabricated, based on vague newspaper descriptions. When detectives asked him if he'd seen the Essex's number plate, Brown told them it started with 147 – as could anyone who'd seen a prominent photo of the actual plate, 147–121, in a front-page *Truth* article a few days earlier. Ironically, the picture had been headlined 'Tell the Police!' That Miller and co. didn't detect Brown's lies, or do any due diligence on their witness, even with a simple phone call to Willis Bros, was an appalling dereliction of duty. And their failure was compounded day after day as the 'description' of Australia's most wanted man continued to be circulated as fact.

When 1932 came to a close, there had been thirty-six murders during the year – ten more than the average for the past three years. But it wasn't only the number of killings that had been unusual; it was also the manner of many of these crimes: ferocious, cold-blooded, seemingly with the slightest of motives or no motive at all. A headline in *The Sun* characterised the past twelve months this way: 'Red Year: Heavy List of Homicide Cases'.

The New South Wales police force could claim successes in convicting William Moxley, Alfred Ball and Maurice O'Hara, and in the clearing-up of the Bungendore Bones case. But the Red Year had ended with the killers of Bessie O'Connor, Iris Marriott, Hilda White, Dorothy Thorne and Claude Saywell still at large. It was a dismal result. While the housewife's poisoning and the businessman's bashing would likely now go unsolved, the police had to catch the Park Demon before he struck again.

25

The Grisly Trail of a Killer

As 1933 began, there was renewed hope that the Park Demon would soon be caught. Inspector Prior made a radio broadcast on New Year's Eve using the new ABC network to relay the suspect's description to all of Australia. The next morning, *Truth* had a sensational front-page scoop headlined 'The Grisly Trail of a Killer', which detailed Bessie's last night alive, based on what it had been told by the witnesses who were assisting police:

> Here is the story of the sandwiches, the toll ticket, the horse trough, the cunning request for petrol, the visit to the Silver Grill, the search of Percy Weeks ... Vital, throbbing clues in an amazing crime story from real life ...
>
> *Truth*, which hitherto has graciously refrained from publishing the full facts, now reveals everything in the hope that other persons whose timidity has sealed their lips may come forward.

Around 9.45pm on Wednesday 14 December, *Truth* reported, an unidentified bystander had seen Bessie and a man in the stolen Essex outside her mother's house. This girl, whom the witness knew as the 'athletic pride of Redfern', had gone inside to change out of her swimmers and into a dress. Meanwhile, the bystander took stock of the man behind the wheel and struck up a casual conversation with him:

> The car driver had one hand carelessly flung over the back of the seat, and whatever light filtered through the car windows [was] captured by a shiny metal object. The man was wearing a gold ring!
>
> No doubt the murderer is reading *Truth* today with prickling spine. He will want to discard that ring. If *Truth* readers know of a man discarding a ring today – phone the police with urgent haste.
>
> However, as he sat there idly talking he said that he had some drink in the car, and he offered a drink to the person who was so keenly examining his pale, intellectual features.

Elizabeth Hamilton Watts was revealed as the owner of the kiosk at Tom Ugly's Point who'd sold sandwiches to Bessie less than an hour later. 'I was attracted by her good looks, her well-formed features, and her glorious tumble of nut-brown hair,' she told the paper. Mrs Hamilton Watts also remembered the amber-coloured beads Bessie wore around her neck. But it was the kiosk proprietress's annoyance that led her to recall the time precisely:

> I hate cutting sandwiches – I would rather scrub a floor – and as I turned from the counter I looked at the clock. It was just on 20 minutes past 10 o'clock, and I thought to myself, 'The cheek of asking for sandwiches at this time of the night.' I cut the sandwiches and as they were being parcelled up by one of my assistants, I walked out on to the verandah, and standing beside the door, just beyond the rays shed by the interior lights was a tall, thin, rather good-looking young man. He was quite cool and calm, but he appeared to be watching the pretty girl at the counter with a strange fixity. His eyes were riveted on her.

This was a lot more detail about the killer than had previously been vaguely attributed to this previously unnamed witness. Mrs Hamilton Watts told *Truth* that Bessie had paid one shilling for the sandwiches, left the shop, joined the man and walked across to the car.

Their next witness was toll booth operator Bert Cook. At 10.25, he'd sold a ticket – number 196112 – to the killer so he could pass over Tom Ugly's Bridge. Cook didn't get a look at the driver or his passenger, but he was certain it'd been the Essex. This was vital evidence, as *Truth* explained:

> How is it known that this was the ticket the Park Demon bought? The ticket was found near the body. It is one of those insolent clues that the murderer distributed about as if to mock and taunt the police who have so fruitlessly hunted him. Why didn't he discard the toll ticket as 99 per cent of motorists do? And if he put it in his pocket, why did he drop it near the dying girl? Was it an accident or was it the shameless scorn of a cunning and calculating maniac?

After battering Bessie and leaving her for dead, the maniac drove the Essex to a horse trough near the Sylvania side of Tom Ugly's Point. There, according to *Truth*, he'd stopped to wash bloodstains from the outside of the car. A Mrs P McGrath, whose front bedroom overlooked the trough, had been awoken by the car's engine and peeped through her curtains. *Truth* again combined reporting and speculation: 'Then the headlights were dimmed as the driver got out to erase the signs of his satanic crime. It was just after midnight, and Mrs McGrath was tired. She slipped off to sleep. Had she remained awake she would have seen the ghastly procedure.'

Yet the most extraordinary encounter echoed the midnight driving done by Moxley as he searched for petrol in a stolen car after committing his double murder. Bus driver Percy Weeks, doing his route from Kogarah to Miranda, had noticed the stationary Essex. On his return trip, it was still there, so he stopped and shouted, 'What's up, mate? Anything wrong?' The driver replied: 'Run out of juice!' Weeks said he'd siphon petrol from his bus if the man had a tin. The man didn't have one.

'Mr Weeks, showing more courtesy than is ordinarily found on the road, offered to try to get one for him,' *Truth* continued. 'They came across the bridge together and the stranger walked into the shop of Mr Ted Watson, proprietor of the Silver Grill restaurant.'

The Essex driver asked Watson: 'Do you know where I can get some petrol?'

The shopkeeper described this man to *Truth* as being tall, with pale complexion and well groomed. He'd told him: 'It's after midnight. It'll be hard to get any juice tonight, but you might try at the pub.' The man left the restaurant and told Weeks he'd been unsuccessful. So the bus driver went into the restaurant and told Watson – who he knew well – that he was going to look for a tin. Finding one, he and the stranger returned to the bus and siphoned some petrol. Weeks told *Truth*:

> He seemed a decent enough man. He was well dressed, polite and very well spoken. He displayed no sign of anxiety or agitation, but there was something about him – I don't know what it was – that made me take some particular notice of him. I noticed that there were two fresh scratches down the left side of his face. But they were not the kind of injuries that would alarm anyone or make anyone suspect that the man had been involved in any desperate affair. He thanked me for the petrol I gave him. He seemed genuinely grateful.

Weeks said he told the man that if he followed him to the bus depot at Kogarah, he'd give him enough petrol to get back to Sydney. The stranger accepted the offer. Weeks waited at the depot, but the fellow never arrived. *Truth* thought it knew why. When the Essex was discovered abandoned, the owner had found the tin inside. But the car's tank also contained gallons of petrol. *Truth* mused that the killer had been washing Bessie's blood off the Essex when Weeks had stopped to ask if anything was wrong.

> Displaying the same maniacal cunning as Jack the Ripper when he was nearly caught in 1888, the man gave the obvious answer, 'I have run out of juice.' ...
>
> And having been proffered assistance he mockingly carried his fiendish burlesque further and obtained some petrol. He was utterly without fear, shame, or anxiety. Only a man of supernatural cunning could have acted with such blood-chilling intent to disarm suspicion.

After what it called a 'devilish jest' at Weeks's good nature, the fiend had returned the Essex to near where he'd stolen it in Centennial Park before he 'vanished into thin air'.

If the murderer was to reappear from thin air – in the custody of the police – positive identifications by these witnesses could be what sent him to the gallows. But *Truth* had now put into the public domain details that might compromise a fair trial. Other newspapers would follow suit.

On New Year's Day, a boarding-house keeper in the Wollongong suburb of Corrimal reported that a man had arrived in the area a day or two after Bessie's murder. This bloke's face bore two scratches that he put down to shaving cuts. Sergeant Newland of the local police took him into custody. The suspect was astounded but made no complaint and agreed to be questioned late into the night.

In the early hours of the following morning, Newland called the CIB. Inspector Miller awoke Detective Keogh with a phone call at 3am and ordered him to drive south immediately to collect the man. By the early morning, the suspect was at the CIB and under interrogation. They brought in their star secret witness, Thomas Brown. He told Miller and Keogh that they had the right man.

The Corrimal suspect's reported comments to detectives showed a remarkable heartiness in the face of this identification, but also showed just how widely their unknowingly false description had circulated in just days. 'I'll admit that I answer the description in a lot of ways,' he said. '... I read where one paper said that the suspect is probably an individual who would attract women. He has also been described as well-spoken and well-educated. It is flattering.'

Miller took the suspect's statement about his movements and he and Keogh drove the man to Corrimal to check the details. The man's alibi was rock solid. After seventeen hours in custody, he was released. Unlike others, who would have complained about being sweated by the cops, this chap reportedly exited the CIB saying, 'You are not a bad lot of fellows at all. I have no grudge. You were only doing your job, and it was just unfortunate that I happened to fit the description. I hope you catch the right man.'

This abject failure seems to have finally led the CIB to suspect they'd been duped by Thomas Brown. Traces of this were found in the newspapers on 4 January, the day after the Corrimal suspect was released. It was reported there had been an 'error' in the suspect description – they were not seeking a man '25 to 28 years of age', as specified in the Thomas Brown-supplied description, but a suspect aged thirty to thirty-five, reverting to what had been initially reported. Despite this change, the other physical details from Brown's description were still 'considered accurate'.

Unnamed detectives were deemed responsible for what had happened, and were assigned to other duties. The higher-ups were still in place: Miller and Comans would continue to direct the investigation. But another investigator would now take the lead. The police department said there was no special significance to the change in personnel but detectives freely commented they didn't believe this. It was that clear mistakes had been made.

As *The Sun* explained, 'There was a new development in the investigations in the C.I.B. today when Det-Sgt T. McRae, who has done sterling work in elucidating many recent mysteries – notably the Bungendore Bones mystery – was detailed to join the squad which has been vainly seeking the killer for weeks.'

26

McRae: The Remarkable Criminologist

A year ago, McRae's approach had pulled off the investigative equivalent of finding a needle in a haystack to identify the man who'd become the Bungendore Bones. Now he was going to revert to such methodical practices to find the Park Demon.

Since Bessie's murder, detectives had become blinkered. They believed the killer lived in Redfern, and had canvassed the suburb and surrounds three times without success. They'd also focused on finding a man matching the bogus description. But McRae was looking at it again with fresh eyes. His approach would start not with a person but with a place – the area around Centennial Park. Hilda and Iris had been killed in the vicinity; an Essex had been seen in a neighbourhood dead-end street the night Iris was murdered; and Iris's clothes had been dumped there, as had both of the stolen Essexes. McRae felt sure the killer lived nearby. He knew the roads and where cliffs and dead ends were. If he'd had a scratched face or bloodstained clothes, he wouldn't have wanted to walk far after dumping the cars. The search would begin at Cook Road, where Mr Downey's Essex had been stolen from a garage with a door opening onto a dark lane. It would radiate outwards from there. Men under McRae's command would go house by house, 'checking up' on every male resident between the ages of twenty-five and thirty-five.

If that meant speaking to as many as a thousand men, so be it – because it ensured the killer would sooner or later come face to face with detectives. If he tried to leave or move, he'd just put a target on his back.

The new strategy was announced in the press, with the public asked to report any man in this age range making a sudden departure from the area. McRae's new plan, *Truth* reported, developed with 'bewildering speed' and he 'was soon dashing around the Paddington and Centennial Park areas'. The paper's reporter said his path intersected repeatedly with that of McRae and the squad he'd formed with men he trusted – Detectives Swasbrick, Comans, Payne, Wiley and a couple of young constables – as they followed up new information.

Less than twenty-four hours after taking charge of the Park Demon case, McRae was talking to a resident near Cook Road and being told about a young man named Eric Roland Craig. He had just yesterday moved from a house in nearby Victoria Avenue, Woollahra, that he shared with his wife and two infant daughters. McRae ordered his men to look into Craig's whereabouts. By the following afternoon they had his new address: 386 Moore Park Road. It wasn't out of the search area; Craig hadn't fled.

But by this time, McRae would've had Craig's record. Learning he'd been a soldier at Victoria Barracks was of interest; Hilda White had been reported as a favourite of local artillerymen. What was also of note was that Craig had been kicked out of the army in April 1931 for his theft of an officer's car. He'd been convicted, though he paid fines to avoid a month in prison. That the police were looking at links between Hilda's murder and the slaying of Iris and Bessie – and that the killer was a car thief – led McRae to order his squad members to watch Craig's residence and pick him up when he appeared. McRae wasn't going to be part of this stakeout; with his photo in the papers so often, he didn't want to risk the suspect recognising him.

From five o'clock on the afternoon of Friday 6 January, Wiley, Swasbrick and two constables sat in a police car and watched the Moore Park house. After two hours, they saw Craig leave. The fellow was about five-foot-six, with fair hair and fair complexion, and a narrow face. In other words, he didn't match the circulated description. Not that they had much faith in that, after the Corrimal suspect debacle. Swasbrick and a constable followed Craig, grabbed him and took him to Paddington station.

On the way, Wiley asked Craig if he had any property in his house for which he couldn't account. He said no. At the station, he was handed over to McRae, while Wiley and Swasbrick went back to the suspect's residence. There they questioned Craig's young wife, Mary. Searching their rooms, they found a fawn cardigan matching the one stolen from the Essex they believed had been used in Iris Marriott's murder. They also took into custody a flashlight like one taken from the car.

Learning this at Paddington, McRae sent an urgent message to the CIB to say he was bringing in a suspect in the murder of Iris Marriott: twenty-five-year-old Eric Roland Craig. Arriving in a car, McRae and Craig were surrounded by a phalanx of detectives, who escorted them to the first-floor offices. Through Friday night and into the early hours of Saturday morning, Craig was interrogated by McRae, Prior, Miller, Keogh, Comans and others. While they had no evidence to connect him with Hilda White, they wanted to know about the murder not only of Iris Marriott but also of Bessie O'Connor.

Under this intense pressure, and shown the cardigan, Craig made a startling confession – and a frustrating denial. Yes, he'd killed Iris; but no, he hadn't murdered Bessie. McRae and his colleagues were gratified to hear the former, but they didn't believe the latter.

At five on Saturday morning, Prior and Miller went home to get some sleep. But there was no rest for McRae or for Craig. As the summer sun rose over Sydney, the detective and a small band of police drove their suspect to the place in the city where the Essex used in the murder of Iris had been stolen. From there, they followed a route to Queens Park, where she'd been killed. Then McRae took Craig to where Iris's clothes had been found. Next, they drove him to the national park, where Bessie was left for dead. Returning to the CIB, McRae and his suspect got a few hours' sleep. Then the interrogation began afresh. Detectives headed out to retrieve witnesses who'd seen the man with Bessie on the night of the fatal attack and who was later seen with the Essex. They were asked to pick the suspect out of a line-up. The results would be contentious. Mary was brought in and questioned about her husband's movements. After being interviewed for hours, she was ushered from the station without being allowed to see Craig.

At 3.30pm on Saturday, Craig was led into the dock at Central Police Station. McRae read out the charge – that on 9 December 1932, at Queens Park, he had murdered Iris Marriott. The detective led the accused to a cell, where he'd remain until Monday morning, when police would seek his remand in court.

With Iris's killer behind bars, McRae stepped out of the CIB and lit a cigarette. Despite having barely slept in three days, he looked dapper in his three-piece suit, striped tie and hat, as did the comrades alongside him: Detective-Sergeant James Comans, Detective-Constable Arthur Burns and Detective-Constable William Payne. A news photographer snapped these men mid-stride, the picture running in the centre of *The Sunday Sun*'s front page the next day under the big banner 'Married Man Stands Charged with "Park" Murder'. The photo of the victorious police – which featured an inset close-up shot of McRae – had its own headline: 'Going Home for Well-Earned Rest'. Or, as the case may be, the pub – the inset was tightly cropped from another otherwise unpublished photo taken that day that showed McRae standing in the doorway of the Lismore Hotel, just around the corner from the CIB, having a chinwag with another bloke.

~

The man McRae had charged with Iris's murder was born Eric Roland Joseph in September 1907 in Carlton, Melbourne, to unwed woman Leah Joseph. In 1916 she'd marry a man named Vivian Craig, who'd give the boy his surname.

As a teenager, he learned about motorcar repairs when apprenticed at several garages in Melbourne. In 1923, following his mother and stepfather's separation, Eric and Leah moved to Sydney, where he worked as a chauffeur. In 1925, Craig enlisted in the 1st Battalion (East Sydney Unit) militia; in March 1927, he enlisted in the permanent military forces for five years. Stationed at Victoria Barracks in Paddington, he was trained as a bombardier with the 1st Field Artillery.

In October 1929, Craig married Mary Tobin, who was just fifteen years old. Three months later, Mary, not yet sixteen, gave birth to a daughter they named Valma. A second baby, Robert, was born the following year. Craig seemed at home in uniform, as *The Daily Telegraph* reported: 'He was a most efficient soldier, known as the bombardier who could assemble the firing mechanism of a big gun's breech lock in faster time while blindfolded than most men could do otherwise.'

Craig was also an athletic bloke, representing the barracks in rugby union and playing Australian Rules and cricket with local teams. A social fellow, he was a popular partner at military dances.

Despite his seeming military aptitude, Craig was cautioned for taking an officer's car without permission in April 1930. When he reoffended, a year later, he was discharged from the army, charged, convicted and paid a hefty £11 fine. It wasn't a good time to lose his soldier's salary – with the Depression by then having pushed unemployment over twenty per cent. With him out of work, Mary took the babies to live with her people in the country. Left to his own devices, Craig relied on the dole and did odd jobs. But being alone in straitened circumstances didn't seem to faze him too much – in his wife's absence he reportedly went to plenty of dances and kept a pocketbook with the names and addresses of girls and women he took out.

Mary and the children returned in autumn 1932 and the family rented rooms from a woman in Victoria Street in Woollahra. Most recently, Craig had worked as a counter assistant at Lowes in the city during the Christmas rush. Then, on 5 January, the very day McRae focused on the Centennial Park area and any men who'd suddenly shifted premises, their landlady moved to Paddington – and Craig, Mary and the kids went with her. He hadn't fled in fear. The timing had been bad luck – and very good luck for McRae.

~

Truth had so far trumped its competitors with exclusives in the Bessie O'Connor case – and now continued its dominance with a Sunday 8 January front-page scoop. The reporter who'd been shadowing McRae cast him as the hero of the hour:

> The events of the week were dramatic. The Criminal Investigation branch was plunged into the deepest despondency. Every theory and clue and suspicion had been carefully examined. Not the slightest success was achieved. And then Detective-Sergeant McRae was added to Detective-Inspector Miller's homicide squad. McRae in the past two years particularly has created a remarkable record of success in murder cases, but his task looked hopeless. So much time had elapsed since the crimes, and he had not the foundation of data possessed by the man who had been on the job for weeks.

But this 'remarkable criminologist' had triumphed within twenty-four hours. *Truth* claimed its man alone had been on the spot when McRae's ambush nabbed Craig. The paper also said it knew exactly what the alleged murderer had told detectives during his long interrogation.

Truth had a genuine exclusive – and, as had been the case with Moxley, their access could only have come from McRae and his superiors Prior and MacKay. The paper was privy to 'one of the most remarkable statements in the history of Australian crime', yet it was not yet at liberty to print the details. But that didn't stop them from offering a juicy alternative, with its 'exclusive description of what possibly happened on the night that May Miller was lured to the Park of Death'. This not-so-speculative 'possibly' version had a Mr and Mrs Gallard, at eight on the night Iris died, finding their Essex stolen from where they'd parked it in the city. The thief had driven the vehicle towards Paddington, where, on Cook Road, he was hailed by a woman. He stopped, she hopped in and they drove to a dead end near Queens Park. They got out, walked into the darkness and sat near a coral tree. As *Truth* put it: 'The woman wanted money ... A sordid story, but a story of real life. There was an altercation, a violent storm of words. But a billet of wood, a piece of heavy timber, was tragically close at hand.'

This was indeed what Craig had told McRae: that he'd killed Iris Marriott, but it had been after provocation.

~

While Craig's wife, Mary, hadn't been able to see him on Saturday afternoon, she was allowed to visit him that evening. *The Sunday Sun,* which had already cast the frail young woman as a 'tragic figure', reported she and her husband spoke through the bars of his cell, while a police guard stood sentry nearby. Craig also received legal counsel over the weekend.

On the Monday morning, at Central Police Court, Craig was denied bail and remanded to Long Bay to await the inquest into Iris's death. The newspapers reported detectives were still working to trace Bessie's killer, but it was clear the focus had narrowed to Craig: some investigators who'd been working up to sixteen hours a day on the case had been given the day off; other colleagues seconded to the murder squad had been returned to routine duties. But a core group – led by McRae and Comans – was focused on interviewing, or reinterviewing, the witnesses at Tom Ugly's Point who'd previously described seeing Bessie and a man on the night she was murdered. They conducted another line-up, but no one identified Craig. Yet their tenacity wasn't in doubt, as evidenced by *The Sun*'s laudatory headline: 'Never Let Up – Murder Squad Has Busy Life'.

Despite the failed line-up, the murder squad's efforts were about to pay off, if *Truth*'s next scoop was to be believed: 'Bessie O'Connor's Murderer May Be Unmasked! Known Suspect to Be Charged Within Few Days'. The article recounted the killer's encounters with still-unidentified 'witness' Thomas Brown. That he was included suggested the paper's source didn't yet know he was lying. *Truth* also told of bus driver Percy Weeks and Silver Grill owner Ted Watson meeting the murderer in his quest for petrol. Here *Truth* laid out detailed inside information:

> While chatting at Tom Ugly's during that considerable time which elapsed before the crippled car moved off, the killer had mentioned the names of people whom he knew and made other singular references. He forgot that he had made these remarks or that they might have any police significance and evidence value. And when a suspect was recently trapped into a cunning talk with one of the detectives, he mentioned the same people and repeated sentences which had been used at Tom Ugly's Point.

Yet *Truth* was also clued-in to the weaknesses in the police's investigations:

> Most of the people who saw the killer at Tom Ugly's Point now declare that they are unlikely to be able to recognise him again after the lapse of weeks and because of the fact that they were in the dark when they spoke to him. It is unfortunate therefore that there is not likely to be any definite identification by the witnesses of Tom Ugly's Point. This is a great disappointment to the detectives.

That week, there was another great disappointment for detectives overlooked for promotion by Commissioner Childs, who had seen fit to bump up eighteen men who worked on the administrative side of things. Officers who missed out in the course of ordinary promotions had the right to appeal. But the same didn't apply to the commissioner's 'special' promotions like these. The Police Association of New South Wales announced it would appeal the unfairness of this to the chief secretary. As *The Daily Telegraph* reported, the detectives were particularly sore that one of their number had been snubbed:

> The case of Det-Sergeant T. McRae had caused much discussion. Regarded as one of the most able officers in the C.I.B., McRae, who solved many big crimes, including the Bungendore Bones mystery, and was one of the central figures in the May Miller murder arrest, is senior to several who were promoted.

~

On Friday 20 January, Eric Roland Craig appeared in the City Coroner's Court before Mr Herbert Farrington, who'd replaced Edwin May, to face the charge that he had murdered Iris Marriott. While the accused's wife and mother were there to support him, Mary Craig soon retreated outside, where she told *Truth*: 'I am terribly unhappy.'

Opening for the police, Inspector Miller described the murder scene, explaining how he'd inspected Mr Gallard's stolen Essex and made a list of items stolen from the vehicle that included a torch and woman's cardigan. When Craig was taken into custody at the CIB, Miller testified, he'd volunteered his movements between 8 and 16 December in a statement taken down in writing and now produced in court.

On the night of Iris's murder, Craig claimed, he'd had dinner with his wife and children at about six o'clock before going out about forty-five minutes later. He'd roamed the city – from Oxford Street to Liverpool Street, into George Street, along Market Street and into a billiard room opposite Lowes in Pitt Street – before returning home at eleven. Craig said his brother-in-law had been there, drunk, and he'd sent him on his way before going to sleep with Mary. He hadn't left the house again that night.

The next five days had been similarly innocent. On the evening of 14 December, the night of Bessie's murder, he'd had dinner around six and gone for a walk until 8.10pm. When he arrived home, Mary told him a mate had stopped by. Craig had decided to go to the friend's house – but also got a shilling from his wife so he could go to the pictures. Neither finding the friend at home nor going to the pictures, Craig returned home around 10.15pm and went to bed with Mary. The next day he spent at home.

At the CIB, once Craig signed his statement, McRae joined Miller to continue the questioning. McRae reminded the suspect he'd said he owned three torches. But there had been four discovered in his rooms. McRae produced the suspect flashlight in the interview room and Craig explained: 'I forgot about that one. I found it in Centennial Park, just inside the Queen Street gates, when I took my little girl for a walk, on December 10.' McRae said the torch they were looking at had been pinched from an Essex stolen in the city on the night of 9 December. Craig replied: 'I know nothing about that.'

McRae had then produced the fawn cardigan and said: 'This was also found in your room tonight.' Craig claimed it was Mary's. McRae told him she'd denied it was hers. The detective had pressed: 'Well, how do you account for the torch and jumper?' At this the suspect had relented: 'Oh, well, I did steal the car.'

According to Inspector Miller's evidence, Craig said he couldn't remember what time he'd stolen the Essex, and that he'd taken it for a short spin up Oxford Street to Fullerton Street, where he'd left it, taking the torch and the cardigan and walking home. McRae countered by saying that the latest the car had been stolen was 8pm, when its owners realised it was missing from the city. It had been found at 1.30am by a nightwatchman – and its engine had still been warm. Craig had described a joyride that would have lasted maybe twenty minutes, but the evidence pointed to him having had the car for at least five hours.

McRae told Craig the police believed the Essex was used that night in connection with the murder of Iris Marriott. The suspect allegedly then said: 'I know what is coming next.' McRae asked what he meant. Craig put his hands on his head and repeated the same words two or three times: 'I must have been mad. I killed her.'

Miller told the court McRae had warned Craig he was going to be charged with murder and that he wasn't obliged to say anything. But the suspect was prepared to have a statement taken down.

At this stage in the inquest, Craig's solicitor, James Desmond, cross-examined Inspector Miller about this statement and the circumstances under which it had been made. Rightly, he said his client had been subjected to a long and exhausting interrogation. Desmond suggested that after Craig's first voluntary statement about his movements, Miller and McRae had put the screws on him, saying he was a murderer, that he was either a liar or mad, that he should talk because his wife had already told them everything, and that his fingerprints had been found on the car. Miller denied all these allegations.

Desmond wanted to know if Miller had used the deceased's unfortunate profession to squeeze a confession from the accused. Had Miller said to Craig, 'She was only a trollop – if she attacked you, you have a loophole of self-defence'?

This was a familiar claim: the idea that the detectives had secured a confession by suggesting the accused might not be in too much trouble after all. Miller denied it. He said that when Craig made his second statement, he seemed like a man relieved to get something off his chest. This was a familiar counterclaim: the idea that the accused had been happy to unburden his guilty soul by making a voluntary confession.

Craig's alleged statement was read to the court. It followed the detail of the first one until he left the billiard room, after which he described stealing the Essex and recounted the routes he'd driven until he came upon Iris 'standing in Green's Road'.

> She whistled to me and I stopped the car. She walked up and got into the car and said, 'Will you drive me home? I'll tell you where to go.' I said, 'All right,' and drove up Park Road to Queen Street, along Oxford Street, Woollahra, past the tram shed to Dennison Street. She said, 'Go straight down till you come to the park.' I drove down Dennison Street to Queen's Park. When we got to the corner near the park she said, 'Turn up this way.' I turned up to the left along Victoria Road to a dead-end, and she said, 'I live over there,' pointing to a house on the opposite side of the street. She said, 'What about coming into the park for a while, love?' I said, 'All right,' and we got out of the car, which we left on the right-hand side of the road, facing the steps. We walked through some long grass under a white railing. She led the way. We went under a coral tree and sat down.

Most newspapers were coy about the rest of the statement, intimating that Iris wanted payment for sex and Craig had refused because he didn't have any money. *Truth* reported it accurately:

> She said, 'Haven't you any money at all? You didn't bring me out here for nothing.' I said, 'I did not bring you. You said you lived here.' With that she stood up and said, 'You are a bastard of a man bringing a woman all this way. For two [bloody pins] I will kick you.' I started to laugh. With that she slung a punch at me. I said, 'You dirty [bitch].' I stepped in close to her. She brought up her knee and hit me on the thigh with it.

I knocked her down with my fist and I lost my head. I think I must have gone mad. I picked up a piece of wood and hit her with that. After I had seen what I did, I got frightened and tried to hide her in the bush, I took her clothing off as I thought they would not know her. I took her shoes and stockings off and took her overcoat and bloomers and her underslip and rolled them in a bit of paper which I got in the car and drove around the first street on the right and ran into a dead-end.

I backed the car back and went up the next street along and into a street where there was a plantation. I stopped the car near the plantation, got out, and threw the leather bag on to the grass. I also put her clothing on to the lawn of the plantation.

I then went up Bourke Street and finally left the car in Fullerton Street and went home. I had some blood on my hands and washed them under the tap outside the kitchen. The only things I took out of the car were a torch and sweater, shown to me by Detective-Sergeant McRae.

Craig apologised and rationalised:

I am sorry for what I have done. I have been mad ever since. I don't know what came over me, I seemed to go mad when she kicked me with her knee. I have been shown a photo of a woman by Detective-Inspector Miller, but I cannot say if she is the woman I picked up in the car. I have read over this statement and it is true and correct, being made of my own free will. There has been no promise or threat or inducement made to me by Inspector Miller to make this statement.

Craig had signed the statement, which was then witnessed by McRae. The inquest heard from other witnesses: a man who saw the Essex stopped at Queens Park at 9pm on Friday; the teenager who found the body at 10am on Saturday; the first sergeant on the scene; the man who'd found the clothes in the newspaper on the nature strip; another man who'd found more items stolen from the car in a discarded leather bag; Mr Gallard, who identified the stolen torch, and Mrs Gallard, who said the cardigan was very similar to the one she'd left in the car, which had a stain on it she'd tried to remove with ammonia; and the nightwatchman who'd found the vehicle with its engine warm.

The most potentially devastating testimony came from GMO Dr Palmer, who described the eight separate wounds that had shattered Iris's skull and destroyed much of her brain. He testified that all but the first blow had been delivered when she was already facedown on the ground. Further, Iris had been so small and light that she was unlikely to be a physical threat to any man in the confrontation described. Dr Palmer put her at five-foot-one and ninety-eight pounds. But Iris's 1929 police record – under the alias 'May Miller' – had her as three inches taller and twenty pounds heavier. Meanwhile, her 'violent temper' and previous ear-biting assault had already been recalled by the press.

Detective Wiley testified that, before dawn on the Saturday, in the police car that was to take Craig on the tour of the crime scenes, the accused had admitted:

> I am glad I have told you everything. I have been nearly out of my mind and frightened to go out of the house. I was up the street a few days ago doing some shopping for the wife. I ran into a policeman and went cold all over and nearly collapsed.

McRae was last to give evidence. He testified about the interrogation, the statements and the visit he'd made with Craig to Queens Park, where the accused had again described how Iris had kicked him and he'd lost his head. Craig, he said, had shown him where he'd battered her, where he'd dragged and left her, after stripping her in the hope she wouldn't be identified. The accused had shown McRae where he'd dumped the clothes wrapped in newspapers; the disappearance and reappearance of this evidence was explained as the result of someone finding it and, when they realised what the parcel contained, returning it for the police to discover. Craig had also shown where he'd thrown the log he'd used to kill Iris, but this couldn't be found amid the bushes.

McRae hadn't finished his evidence when the coroner adjourned court at 5pm. After emotional scenes with his wife and mother, Craig was not returned to Long Bay, as was protocol, but placed in a cell overnight at Central Police Station. The next morning, McRae sprung his surprise: he placed Craig in another line-up and then took him to Central Police Court and charged him with the murder of Bessie O'Connor at the national park on or around 14 December.

It all happened so fast. *Truth* reported: 'Craig appeared dazed. He was livid and he appeared like a man walking in a trance as they charged him with another murder.'

When the inquest into Iris's death resumed, defence counsel James Desmond first established Iris Marriott's criminal record under the name May Miller before he cross-examined McRae in a bid to show that his client had been cajoled and tricked. Once Craig had made his first voluntary statement, he asked, had the detective said to him, 'You are either a fool or the biggest liar I have met'? McRae said no. How about, 'Your wife has told us everything'? He denied this too.

Desmond asked if McRae had lied to Craig by saying his fingerprints had been found on the car linked to Bessie's murder.

The Arrow described a tense moment: 'For a moment the burly police officer shed some of his usual imperturbability.' Then McRae answered scornfully: 'If his fingerprints had been found, he would have been identified within two minutes of their reaching police headquarters.'

Desmond shot back: 'I am not asking that. Was that said to him?'

McRae still didn't answer directly: 'No detective who knew his business would make such a ridiculous statement. Craig would know that his fingerprints were in the records.' Yet McRae did say the accused had asked about Iris on the drive to Queens Park. The detective admitted: 'I informed him that she had once either bitten, or attempted to bite, off a man's ear. I said that she was one of the unfortunate class. He then said, "I would not have tackled her if she hadn't tackled me."' Certainly, McRae saying this was misjudged. But he hadn't told Craig more than had been in the papers recently. If the killer had been following the crime in the tabloids, he would have known he could use Iris's past and occupation in his defence.

With the Crown's case closed, James Desmond did exactly that: 'This woman was given to deeds of violence. I put it to Your Worship that Craig was goaded into the loss of his reason by this woman for not getting monetary recompense for the sale of her poor tarnished body.' Desmond said there no was evidence to support a charge of murder – at most it was nothing more than a case of manslaughter, and manslaughter caused by the provocation of the dead woman, provocation so extreme that his client didn't deserve to stand trial for what had been an act of self-defence.

The coroner didn't agree at all:

> As to what actually took place, we have only the statement made
> by Craig. In that he says that, after certain remarks and threats
> by the deceased, he struck her, and then with a piece of wood he
> bashed her skull. To my mind it was a most fiendish murder.

A fiendish murder for which he was committed to stand trial.

27

I'm Sorry, I Can't Admit That

Craig was back in the same court the following Monday for the inquest into Bessie O'Connor's death. There were to be twenty-six witnesses for the Crown. The most heart-wrenching was Patience O'Connor, who sobbed as she was shown Bessie's torn and blood-stained clothing, and as she described the last time she saw her daughter alive.

Tom Ugly's Point kiosk owner Mrs Hamilton Watts, who'd participated in a line-up and identified Craig, confirmed that the deceased was the girl who'd come in and ordered sandwiches. Asked if she'd since seen the man Bessie had been with, she walked to where the accused sat and put her hand on his shoulder. It was a dramatic moment but proved nothing: Craig was sitting in the dock, where any witness would expect to see the man they were supposed to identify, and Mrs Hamilton Watts's identification would only be as good as the rest of her evidence.

Barrister James Kinkead, who'd successfully defended Thomas Jenkins on the charge of murdering bush-camp bully Michael Desmond in mid-1932, asked Mrs Hamilton Watts when she'd first been interviewed by detectives. It was on 16 December, she said. And how tall had she said the man was then? About five-six or five-seven, she replied, which matched Craig.

'Did you tell the police that?' the barrister pressed.

'I'm not sure,' she admitted.

'Did you not tell the police you thought the man was five feet, ten inches?'

Mrs Hamilton Watts said again: 'I'm not sure.'

And how had she described him on 16 December, the barrister asked.

Mrs Hamilton Watts told the court he had a broad face and Irish features, which was taken to mean dark hair and dark complexion. Yet Craig had a long, thin face with fair hair and skin.

Kinkead asked Mrs Hamilton Watts if she knew that a man had been arrested in connection with the death of Iris Marriott. She did. Had Mrs Hamilton Watts seen a photo of him prior to the recent line-up?

'Yes,' she said. 'I saw one in *The Sun* or *Truth*.'

Kinkead asked if she was short-sighted; Mrs Hamilton Watts claimed she was not. 'Why then are you wearing glasses?' he asked. The witness said it was to hide puffiness beneath her eyes.

When Kinkead requested that Mrs Hamilton Watts's original police statement containing her description of the man she'd seen with Bessie be produced for the court, Detective-Sergeant Comans was called, but he claimed he didn't have this evidence in his possession.

It was an inauspicious start for the police. It looked as though they'd sloppily – or deliberately – relied on an unreliable witness, whose memory was tainted by what she'd seen in the newspapers. Worse, they seemed to have covered this up.

Government medical officer Dr Sheldon gave evidence about Bessie's wounds, saying she'd been hit at least ten times with a tomahawk or blunt instrument. George McNamara told of finding the grievously injured girl in the bush. Sutherland's Detective-Constable William Payne testified about the tyre tracks, which had been matched to the Essex stolen from Centennial Park, and of finding the toll ticket at the crime scene. Payne also said he'd been among the police who took the accused to the national park on the morning after his arrest. As their car was pulling up, the officer said, Craig had become very agitated, pleading, 'Oh, don't take me down there.'

The police did not produce Thomas Brown as a witness. Letting him anywhere near a courtroom would, they knew, subject them to ridicule and hurt their case against Craig. But James Kinkead didn't know the man was a fraudster. He sought advantage for his client by getting Payne to admit the accused looked nothing like the man in the widely circulated description provided by Brown.

The inquest next heard evidence that *Truth* had obliquely described even before Craig had been arrested for Bessie's murder. Detective Payne testified he'd been at Central Station when the accused had mentioned knowing folks at Liverpool. Seeing an opening, Inspector Prior had said: 'I know some people there too. Whom do you know?' Craig had said people surnamed Stone, who lived in Railway Street. Keeping it conversational, Prior asked if he knew anyone who kept a hotel there. Craig replied: 'I know a widow lady with three daughters who keeps a hotel.' This linked to what the court was about to hear.

Witness Gerald Stiff told the court that he and a chap named Alf Brown had been outside the kiosk at Tom Ugly's Point when they were approached by a man on foot who said he needed petrol. They'd pointed him to a bus and suggested asking the driver. In Stiff's account, he'd seen the bus driver siphon some fuel into a tin. Then the stranger had supposedly told Alf Brown his name was Stone and that he needed to get back to Liverpool, where he lived on Railway Street. Alf had driven the fellow back to an Essex – but instead of heading in the direction of Liverpool, he'd driven towards the city.

It was a garbled account – and some such details had already been in *Truth*. Stiff's credibility was done no favours when he acknowledged that he'd picked Craig out of a line-up only as being 'as near as possible' to the man he'd encountered.

When Alf Brown was called, he clarified things a little, saying he had offered to drive the man back to his car. 'I asked him how long he had been out of petrol and he replied that he had come a good long way down the hill with the engine switched on.' Brown said that meant he'd have to put some petrol in the carburettor. But when Brown took the top off, petrol flowed out – indicating the car wasn't out of gas at all.

'Then I told him to look at his gauge, and he went round to the back of the car to see,' the witness explained. 'I said to him, "The gauge is not there; it is on the dash inside the car." This had further aroused Mr Brown's suspicions. 'With that, I asked him if he had stolen the car.' The man denied it and said he was a travelling salesman. Accepting this, Brown had investigated what was wrong with the car. 'I found that the fan-belt had come off the bottom roller and knocked the ignition wire out of the contact,' he said. 'I fixed that, and the engine started off. I took the fan-belt off altogether and gave it to him. Then he drove off.'

Contrary to what Gerald Stiff had said, Brown testified that the man had not told him his name. But he had said he lived in Railway Street, Liverpool, and that he knew a red-haired family there – a widow named Mrs Summergreen and her two daughters – who kept a hotel. The prosecutor asked Alf Brown to walk around the courtroom and see if he could find anyone who looked like the man. The witness did as asked and indicated the defendant, but with a qualification, that he was 'nearest to him in side appearance' – that is, in profile.

On the third day, Lionel Downey testified that the Essex was found not far from his house, smeared with blood inside and out. A large tomahawk was missing, but its leather blade guard was in the car, along with an empty oil tin. Old underpants he'd used for cleaning were also gone from the car; they were those produced in court and now bloodstained. He also identified the oil can he'd discovered in the Essex, and testified that strips of the vehicle's fanbelt had been on the back seat. When the Essex was found, Bessie was yet to be discovered, so the police had done only a perfunctory check for fingerprints, and Downey had soon after washed away all the blood.

Ted Watson, the Silver Grill owner who'd provided the tin at the insistence of bus driver Percy Weeks, testified that he'd stood two feet away from the petrol-seeking stranger and got a good look at him. 'That man I now identify as Craig,' he told the court confidently, 'and I picked him out in a line-up at Central Police Station.'

But under cross-examination, Watson admitted that when he was first interviewed by police, he'd said he wasn't sure he'd be able to identify the man as he hadn't taken particular notice of him. One month later – and having read the papers – Watson had attended a line-up that included the accused. Even then, this witness – who had just expressed certainty – had said he couldn't positively identify anyone, though Craig most closely resembled the man he'd encountered. During the line-up, the accused had even been asked to say, 'Where can I get some benzine?' but Watson couldn't recognise the voice.

Bus driver Percy Weeks testified how it'd been near the Silver Grill that a man had asked where he could get petrol and he'd agreed to give him a gallon. Weeks identified the oil can produced as the one he'd got from Ted Watson. Asked if he'd seen the stranger since, the bus driver looked at Craig and said: 'Yes, I think that is the man, but I cannot swear to it.'

Even this tentative identification unravelled quickly. Defence barrister Kinkead asked why Weeks hadn't picked Craig from the line-up. 'Well,' the bus driver said, 'I'm a bit nervous in these things and at the line-up I did not like to say he was similar.' Kinkead asked that the original description Mr Weeks had given to police be read to the court: 'Slight build; about five feet eight or nine; dark complexion ...' Under questioning, the witness now had to admit that Craig wasn't tall enough to match the man he'd seen, and that he was fair, not dark.

Grace Stone of Liverpool said she'd known Eric Craig since October 1928, when he'd been at the military camp at Liverpool and had visited her and her daughters with another man named George Graham. Margaret Summergreen, who worked in her mother's Golden Fleece Hotel, said Craig's face looked familiar, though anyone saying any member of her family had red hair didn't know them very well.

On the fourth day of the inquest, Detective Comans testified that on the morning of 7 January, Craig had said to him: 'It is no good asking me anything about the murder of Bessie O'Connor for I did not do it. I have told the truth about the other case, and my conscience is now clear.'

Comans had said to Craig: 'I understand that you told detectives at the CIB last night that you knew a Mrs Stone in Railway Street, Liverpool, and you also knew a widow woman there with three daughters.' The accused agreed he'd said those things. Comans asked if anyone had gone with him to visit the Stone family. Craig told him he'd been with a man named George 'Jock' Graham.

Craig had mentioned this fellow before to McRae. The way Craig described him tallied almost exactly with the false description of the killer circulated in the newspapers.

Comans had told Craig that when witnesses had spoken to the suspected killer at Tom Ugly's Point, the man had supposedly claimed his name was Stone, he lived in Railway Street, Liverpool, and he knew a widow with three daughters who kept the hotel there. Craig replied: 'Well, Jock Graham would know all that.'

Comans pressed: 'Can you tell me any other person who would be likely to possess the same information about the Stones and the widow woman?'

Craig had to admit it was unlikely. If he was trying to infer his Liverpool companion was the killer, he'd walked into the trap Comans had set. The detective now told Craig that Jock Graham had been located, interviewed and cleared. Further, he looked nothing like Craig's description. Comans said to the accused: 'I put it to you that it could only have been you or Jock Graham who was seen in a stolen car at Tom Ugly's Point on the night of December 14, and Graham has satisfied us that it was not him.'

Craig had supposedly replied: 'I can't say anything.' Kinkead asked Comans about witness Thomas Brown. The detective told the court this man had provided the widely circulated description of the murder suspect – and admitted it did not match the accused.

Detective Wiley testified about being among the police who'd taken Craig to the national park. The accused had been agitated and, when asked if he'd been there with Bessie, had replied: 'I can't say anything.' On the way back to Sydney, Craig had worried he was about to be put face to face with witnesses. Wiley had asked: 'Do you want to be confronted with them?' Craig had allegedly replied: 'No. I will have a better chance if I am lined up for identification. It will be fairer to me as they will say anything for £250.'

McRae testified last again. He told the court Craig had confessed to killing Iris Marriott, but when asked about Bessie had said: 'I'm sorry, I can't admit that.' Craig had stood by his story in that first voluntary statement – the one in which he'd lied about Iris. He maintained he'd gone out for a while but had been home in bed with his wife by the time Bessie was at Tom Ugly's Point. McRae told the court he'd outlined to Craig why he didn't believe him, saying: 'I will show you the points of similarity of both these offences.' McRae had gone through his list: the use of a stolen Essex car, the taking of a woman unknown to him, the use of a secluded spot, the method of attack with a blunt object, the dragging of victims by their feet, the stripping of the women, the disposal of clothing, and the dropping of the stolen cars near where they'd been stolen and near where Craig lived. To these he added the remarks about the Stone family and hotelkeepers at Liverpool that had been made to witnesses, and then also to Prior and other police.

McRae testified that Craig had replied: 'I can see it. It looks very black against me. I admit that I did kill May Miller, but I cannot admit that I did the same thing to Bessie O'Connor.'

With the police evidence concluded, the coroner asked Craig if he wished to give evidence. He and Kinkead had a whispered exchange. Craig stood and said: 'On the advice of my counsel, no.'

The coroner delivered his verdict: Eric Roland Craig had murdered Bessie O'Connor. He would face trial twice, on separate murder charges. If the Crown couldn't hang him for Iris, they might get him for Bessie.

28

If at First You Don't Succeed, Trial and Trial Again

On Thursday 16 March 1933, Craig was in Sydney's Central Criminal Court to face trial for Iris Marriott's murder. In a distinct voice, he pleaded, 'Not guilty.' Prosecutor Leslie McKean opened the trial by telling the jury that 'all the circumstances point to murder, and murder alone'. To prove this, one only had to look at Craig's confession. But the accused's barrister, Sidney Mack, countered by stating that his client's defence was simple self-defence.

During this first murder trial, the witnesses – civilian and police – repeated their testimony from the inquest. Again, Dr Palmer impressed upon the jury the savagery of the attack against a small woman. All the head wounds had been down to the bone, each one had fractured the skull, and almost certainly each blow would've been powerful enough to knock a person down and render them unconscious. It hadn't just been a kill – it had been overkill. Dr Palmer's testimony was meant to head off the argument that Craig had killed Iris accidentally, while justifiably protecting himself.

With the Crown's case concluded, Craig made his unsworn statement from the dock. 'I did not think I'd kill this woman,' he said in a barely audible voice. 'I never saw her in my life before. I would not have touched her if she had never attacked me.' Then, more loudly, he claimed: 'She came at me like a fury, as I told the police. That's all, gentlemen.' Craig sat, wiping tears from his eyes, and his wife, Mary, suddenly rose, left the court and didn't return.

The defence produced a parade of character witnesses to testify that the man who'd just confessed to bashing a woman to death, apparently because she wouldn't provide sex for free, was a good, helpful, sporting and calm-tempered gentleman – one who'd even once stood up for a battered wife. Against this backdrop of decency rendered defective for a deadly moment by the need for self-defence, Sidney Mack didn't just argue that his client ought to see the charge dropped to manslaughter: he wanted acquittal.

The Crown had not established a motive for murder, he argued, and if the accused had feared grievous bodily harm, he'd had the right to use whatever force necessary to protect himself. Mack cited Iris's threat to kick Craig, and noted that she'd followed through. He told the court she'd once bitten a man's ear off. That was a furious act – and surely the jury could believe Craig when he said that she came at him like a fury. Convict this man of murder, Mack said, and he might go to the gallows.

The barrister didn't have to summon Moxley's ghost, but he was surely haunting the courtroom. That tortured soul was no more, sent to the noose by twelve men good and true, who had sat in the same box as the present jury. If they convicted Craig and he hanged, Mack was asking them, could they, in dead of night in years to come, be certain they'd given him fair justice? 'When a man is dead,' he warned, 'he cannot be brought to life again.'

Crown prosecutor McKean didn't try to rebut the character witnesses. Instead, in an echo of how Moxley and Ball had been compared with Frankenstein's monster, he invoked another recent fright flick to recast their evidence in an even more sinister light:

For all we know, it might be another case of Dr Jekyll and Mr Hyde. He was known to these people as a man of absolute decency, who wouldn't say 'boo' to a goose, and was trustworthy among women. Who would know what he practised in secret – a man who leaves his wife and children at home, kisses his wife goodbye, then goes out and steals a car, and picks up a woman of the streets? We don't know what was in his mind when he took the woman into the park. There are such things as perverts.

McKean reminded the jury that, by his own statement, this Mr Hyde had initially laughed when Iris had insulted him. Then he'd battered the tiny woman – and kept bludgeoning her when she was on the ground, facedown, unconscious, defenceless, her skull already shattered. Rather than seeing what he'd done and admitting this supposedly justifiable act, Craig had calculatingly covered up his crime, dragging and stripping his victim, washing her blood off his hands in his kitchen sink at home, before climbing into bed beside his young and unsuspecting wife.

'Could you imagine anything more horrible than that?' McKean asked the jury. 'Could you imagine any jury of decent men reducing the charge of murder to one of manslaughter?'

But that was exactly what they did. The jury retired at 4pm and returned four hours later to convict Eric Roland Craig of manslaughter. The judge, Mr Justice Augustus James found this difficult to fathom. In sentencing, he said:

> I cannot quite see the facts the way the jury have found them. At the same time, I am bound by their finding ... It is absolutely inadequate to say that you feared you would lose your life or that you would suffer grievous bodily harm at the hands of this little woman. It does not appeal to my intelligence in any way whatever.

The jury must have taken that view. They may have done it on the ground of provocation. It seems to me that the provocation was quite inadequate.

He couldn't overturn the verdict, but he could do the next best thing: 'In the circumstances, I cannot do less than sentence you to 20 years' penal servitude.'

Craig had avoided the gallows. On a twenty-year sentence, he could be out in fifteen with good behaviour – or even earlier if he successfully petitioned for release. But he still might hang if found guilty of murdering Bessie O'Connor.

~

The Crown opened its second bid to put a noose around Craig's neck in the Central Criminal Court on Wednesday 29 March 1933. Justice Halse Rogers presided, with Leslie McKean again prosecuting and Sidney Mack returning to lead the defence. The Crown's man opened by telling the jury the case would hinge on the question of identification. If they were satisfied various witnesses had seen the accused as they claimed, then the verdict had to be murder.

Government medical officer Dr Sheldon detailed Bessie's many head wounds, each caused by a separate blow from a tomahawk or hammer. The jury wasn't supposed to think beyond the evidence before it, but everyone knew Iris Marriott had been killed in exactly the same way.

The court heard much of the same evidence presented at the inquest. But numerous witnesses were even less convincing. Tom Ugly's Point kiosk owner Mrs Hamilton Watts again told of her encounter with the killer, and again identified Craig in the dock. But, as Mack's questioning revealed, she knew all about him from the newspapers. To demonstrate her unreliability, the barrister pointed at his colleague, Mr Kinkead, and asked the witness if she'd seen him before. Mrs Hamilton Watts said he looked familiar. 'Don't you remember that Mr Kinkead cross-examined you at the Coroner's Court?' Mrs Hamilton Watts wasn't sure. If she couldn't be sure about a man who had questioned her at length in full light relatively recently, how could the court trust her identification of a man she'd seen fleetingly in darkness longer ago?

Gerald Stiff admitted he didn't know if he'd seen the man he'd encountered again – and he wasn't sure if he was in court. His mate Alf Brown said he didn't see the man either – and that he hadn't picked him out in the line-up. New witness Frederick Harvey said that at 10pm on 14 December a sedan car had pulled in to his Brighton-Le-Sands service station, with a man at the wheel and a young girl in the passenger seat. Mr Harvey *had* picked Craig out of a line-up at Long Bay for Detective McRae – except that had been less than a week ago, and more than three months after the fact.

Further, his identification had been shaky. Sidney Mack cross-examined: 'Didn't you say at Long Bay, "This is the nearest type of man, but he was a little more tanned than this man and he wanted a shave?"' The witness agreed.

On the second day of the trial, Craig's wife, Mary, corroborated his alibi, saying that on 14 December he'd gone out around 7.45pm, come home at 8.20pm and then she'd given him one shilling to go the pictures. He'd returned not later than 10.30pm, and they'd had a cup of tea and then gone to bed. Craig had been there when she'd woken up.

But her testimony conflicted with what she'd allegedly said during police questioning.

McKean asked: 'Did Detective-Sergeant McRae ask you whether your husband left you alone much at night?'

Mary agreed that he had.

'And did you tell him "He's never at home at night"?'

She denied this.

McKean pressed: 'Did you say, "I know what he's done to me. A little more won't hurt"?'

Mary denied this too.

McKean didn't let go: 'Would you swear that you did not say it?'

She faltered: 'I cannot remember.'

Mary also said she couldn't remember if she'd given up asking about his nights out because he would 'only tell her lies'. Had Mary told the police that Craig's mother had taken a suit of clothes away? She denied it. Had any of her husband's clothes been removed by anyone other than the police? Not to Mary's knowledge. Her friend Lily and her husband's friend Jack both corroborated Craig's version of events: they'd been at the house in the early evening and seen him. But the world only had his wife's alibi for his whereabouts later than that night.

Charles Lawrence took the stand. On the night of 14 December, he'd seen a car pull up on the corner of Eveleigh Street in Redfern. A girl got out and walked towards Holden Street. Unlike in the *Truth* exclusive months ago, in which he'd been quoted as certain it'd been Bessie, now he could only say he was pretty sure it had been her. A man had got out of the car and asked him if he had a match. Lawrence did. The bloke lit his smoke and they chatted for three minutes. The witness told the court he'd seen the fellow's face by the flare of the match – and by the glow of nearby electric streetlights. At a Central Police Station line-up, Lawrence testified he'd said: 'The man isn't there. I could pick him in half a million.' He'd been asked to select a man most like the bloke he'd seen. Mr Lawrence told the court he picked out a man standing three away from Craig.

Under cross-examination, Silver Grill owner Ted Watson admitted he'd first told police he wouldn't be able to identify the man who'd come into his place wanting petrol. Regardless, he now again identified Craig in the dock, adding, over Mack's objection, 'I say he is the man who was in my shop.' The defence counsel elicited from this witness that he'd seen photos of Craig in the newspapers; Watson's 'identification' was thus worthless, Mack told the jury. Bus driver Percy Weeks also stood by his shaky identification, even as he admitted he hadn't picked out Craig in the line-up but only at the Coroner's Court, though he hadn't been able to swear to it even then.

McRae was last to testify. There wasn't much to tell the court. Under questioning, Craig had denied killing Bessie. When McRae charged him with her murder, he'd responded: 'It is a lie.'

Speaking from the dock, Craig maintained his innocence. He said the night of Bessie's murder he'd gone out for a few hours, just as his wife had described. Visiting a friend's house but finding the man not home, he'd walked as far as West's Pictures on Oxford Street (which, of course, had been Hilda White's favourite film palace). But Craig hadn't seen a movie. He'd returned home by 10:15pm. Craig told the jury he'd not done it – and moreover he'd have no need of anyone's help with fan-belt repairs:

> I did not murder Bessie O'Connor. I did not even know her. I have never been out with her. The statement I have given to the police is absolutely true. I have been out of work for over eighteen months, and when I was leaving home I had no money. My wife gave me one shilling. That is all the money I had when I left home. Before leaving home that night I had a shave. I do know something about running repairs to a motor. I have chauffeured for various people in Sydney. Of this charge I am absolutely innocent.

On Friday, the trial resumed for final arguments. Sidney Mack raised Thomas Brown, the witness whose description had been so central to the investigation, but who at the line-up had said Craig was not the man he'd seen. Mr McKean countered: then why hadn't the defence called him? 'It is an extraordinary thing,' he mused. Mack reiterated the many problems with the Crown's witnesses. Craig's alibi was corroborated by his wife and two friends. There was no other evidence. The jury had to acquit.

For the Crown, McKean said no one doubted Mrs Hamilton Watts had seen Bessie at her kiosk. The court had heard that Craig had driven her there in the car that was later placed at the crime scene, and that was seen leaving the area in suspicious circumstances. McKean reaffirmed the validity of the testimony from numerous other prosecution witnesses. The jury had to convict.

The case hinged on identifying the driver. Concluding his summation, Justice Halse Rogers told the jury they had to answer the question: 'Who was that man?' The jury retired at 2.45pm. Just over five hours later, they returned to say that they would not be able to reach a verdict. But the statute was clear that in such cases they needed to deliberate for at least twelve hours. They were sequestered overnight. When April Fool's Day dawned, nothing had changed. With a hung jury, the Crown would have to put the accused on trial again.

Eric Roland Craig would remain in custody until he faced court again for the murder of Bessie O'Connor.

~

Nearly four weeks later, the sequel got started before Justice Colin Davidson in the Central Criminal Court, with Eric Craig again prosecuted by Leslie McKean and this time represented by barrister William Curtis. McKean again said it was murder or nothing – and he asked the jurymen to put out of their minds anything they'd heard or read about the case. By now that was easier said than done. The Crown's evidence and roll call of witnesses remained the same, while the defence tried new lines of enquiry and attack.

Curtis delicately questioned Patience O'Connor, who admitted Bessie hadn't told her everything – including that she might let herself be picked up – and acknowledged that she didn't know who her daughter knew, or if she knew Craig. Service station owner Frederick Harvey was asked how, given he had 150 customers a day, he was so sure, three months after the fact, that it'd been Bessie he'd seen that night. The witness denied insinuations that he had been motivated to come forward by the reward, and said he wouldn't take it if offered because he wasn't a 'bloodsucker'. Silver Grill owner Ted Watson's identification of Craig took another hit when he admitted he'd only seen the man for two minutes in the dark. Doubts were raised over whether the stolen Essex had really been devoid of fingerprints – or whether the police were simply hiding that they'd not found Craig's.

Curtis alleged that Detective Payne and other police had taken Craig to the national park to frighten him into a false confession. The officer denied it. The defence asked Payne about Thomas Brown and was given his statement. The barrister elicited from the constable an acknowledgement that Brown had failed to identify Craig in a line-up. Probing, Curtis asked, 'Was that the reason why Brown was not called?' Payne said it wasn't. But the defence barrister wasn't leaving it at that – and he intimated that when he called this man, his evidence would be sensational.

From the dock, Craig again denied murdering Bessie, and again stressed his driving and mechanical skills to impress upon the jury that he wouldn't have needed help fixing a fanbelt. Mary corroborated his alibi once more, but came in for intensive cross-examination on whether she'd been told what to say by her husband. When would she have had the chance? McKean focused on Mary seeing Craig three times a week at Long Bay Gaol. But during these twenty-minute visits, she told him, it would've been impossible for him to instruct her because there was always a warder present. Yet this would have hardly been convincing to anyone who'd read of *Smith's Weekly*'s reporter's visit with Moxley, with the guard supposedly monitoring them characterised as 'deaf, dumb and blind'. McKean also wasn't recorded as raising the first opportunity Mary had to speak with her husband: the night of his arrest, at Central Police Station.

McKean tried to undermine Mary's corroborative claims that Craig knew his way around cars. Under questioning, she told the court she'd seen him partially dismantle an engine, but said she hadn't known him when he was a chauffeur; indeed, she admitted that she had written to a man seeking a reference about her husband's mechanical ability because it would 'assist him very much in his trial'. Mary again denied telling McRae she didn't know what Craig did with his evenings, and that she'd washed his clothes after the night of 14 December, and that anyone else had taken some of his clothes from the house. She maintained her husband had gone for a walk and had acted perfectly normally on his return around 10.20pm.

Defence barrister Curtis scored significantly against the prosecution. The judge had to order the jury to retire while Detective-Sergeant Comans admitted he'd told Craig during questioning, 'We have information that you are the man who picked this girl up on her way home,' when in fact there was no such evidence. The judge ruled that Comans had to withdraw as a witness. Curtis tore into Detective Payne for intimidating Craig at the national park after his all-night interrogation, a 'torturing, wearing-down process'. Bellowed Curtis: 'Then you took him out to the scene of the murder, graphically describing what had taken place saying, "Here is where the pool of blood was ... Here is where she was dragged through the sand." What was that done for?'

Payne answered: 'Just to show him.'

The third day of trial began with a bombshell when Curtis called Thomas Brown.

The witness told his story of working as a travelling boot salesman for Willis Bros and his close-up encounter with a scratched-faced man who had blood on his shirt and who needed help to fix the fanbelt on an Essex. Brown told the court he'd given the police a detailed description, and Curtis read it to the court. It described a man who was taller and darker than his client. Further, Brown testified that on 7 January he'd gone to

the Craig line-up and had definitely not seen the man he'd encountered –
nor was he now in the courtroom. Curtis elicited that Brown hadn't been
called at the inquest or the first trial, and had only been contacted by the
defence days ago.

This fresh witness was sensational. It seemed the Crown had tucked
him away because his compelling eyewitness evidence proved Craig
could *not* be the murderer. But William Curtis – who'd spent two days
demolishing shaky prosecution witnesses – had just stitched himself up.
Indeed, it's likely he had been deliberately stitched up by the police. On
cross-examination, McKean demolished Brown's story as a complete
fabrication. The witness now tried to claim he was shielding someone –
that he'd given his statement on behalf of someone else, now out of the
country, who actually *had* seen the killer.

McKean held Brown's police statement high. 'Are you aware that you
have committed deliberate perjury?'

The witness stammered: 'I didn't think I was doing any harm at the
time.'

'And you gave all that description – and all lies?'

'Yes,' Brown answered.

Truth slowed the shock moment right down for readers:

> A murmured gasp of astonishment, a whisp of sound like the
> sigh of the surf on a distant shore, swept over the public gallery;
> his Honor – severe and scarlet robed – drew his lips into a tight
> straight line and turned eyes upon the false witness; Craig, the
> accused, moistened his lips with his tongue; Mr Curtis, King's
> Counsel briefed for the defence, sat back sharply as if he had been
> struck across the face; Mr McKean, King's Counsel for the Crown,
> raised his right hand in an emotional gesture ... the jurymen
> glanced at each other in confusion.

Curtis foolishly tried to establish whom Brown was shielding. But the judge ruled it immaterial, as whatever he said would merely be another lie.

As he was being led from the court, Brown was suddenly seized by paralysis. 'Oh, I can't move,' he cried. 'I've been poisoned!' He was rushed to hospital. Brown hadn't been poisoned, but a three-year sentence for perjury lay in his near future.

In the wake of this humiliation, Curtis appeared at first shattered, saying he'd been shamefully tricked by police into calling the false witness and had suffered one of 'the greatest blows that I have ever had'. But he tried to turn what had happened to his client's advantage, arguing that the police resorted to such dirty tactics because they had 'not one scintilla of evidence' against Craig; in their desire to get a conviction in a crime that would otherwise go unsolved, they had 'gone out of their way in methods which are a disgrace to British justice'. What the jury had witnessed was an extension of how the police had hounded his client, torturing him with prolonged interrogation and a bullying visit to the national park. Then, this last affront. 'I say it doesn't discredit him,' Curtis thundered, 'but stands to the eternal disgrace of the police who were responsible for that dirty trick.'

Curtis concluded his summation by saying that not one prosecution witness had given an untainted identification – and that no one had been able to show that Mary Craig was lying or that she'd been instructed by her husband while visiting him at Long Bay.

McKean responded by saying he was stunned that Curtis had swallowed Brown's story – and he claimed he'd yesterday warned the defence that this witness wasn't to be trusted. Why hadn't the Crown called him? It was obvious! McKean said Brown was a 'moron' likely seeking the limelight or the reward. McKean said that attacking the police was a tactic to distract the jury – he reiterated the identifications of Craig and explained Mary's alibiing her husband as the understandable action of a dutiful wife.

Despite what seemed a very real instance of the prosecution luring the defence into the false witness trap, Justice Davidson dismissed Curtis's allegations of dirty tricks. As for the all-night interrogation followed by a daytime tour of crime scenes, His Honour allowed that if such practices were pushed to an undue limit, they might constitute torture. Yet much of what Curtis was talking about had to do with Iris Marriott, and these were 'matters about which we are not concerned'. Further, Craig himself had not claimed to have suffered at the hands of police.

For the second time on a Friday night, a jury was locked up to deliberate – and for the second time on a Saturday morning they had to inform the judge there was no way to reach a verdict.

After the high dramas of the second trial, the prosecution and the defence had arrived at another stalemate. Eric Craig was remanded in custody while the Crown decided whether to press ahead with a third trial. The delay in this decision might have signalled doubts. But two weeks later, on 16 May, the attorney-general announced that Eric Craig would again face court. All the witnesses were to tell their stories all over again. McRae would also be back in the box under cross-examination.

It's likely, though, that McRae didn't pay too much attention to the announcement, stained as he was that day by the blood of a terribly gunshot man, soon to be Sydney's latest murder victim.

29

A Well-Oiled Machine

'Eastern ... Eastern!'

Just after midnight on 16 May, the Central Police Station operator's voice crackled over the wireless in the big eastern district car that was tonight under McRae's command. MacKay had delivered three such powerful vehicles – capable of receiving and transmitting – late the previous year, and they patrolled continuously. 'Eastern ... Eastern,' the operator continued, 'hold-up in Old South Head Road.'

McRae and his three-man crew had been cruising south on Anzac Parade in Kensington. The driver slammed on the brakes, turned the car around, switched on the red blinking 'Police' sign and set the siren shrieking. Pedal to the metal, they hit eighty-six miles per hour through the streets, as more information came over the airwaves: a man had been shot near the corner of Curlewis Street, with the suspects reported to have driven away in an old green or blue car. These details were being beamed all over Sydney: 'All city stations being circulated!'

McRae's patrol car screeched to a stop at the crime scene within three minutes of receiving the first message. A frightened crowd was gathered around a spot on the footpath. McRae sprang from the vehicle and brushed through these white-faced people in their dressing gowns and pyjamas. On the ground lay a man in evening wear. His shirt was soaked with blood. McRae tore it open, found the bullet wound, on the left side of the chest, and did his best to staunch the bleeding. The local who'd called the police had also called an ambulance. Before it arrived, McRae asked the wounded man his name.

'John Rowland,' the fellow gasped.

'Who did it?' the detective asked. 'Why did they shoot you?'

But the victim, who had lost a lot of blood, was in shock and incoherent.

McRae asked bystanders what they'd seen or heard. One reckoned he'd seen the victim thrown from a car. Another said he'd heard a woman scream. A third claimed a sports car belonging to a local chap had passed by right at the moment of the gunshot. Put together, it sounded like John Rowland had got into an argument with a man over a car and/or a woman.

McRae asked Rowland if he'd been in the car and was thrown out. He didn't deny it. How many men had attacked him? He wasn't sure. Where did he live? The man mumbled three different addresses. Officers went racing to these places. In one, just a couple of hundred yards away, they would find Rowland's young wife and their baby son.

John Rowland was thirty-one, a successful salesman and a naturally cheerful fellow who rarely drank. Half an hour after McRae found him, he was in St Vincent's Hospital, pain eased with morphia, able to give a dying deposition to another detective. That night he'd been at his Masonic Lodge. A friend had given him a lift to Old South Head Road. Rather than put his mate out by having him drive all the way home, John had said he'd get out and walk the rest of the way. It wasn't far. He set out, carrying his attaché case, which held his lodge regalia.

A car had pulled up beside John and two men got out. One whipped out a revolver and said: 'Stick 'em up!' John wasn't going to let himself be robbed. 'You go to the devil!' he said as he swung his attaché case at the man. The car's driver said: 'Let him have it!' The gunman took a step back and fired a single shot.

The bullet ripped into John. He fell to his knees, let out a cry and rolled to the edge of the gutter. 'Murder!' he managed to call out. 'Help!'

The two men sped off. John hadn't got a good look at either because it was dark. Having recounted what he remembered, he was too weak to sign the statement. John just wanted to go to sleep. Doctors couldn't be sure of the damage – his condition was too grave for an X-ray. The bullet was in his chest somewhere. Given he couldn't move his legs, it was assumed it had hit his spine. The doctors said John would never walk again – if he survived at all.

Around the time John was giving his statement, a dirty old green Chrysler tourer was found abandoned in the city by a beat constable who recognised it as the possible getaway car from the wireless broadcast. The engine was still warm. He'd missed the men by maybe fifteen minutes. By morning, detectives knew the Chrysler had been stolen in Eastwood early the previous evening. After this theft – but before John Rowland was shot – two bandits had used the car in two separate crimes in Strathfield. In both cases a gunman held a revolver to a young man's chest while his accomplice rifled the victim's pockets. The total haul? Less than two shillings. This was enough to buy each bandit a packet of smokes – and enough to get both up to fourteen years behind bars.

Inspector Prior formed a squad. Given the shooting happened in Area B – the Eastern Suburbs – Lynch had command of McRae, Allmond, Comans, Burns and others. The MO section produced a list of known hold-up men and bag-snatchers, and the most likely of these would be followed up pronto. The newspapers talked up the system's efficiency. But it wasn't really made for a case like this. Everything about this shooting screamed amateur hour. Experienced gunmen wouldn't risk a long stretch – let alone the noose – for the pocket change to be had in such street robberies. A professional villain wouldn't panic and fire; he'd pistol whip the victim or simply make his escape. Thus, the Modus Operandi record results might well not include the most probable culprits: a couple of larrikins whose ill-conceived caper resulted in a capital crime.

Though it didn't yield fingerprints, the stolen Chrysler was the best lead. As it was pinched from Eastwood, it stood to reason that one or both of the culprits lived nearby, or at least were known in the area. The other important clue was lodged in John Rowland's chest. If the bullet could be removed, it might be matched to a recovered pistol or revolver. But there was no way to operate on the victim and retrieve this evidence. At least not while he was still breathing.

A £200 reward was announced. Police used this announcement to try to drive a wedge between the bandits. 'We have hopes,' an unnamed detective told *The Sunday Sun*, 'that the driver of the stolen car, who probably did not wish for a killing, will eventually come forward and tell his story.' These moves didn't shake anything loose. Prior, Lynch, McRae, Comans and other detectives focused on visiting houses in the Eastwood and Epping area, around where the car had been stolen.

Science might have made mighty strides in forensic ballistics but antibiotics were still a decade away. John Rowland's wound became gangrenous and he developed septicaemia. He died on Thursday morning. The reward was upped to £500 in the hope the public would turn in the men who were now murderers.

Dr Palmer conducted a post-mortem. The bullet had gone through both of Rowland's lungs, hit his spine and lodged near his heart. The GMO retrieved the slug for analysis. Ballistics found it was a very rare nickel make. Detective-Sergeant Colin Delaney and Detective-Constable Albert Crosbie were given the job of finding the records of every licensed revolver owner in Eastwood, Ryde, Epping and Dundas. There would be more than 500 homes to visit.

Truth gave the story front-page treatments, breathless in its assertions that if these two killers weren't collared quickly, they'd rob and murder with impunity – no one would be safe. Under the headline 'Murderous

Bandits Menace Public', an unidentified writer wasn't sure whether to hate or pity these 'depression crooks' – a 'new type of shiftless, workless, penniless, ambitionless young men'. He said many had left school and gone straight onto the dole. 'They are loose morally, intellectually and physically. It is a tragedy!'

Shortly after this front-page article – which may have given the wanted men an idea of what to claim in defence, should they be caught – Prior, McRae, Delaney and Crosbie visited an Eastwood residence, following up on a gun whose owner had been at this address. There, householder John Bellamy told the detectives the revolver belonged to a young man named Claude William Wallace, whom he'd known for about a decade.

Back then, Claude, aged fourteen, had befriended Bellamy's sons, and had later moved in with the family because his own parents had supposedly abandoned him. Claude had departed two years ago, leaving behind a Gladstone bag containing an automatic pistol and a few cartridges. Mr Bellamy found it and gave the gun and ammo to his son-in-law Arthur Peake so he could destroy them. But he had forgotten to do so.

On 15 May, Claude Wallace had shown up to get his gun and bullets. Arthur Peake had asked if he could keep a couple of cartridges for his son, who collected such items. Wallace agreed and was on his way. This was hours before the Strathfield stick-ups and the shooting of John Rowland.

McRae took the cartridges given to the kid: they contained the rare nickel type of bullet. Once the CIB pulled Claude Wallace's criminal record, the murder squad had its prime suspect for the shooting. As suspected, he was a petty crook. Further, given Wallace had been mates in gaol recently with a twenty-six-year-old named Eric Newlyn, who had form that might see him do stupid stick-ups, they had their potential accomplice.

Newlyn was found fast, living in a hut at Baulkham Hills. But detectives wanted to nab both men at once. So they kept an eye on him and waited for a crim as reckless as Wallace to pop up. He didn't disappoint.

Around 9.30pm on Saturday 3 June, Detective-Sergeant Len Allmond was in charge of the western district's wireless patrol car as it cruised along Parramatta Road in Annandale. When a tourer passed them, the cops checked the licence plate – and found it had been reported stolen earlier that night. When they tried to catch up to the car, the driver floored it and the chase was on, with both vehicles hurtling along the main road at 60 miles per hour.

Siren screeching, police light flashing, the police pulled alongside the stolen car. Allmond leaned out, pointed his revolver at the driver and shouted, 'We are detectives! Pull up!' But the man put on more speed. Allmond yelled stop a few more times, adding, 'I will shoot you if you don't pull up!'

At this the driver eased off the accelerator, to 40 miles an hour, then threw open his door and jumped. He tumbled about a dozen yards on the road. Remarkably, he wasn't badly hurt and, as his abandoned car went out of control into a post, he jumped to his feet and ran into suburban Annandale.

Allmond and another detective fired a shot each. Both went wide. After a lively foot chase, they caught their man hiding under a hedge. They'd collared Claude Wallace, the wanted murder suspect.

Allmond called this in to the CIB. Prior, Lynch, McRae and Comans came in to Central Police Station and then drove out to Baulkham Hills and surrounded Newlyn's hut. On a signal, they raided. There wasn't a sequel to the earlier thrilling drama – Newlyn was caught asleep in his bunk.

Just after midnight, Wallace faced interrogation by McRae. Initially, he denied everything. Then McRae told him Arthur Peake had handed over two bullets that fitted the pistol and were of the same sort as the one dug out of John Rowland.

Then Wallace told his version of what happened. 'I shot him,' he said. 'I shot him on the spur of the moment.'

Wallace claimed he hadn't known the gun was loaded. He admitted he'd suggested to Newlyn they rob the man they saw walking along Old South Head Road. But only because they were hungry and broke. When John Rowland rushed him, Wallace had backed away, hit a tree or a tree guard and the gun had gone off. Newlyn had been in the car and didn't have anything to do with the shooting. Wallace said he'd rolled the shot man over and wanted to help him. But people had come running and he'd panicked and they'd sped off in the stolen Chrysler.

McRae had heard it all before. Just like Maurice O'Hara, who'd 'accidentally' shot Frank Chaffey. At least the jury had had the sense to convict him of murder, even if the death sentence had been commuted. Now, as then, McRae needed the murder weapon. He asked: 'Have you still got the gun that you say you shot Rowland with?' Wallace said he'd thrown it under the hedge when on the run from Allmond and the other cops.

Prior went out to Annandale and retrieved the automatic pistol. They could now match it to the bullet from the murdered man's body. If Wallace tried to retract his confession, his defence would have a hard time explaining how he'd known where the murder weapon was hidden.

Under questioning, Newlyn told much the same story – but he also allegedly confessed to having been part of the two stick-ups in Strathfield earlier on the night of the shooting. On Monday 5 June, both Wallace and Newlyn were in court, charged with murder. They were remanded in custody, the latest men looking at a death penalty.

~

Eric Craig's third trial began the following day, before Justice Stephen. Leslie McKean would again be telling the jury the things he'd told their predecessors about murder being the only acceptable verdict and keeping open minds. William Curtis was again representing the accused. *The Sun* likened the trial to a well-rehearsed performance, the Crown and defence knowing their lines and delivering them with passion and conviction. But there was new evidence when Dr Stanley Milton King, government microbiologist, testified that his examination of Bessie had revealed semen in her vagina – which was used by the prosecution as evidence that the accused was a sex maniac, rather than the result of the victim's sex work.

As for the witnesses, they were increasingly exhausted – and sometimes confused – at having to recount their testimony and have it cross-examined and compared with what they'd said – or hadn't said – in police statements, at line-ups, at the inquest and the two trials. Tom Ugly's Point kiosk owner Mrs Hamilton Watts perhaps spoke for many when she said: 'I'm absolutely tired of it. I'm afraid I have made some misleading statements through being cross-questioned.' Under intense cross-examination that again cast doubt on his motivations for making his belated identification of Craig in a line-up, garage owner Frederick Harvey said: 'I didn't want to be dragged into this case.' But McRae reaffirmed that the man had been credible, testifying that when he'd placed the accused in the line-up, he'd instructed the potential witness: 'If you see the man who called at your garage, I want you to place your hand on his shoulder.' Harvey had done so, though he'd said: 'I thought he was slightly taller than he is, and he appeared to be a little more sallow … I told him owing to his radiator boiling, his fanbelt wanted adjusting. The man replied: "I know what is wrong with my car, and I can fix it."'

Curtis argued that the newspapers – *Truth* the chief among several culprits – may have influenced recollections through their reporting. He tendered chronologically ordered copies from the time of the murder onwards 'to show what knowledge could have been in the people's mind when they went to make identification'. He again hammered Sutherland's Detective Payne for how, after twelve hours of relentless questioning, Craig had been bullied and frightened at the national park. Payne denied he and the other detectives had done anything wrong. They'd simply shown the accused the murder scene and asked whether he'd killed Bessie.

From the dock, Craig made his denial – almost word for word repeated from the second trial – and his statement was followed by Mary's usual corroboration. McKean this time tried a new angle to explain how she'd come up with the alibi: 'Although you did not see your husband alone after his arrest, your former solicitor and his clerk had private interviews with your husband in the gaol and there was ample opportunity for you to find out what he had told them?'

Mary, no doubt more exhausted than anyone, replied that yes, there had been such an opportunity, not that it had happened.

On 8 June 1933, the final arguments were repeated. Curtis attacked the police and said that if Craig were convicted on nothing more than faulty identifications, which relied on memories that could be influenced consciously or unconsciously, then no one's freedom was safe. Mr McKean said disparaging the police was the ploy of a defence counsel with nothing else, and reminded the jury that only the far-from-impartial Mary could alibi the accused in the hours that mattered.

Summing up, Justice Stephen's comments included the note that if Craig had said on approaching the national park, 'Don't take me there,' it would just as likely reflect innocence as guilt. The jury retired at 2.17pm. Five and a half hours later, they were back.

Eric Roland Craig was guilty of the murder of Bessie O'Connor.

Justice Stephen asked him if there was any reason the court shouldn't pass sentence of death.

'I am absolutely innocent,' he said, 'and I still hope to have time to prove it yet.'

That clock was now ticking, because Craig was sentenced to hang by the neck until he was dead. While other death sentences had been commuted, his crime was on a par with Moxley's, and it seemed he might swing.

~

Was Craig guilty of both killings – and were his convictions justified? The first judge thought he'd murdered Iris, disagreeing with the manslaughter verdict. And if Craig had deliberately killed her, regardless of motive, then, just as McRae had noted, it was hard to credit that less than a week later someone else could have committed an almost identical crime.

Craig's claim that he'd killed Iris but was innocent of Bessie's murder had to be seen in light of what the newspapers had reported by the time of his arrest. Iris's profession and violent past were well known, and he might've expected to get a minor sentence for manslaughter or be acquitted entirely with his self-defence argument. Bessie was a different story. Picking her up in the car, he perhaps thought he could get sex without paying – or in return for the shilling he gave her to buy sandwiches at the kiosk, the shilling his wife said she'd given him for the movie he didn't see that night. Perhaps Craig hadn't set out to murder Bessie and – similar to Iris – had become enraged in the national park. If this girl was just another streetwalker, she wouldn't be missed. Well hidden in such a remote spot, her body mightn't be found for a long time, if ever. Instead, Bessie was soon known to all as an innocent sixteen-year-old swimming champion fatally battered by the Park Demon. There was no way Craig could argue provocation or self-defence. Any confession would mean the death sentence. Yet admitting he'd killed Iris – in self-defence – in the same breath as denying he'd murdered Bessie might make it seem he was being honest about the latter accusation.

Even if all of that were true, it was purely speculative. Undoubtedly Craig's murder conviction was a miscarriage of justice. The case hinged on identification and Bessie could feasibly have been the victim of a copycat. In the two failed trials, the witness testimony had been very far from being beyond reasonable doubt. And the Crown had absolutely nothing else besides this roll call of faulty remembrances. Nothing had changed in the third trial. Ironically, if Craig *had* been convicted of murdering Iris and subjected to an automatic death sentence, the Bessie O'Connor case might not have even proceeded. Even if such a death sentence was commuted, no one in 1933 would have expected him ever to be released. But twenty years for manslaughter? That might see him out well before he turned forty.

McRae and his colleagues may have felt so sure Craig had murdered Bessie that they were determined to convict him by any means necessary. Did they instruct or induce witnesses to identify him in line-ups? Possibly. But if so, they also weren't very successful, given how their testimonies played out. At the very least, having been present at line-ups and interviewed witnesses, McRae had to know they weren't certain in their identifications of Craig, and that his defence would likely discredit much individual testimony. *Truth* had said as much even before he was arrested for Bessie's murder. But the police and Crown were hoping the collective weight of these shaky identifications would sway the jury – especially one that knew Craig had confessed to and been convicted of the almost identical killing of Iris Marriott. It took three trials to prove them right. Not that it made it right.

Despite the similarity of the crimes to the murder of Hilda White, police had nothing that tied Eric Craig to that crime. Her case would remain unsolved.

In the months that followed the guilty verdict, Craig appealed his conviction for Bessie's murder in the Supreme Court. It was in these proceedings that Patience O'Connor revealed what she knew of her daughter's secret life, and claimed she'd never admitted these things before because she'd never been asked. Craig's appeal was unsuccessful – and he was denied leave to appeal to the High Court. The Howard Prison Reform League would protest against the death sentence he now faced, on general grounds of Christian opposition to capital punishment, but also because two failed trials signalled there were doubts about his guilt. Should anything new come to light, you couldn't un-hang a man.

Despite the barbarity of the crimes for which he was convicted – which were surely on a par with those of Moxley, but with fewer mitigating circumstances – Craig's death sentence was commuted to life in prison in mid-September 1933. His file was marked 'never to be released', but this didn't bind future governments. And Craig would see freedom again.

The first time was in October 1941, when, having supposedly become deeply Catholic, Craig escaped from Bathurst Gaol after fashioning a rope from hemp lattice and hiding it inside the organ he'd piously been playing in the chapel. One hundred police joined the search. A maniacal murderer on the loose was a good, if short-lived, news story; Craig was recaptured the morning after his escape as he walked along a road ten miles from the prison.

Despite how his file had been stamped, Craig was paroled in 1957. As outlined in Tanya Bretherton's detailed study of his case in her book *The Killing Streets*, he changed his name, lived in Sydney and, ironically, got a job on the fringes of law enforcement. Eric Craig died in 1965. He wasn't suspected of any further crimes.

That wasn't to say Craig's actions didn't contribute to the death of another young woman. Mary Tobin had been just fifteen when she married Craig. By the time she was sixteen, she had two children. Three years later, she stood by her husband as he admitted killing a sex worker, and then as he was convicted of murdering a girl just a few years younger than she was. In September 1933, upon learning that his sentence had been commuted, Mary Craig, who had been supportive of her husband throughout his ordeal, gave an interview to *The Daily Telegraph*. 'I am a prisoner, too,' she said. 'No one seems to realise that. They have put him in gaol for the rest of his life. They don't realise that they have put me in gaol, too, for the rest of my life.'

It was a lengthy interview in which she talked about visiting Craig, the nightmares she'd endured and the hard work she was now doing as a waitress to support her two babies. Nowhere did Mary say she believed her husband was innocent. Perhaps she believed it didn't need to be said. But Mary did claim police checking in on her 'welfare' was tantamount to harassment, saying McRae and Detective Wylie were particular problems. They denied the allegation. Whatever Mary – now living under an assumed name – believed about her husband, she remained in written contact with him until March 1942, when she filed for a divorce that was granted six months later on the grounds he'd never be released.

Not that Mary's 'freedom' changed much: she had struggled to make ends meet as a single mother for the past decade and would continue to do so. In mid-1948, with her children approaching adulthood, she married a painter named Kenneth Mann. But the relationship was short-lived; by 1950 they were living apart. Understandably, Mary had long been plagued by depression, and in late July that year she became further distressed because her now twenty-year-old daughter had gone missing. On the last day of the month, Mary gassed herself in the kitchen of her Randwick flat. She left a note described by *The Sun* as revealing a 'touching story of Mrs Mann's hardship in rearing her children, and her hard struggle prior to her second marriage'. If Mary had been trying to escape her past, it followed her in death, with a typical headline reading 'Killer's Wife Found Dead'. Despite all she'd been through, she was just thirty-six years old.

~

Back in June 1933, Mary Craig had featured heavily in *Truth*'s wrap-up of her husband's conviction. The latest iteration of her evidence was published, accompanied by two photos of this young woman who had two tragic decades still left to endure. Also on that page – as though passing the baton – were photos of John Rowland's alleged killers, Claude Wallace and Eric Newlyn, looking every bit the grim-faced 'depression crooks'. They seemed even more thuggish a couple of weeks later in *The Sun*'s courtroom sketches as the inquest into the murder began.

Bondi witnesses told of hearing angry words and the gunshot before finding Rowland bleeding on the roadside. John Bellamy and Arthur Peake described Wallace retrieving the automatic pistol. McRae give evidence of his interrogations of Wallace and Newlyn, and their statements were read for the court, while Allmond recounted the dramatic circumstances of the car chase. But the most poignant testimony was John Rowland's dying deposition.

While that was emotive, the last witness was all science: he was the CIB's forensic ballistics expert, Sergeant Herbert Hanlon. He testified how he'd received the death bullet and made tests with the automatic pistol the accused had thrown into the hedge. Hanlon had fired the bullet that had been in the gun's chamber, shooting it into water so it wasn't damaged. Hanlon similarly fired one of the cartridges that had been given to McRae by witness Arthur Peake. The markings on both test bullets showed unusual rifling, very similar to that of the fatal bullet. Further, their weight and size were identical.

Hanlon had combed the city, trying but failing to buy more of this make of bullet, which he believed had been manufactured before the war in Belgium. In other words, these bullets were vanishingly rare in Sydney. Much was made of this ballistics evidence, which was the first real use of the startling new police science that was as exact as fingerprinting. Wallace and Newlyn were ordered to stand trial in September.

~

Just a week after forensic ballistics took centre court, the New South Wales police had a new and far more appealing weapon in the war on crime.

After more than a year in training, Constable Adam 'Scotty' Denholm and Constable Reilly officially introduced their Alsatian dogs, Tess and Harada, in a demonstration of the new squad MacKay had instituted as a response to the deficiencies of the Moxley manhunt. When officers posing as crooks threatened their trainers with guns, these dogs ferociously attacked the threats – and they didn't back down when blanks were fired. But as soon as Scotty and Reilly gave the word, their canine charges broke off their onslaughts and returned to docility. As *The Sydney Morning Herald* reported:

> The dogs were almost human in the way that they understood the orders of their trainers. After giving the command, 'Stay there', the trainers walked away, leaving the Alsatians with a group of men. The dogs allowed the men to approach and stroke them, but would not budge an inch from the position they had taken up. After the trainers had gone some distance away, they said in a quiet, ordinary voice, 'Do not let anybody touch you.' The dogs immediately understood and any attempt by the group of men to approach or touch them was met with an angry snarl.

The dogs could track men, articles and parcels by their scent – and chase crooks and pin them down until they were arrested. But these dogs were absolutely placid and friendly otherwise – and were particularly good with children.

In mid-August 1933, the wisdom of MacKay's initiative was proved beyond doubt. Tess and Scotty were called out at night to look for a man who'd gone missing in bush at Dee Why. Taken to where his truck had been found, the Alsatian sniffed a coat belonging to the lost fellow. *The Sun* reported:

> Tess immediately showed signs of excitement and set off at a smart trot, followed by the party, flashing torches and using lamps to assist their passage over the rough ground with precipitous gullies at many points. After two hours, in which they covered four

miles, Tess found the man alive and unharmed at the bottom of a gully, and Scotty climbed down to his aid. Commissioner Childs ordered that the dog squad henceforth take part in any missing persons search.

In the decades ahead, Scotty and his dogs became stars. Many lives were saved. In 1941, he and his dogs joined the hunt for prison escapee Eric Craig. Though that chase ended peacefully, other scents led to tragedy. The most horrific was Scotty and Tess's discovery of the body of six-year-old Marcia Hayes, murdered on Christmas Eve in 1937 in Windsor. She'd been raped, strangled and dumped in a river in a sack. Dorothy Denzel had suffered a similar fate, and in an awful coincidence her father knew the Hayes family; he drove them to the funeral, consoling them as they collapsed at the graveside. Like his daughter's murderer, Marcia's killer was to hang; sixty-five-year-old Alfred Spicer's May 1938 execution would be the second-last in New South Wales.

As grim as some of the dog squad's work could be, it was an undisputed public relations triumph for the New South Wales police – perhaps second only to MacKay's other enduring initiative, the Police Boys' Club in 1937, which evolved into the Police Citizens Youth Clubs (PCYC) in later years. At the Easter Show, the annual Police Carnival and other big public events, Tess, Zoe, Disraeli and the rest performed incredible feats – such as jumping through flaming hoops, climbing ladders to fire fixed guns and responding to commands delivered via radios – and were captured in action by newsreel cameras for audiences all around Australia. By 1948, Scotty was the subject of a memorably titled book, *The Cold Nose of the Law*. After he retired from policing, he would have a successful career training animals for Australian films and television – including that major cultural export, *Skippy the Bush Kangaroo*.

~

Two weeks after Scotty and Tess saved the man in the bush at Dee Why, Wallace and Newlyn stood trial together for the murder of John Rowland. The Crown's witnesses and evidence were the same – including those forensic ballistics. Both men pleaded not guilty.

Wallace gave an unsworn statement from the dock. He said on 15 May he'd gone to Arthur Peake's place looking for work. Peake had offered him the revolver because he had no use for it. Wallace, the good citizen, said: 'If you don't want it, I'll put it in at the police station.' He'd slipped the pistol into his pocket, not knowing it was loaded. Leaning in to the 'depression crook' idea, he told the jury he had 'got a car' – that is, stole one – and was driving about aimlessly with Newlyn.

'I had had nothing to eat since the morning before,' he told the jury. 'I had no clothes after paying two weeks' board. I had got cards printed and tried to get honest work. I couldn't get work anywhere. I intended to get benzine for the car and to get out to the country.'

Wallace had then seen Rowland and told Newlyn to stop. 'Pull up here, we've had some bad luck and we might be able to get enough to help us.'

He'd jumped out and pulled out the automatic pistol.

'Put your hands up,' Wallace said.

Rowland had yelled.

'Don't be silly,' Wallace told him. 'I've got a gun.'

Rowland had shouted: 'You'll get nothing from me – police!'

Wallace said: 'Don't sing out, I'll let you go!'

He'd been backing away when he hit a tree or tree guard and the gun went off. 'I jumped sideways when I saw a flash and heard a report,' Wallace said. 'The man fell over. I turned him over. The police say I pointed the revolver at him. I said, "No, I had it over his head." I didn't know it was loaded ...'

Wallace said Newlyn hadn't said anything – let alone 'Give him one!'

Newlyn told the court his part of the story, including, 'Until I heard the shot, I didn't know Wallace had a gun.' He, too, claimed they'd wanted to help Rowland but were scared and drove away. 'I had no intention of robbing anyone.'

But with that last claim, Newlyn opened the door for prosecutor, Leslie McKean, to seek admission of another statement Newlyn had made to McRae. This was him confessing to have stuck up two men earlier in the evening – a blatant contradiction of what he'd just told the court. McRae was recalled to testify about this confession. Newlyn's statement was admitted – and the two young men they'd robbed then also testified. Both identified Newlyn. One also identified Wallace. The other couldn't, saying the gunman who robbed him wore a white handkerchief as a mask.

The jury returned a verdict that both the accused were guilty – but of manslaughter, not murder. As *Truth* would say, all of New South Wales 'was dumbfounded and amazed' by this latest decision from a 'chicken-hearted' jury. Certainly the judge, Mr Justice Kenneth Street, was appalled.

The jury might have second-guessed themselves when the records of the men they'd just spared the death penalty were read out. Not that the court heard all the details, but both had had colourful criminal careers. On Christmas Day in 1928, Wallace, then nineteen, who a year earlier had married a fifteen-year-old, got up from lunch with his in-laws to go out and buy a packet of cigarettes. His young wife never saw him again – until his picture was in the paper for murder. He'd been found guilty of stealing a truck, and of numerous counts of breaking-and-entering – just a fraction of the crimes he was suspected of committing. In 1931, Wallace had stolen a car, crashing it and crawling free moments before it burst into flames.

Wallace had then actually given himself up to the cops, saying, 'I want to get done with all this trouble. I'm going to turn over a new leaf and make a fresh start.' This was possibly a ploy to avoid being charged with more serious offences. According to the police report, he'd carried a gun when committing his crimes – likely it was the one he'd left with John Bellamy before turning himself in. Wallace had got two years and four months – and had retrieved his pistol soon after his release.

Meanwhile, starting in October 1929, Eric Newlyn had been in and out of prison – but mostly in. He was convicted of stealing a hat from a man's head, of ripping off a truck loaded with paint, and of stealing a car and a huge amount of tobacco, burying the latter in a cave at Baulkham Hills. His final caper – the one that put him in prison – was stealing a truck, one of six he intended to nick so that – much like his mate Wallace's professed dream – he could move to the country, go straight and live a quiet life.

Reading their records, Justice Street knew that Wallace and Newlyn hadn't robbed John Rowland on the spur of the moment. Whether they'd intended to kill him or not, under the definition of the law they were both guilty of murder. While His Honour had to abide by the jury's verdict, he gave both men life sentences – though they'd be eligible to apply for release in twenty years.

Putting Eric Craig, Claude Wallace and Eric Newlyn behind bars were wins for the New South Wales police – as was the dog squad's finding the man lost in the bush. New crime-fighting tools – forensic ballistics, super-fast wireless cars, canine constables – were being coupled with the time-honoured techniques of beating the footpaths, house-to-house searches and sweating suspects in lengthy interrogations.

But even these celebrated convictions would pale in comparison with the processes McRae used to solve his next murder, an investigation that would justify his promotion to chief of the Homicide Squad.

30

The Human Glove Mystery

The late afternoon of Christmas Day 1933 was sunny and mild in Wagga Wagga, perfect for fishing on the Murrumbidgee River. That was what two local mates were doing in a canoe when they were engulfed by a choking stench. The source was a horrific bundle caught on a branch. Decaying buttocks protruded from the water. But from the waist up, the corpse was inside a chaff bag.

Detective-Constable Joseph Ramus, a local policeman, was to take charge. Born in 1898 and raised in Corrimal, he'd joined the force when he was twenty-one and was on the same sort of career path as McRae. Ramus had worked towns in the Riverina and been stationed in Wagga since 1929. As the rest of Australia put its feet up for Christmas night, the young detective, along with a Constable Walsh, Wagga's government medical officer Dr Weedon and a few other unlucky souls, headed out to do their grisly duty.

The policemen brought the body – which was flyblown and falling to pieces – in to shore. Preliminary examinations at the river and morgue had it that the dead man was likely in his mid-forties, stood around five-foot-seven and had been solidly built. The decomposition was so advanced that the doctor believed he might've been in the water as long as two months. But even without this putrefaction, identification would've been difficult: his face and skull and been caved in and broken open.

Had these injuries been done before or after he went in the river? The fact there was no water in his lungs suggested he hadn't drowned. The chaff bag also pointed to foul play. Yet, tragically, men in these times did throw themselves into rivers inside sacks so they couldn't swim free if they had second thoughts. The man could have jumped from a bridge or tree, hit rocks or a log, been killed instantly and not inhaled water. Arguing against this: he would have to have hit his head very hard to cause such damage, and the chaff bag hadn't been torn by any such impact. The doctor thought he'd been battered with the back of an axe or tomahawk. Then he'd gone into the bag, then he'd gone into the river.

Ramus was looking at his first murder. As ever, it began with identification. Who was the dead man? Ramus – and his boss, Inspector Stuart McIntosh – made some assumptions. He was wearing dungaree trousers, a grey shirt, Blutcher boots and the sort of dyed military-style tunic handed out to men in need. He'd likely been one of the tens of thousands of blokes roaming the countryside looking for work. But any dole rations or work orders bearing his name weren't in his rotted pockets. There was nothing else distinguishing – no tattoos or unusual dentition – that might jog memories or match a charge sheet or criminal record. The only thing that stood out was that he wore his dark hair long for a man. As for fingerprints? All that remained of the skin on the left hand was a scrap of the thumb. The skin of the right hand, meanwhile, was completely gone. To try to establish the bloke's identity, Ramus would talk to locals about any swaggie who'd suddenly vanished in the past two months. But the detective was up against it, because in that time the Murrumbidgee had experienced a couple of flood surges. This meant the man might have gone into the water as far as eighty miles upriver, near Gundagai. Ramus was going to need help.

The usual calls were made to the CIB, and McRae was ordered onto the case. He'd take the night train and have as his partner Detective-

Constable Albert Crosbie, who'd done sterling work tracing the revolver in the Rowland case, and who was now being trained in murder investigation.

While Ramus awaited the arrival of the CIB men, he and police from Wagga and Gundagai roamed the countryside. Unemployment had peaked in New South Wales at 32 per cent in 1932, and things had gradually been improving since then as Australia made a slow but steady recovery from the Depression. But despite an upbeat Christmas editorial in Wagga's *The Daily Advertiser* about bad times being on the way out, there were still unemployment camps in town and dozens more dotted around the district. Cops visited all of these hardscrabble camps, where down-and-outers lived rough side by side, without a lot to keep them occupied except each other's business and strangers passing through. No one knew anything – or anyone who might fit the fairly generic description.

The CIB men reached Wagga the next morning, with a reporter and photographer from *The Sun* tagging along. By then their rival, *The Sydney Morning Herald*, had already made its view clear: 'Detectives have been set an almost impossible task in solving the mystery.' McRae, Crosbie and Ramus headed to the hospital, where they assisted in a three-hour post-mortem. Dr Weedon removed a scrap of thumb flesh for the CIB fingerprint experts. It was a long shot, but worth trying. He concluded that the skull had been split open by one or two blows, and death had been mercifully instantaneous.

McRae and Crosbie went to the police yard to inspect the dead man's clothes and the chaff bag, *The Sun*'s photographer taking shots as they worked amid the stink of the rotting evidence.

McRae needed the river discovery site thoroughly searched. It was another tragic waterway, the first of many that dated back to his childhood. At least McRae's age and seniority had their advantages, and so it was Crosbie who donned a bathing suit to swim among snags and dive to the bottom of deep and dangerous holes. Disappointingly, he didn't find the murder weapon, bringing to the surface only a swaggie's mattress, which was believed to belong to the victim and bore what seemed to be bloodstains. But on the shore, Ramus made an astounding discovery. Half in and half out of the water was the decomposing but completely intact epidermis of the dead man's right hand. A human glove – fingernails still attached.

McRae thought the man's tunic sleeves, which were tight at the wrist, might have been responsible. When his flesh swelled, the skin had been sliced through, slipped free and swirled away.

It couldn't be a coincidence that it washed up there. Ramus suspected it had been in the chaff bag and had slipped out unnoticed when they were bringing the body from the river. But it was a Christmas miracle it hadn't swirled away since then. The trio of detectives knew what they had. Some quirk of fate – water, weather, whatever – had preserved the skin so well that fingerprints *might* be taken. McRae ordered it photographed, carefully wrapped in cotton and assigned a constable to take the hand epidermis and the thumb scrap on the next train to Sydney. The discovery of the 'Human Glove' was a tabloid sensation.

While the detectives awaited word from the fingerprint section, the CIB had good news. McRae's promotion had finally come through; he was now Detective-Sergeant Second Class, designated also as Chief of the New South Wales Homicide Squad. *Truth* commented that his 'recognition is belated. For years he has been doing outstanding, clever work, but he has not received the just reward of quick promotion.' Crosbie also had reason to smile – he'd been bumped up to Detective-Constable First Class. He'd been promoted alongside Detective-Constable First Class Darcy McDermott, who'd worked with McRae on the Thorne poisoning. Both young men – like Scotty Denholm – also had MacKay's favour as 'bright young men' of the force.

Commissioner Childs, who'd started the CIB fingerprint department thirty years earlier, meanwhile had a protégé in the bureau's new top man,

Detective-Constable John Walkom. Promoted to the post in the middle of 1933, he was just thirty-five and reputed to be the youngest fingerprint chief in the world. This would be an unprecedented test of his talents. The human glove was like parchment, and his attempts to print the fingers failed. So, using warm water, Walkom gently softened the skin until it became malleable. But now it wasn't possible to print from these floppy, boneless fingers.

Clearly a man with strong stomach, Walkom donned a thin rubber glove and carefully slid his own hand inside the dead man's skin to print each finger of the human glove. Was it a ghoulish stunt or a world-first piece of forensics? The answer would depend on getting a match from the 200,000 records on file. Working on the assumption that major crooks who were murdered wouldn't be reported missing, the fingerprint department began with them and worked through to minor offenders. Childs would claim the search took three hours.

Though it was initially kept from the press, McRae now had a name to work with. Percival Smith, thirty-five, originally from Carlton, in Melbourne, had been fingerprinted in Albury in March 1931 when he'd been charged with obtaining food relief under false pretences and got one month in gaol. Eighteen months later, in September 1932, he'd been printed again in Young, eighty-five miles north-east of where he'd been found dead in Wagga Wagga.

McRae, Ramus and Crosbie made enquiries with other Riverina police, learning Percy had drawn food relief in Cowra and Young in May and June 1933, and then in Barellan in October and November. Constables at various stations recalled him clearly: he had long hair, drove a four-wheeled black covered wagon pulled by a half-bay horse, and he travelled with two dogs. McRae traced him to Narrandera, with witnesses saying Percy had camped on the town common for about a month from 25 October.

On McRae's advice, Inspector Prior released Percy's identity and description to newspapers and radio stations around Australia. *The Daily Advertiser* in Wagga Wagga ran the details of the man, his wagon and his animals. Wagga horse dealer Charles Seymour read the article in disbelief. On 19 December he'd bought that wagon and horse from a local auction house, which had sold them on behalf of their owner. Earlier that same day, this owner had personally sold Charles a horse blanket. Since then he'd only used the wagon when driving it home from auction. On that journey, his son had found dole and ration cards stuck between the canvas and the side of the wagon. They hadn't meant anything at the time. Now they did because they bore the signature 'Percy Smith'. After reading the *Advertiser*'s article, Charles took a closer look at the wagon and found bloodstains. He contacted the police.

According to Charles, the seller claimed to have bought the wagon, horse, blanket and other things at The Rock, a small town twenty miles south-west of Wagga. This man's name? Edward 'Ted' Morey.

Wagga police knew exactly who Charles was talking about. Just two weeks ago, Constable Walsh had collared Morey for drunkenness and receiving stolen property. For these latest offences, he'd been sentenced to fourteen days in the lock-up. Morey had been released that very morning.

With the blanket taken into evidence and the horse and wagon impounded, Inspector McIntosh told Walsh to go find Morey. The constable knew where to look: Tent Town. This Spring Street settlement in Wagga would be described by *The Sun* as 'one of the most dismal of all unemployed camps in the country centres. Huts and tents made of odds and ends of materials, with here and there a more substantial low hut, are spread over the flat ground abutting a rubbish tip and the large stockyards'.

Walsh found Morey at Tent Town matriarch Susan Pearce's place. They were family: her daughter was married to his brother. Morey asked Walsh what the trouble was. Told about the wagon and horse, he said he'd bought them at The Rock from a man with whom they were both acquainted. 'You know, big George McDonald,' Morey said. 'You arrested him outside the Riverina Hotel when he was working on the bridge job.'

Walsh knew George McDonald. But he took Morey in for questioning anyway.

~

Edward Henry Morey had already left murder, madness and heartbreak in his wake – perhaps without even knowing the carnage he'd triggered. Born in April 1897, he'd lived most of his life in the Central West and Riverina. Ted was easy on the eye but he was reckless and left others to pay the price. After enlisting for the Great War in June 1916, he deserted the following year, got a seventeen-year-old orphan named Jessie Thompson pregnant, and then deserted his teen bride and baby daughter, Dorothy, to re-enlist in the army – only to desert again in September 1918.

Morey was on the run not only from the military authorities but also from the young wife and child he'd abandoned. In Sydney, Jessie worked herself to the bone just to stay on the breadline during the Spanish flu pandemic. When little Dorothy got sick, she was refused hospital treatment because it was discovered she had venereal disease. Likely this had been acquired at birth from Jessie, who believed she'd been infected by Morey. Jessie was also unable to get state assistance until she found her husband, but despite her repeated requests, police couldn't or wouldn't track him down.

Eventually, Jessie cracked and tried to strangle Dorothy, the child barely surviving. 'I had no place to go to,' Jessie said when confessing to a constable. 'I was penniless and homeless.' Her horrific circumstances saw her acquitted. Months later, in a cheap city room, she gave birth to another daughter – and killed the baby because she had to go to work. 'I did not know what to do,' she said. 'I was nearly out of my mind.' Jessie was acquitted on the grounds of temporary insanity.

Newspapers everywhere – including Wagga's *Daily Advertiser* – carried stories about Jessie's plight. Did Morey know what became of his wife? He couldn't read but he lived in a hearsay, read-aloud culture and so may have known of the tragedies he'd set in motion. But Morey had plenty of problems of his own making: his first recorded brush with the law was in the Riverina in 1919. From then on, he'd rack up conviction after conviction.

~

In the Wagga police station on 4 January 1934, Morey made a statement for Walsh to type. He said he was a labourer and usually got around in his Dodge truck. Morey claimed on 18 December he'd been on the Albury Road near The Rock when he'd seen George McDonald and another man who, George told him, 'was Percy. I think he said Smith.' George had wanted eight quid for the wagon, horse and dogs, along with a harness, a tent, a horse rug, a tuckerbox, toolbox and other items. The reason for the quick sale? George said he and his mate were getting a train to Shepparton to pick fruit.

This 'Percy' had stayed quiet during the deal-making. Morey only had six pounds. But George agreed he could pay the £2 balance next time their paths crossed – and that he was free to sell the goods in the interim. Now Percy had spoken up: 'I don't know about the £2. I don't know this man.' But George assured him: 'He is all right. I know the man.' George had written a temporary receipt. Morey said he couldn't now find this proof of purchase – and the proper receipt he'd been promised hadn't arrived by post.

After staying with the men until just before they caught their train, Morey had driven the wagon towards Wagga, camping overnight because the horse was tired. After visiting Susan Pearce at Tent Town, he'd left the two dogs with her, along with some of the smaller things he'd bought. In

Wagga, Morey said, he sold the wagon, horse, harness and rug to Charles Seymour – and also a tent to second-hand dealer Leslie Peacock.

Having taken Morey's statement, Ramus went to Tent Town to retrieve Morey's truck, the dogs and various items from his lorry and others entrusted to Mrs Pearce. Everything was impounded – the mutts included, now leashed up in the police yard beside the wagon, the horse and the truck.

Returning from Narrandera, McRae examined the evidence and questioned Seymour and other witnesses before interviewing Morey late that night. Despite Morey's criminal record, McRae initially believed him: the story was credible, told with conviction and the man was offering to remain in voluntary custody until police found George McDonald. Narrandera witnesses had told McRae that Percy had gone off looking for work around the end of November with a big man named 'Ryan'. Their description of this fellow matched Morey's description of McDonald. With Morey in custody anyway, McRae issued an arrest warrant for this suspect.

The next morning, McRae took Morey to The Rock and had him show where he'd camped and where he'd bought the wagon. But the more the detective learned from locals, the less and less he believed the man. McRae charged Morey with vagrancy and had him remanded for a week in Wagga. Now he was in custody whether he liked it or not. McRae kept investigating in The Rock that weekend. By the time he got back to Wagga, he was sure Morey was a murderer.

On 8 January, McRae questioned Morey again. He showed him the blood found on the tent fly found among his possessions. Morey claimed it was in whatever condition he'd bought it. How about a bloodstained white shirt? Morey said he'd hurt his ear and it had bled. Maybe those explanations were plausible, but how about the witnesses who'd seen Morey with Percy Smith in The Rock in early-mid December? Hadn't he repeatedly said he hadn't met the man until 18 December, when he bought the wagon? Morey told McRae that people in The Rock must've mistaken Percy for his mate Joe Baker.

Okay, McRae said, if I find George McDonald, are you happy to look him in the eyes?

Morey replied: 'Yes, I will front him any time, and if he says I didn't buy it off him, he is a liar.'

With that, McRae charged Morey with the murder of Percy Smith on or about 16 December 1933.

31

This Case Will Go Down in History

Two days after McRae laid the charge, Ramus found George McDonald and brought him in. This man told McRae he'd been working for the Main Roads Board in Wagga between 11 and 22 December. He hadn't been at The Rock recently and hadn't sold anything to Ted – he hadn't even seen him for about two years.

Early that evening, McRae went to Morey's cell and told him to come to the exercise yard. There stood McDonald. Seeing him, Morey said: 'Good day, George.' McDonald returned the greeting. But now Morey turned to McRae and Ramus and said: 'He is not the George McDonald I meant, he is a larger man that that.' Yet Morey had already said this *was* the fellow he'd meant: the man he knew, who knew him, the man once arrested by Walsh outside the Riverina Hotel.

From witnesses, detectives had learned that one of the last sightings of the two men believed to be Percy and Morey with the wagon had been on a country laneway off the Urana Road on the night of 18 December. This was just 600 yards from where the body had been found. Searching the area, Ramus, McRae and other police found the remains of a fire, bloodstained trousers and horseshoe nails of the same brand as others found among Percy's effects in Morey's possession. McRae believed this was where Percy had been battered to death in the back of his wagon.

Confronted with the trousers, Morey denied they were his. But Susan Pearce told police they belonged to the accused – not so long ago, she'd mended them for him.

Six weeks later, the inquest into the death of Percy Smith opened at the Wagga Police Court. As the proceedings began, everyone traipsed out into the yard to examine evidence too large and too alive to be tendered inside: the wagon, horse and dogs. Such exhibits were unusual. The three dozen witnesses would also be seeing dozens of inanimate items, including the bloodstained pants and tent. Yet nothing could compare with the 'star' piece of evidence: the human glove, now floating in a jar of formalin, which would be set on the coroner's bench at the start of each day of the inquest.

The court heard about the discovery of the body, the cause of death, how the advanced decomposition was due to exposure to heat, air and water, and how the fingerprints had been obtained and used to establish the identity of the dead man. Country constables chronicled their various encounters with Percy over the past few years; Narrandera folks described his arrival and the month he'd spent in their town. All described the same distinctive, long-haired man with the black wagon, bay horse and dogs. Those who had spoken with him said he had a lisp.

One of these witnesses, a thirty-four-year-old invalid pensioner named Moncrieff Anderson, lived on the common near where Percy had camped and had got to know him well enough that his young wife, Lillian, had made a gift of a plate, now produced in evidence as having been in the accused's possessions. Shown the horse rug Morey had sold to Charles Seymour, the witness recognised it as having belonged to the dead man. Moncrieff said he'd also got a look inside his wagon. The first thing he'd noticed was that Percy had hung up a framed photo of Jack Lang. Charles Seymour said it had still been there when he bought the wagon. Poor old Percy had been done to death beneath the gaze of the patron saint of the dispossessed.

From around 13 December, residents of The Rock had seen Percy in their town. He was accompanied by Morey, whom many had known for ten years or more. Percy had got locals to fix his horse's teeth and repair his wagon's shafts. The two men had drunk in pubs with locals, the long-haired man paying for drinks because Morey was skint. He couldn't afford to buy beers any more than he could afford to have the axle replaced on his Dodge truck, then stuck in a garage yard in the town.

One witness testified that Percy had bought him and Morey drinks in a hotel on 16 December. Later that day in the street, he testified, Morey had put the bite on him for a couple of shillings for sausages and bread. After that, no one had seen the wagon man again in The Rock. Morey was also scarce for a few days. But he resurfaced on 20 December, cashed up sufficiently to pay £2/9 for a new axle for the Dodge. He repaid the witness for the food money and even shouted him a beer at the pub. When this man said he'd buy a round, Morey told him: 'No, keep that for tobacco. I have money.'

What had happened between 16 and 20 December? A farmer told the court that on Sunday 17 December, at about 6pm, he was driving his sulky along a road four miles from The Rock when he passed the black wagon. The long-haired man had previously camped near his property and they'd exchanged waves. But he didn't recognise the fellow sitting next to him. Witnesses testified that the next morning the wagon was travelling towards the village of Collingullie. There, about 10.30am, the lisping, long-haired man went into a hotel and bought a bottle of wine, remembered by the hotelkeeper, who took notice of his distinctive half-bay horse. That evening, a labourer saw the wagon parked close to his camp near Urana Road. This was where the bloody trousers and horseshoe nails were later found. Early the next morning, the labourer said, the wagon was gone, its tracks pointing towards Wagga.

Susan Pearce testified that at 8.30am that day Morey arrived at her place in Tent Town, having come from the direction of Urana Road. He told her he'd bought the wagon, horse, dogs, everything, at The Rock for £4, not £6. Now he was going to sell what he could in Wagga, even if he only got five quid. After a quick cup of tea from the pot of a tent neighbour, Morey went off to do business, leaving the dogs and other things in Susan's care. She testified that among the items was the tent fly, the blood on it not yet dry.

Susan next saw Morey on 21 December. He was driving his repaired Dodge and said he'd sold the wagon. After that, from what she'd heard, he was locked up for drunkenness. Immediately on his release, on 4 January, he came to her tent and asked 'if the detectives had been down'. When Susan asked why, he said they might be asking about the murder. Morey asked her son to read aloud from that day's *Daily Advertiser*, which had first carried the identification of Percy Smith. Susan thought it odd Morey had such an interest. He told her he was going to leave town. She asked when, and Morey replied: 'I am going away tomorrow if the police don't arrest me this afternoon.'

Morey was still there when Walsh arrived and questioned him. When he got the chance, Morey had quietly asked Susan to quickly write a receipt for the wagon in the name of 'George McDonald'. Susan refused. Morey had then gone with Walsh. When shown the bloodstained trousers, she confirmed they belonged to the accused. Tent neighbour Lillian McIntyre corroborated Susan's account of Morey's arrival with the wagon. She added that he'd been wearing a white shirt. When he returned two days later, she helped him load his Dodge and noticed this shirt was now bloodstained and in a trunk. When this garment was produced, Lillian said it was similar to the one she'd seen. But the fact it hadn't been stained on 19 December seemed to support Morey's claim that the blood was from a later ear injury rather than a murder victim.

Charles Seymour testified that he previously knew Morey. The man had come to his house at 9am on 19 December, wanting to sell the wagon, horse and harness for £20. Seymour thought the horse was all right but it wouldn't let him see its teeth. Charles declined the deal. But he did pay ten shillings for the horse rug – initialled 'PS' – and this was now produced in court.

Morey had then gone to see Wagga second-hand dealer Leslie Peacock, who paid twenty shillings for the tent, the saw and the pair of reins that had been tendered in evidence. The accused had wanted to sell the wagon. Peacock, who'd known Morey three years, said he was surprised to hear he owned one. Morey replied: 'Oh, yes, I have had one for a long time.' The horse wouldn't show its teeth. Morey explained: 'He is a bit touchy. He has had his teeth done up.' Again, no deal was struck. So Morey went to the auction house, where that afternoon Seymour bought the wagon, horse and harness for £11. He testified about his son finding Percy's dole and ration tickets in the wagon and of later discovering it was bloodstained. The kid had also torn down the photo of Jack Lang.

Microbiologist Dr Stanley Milton King certified that human blood had been found on the wagon, on newspapers beneath its false floor, on the trousers, on a white sports shirt and on the tent fly.

Constable Walsh testified about Morey claiming to have bought the wagon from the same George McDonald whom the policeman had once arrested. Walsh said he'd known the real McDonald for nine years, and that he knew of no other man with that name in the district.

McDonald was called into court and Walsh identified him. McDonald said he'd known Morey for about a decade, hadn't seen him in a couple of years and had not sold him anything in December 1933. The accused was a good fellow sober, he said, but 'would fight his best mate when drunk'. Ramus testified to retrieving the body, and finding the human glove and the bloodstained trousers. He said he'd been present when Morey had told McRae the dogs were named Rover and Pete, claiming he'd been told this when he bought them with everything else from 'George McDonald'.

McRae corroborated much of what the court had heard. Morey, he said, told him he'd bought the wagon using some of the twelve quid he'd earned carting wood in Cowra. McRae's extensive interviews with people at The Rock proved Morey had been lying about not knowing Percy Smith before supposedly buying the wagon from McDonald. Further, Morey's story about the two men catching a train to Shepparton on 18 December was a lie: there was no rail service that day or night.

On the sixth day of the exhaustive inquest, the deputy coroner found that the police had proved Percy Smith had been murdered by Edward Henry Morey on or about 18 December. The magistrate lavished praise on McRae, Crosbie and Ramus. 'This case,' he said, 'will go down in history as one of the most remarkable ever brought before a court in any part of the world.' Morey was to stand trial for murder. The evidence was damning, and people who'd known him for years would next repeat testimony that might see him hang.

Even so, there was a flicker of hope in Morey's darkest days. That's because there was a stranger out there who would support him – *love* him – no matter what. From early April, while Morey awaited trial in Albury gaol, he took comfort in correspondence from a mystery woman.

32

A Shot in the Dark

In the first letter from Morey's secret admirer, read to him by a kindly gaoler, Thelma Smith said she was twenty-four and she'd first met Morey nearly a decade ago, when he'd done her a good turn. Thelma had seen 'Ted' a few times after that, the last occasion being five years ago. While he wouldn't remember her, she hadn't forgotten him: 'Ted, I always liked you. If there is anything you want, let me know. I'll draw to a close. From a friend whose name you did not know.' Thelma said he could reply care of 'L. Anderson, Post Office, Narrandera'.

Morey sent the letter to his solicitor, hoping it might serve as a character reference. Thelma wrote again soon, divulging more about her struggles, and including that she'd recently had a fall and hurt herself. Even so, she was a survivor:

> I am a good woman; not praising myself up, but I have looked after myself since I was 13 years old. I have been in lots of places and I always got on well. I will say goodbye till I hear from you again. I am sending my love and hopes to you.

Thelma said she'd reveal where they'd met when she eventually saw him again. Morey's gaoler took down a reply he dictated to this absolute stranger whom he addressed as 'My Dearest Thelma':

> I am sorry if I have done wrong in sending your first letter to
> the solicitor, dear, but I thought it was such a fine letter for a
> character for me, so I hope you will forgive me, dearest, under the
> circumstances ... I will always think of you, dearest, and you do
> not know what a comfort your letters have been to me.

Promising to call on her personally as soon as he could, Morey signed
off: 'I remain, yours lovingly, Ted. I send love and kisses to you, Thelma.
Xxxxxxxxxxxxxxxx'

Thelma's reply was a real mash note:

> I know nothing wrong of you, only that you are a good fellow and
> would make a good man if some woman got you. I have only seen
> you three times, but I took a liking to you and then it grew to
> what it is now ... I am still thinking of you and I still love you,
> sweetheart. If things go wrong – well, I'll stick to you.

~

Morey went to trial on 8 May 1934 at Wagga Court House. The evidence
from the Crown was almost identical to that given at the inquest. The
prosecution rested at the close of the third day. The next morning, Morey's
defence would fight for his life.

At around seven o'clock that night, a shot rang out in the darkness on
the fringes of Tent Town. A woman cried out, and moments later Lillian
Anderson ran into Susan Pearce's tent. She said: 'Crieff is shot! I heard
someone fire a shot. I saw a pink flash in front of me. Quick: run for the
police. He fell at my feet.'

Lillian – a tiny and girlish twenty-four-year-old – was talking about her invalid older husband Moncrieff, who had two days earlier repeated his evidence at Morey's murder trial. Tent Town men ran to where she'd seen her husband shot. They found him seventy yards away, at a water trough, on his back, unconscious and bleeding from a bullet wound near his left ear. They carried Moncrieff back to the camp, where McRae, Crosbie and Ramus had arrived.

After the detectives quickly examined the victim, he was loaded into an ambulance and rushed to hospital. Dr Weedon said Moncrieff had been shot at close range. There was no exit wound and an X-ray confirmed he had a bullet lodged in his brain. He was going to die.

McRae was mystified. This man's evidence had been helpful in establishing Percy's movements and identifying his wagon. But he'd never seen Morey with Percy at The Rock. Moncrieff had been one of many links in the circumstantial chain – important but not crucial. Even if he had witnessed Morey bashing Percy to death – and had said so in court – why shoot him *after* he'd testified?

McRae interviewed the shocked soon-to-be-widow Lillian Anderson. She and Moncrieff had come up from Narrandera on Monday so he could testify the next day. They'd brought with them their seven-year-old daughter, Joyce, along with some bantam fowls and a few meagre possessions. They'd planned to return home tomorrow.

Lillian told McRae that this evening, after court adjourned, they'd come back to Bob Bowman's hut for tea. Moncrieff had a few drinks and then she'd accompanied him to get some water. At the trough, her husband told her to go and get another bucket. She'd done as he said and was heading back when she ran into Joyce, who was with Susan Pearce's fourteen-year-old daughter, Laurel, and another girl the same age named Frances Jones. Joyce wanted to come with her mum to get water. Lillian said it was too cold and to go back to the hut with the older girls. Lillian had almost reached her husband when she saw the flash, heard the bang and saw him fall. She hadn't seen the gunman, nor did she know why anyone would want to shoot Moncrieff.

Few in Tent Town were going to sleep that night – not with a gun-toting murderer on the loose – and McRae, Crosbie and Ramus interviewed the fearful residents. No one could tell them much. Laurel and Frances both said they'd seen Lillian going back to the trough, holding a bucket in her left hand and clasping her right hand against her long coat. Susan Pearce – star witness at Morey's trial – had been inside her tent and hadn't seen anything. But she did have something for police that was in its own way as startling as the human glove.

Nine letters. Eight were from Thelma Smith, who had made contact at the start of April. Eight were addressed to Susan. The ninth letter was Morey's reply to Thelma, written just last week in the Albury gaol. McRae wanted to know why Susan had this letter. She said Lillian Anderson had given it to her for safekeeping when she arrived in Tent Town. Lillian hadn't wanted Moncrieff to find it. She said she'd retrieve it from Susan before they left so she could pass it on to Thelma when they got to Narrandera. McRae read each of the letters and took them into evidence. The return address on each of those addressed to Susan had been care of L. Anderson at Wagga Post Office.

At daylight, Lillian went to her dying husband's bedside, while detectives searched the crime scene. Ramus found a .22-calibre rifle submersed at the bottom of the trough. It had a spent cartridge in the breech. McRae showed the gun to Bob Bowman. He established it had belonged to Moncrieff. Had Lillian taken this rifle out to shoot her husband? The teenage girls had said she was holding her right hand against her coat. She could have been concealing the gun there. But what was her motive? McRae compared Thelma Smith's letters to a sample of Lillian's handwriting. To his eye, they were identical, and the content of these rambling and misspelled missives gave him all the motive he needed.

McRae, Crosbie and Ramus arrived at Moncrieff's deathbed to question Lillian again. She denied knowing anything about a gun or any letters. Ramus showed her the rifle and said they knew it was her husband's. McRae said the letters were in her handwriting. Now Lillian switched up her story. She'd written the letters for her illiterate friend Thelma, who, she claimed, had just left Wagga. Last night she and Moncrieff had gone out, not only to get water but to shoot feral cats that were preying on their fowls. She'd been carrying the .22. 'I didn't mean to shoot him ... I turned round to the left and I think that the rifle must have got caught in my coat and it went off.'

Lillian said she panicked, dropped the .22 in the trough and ran into camp with her story. Under further questioning, she cracked and admitted she was 'Thelma'. But despite what would be shown as incredibly incriminating content in her letters to Susan Pearce, Lillian maintained she'd shot Moncrieff by accident.

McRae arrested Lillian, took her to the Wagga Police Court and charged her with attempted murder. Yet few took notice of the small, weeping woman in custody that morning; all eyes were on Morey's trial, due to resume in the main court.

~

While the prosecution had spent three days constructing its case, the defence's arguments took just an hour. A groom at the Terminus Hotel said he'd known Morey for about three years and that he'd seen him in the pub's yard with the wagon. Two days later he'd seen him again at the hotel, his ear bleeding and blood on his white shirt, which tallied with what Lillian McIntyre also testified. A farmer told the court he'd offered Morey £5 for eight to ten days' work in early December. But the accused hadn't taken up the offer, and had instead gone off to The Rock. The defence reckoned this showed Morey had no need to murder Percy for money, because work was available if he wanted it.

Morey made an unsworn statement from the dock. 'Gentleman of the jury,' he began in a quiet voice, 'I never murdered Smith.' Everything had happened just as he told detectives. The blood on his shirt was the result of him getting on the booze at the Terminus and hurting his ear. As for the witnesses who'd seen him with Percy Smith, they were mistaken. Morey denied that he'd said anything to Susan Pearce about the murder, that he'd asked her to write a fake receipt and that he owned the bloodstained trousers. 'That is all, gentleman of the jury,' he said. 'I never hurt Smith. I place myself in your hands to say whether I am guilty or not guilty.'

Morey's barrister reiterated that his client had cooperated at every turn, that the evidence was purely circumstantial and that no one in The Rock had known Percy's name, so maybe there had been a mix-up. Playing the familiar card, he said Susan Pearce and Lillian McIntyre's evidence shouldn't be believed, and insinuated that they'd been coached by the cops. Further, detectives hadn't proved how Percy had died: it might've been suicide, accident or manslaughter, or he could have been murdered by someone else.

Summing up for the Crown, William Monahan defended the integrity of the police and Susan Pearce. He said other witness evidence was conclusive: Morey had been seen with Percy in The Rock; the wagon had been seen on the bush laneway; the next morning the accused had sold the dead man's possessions; and he'd lied about George McDonald, just as he'd lied about the bloody trousers found at the presumed murder scene. Monahan said an accident or suicide was too fantastic to consider.

The jury returned in under an hour: Edward Henry Morey was guilty of the murder of Percival Smith. Asked if he had anything to say, Morey maintained his innocence. *Truth* reported:

> The spectacle of the man will never be forgotten by those who saw him. There was a fearful moment when he was sentenced to hang and his right hand involuntarily went up and fumbled with the

knot of his tie. He gulped and his heaving chest revealed how he was panting for breath.

Back in his cell, awaiting transportation to Long Bay, Morey collapsed and cried for hours. In the adjoining cell, Lillian Anderson was also hysterical. Moncrieff had just died, and the charge against her was to be upgraded to murder.

It wasn't reported if these two distraught killers talked through the bars – or if Morey knew the wailing accused murderess was 'Thelma Smith'. Even though he was quickly whisked off next morning to the train, he'd be seeing his secret admirer again.

Escorted to Sydney by Detective-Constable Walkom, Morey couldn't sleep and often shuddered in silent sobs. Were his tears for what he'd done or because he might hang? Or was he an innocent man who might go to the gallows for a crime he didn't commit? If you accepted Morey's story about the other 'George McDonald', then much of the other evidence fitted with his claims. But that meant overlooking that so many people had seen Morey with the very distinctive Percy and his equally recognisable wagon, horse and dogs.

By investigating the 'George McDonald' claim and interviewing so many witnesses, McRae and Ramus had given Morey the benefit of the doubt and done their due diligence. Everything they learned about him matched what they'd known of his record, even if they couldn't put his past before the jury. But his criminal record could be considered by the Executive Council, when it considered whether Morey's death sentence should be commuted.

On 16 May, McRae and Ramus wrote a letter to the Executive Council, summarising what they knew:

> He first came in contact with the police in the month of April 1919 and since that time he has been convicted on 31 occasions.

His convictions include stealing, receiving, assault occasioning actual bodily harm, common assault, illegally use motor car, possession of o'possum skins, use cyanide for the destruction of o'possums and minor offences.

After describing his itinerant ways and criminal associations, the letter narrowed focus to what was most relevant to the Percy Smith case:

He is a man addicted to drink and when in that condition he becomes quarrelsome and very violent. Included in his convictions are five charges of assault and one charge of assault occasioning actual bodily harm and when committing these crimes his modus operandi was hitting men on the head with bottles and pieces of wood.

Morey's form fitted precisely with how Percy was killed. What wasn't in the letter but had made *The Daily Advertiser* was the defence Morey had offered in June 1932, after Ramus arrested him for having forty possum skins in his possession. Morey claimed he didn't know it was illegal to have them. That was pretty rich, given he had two previous convictions for the same offence.

Morey further claimed he had not poisoned the animals but bought the skins from 'Bill Davis', who should be easy to find because this bloke had been locked up for drunkenness. Ramus had remanded Morey for a week while he tried to verify this story. There was no record of any such drunkenness case in the district. Morey was convicted and fined £80.

Unless 'George McDonald' was holed up somewhere with 'Bill Davis', these not-for-trial details seemed to put beyond all doubt that Morey was a murderer who'd say anything to avoid the noose.

McRae's reputation as one of Australia's best detectives was further burnished by the remarkable work he did on the Human Glove mystery.

While the headline-grabbing forensics had established the dead man's identity, it had been the painstaking amassing of witness testimonies that had proved that Morey was a murderer. But McRae rightly shared the credit. In his internal memo summing up the case, he reported to his superiors that Ramus:

> ... displayed untiring energy and ability in the elucidation of this crime. He implicitly followed all my directions and suggestions regarding the case. He was an outstanding witness and is a smart and intelligent detective and as much credit for the solving of this crime belongs to him as to myself.

McRae was also fulsome in his praise of Crosbie, Walkom and other officers. Being in a murder squad meant being part of a team: patting everyone's back and having everyone's back.

33

Death Is Nothing When There Is Love

Morey was in Long Bay Gaol, preparing an appeal to show he'd been unfairly convicted, when the inquest into Moncrieff Anderson's death began on 18 May at Wagga Court.

Like Morey's and Craig's poor young wives, Lillian had been just a girl when she married Moncrieff in 1926. Fourteen and already pregnant, she'd have baby Joyce before her next birthday. Two years later, Moncrieff was smashed over the head with a bottle and rendered an invalid on a small pension. The injury made him prone to drinking, and when he was drunk he became aggressive. Lillian was afraid of him, and he was terribly jealous and wouldn't let her talk to other men. At least, this was what one of Lillian's sisters would later say. But Tent Town's Bob Bowman reckoned the couple appeared on good terms, and Moncrieff's brother James was to deny he'd been a drunk and said Moncrieff had treated Lillian well.

At the inquest, Detective-Constable Joe Ramus testified about Lillian changing her story and saying she'd shot her husband accidentally. McRae said he'd then asked her about knowing Morey and writing letters. Lillian had made denials and then, confronted with her handwriting, claimed she'd written them for Thelma Smith, whom she'd known for a decade, and who, inconveniently, was now nowhere to be found. Then, McRae testified, Lillian had cracked, confessing: 'I have told lies. I am Thelma

Smith. I have known Morey for eight or nine years. I met him at the Riverina Hotel but he did not know that it was me writing to him.' Yet Lillian had maintained she shot her husband by accident. But the letters McRae had seen made this impossible to believe.

The court was first read the letters 'Thelma' wrote to Morey. They also heard his reply. Susan Pearce testified she'd been given this letter by Lillian for safekeeping. On the day Moncrieff was shot, the accused had asked about it in her latest letter to Susan, in which she also said her husband was a mongrel who beat her. All eight letters that 'Thelma' wrote to Susan were read in court. They were startling and increasingly deranged.

'Thelma' had started her letters to Susan by claiming to have known 'Teddie' for ten years. She wrote that she was now pregnant to a violent mongrel named Jack Hargraves, who wanted to marry her. Jack beat her and threatened to kill her because she was in love with Ted Morey. But back in June 1933, Thelma wrote, it'd been a drunken lecher with a lisp named Percy Debit – aka Percy Smith – who had wanted her for his wife. So, if Ted had killed Percy Smith, then he'd done the poor sod a favour.

Thelma wrote that she believed Ted was guilty and she wished she could get rid of the evidence that would be used against him, particularly those bloodstained trousers. But even if he was convicted, she'd wait for him. As the letters to Susan continued, Thelma told her of beatings she'd suffered as Jack pressured her to marry him – which she'd never do. Susan, she said, should reply to her care of 'Lena Anderson', or else Jack would get her mail and there'd be even more hell to pay. Lena, Thelma confided, was the wife of a witness against Morey – and Lena's husband knocked her around too, even though 'she's a clean little thing; too good for him, I think'. Her last letter to Susan lurched further into fantasy to describe the last time she'd seen Ted:

> Even the day he said goodbye to me, I put my arms around his neck
> and cried to him to stop with me, and he said, 'Look, Thelma, I

love you and you only and death is nothing when there's love, so I can't put up with you telling me what to do.' Poor Ted. Does he think of my words now?

And, seemingly forgetting she was supposed to be Thelma, Lillian wrote what sounded very much like a request that Susan Pearce organise an assault on her actual husband:

> [Moncrieff] Anderson was going to hit me. I would go to the police only Ted's in enough bother with them. I would like to see him get his guts kicked out ... Put someone up to kick Anderson to pieces and I'll know nothing. You'll know nothing. If Ted hangs, I'll die. Life won't be worth living.

Hours after Susan received this letter, Lillian had shot Moncrieff Anderson in the head.

Lillian was tried for murder at Sydney's Central Criminal Court on Monday 18 June 1934. The prosecution called the same witnesses – police and civilian – who'd testified at the inquest. The letters were read again. The defence called Long Bay Gaol's prison surgeon and a Macquarie Street specialist, who'd both examined the accused while she was in custody. They reported that Lillian was erratic, emotionally unstable and had the mentality of a twelve-year-old girl. She was the sort of childish personality that fell deeply in love with movie stars and the fictional heroes they played – and this was the sort of fantasy Morey had become to her. Nevertheless, the two doctors had concluded that Lillian was sane.

Matilda Anderson – the wife of Moncrieff's brother James – testified that Lillian had said Moncrieff hit her, and had shown the bruises these beatings inflicted. Morey was called by the defence. Asked if he'd ever seen the accused before, he firmly said he had not. 'Did you ever know anyone by the name of Lillian Anderson or Thelma Smith?' Morey said no – and was returned to Long Bay.

Presumably, the defence called Morey to show that Lillian's letters were pure fantasy, and thus to lessen her motive for murder. In another dramatic turn, her defence barrister called the accused's little daughter, Joyce, who was sobbing as she entered the witness box. Lillian wept. So did many women in the court. A juryman also dabbed away tears. Lillian's barrister said he couldn't go through with the questioning because the child had suffered enough. Joyce was led from the court, her wails echoing through the building. It was likely this had been a cynical ploy to remind the jury that the accused woman was a mother.

Lillian spoke from the dock. Rather than the usual sort of unsworn address, which simply repeated denials already related in police evidence about statements the accused had made, she dropped a bombshell. Lillian said Percy Smith had actually come to Narrandera common in December 1933 – one month later than had been firmly established in Morey's trial. Moncrieff had argued with him, she claimed, and Percy had left shortly after. Moncrieff had followed and returned a few days later with a bloodstained shirt. Her husband wouldn't say what had happened.

Then a letter had arrived for Moncrieff. He was illiterate, so she read it to him:

> Well, mate, I got rid of the turnout which you left me with; I sold it for so much I've got £6 on me. I am enclosing you £3 and I am keeping £3 ... You were a bloody mug. Why didn't you tell me what was in the wagonette? I got rid of it to a fellow and I told him to take it and sell it and I would him send him a receipt through the WPO. And if there is anything about it, I know nothing, you know nothing, nor my mate.

Lillian said Moncrieff tore up the letter. When Percy's body was found, he warned her to keep her mouth shut – which she'd done out of fear, as McRae made his investigations at Narrandera. Later, Lillian told the court, Moncrieff confessed he'd caught up with Percy, they'd got drunk and argued, and he'd hit him, first with a bottle of wine before finishing him off with a tomahawk. Moncrieff put him in the chaff bag and dumped him in the river, making the mistake of leaving a pair of bloodstained trousers. On his way back to The Rock, he'd met two swaggies – one tall, one small – and given them the wagon and goods to sell.

When Lillian and Moncrieff had been in Wagga for the inquest and trial, he'd kept close watch on her so she couldn't reveal anything to McRae or to Morey's defence lawyer. On 10 May, he was drunk and hit her, which was par for the course. But, reaching the water trough that night, she saw Moncrieff had the .22 and intended to kill her: 'When I stopped, I heard [a] click, and when I did, I just happened to look and I saw the rifle. I grabbed for the rifle. When I did so, I do not know what happened. But if I shot him, it was accidental.'

Lillian told the court she remembered nothing until McRae questioned her the following morning. He'd frightened her and she told him lies. As for why she wrote the eight letters to Susan? They were apparently Moncrieff's doing; he'd stood over her, telling her what to write. The 'logic' was impenetrable:

> He said, 'I want to get all the evidence I can against that fellow that had the wagonette.' He said: 'I want you to write letters to Mrs Pearce', which I did. He told me the things to put in the letters and not to claim my own name. When I wrote them he said, 'You are going to get into serious trouble.' I said, 'What for?' He said, 'For writing letters under a false name.' No doubt I did put some things in the letters and a good lot of it he told me to put in. He said he wanted to get all the evidence he could to clear his own shoulders when he told me what he had done.

In terms of fanciful defences, it rivalled Moxley's story about Snowy Mumby, not least by rewriting the timeline of Percy Smith's arrival in Narrandera and ignoring Morey's well-documented time with the man in The Rock. The Crown argued that Lillian's story was merely the continuation of an obsessed woman's deranged fantasy, meant to save herself and the murderer she imagined was her lover.

The defence argued that the letters and everything else to do with Morey was completely immaterial. The prosecution had presented a weak circumstantial case. All that mattered was this: did Lillian shoot her husband deliberately? She was a brutalised young wife who'd grabbed reflexively in self-defence when her beastly husband pulled a rifle on her. Moncrieff Anderson's death was a tragic accident, and she'd initially lied to the police because she was a panicked woman in shock.

A jury had decided Morey's fate in less than an hour. Now, the dozen men deliberated all afternoon and through the night. They couldn't reach a verdict.

~

A retrial was ordered, commencing on 25 July at the Wagga Court House. After hearing all the evidence again, the new jury deliberated overnight. The next morning, their foreman announced they couldn't agree. This legal impasse saw Morey seek leave to appeal against his conviction. Whether he lived or died might hinge on the outcome of Lillian's case. If juries couldn't find her guilty, that meant they accepted – or at least didn't reject entirely – her story that Moncrieff had killed Percy Smith and given the wagon to two men to sell, one of whom might have called himself 'George McDonald'.

~

Lillian's third trial began on 5 September in Wagga Court and repeated what had been said previously. The accused made another impassioned plea of accidental self-defence, saying she saw Moncrieff with the gun and reacted instinctively to grab it: 'I had no intention of doing him any harm. I never murdered my husband and will say so to my dying day.'

The new jury debated overnight and returned to the court the next morning to say they needed more time. An hour later, they requested another extension. When this third jury came back a third time on the third day of the third trial, they had decided that Lillian Anderson was guilty – but only of the manslaughter of her husband.

Justice Horace Markell said he'd never heard a worse case of manslaughter. He would have imposed a life sentence if not for her low intelligence and the fact she'd had very little chance in life. Instead, he gave Lillian Anderson twenty years.

~

After Lillian's conviction, Morey was denied the right to appeal. Despite McRae and Ramus's letter, which made it clear Morey had been a veteran violent criminal before he murdered Percy Smith, the Executive Council commuted his death sentence to life imprisonment. Like Craig, he was 'never to be released'.

The gruesome exhibit that was the human glove had a long posthumous life in its jar of formalin as part of a post-war New South Wales police exhibition that toured the state. The puffy thing – which was slowly going to pieces – was even displayed at the Easter Show in 1950.

By then, Lillian Anderson, having been released in 1944, was living in obscurity. Still protesting his innocence, Ted Morey was set free at Christmas in 1953 because he was suffering tuberculosis. The conditions of his freedom were that he get treatment at a private hospital and not run afoul of the law, lest he serve the rest of his life sentence. Morey recovered from his TB, was released from hospital, moved to Orange and was convicted in March 1955 of driving a truck while drunk without a licence. The judge had no choice but to send him back to gaol. Morey spent the rest of his life behind bars, dying in North Ryde Psychiatric Hospital in November 1977 at the age of eighty.

34

The Pyjama Girl

For a frustrating week, Lillian Anderson's third trial kept McRae from the most famous Australian murder case of the 1930s. But once he began investigating, he'd never be able to shake it.

Around nine on the morning of Saturday 1 September 1934, about four miles north of Albury, a local man named Tom Griffith made a horrific discovery. The twenty-three-year-old was leading one of his family's prized bulls home from the Holbrook Show. As the beast had a sore hoof, they took the grassy verge beside the Howlong Road. Not far from home, in the shadow of a brick culvert, Tom saw a human body. The head and shoulders were hidden inside a charred sack. But there was no mistaking glimpses of torso and thighs clad in scorched scraps of colourful material, and lower legs crammed into the open mouth of a narrow drainage pipe. Terror-stricken, Tom tied up his bull, hailed a local who was riding past, borrowed the fellow's bicycle and rode home as quickly as he could to phone the Albury police.

Inspector David Goodsell, Detective-Sergeant George Cleaver and the local government medical officer Dr Leslie Woods were soon on the scene, noticing the area around the body smelled of kerosene and that there was an oily substance on the grass. Inside the pipe, the feet were badly burned, as were the thighs. The men eased the upper half of the body from the sack and unwrapped a partly burned towel around the head.

The officers and doctor gazed on the face of a young woman. She had a small circular injury beneath her right eye, a larger wound beneath her left eye and a terrible penetrating injury that exposed the brain on her left forehead. There were other fracture wounds to the left side of her head. She'd been bent – thighs up to her chin, hands behind her head – and her shins and feet put into the hole. A blaze had been set with the accelerant, but the fire had died down before the body was charred beyond recognition. It would probably have been doused by rain, for there was standing water in the ditch. On close examination, what remained of the canary-coloured material appeared to be pyjamas. There was also a fragment of a Melbourne newspaper in the drain. But the body was in New South Wales, so the Albury detectives called the Sydney CIB.

With McRae due in Wagga Wagga to give evidence in Lillian Anderson's third trial, Childs and Prior conferred and sent Detective-Sergeant Len Allmond, veteran murder investigator, with Detective-Constable Darcy McDermott, who'd assisted McRae in the Dorothy Thorne investigation. Until they arrived, the victim was to be guarded in situ. The story was big news in Sydney's *The Sun* that evening – and, as with the Human Glove case, the paper sent a reporter and photographer on the train with the police. Given the murder scene was closer to Melbourne, it was also a big story in that evening's *Herald*. But it'd be the Sydney tabloid, in its Sunday edition, that dubbed her 'Pyjama Girl' in its front-page headline.

Readers of both papers learned what she'd looked like in life: about twenty years old, pretty, blue or grey eyes, pencilled eyebrows, fair complexion, good teeth with no fillings, manicured fingernails, light-brown bobbed hair, standing around five-foot-three and weighing maybe eight stone. They read what was known of the sack, towel and pyjamas.

From the girl's appearance, local police believed she'd been from the city rather than the country, perhaps even an actress or a singer.

While the Albury detectives waited for Allmond and McDermott, they began chasing up reports of local girls reported missing recently, and interviewing folks who lived near the culvert to see if anyone remembered seeing anything unusual in the past few days. They'd soon speak to a man who'd driven past around 2.30am the previous Wednesday – 29 August – and seen flames flickering up from the culvert. He'd assumed it was a swaggie's fire for boiling a billy. Other drivers who had passed by as early as 1am reported seeing nothing. This suggested the time frame in which the murderer – or murderers – had tried to burn the body before rain soon after 2.30am thwarted the attempt. Tyre marks on the grassy verge indicated a car had skidded, perhaps as the culprit took off, fearing passing drivers might remember him.

Allmond and McDermott inspected the scene and then supervised the removal of the body to the Albury morgue for Dr Woods to perform the autopsy. He believed she was twenty-five to thirty years old. Her death had been caused by a fractured skull – she'd been hit about seven times, likely with a tyre lever or similar weapon. Her hair had been dyed, showing dark at the roots, and, contrary to initial observations, she'd had some work done on her teeth, so they would need to follow up by investigating dental records. As she'd been wearing pyjamas, and her injuries had been inflicted on the left side of her head, it was theorised that she'd been asleep when battered, so somewhere there had to be a bloodstained mattress. And a well-groomed girl like this surely had plenty of clothes, accessories and jewellery. Had the killer disposed of this evidence already?

As always, identifying the victim was the immediate priority. Compared with the Bungendore Bones case, there was plenty for Allmond to work with. He ordered the fingerprints be taken, but a comparison with those on record at Albury turned up nothing, so copies were sent to Sydney and Melbourne. Even if her prints weren't on file, the police were still miles ahead of where they'd been with the Human Glove case. Once the fire was out, the towel had helped preserve her features. As *The*

Sun put it that day: 'Anyone knowing the girl would be able to readily recognise her face.' Her distinctive outfit could also be the key: 'Anyone knowing a girl owning white pyjamas with yellow borders is asked to communicate immediately with the police.'

Allmond decided to pursue an 'unusual' strategy – allow the public to see the body. Given that a positive identification might rely on an eyewitness viewing the corpse, he had to ensure it was preserved for as long as possible, so he had it packed in 250 pounds of crushed ice. That night, and on Monday, Albury people queued up to see her. Those not up to gazing directly on the poor woman could look at photographs of her face. Hopes for an early breakthrough were dashed. No one knew her. Already questions were being raised about how long the Pyjama Girl's features could be kept intact, with *The Sun* reporting: 'If identification is delayed, the head may be preserved in spirit.'

Allmond didn't think the killer or killers were locals. No one who knew the area would choose the culvert beside a well-travelled road as the best spot to dispose of a body. While it wasn't visible from the road, the flames had been, and there was open country – not a tree or bush in sight – for hundreds of yards in all directions. Why not dump her in the Murray? Or in one of the nearby lagoons? Allmond envisaged a stranger driving long miles through the night, and then – perhaps fearing coming into Albury up ahead – pulling over in a panic to hurriedly go about the burning. Arguing against this was the picture of a killer risking a long journey with a dead body, passing by any number of better bush hiding spots. It was three hours from Melbourne, three times that from Sydney; Allmond figured it was more likely the murder had been committed within a radius of fifty to seventy miles.

With no one yet identifying the Pyjama Girl, Allmond and his colleagues worked with the little they had. The towel had a laundry mark – RIW or RIN, QIW or QIN – and the sack still bore part of a stencilled DE. These details – along with an update on the girl's dentition, to include she'd had wisdom teeth excised and a gold filling and gold inlay – were circulated in the newspapers. *The Sun*'s photographer captured the lonely crime scene, the detectives examining the evidence, and took close-ups of the tyre marks and pyjama and towel remnants, returning to Sydney by Monday 10.15am so the pictures could be in the paper two hours later. He'd also taken post-mortem photos of the girl, which were used for a line portrait of the victim run on the front page the following day, along with the headline: 'Do You Know This Girl?' But evidently Childs and perhaps *The Sun*'s editor weren't satisfied with the likeness, as more photos were supplied and the day afterwards a more lifelike illustration – close to photographic in style – appeared in the paper.

Fingerprint records in Sydney and Melbourne turned up nothing. This disappointment was reported in all the newspapers. But what police keep secret – in order to weed out cranks making false confessions – were the results of Dr Woods' X-ray of the Pyjama Girl. It revealed that the small wound beneath her right eye was caused by a bullet that had deflected down and become lodged at the left side of her neck, below her skull. Dr Woods performed a dissection to retrieve the slug, but concluded this wound hadn't been fatal. This injury, which was on the right side of her face, taken with bruising to her body, suggested she hadn't been asleep when attacked and had possibly fought back. But the bullet – identified as having been fired from a .25-calibre Webley & Scott automatic pistol – might prove crucial, as had been the case in the Rowland shooting. Detectives in New South Wales and Victoria set about locating and testing every pistol of this make on their registers.

Up at Wagga Wagga, McRae was surely following every development, especially as his colleagues Detective-Constable Ramus and Inspector McIntosh were enlisted in the search, following up a 'theatrical pair' who'd married in the town recently. The bride was apparently the spitting image of the Pyjama Girl. Happily, she was alive and well. But, given Wagga was just eighty miles up the road from Albury, Ramus and McIntosh would continue to look into show people in the Riverina and the young women who sometimes travelled with them.

By Wednesday, 250 people had seen the body on ice and another 400 had seen the photos. Thirty reports of missing women and girls with light-brown hair had been investigated by Allmond, McDermott and Cleaver. All had been traced or ruled out.

A circular with the case details and three post-mortem photos – two front-on, and one profile – was posted to every police station in New South Wales. Albury dentist Francis Jackson did an extensive examination of the Pyjama Girl's mouth. Wisdom teeth didn't usually come through until eighteen; the two the girl was missing had been removed no more than five years ago, he reported, so she was no younger than twenty-three. Jackson also described the work done on six teeth in minute detail. The dentistry was top-notch, which suggested she was – or at least had once been – in good financial circumstances or from a well-off family.

Jackson extracted the six teeth that had had dental work. Then, battling blood, saliva and what seemed to be sand in the cadaver's oral cavity, he took dental moulds of her remaining upper and lower teeth. From these, he made casts, setting her six real teeth into position beside the plaster ones. His creation was photographed and the pictures circulated to dentists around Australia. To these professionals, it would be as unique as a fingerprint. 'They are the finest set of teeth I have ever seen and any dentist treating them should remember the girl,' Jackson said. His work was acclaimed as a first in Australian crime detection. But the pistol tracing and testing – involving hundreds of guns – hadn't turned up the murder weapon.

Hundreds of people contacted the Sydney and Melbourne CIBs with information about missing wives, daughters, sisters, friends and girlfriends. Each report would have to be followed up. But by the time they had been investigated, the police were still no closer to putting a name to the face now known all over Australia.

35

The World's Greatest Mystery

On Friday 7 September, at Wagga Wagga, with Lillian Anderson convicted of manslaughter, Tom McRae was ordered to Albury to take charge of the Pyjama Girl investigation. By the following morning, he'd arrived at a place that had to bring back memories both sweet and sad. A quarter of a century earlier, this had been his first wife Mildred's home town. McRae was met not only by Allmond and McDermott but also by Inspector Prior, who'd come down from Sydney. Once the CIB chief had conferred with his men and met the Albury police, he officially requested assistance from his Victorian counterpart, General Thomas Blamey, who agreed to put his officers under the direction of the New South Wales detectives.

It had been a week since the Pyjama Girl was found. A £250 reward was announced – with *Truth* posting its own £100 bounty for information leading to the killer. While an Albury sergeant was daily replenishing the ice that kept her chilled, she couldn't be kept this way indefinitely; already her features were beginning to contort and there was talk she'd need to be buried in a few days. Rather than the proposed solution – decapitation and preservation of the head in a jar of formalin – McRae had a better idea. It'd never been tried before with a murder victim, but they could have her embalmed. Done well, she might be restored to a more lifelike appearance, and she'd be available for identification purposes for as long as it took. McRae suggested that, if identification still proved elusive, she could be taken to Sydney University, where Dr Burkitt, who'd assisted on the Bungendore Bones case, might analyse her and provide more information.

In Sydney, funeral director Charles Kinsela volunteered to do the work. His family had been in the business for a century, and he'd recently visited America to learn the latest embalming methods. Preserving the Pyjama Girl would be a challenge – and a publicity opportunity.

In Albury, McRae and colleagues followed every lead. A Wagga motorist viewed the body and said there was a 'striking resemblance' to a girl with a male companion to whom he'd given a lift to Albury on 20 August. A member of a sideshow troupe said that, a day or two before the murder, he saw a woman like the Pyjama Girl try to flee a car on a remote road north-west of Albury, only for a man to bring her back to the vehicle.

McRae and colleagues investigated these and plenty of other stories of men and young women arguing in cars parked on various roads on the night the body was dumped. Police searched the Murray River's banks, looking for personal effects, bloodstained foliage or anything else. Every farmhouse within several miles of the road from Albury to Corowa was visited. McRae directed that police begin canvassing every house in Albury, which had a population of 11,000. Hundreds of district people had by then inspected the body. Still they kept coming, all day long, despite drizzling rain.

Truth – which, like *The Daily Telegraph*, ran its own 'official' illustration of the Pyjama Girl – was typically verbose when it set out everything known about 'the most dastardly crime of a generation', committed against the 'perfect specimen of a young Australian girl on the threshold of womanhood'. It called on readers to play detective, because 'everyone can join in this hunt for the murderer by reading carefully through this newspaper's story today, and sifting the clues and theories'. The paper had an eye on circulation but was also doing the police's bidding with such appeals.

But with hundreds of missing-girl reports flooding in from all over Australia leading nowhere, what was increasingly difficult to understand was why *no one* had missed the Pyjama Girl. McRae and Allmond wondered whether she had been killed by one family member and the rest of the clan had clammed up. Certainly Sidney Morrison's people had known he had a .22 and was distressed and depressed before he disappeared. They hadn't come forward to say he might've been the Bungendore Bones – and even after it had been proved it was him, they wouldn't accept the shame of suicide. How much more motivation might a family have to protect a father, husband, brother or son, particularly if such a man also made threats against them?

While his colleagues continued their enquiries in Albury, McRae on Monday 10 September went to Melbourne with the pyjamas, the sack and the towel. The towel was identified as having been made in Japan; a large number had been imported into Sydney and Melbourne the previous year. At Melbourne police headquarters at Russell Street, the laundry mark was subjected to UV rays; the best analysis said the letters were 'RCO'. This information, along with details of the case and photos of the towel and laundry mark, would be used in queries made to hotels and boarding houses.

Further, under McRae's direction, Detective-Constable Alfred Wilks, whose duty was correspondence relating to identification, liaised with the secretaries of the New South Wales and Victorian associations of laundry owners, with details sent to all their members. No one identified the towel or the mark. To McRae this suggested it was a private mark used by an unregistered laundress working from home.

UV analysis revealed the sack's 'DE' stencil was part of the words '1st GRADE' below the letters 'DALM'. McRae concluded the missing letters would've spelled 'DALMORE'. Dalmore was a potato-growing district in Gippsland, but this revelation didn't help much because these sacks were very common all over Victoria and the Riverina.

Meanwhile, the pyjama fragments were reported to be made of crepe thought to have been imported from China. There were illegible markings on a hem that might be the letters A, M, C and/or O and spell part of a name like 'Pamela' or 'Cameron'. A Sydney merchant told Crosbie and Wilks that he was sure the design included a dragon embroidered in white silk on the coat. The consignment had been imported around 1930. But they weren't rare – sold in New South Wales and Victoria, in city and country stores, for 27/6. A photo of such a coat was printed in the papers, *Truth* putting a model in the dragon design on the front page. Analysis on the hem characters would continue.

On 12 September, Charles Kinsela and his son Charles Jr arrived in Albury to do their best with the Pyjama Girl. In case the 'experiment' didn't work, a Sydney constable took a plaster cast of the girl's head. Over ten hours, the Kinselas wielded their tubes and chemicals, powdered her face, rouged her lips, pencilled her eyebrows, darkened her eyelashes, shampooed and styled the hair. The operation was reported as a success. *Truth* claimed of the 'little Cinderella': 'Were it not for that waxen pallor of death, the unknown pyjama girl might be in a doze, for she looks so natural.' It was another historic day in Australian policing. *The Herald* in Melbourne reported: 'This is the first time in the annals of Australian crime that a murder victim's body had been embalmed, and it is the first time, also, that a plaster cast of a victim's face has been taken by the police.'

But Charles Kinsela Jr gave a detail that was at odds with the description now in circulation for weeks, one that might also cast doubt on the idea that the girl was a sophisticated glamour, telling *Truth* that, in his opinion, her nails 'had not been well manicured, as was officially announced. The nails were short, rather rough, and dirty.'

While the Pyjama Girl was now embalmed, she'd still be kept on ice in Albury. If it proved necessary to take her to Sydney, McRae wanted her preserved in formalin. So far, 500 people had viewed the body, while thousands had seen the photos. Detectives working out of Albury, in conjunction with their colleagues in Melbourne, Sydney and other state capitals, had traced 350 missing girls – with a dozen or so still unaccounted for.

Hopes were repeatedly raised and dashed. Seven witnesses in Sydney – including a King's Counsel – swore the girl had worked for a Waverley doctor before vanishing. She was quickly found, alive and now employed as a maid in a city restaurant. A woman said her friend Beryl Cashmere had definitely owned the pyjamas and had gone to Albury. For a few days she was a good bet as the murder victim – but was then found in her native New Zealand, having never even been to Australia. In Sydney, a married man burst into tears when he saw the photo. He was sure it was his wife, missing for a year, and the dental work resembled hers. Within thirty-six hours, the police had found the wife – and the grateful husband promptly declared he was going to divorce his runaway missus.

Sydney dentists contacted police to say they'd worked on the Pyjama Girl's mouth. But each was mistaken. By mid-September, almost every house in Albury had been visited, and most in Wodonga. Up and down the Hume Highway, restaurant and garage owners were asked about any driver behaving unusually around the time the killer had tried to burn the body. Police on road duty were asked about any motorist who'd hurried away or been nervous when spoken to. They checked every interstate car that had passed through Albury in the past two months, as such border-crossing visitors on the Hume were required to stop and get a sticker. The reward was doubled to £500. It included a free pardon for any accomplice not directly involved.

McRae had cracked the Bungendore Bones with the help of Scotland Yard. If no one in Australia had missed the Pyjama Girl, it was reasonable to think she might be from overseas. From the third week in September, Wilks began sending requests all across the globe. Over the next month, police chiefs in London, Paris, Berlin, New York, Los Angeles, Shanghai, Hong Kong, Manila, Pretoria and eighty other cities would receive the case files – photos, fingerprints, descriptions, everything. Cables came back with the names of missing women who might conceivably have gone to Australia. They were either found alive and well or were eliminated. The best lead, a young Englishwoman last seen in Shanghai, was found in Brisbane. She was a wanderer and unaware that for a few days she'd been the focus of the biggest murder investigation in Australian history. Police continued to visit hotels, boarding houses and laundries, wheat and potato merchants, as the number of letters and missing girl reports continued to rise.

On 11 October, with some 1000 people having viewed the preserved body and the Albury witness pool exhausted, the Pyjama Girl was sent to Sydney University and placed in a zinc-lined, coffin-like box filled with formalin. She had a collar around her neck, so she could be lifted from the fluid for witnesses. But before any such viewings, Dr Burkitt made his examination and a week later provided new details to narrow the search slightly. She'd been within two years of twenty-five, and had stood an inch on either side of five foot. But what was particular were her ears, their edges imperfect, both with very little in the way of lobes. This was reported in the papers – and a revised sketch, with a fuller face, was released. The more definitive age range would be used in another widescale strategy: tracing every woman who'd failed to vote in the September federal election.

As police set about this mammoth task, McRae finally had an answer about the markings on the pyjamas. They were Chinese characters that translated as 'Hung Ching Kee', the name of a small factory in Shanghai. They'd supplied huge numbers of these pyjamas and the clue didn't lead anywhere.

On 23 November, after two and half months in Albury, McRae was recalled to Sydney. But he'd barely had time to see his wife when he was off again, checking fruitless information in Newcastle, before returning to interview a crook in Long Bay. In December, in London, *The Dental Magazine and Oral Topics*, which was circulated to dentists throughout the world, ran the Pyjama Girl story over three pages – including, of course, photos of the remarkable work that Francis Jackson had done on the teeth, mould and description.

New Year's Day 1935 marked the fourth month since the Pyjama Girl's body had been found. But there was now hope of a breakthrough. Playing his cards close to his chest, McRae had a good lead and was on the train to Wagga Wagga, before he went on to Albury, then to Melbourne, then back to Sydney and up to the North Coast and Northern Rivers. *Truth* reported that McRae was now on a 'roving commission' to follow his own 'lone-hand enquiries unhampered by instructions. He will be able to go where he likes in the pursuit of the new trail and all police facilities, such as fast motor transport, will be at his complete disposal.' McRae's hush-hush investigations had been the result of a woman positively identifying the Pyjama Girl and naming a man last seen with her. McRae tracked this suspect to northern NSW, where he detained and interviewed him. But the fellow had a rock-solid alibi – he'd been in hospital from 29 August to 5 September. The lookalike woman he'd been seen with was also determined to be alive. The man was released. McRae was back at square one.

In Sydney, an average of four people a day gazed on the Pyjama Girl, glazed face dripping with formalin, before they shook their heads and said: 'No, I don't know her.'

By the end of January 1935, some 1000 missing girl reports had come into the investigation. McRae would henceforth investigate the Pyjama Girl while also being available for other cases. In mid-February he worked grisly back-to-back tragedies, the first involving a country man gored to death by a bull and the second a horrific city murder-suicide. In April, eight months into the case, an Austrian countess who'd visited Australia in 1929 was thrown into the mix as a possible Pyjama Girl. It took a day to establish that she was living with her count on the other side of the world. A few days after that, Australia had a new mystery to fascinate in a case known as 'the Shark Arm Murder', which Allmond and McDermott would help investigate. By July 1935, McRae had covered 4000 miles, and around 5000 letters had been received, making for a stack of files that stood up to his shoulders. Total expenses for the investigation – salaries, travel, accommodation, postage and more postage – had reached £10,000. During that time, in addition to the usual hoaxes, cranks, psychics and astrologers offering to assist, five swaggies had confessed to the murder and had been released.

The first anniversary passed without any breakthroughs. By the time the second anniversary approached, the most promising possible Pyjama Girl was a German lass named Emmie Behrendt, last been seen in Sydney in 1934. It was mooted that Commissioner MacKay, who'd succeeded Childs in March 1935, might make personal enquiries about her while in Berlin, where he was studying the policing methods used by those Nazi models of investigative efficiency.

In 1935, Walter Warneford, who'd infiltrated the New Guard for MacKay and who was still on the police payroll, provided a Pyjama Girl tip that came from his housemate, George Kemphe. Kemphe thought the dead girl was English immigrant Linda Platt, twenty-five, who, though married already back home, had wed an Italian man named Antonio Agostini. Linda had unusual ears and was known to have pyjamas like the famous pair. Her husband, once a waiter at Romano's restaurant in Sydney, had a violent temper and had threatened to kill her. Linda's husband was now in Melbourne and she'd not been seen for some time.

Warneford's informant hadn't come forward earlier because the person didn't want to get Linda in trouble for bigamy. Wilks arranged a viewing – and Kemphe thought it closely resembled Linda. But extensive enquiries in Melbourne, including interviews with her Italian husband

and follow-ups by Wilks, led him to conclude she didn't resemble the Pyjama Girl. She had different dental work, brown eyes rather than blue, and a much longer nose.

In May 1937, McRae had another promising lead when Jeanette Routledge, from Bomaderry, said the Pyjama Girl was her illegitimate daughter, Anna Philomena Morgan, who'd left home in 1930 at the age of eighteen. McRae took the witness to the University of Sydney, re-enacting a ritual he'd performed countless times by now. Warning the woman the body she was about to see may not be her daughter, he led her to the coffin of formalin. Mrs Routledge would say:

> The body was hooked out of the liquid by him in my presence. I looked at the face, which was battered and hideously mangled, and I was too overcome with horror to inspect it. I had an overwhelming desire to get out of the room and out of sight of the body, and I therefore said to the police officer, 'I cannot recognise her. She is not my daughter.'

While the Pyjama Girl case remained unsolved, it hadn't reflected badly on McRae, who'd had notable successes over the past two years.

In November 1935, McRae, now working under Commissioner MacKay, led the investigation into the murder of a man he'd known: sixty-five-year-old Montague Henwood. This veteran industrial advocate was the state's Conciliation Commissioner, and his body had been found thrown beside railway tracks in the Blue Mountains.

It wasn't long before McRae and Wilks traced the killer, who'd used one of his victim's cheques, and seventeen-year-old Edwin John Hickey made a handwritten statement confessing to the crime. But he claimed Henwood had gone crazy in the carriage and attacked him first. Hickey said he lost his temper, battered the man to death with a bottle, robbed his corpse and tossed it headfirst from the train. McRae didn't believe the self-defence claim. Neither did the jury, who opted against a manslaughter conviction. The boy was sentenced to death. It was reported that if Hickey hanged, he'd be the youngest person ever executed in New South Wales. Leaving aside early colonial executions, this was likely true.

A vocal campaign for mercy was led by Jack Lang, Labor opposition leader, and Donald Grant, MacKay's old IWW enemy and now a member of the Legislative Council. They even appealed to Prime Minister Joe Lyons to intervene. In addition to Hickey's age, they argued that hanging him would be a travesty given so many others had recently been saved from the gallows, either because they received manslaughter convictions or their death sentences had been commuted. This roll call included Maurice O'Hara, Eric Craig, Claude Wallace and Eric Newlyn, Ted Morey and Lillian Anderson – all killers that McRae was largely credited with catching.

But before the New South Wales Executive Council made its final decision on Hickey, the homicide chief had another murder file on his desk: the February 1936 Darlinghurst shooting of garage owner Norman Stead during a robbery gone wrong. There were echoes of the John Rowland murder: two youths seen running from the scene, having stolen just £8; the victim killed by a bullet through the lung, fired in a panic when he resisted; one thug thought more responsible than the other. Detectives Wilks and Allmond soon had twenty-one-year-old John Leighton Massey in custody. He confessed that he'd had his confederate, twenty-two-year-old Aubrey Potter, dispose of the .25-calibre pistol used in the murder. But Massey had forgotten about an incriminating bullet in his pocket. Following the usual playbook, he said he'd only decided to rob the garage because he was broke, that he'd only carried the gun with the intention of scaring his victim, and that it'd gone off by accident during a struggle. McRae scooped up Potter and took his corroborative statement about the whole sorry business.

But this jury would not stand accused of being chicken-hearted: they found both young men guilty of murder. They were sentenced to death.

Around this time, there were four further recently convicted murderers in the shadow of the gallows – including two other seventeen-year-old boys, who'd separately killed graziers near Wagga and Tamworth.

On 14 May 1936, young Edwin Hickey was hanged at Long Bay Gaol, the first execution since Moxley. The huge backlash likely helped save the four other murderers – including the teenagers – who were reprieved by the Executive Council. Potter also dodged the noose, his sentence reduced to fifteen years. But there was no mercy for John Massey, who went to the hangman on 15 June.

~

Though he'd been homicide chief for three years, McRae was only promoted to Detective-Sergeant First Class in April 1937. When a magistrate next saw him in the witness box, he asked if it was correct he'd been bumped up. *The Daily Telegraph* reported that McRae answered with a modest yes. The magistrate then offered a 'remarkable tribute', breaking protocol to say: 'Allow me to congratulate you on a very merited promotion and I hope that very soon you will be promoted to commissioned rank, which you so richly deserve.'

But this period was less favourable for MacKay, whose reputation was tarnished in 1936 by a royal commission into illegal gambling and by his victimisation of a constable, which led to another royal commission the following year. The Police Association of New South Wales, which MacKay had created, was also turning against him for his dictatorial ways and blatant favouritism.

~

In January 1938, the coronial inquest into the Pyjama Girl's death was finally held at Albury. Unlike other such murder inquiries, which typically saw dozens of people testify, there were only four witnesses: Tom Griffith, the lad who'd found the body; Constable Kelly, the Albury cop who was first on the scene; Dr Woods, who'd done the autopsy; and McRae, who'd led the investigation since the end of the first week. Only now was it revealed that the Pyjama Girl had been shot in the face, the bullet lodging in her neck. Other than that, McRae's long testimony set out what he and his colleagues had done and the dead end at which they'd arrived. All up, some 3000 files of women and girls reported missing in Sydney and Melbourne, plus more from other states, had been investigated.

McRae said he believed it was as possible the victim had been killed in New South Wales as in Victoria. But he was no closer to identifying her. Yet he didn't believe, he said, that she should be buried even now. 'I consider that, in the interests of justice, the body should be kept as long as possible in case her identity can be established in the future,' he said. 'It is apparent [that] if she were buried, all means of identification would be lost. Enquiries about the identity of the woman and the manner and place in which she met her death are being continued.'

The coroner said that even though they had failed, New South Wales could offer nothing but unstinting praise for McRae, Allmond, McDermott and Wilks – and all the police involved – for their 'unceasing effort, and the exceedingly painstaking and exhaustive steps they have taken'. The magistrate's sad duty was to rule that the unidentified woman had been murdered by an unidentified person or persons.

Straight after the inquest, Wilks reviewed all the files in Sydney to see if anything had been missed; Bowie and McRae did likewise in Melbourne. With the Pyjama Girl back in the public eye, sixty more people came forward to view the body, and there were 150 additional missing persons reports from all over Australia. One of these was from Antonio Agostini, who saw Wilks at the CIB to ask for help tracing his missing wife, Linda. He was shown the body at Sydney University and said that while there was some resemblance, it wasn't her. One of Linda's friends viewed the Pyjama Girl and said it wasn't her – and when Linda's dentist was traced, he said her dentition didn't match. But Wilks didn't rule her out. Linda Agostini was one of the 125 missing women who hadn't been traced in the past three years.

Superintendent Prior would announce that nothing had come from these renewed efforts. Shortly after this, in March 1938, 'Silent Bill' announced that he'd be taking extended leave before his retirement. It was the end of an era. Prior had joined the New South Wales force just after Federation, before fingerprinting was used, and was saying farewell nearly forty years later, when detectives could rush to a crime scene by plane. Prior had not only served well in fighting crime and leading his detectives, but through the 1930s he and his second wife, Katherine, had every year organised the glittering CIB ball for charity – an event that received considerable press coverage and helped burnish the force's image.

Prior's decision to retire coincided with a stressful time in his personal life. In late 1937 Katherine had become sick, was hospitalised at Royal Prince Alfred and had a successful operation to remove a growth. In February 1938 she went to convalesce at her sister's house in Yass. Prior remained living in their Dulwich Hill home while he finished up at the CIB, and they wrote regular affectionate letters. In May 1938, he visited his wife at Yass for two weeks. While her physical health was improving, she'd become convinced she had a 'growth' inside her body, even though the doctor assured her this wasn't the case. On 10 August 1938 Katherine shot herself through the heart. She was forty-seven.

Prior's retirement became official the following April. He would marry for a third time, and be survived by this wife, Agnes, when he died suddenly at his Dulwich Hill home in August 1944, aged sixty-five. Despite his many contributions to the city and state, the newspapers marked the former CIB chief's passing with only the briefest of articles.

~

In May 1938 the reward for information leading to a conviction in the Pyjama Girl murder was raised to £1000. There would be £500 for anyone who could identify the dead girl. Late that year, determined to see the case solved, MacKay took it over personally. He'd soon appoint new detectives, instructing them to ignore previous investigators' conclusions when they reviewed the files. This included tossing out McRae's rejection of a crank named Dr Benbow, who'd persisted with numerous theories, and McRae's and Wilks's belief the Pyjama Girl was neither Philomena Morgan nor Linda Agostini.

But for the time being, McRae would still be on the case, showing potential witnesses the body at Sydney University. Publicity at this time included a four-page pictorial spread in an October issue of recently launched *Pix* magazine, under the headline 'World's Greatest Mystery'.

In December that year, McRae went to visit his mother, who was sick in Adelaide. During the visit, he took the opportunity to go to his boyhood home town of Strathalbyn, where he still had kin, and where his father, who'd died in 1927, and his little brother, who'd drowned before the present century even started, had been laid to rest. While in South Australia, McRae spoke to the Adelaide papers, *The News* calling him 'one of Australia's foremost criminal investigators'. He remained confident he'd solve the Pyjama Girl case. If only someone would one day identify her in the formalin bath. The article lionised McRae:

> Tall and powerfully built, Detective-Sgt. McRae has a deliberate way of speaking that belies the keenness of his brain and eye and the shrewd deduction that have placed him in the vanguard of Australian detectives. If he ever gets the time to write his memoirs, there is little doubt that the book would be a best seller.

Perhaps he could even be a movie character. In August 1939, in the weeks before Hitler's aggression triggered another world war, cinema audiences saw McRae in a narration-driven short film, *The Pyjama Girl Murder Case*. Produced with the approval of MacKay, McRae and Wilks, it was made by Rupert Kathner, later reputed as Australia's worst movie director.

Despite various factual errors and some dramatic licence, the little documentary was a reasonable low-budget attempt to convey the basics and renew public interest. It chronicled recent efforts to drag lagoons near the culvert, which had turned up clothes that might have been worn by the Pyjama Girl, with recreations of these garments then shown adorning a mannequin. The film also used a stand-in for McRae in an inquest sequence, telling of the body dumping, which was also re-enacted in darkened roadside shots. The detective was credited with recommending that the body be preserved at Sydney University, and scenes showed witnesses shaking their heads sadly as they gazed upon the unseen Pyjama Girl in her formalin coffin. Hopes the film would lead to anything new weren't realised.

At the time *The Pyjama Girl Murder Case* portrayed McRae up on screen, he had just turned fifty-three and was on track to make inspector. He still had years before he retired and he was sure to put a lot more killers behind bars in that time. Maybe he would finally solve the Pyjama Girl case. But in mid-September 1939, as he was taking a carload of woman witnesses to look at the embalmed girl, McRae didn't realise he was acting in a crucial scene that would help write the third act of his life.

The mystery of the murdered girl had been McRae's main focus for five years. Now his last case would see him in all the newspapers like never before and consume the rest of his life. For McRae, the Pyjama Girl was nothing compared with 'the Lady in Grey'.

36

The Lady in Grey

Freda Agnes Smith was a photogenic blue-eyed brunette who might have been cast as a tragic heroine – or a femme fatale – in Hollywood movies. Certainly the most famous part of her life was like something in a film noir based on a pulp novel.

Freda was born in September 1915 in the little northern New South Wales town of Boggabri. Her father, Walter, was a country constable. Like the McRaes, they moved wherever he was transferred, with Freda attending primary schools in villages around the state. When it came time for her intermediate education, she boarded at Catholic convents in Goulburn and Dee Why. After finishing school, she stayed in Sydney and worked as a stenographer.

In winter 1932, visiting her family at Stroud, near Newcastle, where Walter was now a police sergeant, Freda met and fell for electrical mechanic Tom Caesar. They married in June 1936. He got a good job at the Chullora Railway Workshop in Sydney and they lived in Kensington, where Freda doted on her tiny Pomeranian, Princess Wicky. By then her dad, Walter, was a sergeant working at nearby Daceyville station.

Freda's husband was a jealous type. In mid-1938 he heard she had been 'talking' to local constables. So he enlisted a Daceyville cop mate to keep an eye on her – and also got a fellow railway worker to spy on Freda.

Serious trouble erupted on 6 October. Tom had supposedly told Freda's folks she was in a private hospital following an abortion – then a serious crime. Wearing his police uniform, Sergeant Walter Smith – along with his wife, Agnes, and their other daughter, Thelma – fronted his son-in-law at the Kensington house. He demanded to know Freda's whereabouts. Tom wouldn't tell him. A fight broke out. Tom later claimed Agnes and Thelma had come armed with a gun and a knife, and in self-defence he'd pushed them from his house. The Smith women denied this. They said Tom punched Agnes in the face and threw Thelma to the ground. Only then had Walter punched out his son-in-law. He'd been about to beat the life out of Tom when half a dozen police officers arrived to break up the brawl. Statements were taken long into the night.

In the aftermath, Tom wrote a letter of complaint to Commissioner MacKay. He denied Freda had procured an abortion, and said Sergeant Walter Smith was a raving lunatic who would've killed him if police hadn't intervened. Tom claimed that his father-in-law was following him and had threatened to 'get him'.

Superintendent Quinn told McRae to look into the complaint. On 2 November 1938, McRae went to Tom and Freda Caesar's house, which wasn't far from where he lived with his wife, Jean. Tom wasn't home. McRae returned the next day. He interviewed Tom and arranged to take his statement that night in the presence of a shorthand writer. But when McRae arrived that evening, Tom said he was dropping the complaint against his father-in-law, Walter. Freda made tea, which they all drank in the lounge room as a serial played on the wireless. McRae made his report. No action was taken against Sergeant Walter Smith. That seemed to be that.

Eight months later, in July 1939, McRae got a phone call from Freda. The detective wasn't sure who she was. Freda reminded him. She said last year he'd handled the situation with her father very well, and he had said to call if she ever needed advice. Freda told McRae her problem: Tom wouldn't give her any money. Was he allowed to do that? McRae said he didn't think so: a husband was obliged to support his wife. That was the end of the call. Later that month, McRae's driver happened to take him past the Caesars' Kensington house, and he saw Freda watering her garden. The detective had his man stop, and he climbed out and asked how she was getting on with her husband. Freda said things hadn't changed – and Tom was actually at home, off work sick. McRae continued on his way.

On 7 September 1939, just four days after Prime Minister Robert Menzies announced that Australia was again at war with Germany, Freda came to the CIB with a young friend she introduced as Madge James, who said she might be able to identify the Pyjama Girl. As it happened, McRae had already arranged to take a Mrs Dan of Bellevue Hill to see the body that day, and he told Freda and Madge they could come along. At Sydney University, McRae had the Pyjama Girl brought out of the formalin. Neither woman could identify her.

On the way back, he asked the women where his driver could drop them. Mrs Dan got out on City Road. Freda and Madge wanted to go to Oxford Street. On the way, McRae saw some people who looked like university students enter a hotel that he'd been ordered by MacKay's second-in-command, Superintendent James Scott, to keep an eye on as it was suspected of serving underage drinkers. So he had the driver pull over, took the women with him into the pub, bought them all a drink and sussed things out. Satisfied that no action was needed, they all left and McRae dropped them off.

A week later, Freda rang him again at the CIB. Tom was giving her trouble and she wanted to get a job at a hotel. Could McRae recommend her? He said the only hotelkeepers he knew needed experienced staff. Had she done hotel work? When she said no, he said there wasn't much he could do. Later that day, waiting for the tram to take him home, McRae ran into Freda and a woman friend. Freda asked if he'd buy them a drink. To be polite, McRae did, before going on his way.

On Friday 22 September, Freda came to see McRae at the CIB, seeking his help because a man had some of her property and she needed him tracked down. McRae said he'd make enquiries. He wrote down the silent office number – rendering it in a simple code that he explained to Freda. The reason for this, he'd later say, was so it couldn't be phoned by anyone else should they find the slip of paper. But Freda's trivial request for assistance slipped his busy mind. After she left a series of phone messages, McRae made an enquiry but it didn't pan out. He called her back to say so. Freda said she wanted to come and see him. McRae said there was no need: he'd done as much as he could.

On Friday 29 September, Freda phoned four times asking for McRae. Hearing she'd been calling, he told a colleague that the woman was a damned nuisance. If she rang again, tell her he was out. But Freda knew he was there. Around noon, McRae had a visitor in reception. Freda told him she'd left her husband, had taken a job at David Jones and was now living across the road from the CIB at Mac's Hotel. She told McRae she had important information about serious crimes her husband had committed. 'I'm going to tell you the lot,' she said, 'and I don't care if he goes to gaol for life.' McRae asked her to spill, and Freda said she would tell him everything over lunch. He said he couldn't leave the CIB until 1pm. Freda replied that she'd wait outside on Pitt Street.

About 1.10pm, McRae told the shorthand officer he was working with on the Pyjama Girl case that he was going to have lunch with a woman who was about to put her husband in the crosshairs. Outside, he saw Freda and suggested they go to a cafe. She said no because what she had to tell him couldn't be said in public. 'Come across to Mac's with me,' Freda said. 'I have some sandwiches.'

They went to the hotel and took the lift to the third floor. When Freda let him into Room 44, McRae was surprised that it was just a bedroom, rather than a suite with a kitchenette for more permanent residents. Freda told him it was only temporary and to make himself at home. McRae did what he did in his own house – he took off his coat and his hat. Freda poured him a glass of beer from the two bottles she'd bought with sandwiches from Coles. The room's door was open, and a cleaner was working in the hallway. But Freda pushed it closed with a click and then sat perched on the bed. McRae was on the room's only chair, having a bite and some beer.

He said: 'I have not got much time. What about getting on with your story.'

Freda replied: 'Don't bother about that now. Come over here.'

Taken aback, McRae asked: 'Why? What's the game?'

He was demanding 'What's the strong of this?' – an idiom of the day meaning 'What's the meaning of this?' – when there was a knock on the door. Everything happened at blinding speed. Freda jumped off the bed. In one motion, she threw off her dress and flung open the door. Hubby Tom barged into the room, followed by private detective Angus Kellock and Mr Kellock's wife. Freda grabbed McRae from behind, while Tom laid into him with punches until Mr Kellock separated them.

McRae suddenly understood. All these months, Freda had been trying to lure him into a honey trap. 'You bloody little crook,' he bellowed. 'I will have all your telephone messages to get me here turned up and prove that this is a conspiracy.' Tom attacked McRae again, sending his glasses flying. Snatching his broken spectacles from the floor, the detective stormed out.

McRae was back in the CIB at 1.20pm. He'd been gone only ten minutes, and was in the hotel room for just three. McRae told his colleagues what had happened, requested an immediate investigation and made a full report. It was only then that he realised he'd left his cardigan behind in the hotel room. McRae would later say he might have taken it off with his coat or that it might have been pulled off during the fight with Tom.

Detectives were despatched to Mac's. Freda was interviewed. Adultery might be immoral but it wasn't a crime. She wasn't required to give a statement. But she did after being told that anything she said was only for an internal police inquiry and wouldn't be used in court. Over the next few days, Freda made several further statements. And in all of them, her version of what had happened between her and McRae was very, *very* different.

~

Freda agreed that back on 2 November 1938, Tom hadn't been home when McRae came to investigate the complaint against her father, Walter. As Freda sat with him in the lounge room, the detective said her dad was in serious trouble and would likely be fired. McRae said he would do what he could to get Tom to withdraw the complaint and save her father's career. *If* she was nice to him. McRae, then fifty-two, tried to kiss Freda, twenty-three. She didn't let him. When he returned the next day, she relented and they had sex – on his promise that he'd help her father.

Over the next eight months, McRae came to the house for sex two or three mornings a week. Freda didn't enjoy it but she got used to it. When she tried to break things off, McRae said she was jeopardising her father's chances at promotion. She had no idea that her dad's record was by then clean and he was on track for advancement.

Around June 1939, McRae told her he had go to Dubbo to investigate the grisly series of 'bones' murders. When he returned that day in July, the detective hadn't just happened to be driving past her house; he'd been arriving for one of their regular assignations. But Tom was at home sick, so Freda had headed him off at the gate.

Around the time of this close call, McRae told her that the local cops had noted his car parked near her house. So he and Freda had resorted to rendezvous at the CIB, on four occasions having sex standing up against a desk in a third-floor office. The last time had been on Tuesday 26 September – three days before the hotel bust.

Freda admitted she'd been at the CIB on another occasion that month, when she and Marge Varley – which was the real name of 'Madge James' – had wanted to satisfy their morbid curiosity by seeing the Pyjama Girl. McRae had arranged their visit, saying that if anyone asked, she was to say she thought the dead woman might be her sister. Freda said she'd kept her relationship with McRae a secret from Marge by saying he was her 'Uncle Mac'. But there was no such subterfuge at the CIB, where the big detective's colleagues all made a fuss over her as his 'girlfriend' – which she actually did like. On account of what she wore when visiting, they'd even nicknamed her 'the Lady in Grey'.

On the morning of Friday 29 September, Freda saw Marge at the city cafe where she worked and invited her to dinner that night at her Kensington home. They took a walk together and parted at the CIB, with Freda saying she was visiting Uncle Mac. Upstairs, McRae told her to book a room at Mac's Hotel across the road and to get some beer and sandwiches.

Freda did as she was told and they began their rendezvous. She'd been shocked when her husband and Mr and Mrs Kellock burst in. But Freda was far more appalled that – after nearly a year of pressuring her into sex – McRae immediately accused her of trying to frame him. That was beyond the pale – as was his storming out and leaving her. For these reasons, Freda was willing to give a signed statement to Mr Kellock detailing her adultery. With no other paper available, she made this statement on the reverse side of Princess Wicky's pedigree licence, which she had in her handbag. Freda had given her various statements to the police. Tom Caesar, Marge Varley and Mr and Mrs Kellock were also interviewed.

Whatever happened in that hotel room, the Australian public would know nothing about it for more than a year. McRae remained the dogged detective of the Pyjama Girl newsreel, still determined to solve the murder after half a decade. Throughout 1940, newspaper readers learned of his ongoing adventures: investigating the Darlinghurst shooting murder of a notorious razor gangster, chasing down a boy robber in Petersham, and trying to nab a daring cat burglar working fancy homes in Vaucluse. This hero wasn't just catching killers and crooks – he was keeping Australia safe from potential subversion. In mid-June, after Prime Minister Menzies outlawed the Communist Party, McRae led a big squad of detectives in a sensational raid on the Red headquarters in Haymarket.

But in the wake of the Mac's Hotel scene, life had not resumed as usual for Freda and Tom Caesar. Straight after the bust, he'd kicked her out of their home and begun divorce proceedings. But to be legally rid of Freda, Caesar needed to show fault in court – and if he could prove her adultery, he'd be entitled to compensation from McRae. If Caesar won, a jury would then decide how much 'value' they believed he'd lost due to his guilty wife and her lover. This monetary figure, as the judge was to put it, would be determined by Freda's 'capacity as a housekeeper, her value in the home, her capabilities in the management of the financial affairs of the home'. Caesar began divorce proceedings against Freda, with them due to be heard in the Supreme Court on 4 November 1940. McRae was named as co-respondent.

If adultery was proved, McRae wouldn't be going to gaol or the gallows. But his life would be ruined personally, professionally and financially. Not only was Caesar going to drag his name through the mud and put his career at risk, he was seeking the immense sum of £2000 in damages – the equivalent of what McRae had earned over the past five years.

37

He Said, They Said

McRae, famous for putting bad guys away, was now effectively on trial, up against an old nemesis, William Dovey, who'd once defended the poisoner 'Old Bill' and who'd since become a King's Counsel. That a top cop was in such a bind was always going to make a top story – and it got even juicier as allegations of police corruption and counter-claims of a frame-up became public. But what ensured the Caesar court case was the biggest newspaper scandal in years was that it put so much graphic sex on the record, meaning it could be reported in the public interest. This was a thrill in a society where books such as *Moll Flanders*, *The Dubliners* and *Ulysses*, *Brave New World* and *Lady Chatterley's Lover* were still on the banned list.

But the case was even more sensational because it was so wildly at odds with the typical adultery divorce, where a defendant denied wrongdoing while the aggrieved spouse tried to prove infidelity. Freda Caesar – great-looking and a fiery and funny courtroom presence – was admitting *everything* to support the claim of the man who was divorcing her.

Respectable broadsheets and tabloids tried to cover the Caesar divorce trial with little lewd detail, but *Truth* went gangbusters, printing verbatim testimony in most of its salaciousness. Its 10 November report was more than 15,000 words – and that was just the first half of the proceedings. McRae, so long lionised, was captured in purple prose that left little to the imagination:

Catcher of criminals, one of the chief investigators of the Pyjama Girl mystery, hero of many a tough tussle on behalf of law and order, the man on the job in the elucidation of many a perplexing problem, he was now alleged to have found himself in a situation as bizarre and intriguing as any other he would expect to meet in his lifetime – in the bedroom of a city private hotel, attempting to defend himself with one hand, while he grasped with the other, pants that were falling down his leg.

Raising the stakes was the fact that the sex in question was *sinister*. Freda was claiming McRae had coerced her into immoralities that had defiled her decency, destroyed her marriage and disgraced the holy of holies: the CIB offices. Such coercion constituted the more serious accusation of aggravated adultery.

The jury might believe Freda simply because no woman would admit to such shame if it weren't true. Yet that very willingness to sully her reputation might also fit McRae's defence that she was a hussy who'd insinuated herself into his life to lure him into that hotel room to frame him with the help of Caesar, Marge and Mr and Mrs Kellock.

Dovey opened by asking for the police to produce McRae's reports about the original 1938 complaint against Freda's father, the witnesses' statements after the hotel bust, the Caesars' correspondence with MacKay and McRae's own police record of service. Detective-Inspector Sherringham, representing MacKay, who'd ignored a subpoena to appear, told the court he'd been instructed to claim privilege for these files, which would mean neither side had access to them. Dovey said this was extraordinary but perhaps reflective of a cover-up. 'After the co-respondent McRae was caught,' he said, 'half of the police force was lined up on his side in order to frighten off the petitioner.' His Honour reviewed the documents and denied the request for privilege.

Freda told the court how McRae had manipulated her: 'He said that he was married and that he had no kiddies and that his wife was not a strong woman and that he couldn't get all the fun he wanted.'

Truth's account of the first time she had sex with McRae bordered on the pornographic: 'She was wearing just an overall that tied at the back, with scanties underneath. She had no stockings on. She was usually dressed that way when doing her household work.' After that first time, he came to her house on Monday, Tuesday and/or Thursday mornings. Freda told the court: 'That was all he came out for. He would just come in. I knew what he had come for. I got no thrill out of it. He was not a lover. He would kiss me. He used to call me a little bitch.'

The court heard how Freda had tried to end it, but McRae said she was jeopardising her father's upcoming promotion, which she didn't know had already gone through. She told of having sex at the CIB, being known as the Lady in Grey, and how she had come into town that day, seen Marge, invited her to dinner that night and then gone to meet 'Uncle Mac'. McRae had told her to book the hotel room. She'd actually booked two nights, because Caesar was going away for the weekend.

When McRae arrived, he hadn't wanted to waste time, having a little beer before kissing her, calling her a little bitch, taking off his coat and cardigan but leaving his boots on because he was in such a hurry. Freda had removed her jumper, skirt and shoes. They'd been in bed about ten minutes when there was a knock on the door. Freda had thought it was the manager. McRae had yelled: 'Don't go to the door!' But she'd opened it just a fraction, and Caesar and Mr and Mrs Kellock had burst in. The fight had ensued, and McRae had made her angry by claiming she'd framed him and leaving her. Freda signed her statement on her dog's licence paper. 'When I registered poor little Wicky,' she told the court, 'I did not think that she would be brought into anything like this.' Everyone cracked up with laughter.

Freda was a smart and confident witness. But parts of her story were difficult to grasp. Why had she booked two nights at the hotel but supposedly invited Marge to dinner at her house that night? Why had she opened the hotel room door even a fraction while wearing only a slip? Few married women would do that if they thought a manager was knocking, particularly when committing adultery with a well-known detective. Even harder to understand was Freda telling the court: 'After signing the confession, I said we might as well finish the bottle of beer that had been opened and celebrate. They said they did not want any. So I drank it all myself.' Freda had just been caught *in flagrante delicto* – and would likely now be publicly shamed in a divorce trial. What was there to celebrate?

Freda said detectives had interviewed her that afternoon and over the weekend after Caesar had kicked her out of their home. She'd told them if McRae had stood by her she wouldn't have said anything – which seemed a strange claim, given she'd also said she'd been coerced, she didn't like having sex with him, she had tried to end their relationship and she had wanted to celebrate after the hotel scene. Freda told the court she'd asked detectives not to tell McRae her whereabouts because she was afraid he'd shoot her. She also said her experience with the detective had changed her. Before she met McRae, she'd been simple and wholesome. Now Freda liked to drink and smoke and run a bit wild in Kings Cross.

McRae's lawyer, Jack Shand, wanted to know why Freda hadn't known the complaint against her father that set all this in motion had been resolved within a week. She claimed because she hadn't seen him in all that time. So, against her will, she'd had sex with McRae for nearly a year in order protect the father she didn't see, even though he lived in the same suburb? Freda said the police had told her to stay away from her dad. Shand also pointed out that McRae hadn't worked the infamous Dubbo 'bones' murders case – which she claimed he'd told her.

The judge asked Freda to accompany the jury to the CIB and show them the office in which she'd had sex with McRae. She refused. The jury was shown the third-floor general offices. But the room where it happened – or didn't happen – remained unknown.

The defence's big question was this: if this hadn't been a frame-up, how had Caesar and the private detective known exactly when and where to find Freda and McRae? Caesar testified that he'd been suspicious of Freda. She'd started drinking and smoking, which wasn't like her, and he'd kept tabs on her with the help of a few mates. Then he found her diary, which mentioned 'Tom' – and from the context it was clear it wasn't him. On that day in July 1939 when he was home sick, Caesar saw Freda with McRae at their front gate, and said they'd been touching hands, the detective carrying on like a lovestruck kid. His local cop mates also whispered about the old detective spending time at his house. Caesar said he'd heard from as many as eight police – whom he refused to name – that his wife was known as the Lady in Grey at the CIB. He denied she'd told him this detail.

Caesar had contacted private detective Angus Kellock and paid him to watch the house for a few days in early August. Despite Caesar hiring him – and his specific suspicions – Kellock claimed he hadn't known his stakeout target was McRae. In any case, he saw nothing untoward. It had actually been Marge Varley who gave the game away. On Friday 29 September, Marge had checked her roster and realised she had to work at the cafe that night, and couldn't go to the Caesar home for dinner. So she called Caesar at the Chullora Railway Workshop to tell him. In passing, she said Freda was at the CIB seeing her 'Uncle Mac'.

Alarm bells ringing, Caesar left work, raced into the city and found Mr Kellock, who was having lunch with his wife. The trio hired a taxi and scoured the streets and Caesar spied Freda on Pitt Street near Mac's Hotel. 'My God,' he said, 'there is my wife standing over there.' Tom claimed this was 'luck'. Under cross-examination, he said perhaps Marge had mentioned Mac's Hotel was where Freda might be found.

They piled out of the taxi and watched as a big older bloke met Freda and they went into the hotel. Rather unbelievably, Caesar claimed he hadn't known the fellow was McRae. He told the court he raced in, ran up the stairs, saw the lift stop on the third floor and Freda and the big man go into Room 44. Caesar fetched the Kellocks and they stood quietly by the door, hearing murmured talk and then bedsprings squeaking. Caesar burst in, saw Freda in a slip, her hair a mess and her face smeared with lipstick.

'What the bloody hell are you doing here?' he demanded.

She shot back: 'What's that got to do with you?'

McRae was behind the door. 'Never mind me,' Caesar roared. 'I'm only the husband!' Even now Caesar claimed he hadn't recognised McRae, who had his head down. Caesar attacked. 'I did my block,' he told the court. 'I saw red. I got stuck into him. I went for him. I cracked him.' McRae tried to fend him off with one hand while pulling his trousers up with the other.

Angus Kellock separated them, but when McRae accused Freda of being a crook, Caesar lost it again and broke the detective's glasses. As he left, McRae had sworn: 'I'll get you, I'll get you all for this.' Only then did they realise they had his cardigan, which Mr Kellock kept as evidence.

Jack Shand argued that these conspirators had expected McRae to be so mortified he'd cough up cash to ensure their silence. Instead, he'd done what he'd always done – the right thing – by reporting what had happened, demanding an investigation and doing his own detective work. Faced with this, Caesar had doubled down with this expensive divorce claim – some of the money from which, it was intimated, would find its way to Freda down the track. Shand argued that Caesar's story was a stack of lies. He told the court that at around 11.30 on the Friday morning, Freda told the Mac's Hotel management to keep Room 44 for her as she was going to tell a 'girlfriend' to meet her there. She'd then told Marge, who'd called Caesar so he knew which room to go to for the final act of their sting. The private detective and his wife had been roped in to corroborate the story.

Shand said Caesar had just given the court the colourful detail of McRae pulling up his pants. This was crucial evidence of adultery. But he hadn't mentioned this when interviewed by police – why? Caesar said he had, and the statement was wrong. Then why had he signed it? Caesar hadn't read it, because the police had hurried him. Shand asked where the diary was mentioning this 'other Tom'. Caesar said it had since disappeared. Shand claimed Caesar hadn't mentioned the phone call from Marge initially because it was the vital link proving the frame-up.

Shand now told the court that seven weeks after the hotel bust, Caesar had turned up at the McRae home in Kingsford. The detective wasn't there, so Caesar lied to Mrs McRae, saying he was one of her hubby's golfing buddies. That sounded plausible enough. Whenever McRae wasn't working, it was a good bet you'd find him ruining a good walk with a game of golf. Caesar told Jean McRae it'd be to her husband's 'advantage' if he came to see him at his place in Kingsford. But McRae hadn't gone to what Shand intimated was a shakedown attempt.

Under cross-examination, Caesar denied he'd intended to demand money. He merely wanted to talk to McRae and sort things out because he didn't want to lose Freda. By this time, Shand pointed out, Caesar had already started divorce proceedings. So clearly he was planning to blackmail McRae. Caesar shot back: 'I have never wanted to get his stinking money at any time!'

Shand responded coolly: 'If you are so averse to McRae's money, why are you claiming two thousand in damages from him?'

Caesar replied: 'He smashed up my home and everything I loved.'

Marge Varley testified about making the phone call to Caesar. Shand asked why she hadn't mentioned this in her statement to police. She said because she didn't want to get Freda in trouble. Marge denied knowing Kings Cross crook Stanley Godden and other colourful personalities – until they were brought into court and she 'remembered them'. Recalled to the courtroom, Freda made similar denials about these figures, which were soon reversed when she admitted she'd partied with them – sometimes in Marge's company – and much more.

McRae testified to deny any intimacy with Freda, and said their trivial interactions had been at her repeated instigation. McRae said the member books from Eastlakes Golf Course showed he'd been there on mornings she claimed he was at her place. He hadn't even been stationed at the

CIB during two of the months Freda alleged they used an office there for sex. Further, he'd been on holiday for a month after that, recalled only towards the end of August because of the imminent war. As for the office she described – McRae said it was only partitioned from others. With the hallways always busy, no one could do what they'd supposedly done during business hours without being seen.

But McRae didn't produce phone messages from Freda, proving she'd pestered him at the CIB to the point of being a nuisance. What was also curious, given he'd used stings and stakeouts to make his name in the 1920s, was that he didn't set up such surveillance to catch Caesar trying to shake him down – a possibility he must have suspected. Under cross-examination by William Dovey, another part of McRae's distant past was made public to cast suspicion upon his character as a man and as a police officer.

Dovey: 'Is this the first time since you have been in the police that you have been spoken to ... about your conduct with women?'

McRae: 'Yes.'

Dovey: 'Were you ever called upon to make a report?'

McRae: 'When I was lost in Frenchs Forest with a woman.'

Dovey: 'And you were a married man?'

McRae: 'A widower.'

After establishing that McRae had been married to his second wife for years, and McRae 'knew' the woman in Frenchs Forest before his first wife died, the cross-examination continued:

Dovey: '... After you were lost in Frenchs Forest with this lady, you were called in and questioned by the police department?'

McRae: 'No, sir. I made a report concerning my absence. After that report was made, I went into hospital for two months. I asked for an inquiry and to be put back into uniform.'

Testimony for McRae was heard from those King Cross habitués who'd been pals with Freda and Marge: Stanley 'Sloppy' Godden, alleged thief and blackmailer, and his best mate, Bert Sutherland, who boasted about being 'Sex Pervert No. 1' and was believed to own a brothel. They said they'd partied with Freda and she told them of her plan to frame McRae. Just hours after the hotel bust, Sloppy and Bert said they'd seen Freda at a cafe and she crowed, 'We got him today,' laying out how she'd had Marge call Caesar and how she and Caesar had roped in the Kellocks as witnesses. They partied with her that weekend. After that, Sloppy and Bert hadn't seen Freda for about six months, but when they did she said of her extortion: 'Old Mac has not come good yet but I am still living in hope.'

McRae didn't know it, but during the trial he was being tailed by Caesar's team, and one night they'd seen him meet with Sloppy and Bert. Now Dovey suggested he'd pressured these lowlifes to perjure themselves. McRae denied it. He said he'd never met either man until the night he'd delivered subpoenas to them because he'd learned they had valuable information that might help prove he'd been framed.

Asked about Sloppy and Bert, Freda had at first said in court that she didn't know them. But under cross-examination, she admitted they'd tried to get her involved in a scam to fleece David Jones. Freda had turned them down. But she also said they'd boasted about blackmailing a businessman with a false allegation of adultery. It was a striking coincidence. Further, why hadn't she reported these men to her father, the police sergeant? Because it wasn't her business – and besides, she'd been told not to see him. Freda maintained she hadn't said anything to her Kings Cross crook mates about a plan to frame McRae. Immediately after the hotel bust, she admitted, she had seen Sloppy. But Freda hadn't said anything about McRae. There had been no need. 'People all over the Cross knew,' she told the court. 'They pointed me out as the girl who had been caught with Old Mac.'

The Mac's Hotel managers testified Freda had come in around 11.30 that Friday morning. She had inspected Room 44 and asked them to keep it for her because she was off to tell a girlfriend the number. Then she'd come back to pay for it. This contradicted what she'd said about McRae telling her to book a room. Yet Mr and Mrs Kellock testified to corroborate Freda and Caesar's account of what happened in the hotel room, and they denied being in on any conspiracy.

Under Shand's cross-examination, Mr Kellock admitted he had previously worked for the Rex Private Inquiry company. Rex had in mid-1939 become notorious for having hired women for adultery frame-ups; one of the company directors had killed himself rather than face charges. Mr Kellock told the court he'd worked for the firm only briefly, and that he'd quit when he learned they were dodgy, long before the scandal. While it was true he'd been out on his own with Kell's Private Inquiry Agency since early 1938, that didn't mean he hadn't been in on such frame-ups before that. For one thing, if he knew about Rex's illegal practices that long ago, why had Mr Kellock – who proudly advertised as having been a police officer in Glasgow, Victoria and Rabaul – not taken his concerns to the Sydney CIB?

Jack Shand's closing argument lasted over eight hours. Freda was 'as slippery as an eel with a brain that was always working', and had admitted consorting with criminal deviants who just happened to have told of a sex-extortion plot like hers. Freda had tentatively booked the room but only paid for it when she knew McRae was at the CIB and had then told Marge. As for Marge – why ask to speak to Caesar at the Chullora Railway Workshop rather than just leave a message? Why had neither mentioned this phone call initially?

Because it was the link that proved the frame-up, Shand continued. Their planning was shown when Caesar, who initially claimed he had a 'hunch', dropped everything at work, raced into the city, conveniently located the Kellocks during their lunch adjournment from court appearances, and then equally conveniently spotted Freda standing on Pitt Street. Caesar didn't need to bolt up the stairs at Mac's Hotel to see where McRae and his wife went because he already knew they were in Room 44. What Caesar and Freda hadn't counted on, Shand said, was McRae standing up to the extortion attempt. William Dovey also spoke for more than a day, accusing the police of Gestapo methods of intimidation. Dovey told the court he'd learned that before the police tried to deny him and his client access to those files by claiming privilege, they'd given everything to McRae so he could make copies – which he'd done with the help of shorthand writers. This was a blatant attempt to pervert the course of justice. Beyond exposing this, Dovey shot McRae's stories full of holes. There was the ridiculousness of James Scott – who was now Deputy Commissioner and Metropolitan Superintendent – being so concerned with students' underage drinking that he'd ordered McRae to stake-out a city pub. Or McRae claiming Eastlakes Golf Club as his alibi when Freda Caesar lived just 100 yards from the place. Then there was the far graver matter of McRae orchestrating a seedy conspiracy of King Cross thieves and perverts to perjure themselves on his behalf. Whatever good he'd done in the past, Dovey argued, McRae was not fit to remain in the police force.

The Caesar divorce trial had lasted thirteen days – longer than Eric Craig's three murder trials put together. Mr Justice Street gave a careful summation for the jury. This wasn't a criminal trial and so they didn't need to reach a verdict beyond reasonable doubt. Their decision could be based on what they believed most probable.

On 20 November, after deliberating for ninety minutes, they found in favour of Caesar. The jury concluded that McRae and Freda had committed adultery from 3 November 1938 until Christmas that year, from 5 to 31 March 1939, during the third week of September at the CIB, and finally at Mac's Hotel on the day of the bust. In giving these precise times, they were excluding infidelities Freda said had taken place when McRae had been away from the CIB or on holiday, which indicated they had doubts about parts of her story. Nevertheless, the jury found no evidence Caesar had been aware of Freda's infidelity, or that they'd conspired to entrap McRae. In effect, the jury was saying McRae had perjured himself repeatedly, induced others to perjure themselves, and conspired to frame Caesar and Freda as blackmailers.

The jury gave a backhanded slap to Freda's 'value' as a woman by only awarding £200 in compensation to Caesar. McRae would be out another £200 in costs awarded to Caesar – and £1000 on top of that for his own defence and other court costs. With the case finally over, Mr Justice Street blasted the New South Wales police force for its conduct. He'd waited until after the verdict because he hadn't wanted to prejudice the proceedings. His Honour said he was astonished and appalled by what had been revealed. By trying to claim privilege on files they knew they'd already given to McRae, the police had engaged in deceit, displayed contempt for the court and tried to obstruct justice. Mr Justice Street also delivered a milder rebuke to MacKay for not answering the subpoena personally. But His Honour noted that there was a memo with the files dated before the trial from the commissioner and it said they were to be given to the plaintiff if requested. Under the judge's questioning about the request for privilege, Inspector Sherringham said he'd been following orders from Deputy Commissioner Scott.

After this scathing judicial opinion, the New South Wales government would censure its own police force. But MacKay, Scott and other senior officers would face no blame or consequences. On the evening of the verdict, MacKay, Scott and chief of the CIB Inspector Frank Matthews held a conference at the CIB that went late into the night. McRae was summoned from his home at midnight. He threw his suit on over his pyjamas and rushed into the office. MacKay told the state's top homicide detective – who he had known for nearly a quarter-century – that he was dismissed.

On the surface, it was a summary sacking, a shameful swansong to a career spanning nearly thirty years. In reality, MacKay knew the chief secretary was about to fire McRae, and if that happened, he'd be done and dusted. But if McRae was dismissed by the force, he, like any member of the Police Association of New South Wales, had the right to appeal the decision.

MacKay had thrown his old colleague a lifeline.

38

I Demand Justice!

Truth was livid. In a page 19 editorial, it said the New South Wales police were rotten to the core and called for MacKay's head. But *Truth* was also titillated. On the same front page, it had an exclusive interview and saucy photo shoot with Freda, the article continuing inside with more glam pictures. *Truth* had spoken to her at a guesthouse on the coast, where she was lying low. But Freda revelled in the attention and her martyrdom. 'It seems only yesterday that I was a contented wife in my own home with a good hard-working husband!' she said. 'Now I am the Scandal Woman – the confessed adulteress in a sensational case, known as the Lady in Grey.'

Freda said she was like Scarlett O'Hara in *Gone with the Wind*, which she was reading right then as the film version burned up Australian movie screens. Actually, she was even worse off:

> There has been no story of love in my downfall – just a plain seduction without any romantic trimmings, and because I have been dragged down, and have lost almost everything that was dear to me, I am condemned as a cast-off ... What is going to become of me now? No husband, no home, no job – just nothing!

The reporter asked if she couldn't marry again. 'Never that!' she fired back. A man who cheated was sometimes held up a hero. 'But a woman – she becomes untouchable!'

~

McRae began his appeal before the Police Appeals Board in the District Court on 10 December 1940. If he won, he might be reinstated; if he lost, he'd lose everything. His fate was now in the hands of Justice John Clancy and two Police Board members. The same witnesses testified. Freda and Caesar appeared under protest and were denied legal counsel – which led to *Truth* branding the proceedings a 'star chamber'. But McRae was allowed representation and he paid for a bigger legal team that again included Shand, and these advocates aggressively cross-examined witnesses to the point of frustration. Freda, especially, was ropeable at having to give all her evidence again – and again and again – when she'd already testified about all of this in the Supreme Court.

Caesar was forced to deny he'd struck blows on McRae in the hotel room for 'show'. Sloppy Godden stated he'd first met Freda in July 1938 when he 'pirated' her in the street. She'd invited him and Bert Sutherland over to her house – but impressed on them not to come around at night but in the mornings. If true, it undermined her claim it'd been her later involvement with McRae that had corrupted her.

Freda proved a match for learned counsel. Shand asked if she'd posed for *Truth* with very few clothes on? 'Yes,' she said, 'in a bathing costume. Any harm in that, Mr Shand?' He asked if she'd been paid. Freda said no. Then why had she done it? 'Fun,' she said. Shand asked where the 'fun' was in posing for photos. 'Well,' she shot back, 'it was more fun than spending fourteen days listening to you.' The court erupted in laughter. But Freda was serious when she again refused to go to the CIB to point out the office allegedly used for sex with McRae.

Among McRae's police defenders was MacKay. He acknowledged

dismissing the detective so this avenue of appeal would be open to him. While he believed McRae had committed adultery, it had not been aggravated and thus he didn't believe it was a sackable offence. The punishment, he told the hearing, was 'too severe'. The Police Appeals Board should reflect that by giving him his job back. The commissioner related his many achievements, from the 1917 case of goods stolen from the crippled *Cumberland* and mid-1920s robberies they'd worked together, through pretty much every major murder investigation of the past decade. 'I regard the whole of McRae's career as one of outstanding merit and ability,' MacKay said, 'and his dismissal from the police force is a distinct loss to the service.'

But the commissioner's argument was astounding in its hypocrisy: if McRae had committed adultery, then he'd also perjured himself – a criminal offence that had led to the false witness in the Eric Craig case being sentenced to three years in gaol. What McRae thought of this 'support' wasn't recorded but he maintained he had not committed adultery at all.

After sitting for seven days, the Police Appeals Board completed its inquiry on 19 December. It found McRae had committed adultery with Freda. But he'd not pressured her. 'The board has carefully considered this matter,' they said, 'and has carefully observed the demeanour of the woman who has made the charge, and it is definitely of opinion that these allegations are entirely false.' So McRae *wasn't* guilty of aggravated adultery. The board recommended to Premier Alexander Mair that McRae be reinstated.

This was, as *Truth* railed, justice working backwards. The Police Appeals Board's power was limited to deciding whether McRae's punishment was too harsh. But it had effectively retried the case, then 'reviewed' the Supreme Court verdict and found it incorrect. This was as outrageous as the police force trying to withhold evidence in the divorce trial.

On 23 December 1940, the state cabinet refused the recommendation that McRae be reinstated. His career was over. Not only was his salary gone, but he also lost all his superannuation and wouldn't be eligible for the police pension. All up – including compensation, legal costs and lost future earnings and monies – the scandal cost him more than £10,000. In 1940 that was enough to buy four new brick cottages in Kingsford and put a new Buick in each driveway.

McRae, who had little in the way of savings and who was renting his home, made an outburst to *The Sun*:

> What can I do after that? They have taken every penny I had. I haven't a red cent left. I haven't got a quid – not a quid. At 54, after a lifetime in the force, I can't knuckle down yet to facing a future without the work I was specially trained for.

But he still had his wife, Jean, who told the paper: 'I have never lost faith in my husband – and I never will.' MacKay was less sanguine about McRae's future, characterising his punishment as 'tantamount to a death sentence'.

~

Caesar's divorce from Freda was granted in July 1941. She was back in *Truth* five months later with a big photo story announcing she was overjoyed to have married her ideal man after all. He was an artist named Robert Morehead, who soon enlisted and was deployed overseas. While he was serving, in June 1943, Freda had the ultimate scoop for *Truth*: she'd never had sex with McRae.

Freda told the paper the detective had never even *suggested* impropriety. She had framed him – and had tricked the husband she loathed into becoming suspicious by leaving cigarette butts and wine glasses around the house. Then she'd lured McRae to Mac's Hotel to entrap him – and get herself divorced by Caesar. Freda and the *Truth* reporter went to former state treasurer Athol Richardson. She gave a statement but refused to sign it until she was paid. Nevertheless, Mr Richardson took her to the recently elected premier, William McKell, to tell her new version. But as she wouldn't sign the affidavit or confirm its truth to him in person, the state leader refused to believe her – and refused Richardson's request for a royal commission into the matter.

In the wake of this revelation, McRae submitted two sworn witness statements to the government supporting his contention that he'd been framed. Premier McKell still refused a royal commission.

Freda's statement to *Truth* could only be interpreted in two ways. Either she'd told the truth in 1939 and 1940 but was now prepared to lie for money. Or she'd been a perjurer and blackmailer then and had ruined McRae's life.

McRae would keep fighting to clear his name. *Smith's Weekly* ran a supportive front-page article in November 1946 headlined 'Detective Says He Can Prove His Innocence'. It reported that McRae had new evidence, which the paper sent to the government. There was no action. McRae had now been working on his own case longer than he'd worked on the Pyjama Girl.

Freda's second husband, Robert, returned from overseas service in December 1946, she became pregnant and their messy split began a few months later. By mid-1948 she was in court trying to compel him to come back to her and her baby. He wouldn't and their divorce was finalised in 1949. Freda was to fade into obscurity. But she'd find love again, taking the surname of her de facto husband, Fred Lawson. Freda died suddenly of heart failure in Kingsford in July 1963, aged just forty-seven. She was survived by Fred and by her daughter.

~

While the newspapers had usually served as police boosters, from the late 1930s they became more critical of the accumulation of unsolved murders. *Truth* in particular could be relied on for regular articles that listed the roll call of failure – and was now more willing to slate Commissioner MacKay and CIB chief Frank Matthews for their sins. In March 1943, for instance, the paper called for 'some real hard detective work, the removal of nepotism, and advancement for conscientious men who are capable, but have little future in the force under the present regime'. It listed thirty-six unsolved murders, including those of Hilda White, Dorothy Thorne and Claude Saywell. That the earliest of them dated back a dozen years actually meant an average of three unsolved homicides per year. Put that way, the record might seem defensible, but taken together, it looked an appalling indictment. Of course, the highest-profile case remained the Pyjama Girl, which had now been under MacKay's direct supervision for four years.

Billy MacKay would 'solve' the Pyjama Girl case in extremely dubious circumstances. In December 1942, Jeanette Routledge – who in 1937 had told McRae the woman in the formalin was not her missing illegitimate daughter, Anna Philomena Morgan – viewed the body again, changed her mind and asked the New South Wales Probate Court to confirm this so she could administer her daughter's estate. It was a bruising and sensational court case. The police's side of things was hampered because they couldn't call McRae as a witness to discredit the resurgent Pyjama Girl crank theorist Dr Benbow; McRae's disgrace and dismissal meant he could never testify in court again and expect to be believed.

At the start of March 1944, Antonio Agostini, again working as a waiter at Romano's, was brought into the Sydney CIB. MacKay had ordered a review of the dental records, and these and some witnesses – starting with George Kemphe – now indicated that Linda Agostini *was* the Pyjama Girl. In an echo of the Moxley circumstances, the commissioner – who'd also known 'Tony' for years – allegedly told him in private they knew he'd killed his wife and it would be best for him to confess. The suspect did so in the presence of a shorthand writer and Joe Ramus, now promoted to Detective-Sergeant, who had come to fame in the Human Glove case and had taken over as one of MacKay's men on the Pyjama Girl case. Agostini said that on 26 August 1934, at their home in Carlton, Melbourne, Linda had threatened him with a gun. There had been a struggle. She'd been shot and died. Agostini had panicked and decided to dump her. Trying to move Linda, he had lost a grip on her body and she'd bumped down some stairs, which led to her head injuries. He'd then dumped her in Albury.

Since the crime had taken place in Victoria, Agostini was extradited to Melbourne in a police vehicle under great secrecy – with a van following containing the formalin tank containing the body some claimed was his dead wife. A new post-mortem revealed that dentist Francis Jackson, whose work had been so acclaimed, had actually missed two porcelain fillings in teeth that remained in her head. He'd also misnamed a molar's position in his description. So his widely distributed description was incorrect – and the new dentition, supposedly, more closely resembled the known work done on Linda Agostini. A Melbourne coroner decided she was Linda Agostini. But serious doubts remain. As historian Richard Evans has argued in his book *The Pyjama Girl Mystery*, and recently revisited in his authoritative *W.J. MacKay and the NSW Police, 1910–1948: A Dangerous Man*, this conclusion was 'untenable'. For one thing, Linda had brown eyes while the Pyjama Girl's were blue.

Nevertheless, Agostini was tried for murder. During the trial, his defence tried to argue that MacKay had coerced the confession by getting the accused drunk and telling him he'd hang for murder if he didn't claim manslaughter – the classic 'threat and promise' inducement. Agostini testified that when he was 'stuck' in expressing his thoughts, MacKay had 'helped' him. In addition to Agostini's self-defence claim, he also told the court that during his four-year marriage to Linda, she had been an unpredictable and violent drunk who had pulled a gun on him more than once. Yet while Agostini admitted having killed her, and having taken her into the country to dump the body, he didn't believe he'd gone to Albury, and he consistently denied that the Pyjama Girl was his wife.

As MacKay had allegedly predicted, Agostini was convicted only of manslaughter in June 1944. The judge sentenced him to six years. The Pyjama Girl case was considered 'solved'.

In January 1948 in Sydney, MacKay, sixty-two, 'dropped dead', as was the parlance, at his home in Edgecliff. He was succeeded by his deputy James Scott. Agostini was released and deported from Australia in August that year.

~

By the time McRae's most famous case reached its final murky act, he was an obscure figure in Sydney. To keep a roof over his and Jean's head, he worked as a private investigator for insurance firms. It was a huge step down from tracking murderers. Tellingly, McRae listed his occupation on the electoral rolls as 'police officer'. He might have seen himself as one still – just on an enforced hiatus until he could prove his innocence. For, when McRae wasn't earning a crust doing investigative work, or playing eighteen holes at Botany Golf Club, he would be obsessively working on his own case.

In December 1953 McRae saw his name in *Truth* again. His role in the Human Glove case was recalled because murderer Ted Morey was getting compassionate release as a result of his tuberculosis. The newspaper had interviewed Morey, who still protested his innocence. 'I told the police that if they got hold of this George McDonald, they would have the murderer,' he said, telling the reporter what he'd told McRae, the court and the world. 'Certainly they confronted me with a George McDonald, but that was not the man ... The evidence was all circumstantial ...'

Was Morey really innocent and the victim of a great injustice that had ruined his life? Or had he told his own lies so many times they were now his truth? McRae hadn't believed Morey in Wagga in 1934 and probably didn't believe him now. But he might have understood how Morey *felt*. McRae, too, was aged and sick but had never ceased claiming he'd been framed, or lost the hope he might still clear his name.

'Old Mac' wouldn't give up. In October 1956 his solicitor sent his file and 'vital fresh evidence' to the attorney-general of New South Wales with an application for a special judicial inquiry into the dismissal. McRae's lawyer wrote: 'The information now to hand in the light of all the past circumstance is of such a nature as to call for a full and urgent investigation so that a grave miscarriage of justice should not occur.'

The following month it was announced the application was being considered by Premier Joseph Cahill. To prepare for the hearing, a Queen's Counsel took on McRae's case pro bono. The wheels of justice moved slowly – and then ground to a stop. In September 1957, the premier wrote to McRae, saying that his legal counsel had interpreted the request as being for a royal commission constituted by a Supreme Court judge with 'drastic powers' under the law. They said this wouldn't be justified. 'In the circumstances,' the premier wrote, 'it is regretted that your request cannot be granted.'

McRae took his frustrations to *The Sun-Herald*. The paper's editor sent a reporter and photographer to his home on Saturday 14 September. No longer the big, powerful man who'd led his men from the CIB for a beer after charging the Park Demon with Iris Marriott's murder, McRae had recently turned seventy-one and was a stooped and sickly senior citizen who was being treated for heart trouble. The reporter jogged the memories of older readers and introduced younger ones to the man this craggy old codger had been:

> Once the crack chief of the C.I.B. Homicide Squad, top 'glamour' detective of the force, Detective-Sergeant McRae figured in

practically every murder investigation in NSW in the wild 1930s. He once estimated that his photograph appeared in 32 out of 52 weekly editions of a Sunday newspaper. The Pyjama Girl, the 'Human Glove' case, the Craig park murders were some of the famous cases on which he worked. For 17 years since his dismissal, Mr McRae has said that he was innocent. He has worked non-stop to prove it.

McRae told *The Sun-Herald*:

> I will not stop fighting until I get justice. I have been an innocent victim and I mean to clear my name before I die. I am not interested in money. All I want is a rehearing of my case in the light of this fresh evidence I've uncovered. It is sensational. I want the facts brought up in Parliament. I've been fighting for it for 17 years and I'll leave no stone unturned until I get an inquiry before a Supreme Court Judge.

McRae showed the reporter the premier's letter of refusal. He said:

> What do they mean by 'drastic powers'? It seems that the only alternative is that I am to be denied justice. Yet I have six unsolicited declarations from unconnected people, supporting my innocence and telling the story of what happened. The last declaration was supplied a little over a year ago by a man who voluntarily came to see me. He was unknown when the case was heard – now he is vitally linked to it. I believe I put sufficient evidence before the government in 1943 to justify a Royal Commission, which was refused. Now Mr Cahill refuses me. Why?

Whether he realised it or not, McRae sounded like Ted Morey – and Maurice O'Hara, Eric Craig, Lillian Anderson, Claude Wallace, Eric

Newlyn and any number of others he'd put behind bars: condemned but still claiming innocence long after everyone had ceased to care.

Almost everyone. McRae still had one unswerving supporter. Nearly twenty years since his disgrace, his wife, Jean, was still by his side. She told the reporter:

> If I believed my husband had been guilty, I would not be with him today. But I know he is a good and an innocent man. I know what was done to him. It has meant pain, humiliation and suffering for us, and loss of money. My husband had a bad breakdown in health three years ago – I thought he would die. I am fighting back with him.

McRae reiterated his determination to prove the truth in what had been his last case and his longest investigation: 'If I had been the guilty party, I would not draw all this attention to myself – I would have crawled into obscurity by now. I've been fighting since the day they wrongfully convicted me and I'll keep on fighting till the end.'

The Sun-Herald's headline read: 'I Demand Justice!'

~

Despite former Detective-Sergeant Thomas Walter McRae's poor health, one thing about him hadn't changed. If he wasn't working on proving his innocence, he'd be indulging his other innocent obsession. McRae was at Botany Golf Club on the evening of 17 January 1958, having just spoken to a meeting of 150 members, when he 'dropped dead'. His passing merited but a brief report in *The Sydney Morning Herald*, which noted his reputation, his ruination and the long battle to clear his name.

'He died,' the piece concluded, 'as he was about to launch another appeal against his dismissal from the police force.'

A detective to the end – for better or worse.

Epilogue

Was McRae a victim of injustice? There's no way to know. Certainly there were reasons to doubt Freda and Tom Caesar. Yet McRae was also unable to produce evidence to prove his claims of a frame-up – and the police force's obstructions made him look guiltier. The official verdict we're left with is that McRae had done what was alleged in court – just as we're left with the verdicts from juries who'd convicted murderers he'd given evidence against.

Did McRae – along with his brothers in blue – give false testimony to secure some of these convictions? It's possible that he did, though it's not possible to say against who, about what, to what extent or how important such evidence might have been in any given jury's deliberations. What seems most likely is that McRae and his colleagues sometimes made threats and promises to elicit 'certain admissions', and that the resulting statements sometimes suited their purposes and served their belief that the accused people were guilty.

Yet, as shown in most of the cases in this book, there was almost always other physical and/or witness evidence that might be strong enough to sway a jury. What also argues against these police always or even mostly forcing or fabricating admissions were the many murders that weren't solved by a frame-up that would have been supported by such evidence. What stopped McRae from claiming that Eric Roland

Craig had verbally confessed to murdering Bessie O'Connor but refused to make a statement? In light of what the accused admitted about Iris Marriott, such a retracted 'confession' might have rung true, given he couldn't hope to argue self-defence. Similarly, if Alfred Lockyer's allegations about detective intimidation were true, why didn't McRae go all the way by verballing him for the poisoning of Dorothy Thorne? If it was so easy to frame a man, why not do it in these instances? Further, in terms of celebrated solved cases, Ted Morey consistently claimed he was innocent, yet he never accused McRae of misrepresenting what he had said during interrogation – and the detective's job would surely have been easier and a conviction more assured if he had claimed the accused had 'confessed'.

Definitive answers about individual detectives and specific cases are elusive because such practices were by their nature almost always hidden and were predictably denied in court if raised. But what is clear is that the New South Wales Police Force increasingly became a law unto itself under the long reign of Billy MacKay. By the time he tried to 'save' McRae in 1940, MacKay's police force would obstruct justice to protect its own – even if the commissioner believed his own were bent. Regardless of what McRae had or hadn't done, MacKay accepted he'd committed adultery. By default, that made McRae a perjurer who'd tried to frame innocent people for blackmail. But MacKay said that *didn't matter*. And Big Bill wasn't just saying this because it was Old Mac. MacKay had already said this was his general policy three years earlier, at a commission into starting price betting, when he admitted there were bad cops in his force and that recent inquiries had unfortunately made this fact public. 'I want to wipe out this stigma,' MacKay told the commission in September 1937. 'Let us keep our troubles to ourselves and not say to the whole world "We are rotters!"'

MacKay hadn't wanted to remove the stigma by attacking it at the source. He didn't want to shine a spotlight on perjurers, framers, bashers and bribe-takers on his force. This wasn't abstract, either; he knew specific offenders. MacKay was asked during the commission if a police officer shown to have lied to secure an SP conviction would be fit to remain on the force. He had answered: 'I know of cases just as bad and worse and the men are still in the force.' MacKay knew the bad apples – because they hadn't fallen far from his own rotten tree.

The rot had taken a firm hold under MacKay and it would eat more deeply into the force in the decades to come. Following McRae's downfall and death, New South Wales would have other high-profile hero cops who got the job done. But the force they came up in allegedly allowed them to get away with murder while they made money from giving new meaning to 'controlling crime'. Like McRae, men such as Ray 'Gunner' Kelly, Fred Krahe and Roger Rogerson were to be remembered more for how they broke the law than for how they served it.

All of which said, it would be unfair to throw out the work that McRae and members of the various murder squads did during the darkest years of the Great Depression. Juries often convicted because they were convinced by the sometimes brilliant evidence-gathering work done by these men. McRae and his colleagues achieved this during a desperate time, when police cars were few in number, when radio communications were primitive, and when blood couldn't be analysed beyond coming from a blood group. They chased after killers before they could match DNA to suspects and victims; before they could find out who was where and when by consulting ATM and EFTPOS records, traffic cameras and phone GPS locators; before they could access immediate widespread community assistance by making real-time updates and appeals via large news radio networks, 24-hour television stations, internet news sites and social media channels.

What they achieved, they also achieved with the numbers against them. The New South Wales Police Force in 1929–34, even under the ambitious and expansionist MacKay, was poorly resourced compared with today. In 1932, the total strength of the force was 3602, which was 144 per 100,000 people in the state. These days the force has 21,634 employees – 80 per cent of them officers – which is 262 per 100,000 people. During the Depression, the proportionally much smaller force also had a bigger workload of homicide cases. In 1932 – the 'Red Year' – there were 36 murders in New South Wales, ten up on the average of the previous three years. With a state population of 2.5 million, that was 1.44 homicides per 100,000 people. The six-year average was 27 – or 1.08 per 100,000. By comparison, New South Wales, from 2015 to 2019, with a population approaching 8.2 million, recorded an average of 68 murders per year, which was 0.83 per 100,000 people. The differences are substantial – but even more so when taken with changes in police numbers, procedures and technology. McRae and other murder investigators had to do much more with much less.

Put at such disadvantages, it's perhaps remarkable that they caught and convicted as many killers as they did. But exactly *how* they got their men will always be under shadows of doubt.

Notes on Sources

The Murder Squad arose from a series of episodes that I produced for my podcast *Forgotten Australia*. In writing this book, I greatly expanded my research into these cases, added many new ones, and focused specifically on Tom McRae and his colleagues. Material came from contemporaneous articles found at the National Library of Australia's Trove database of historic newspapers, from files held by the National Archives of Australia, the New South Wales State Archives Collection, the Public Record Office of Victoria, the Queensland State Archives and the National Film and Sound Archive, while family history information was accessed through Ancestry.com.au. Special thanks also to Tina Magennis, Information Review Officer, of the New South Wales Police InfoLink Unit, for guidance about extant departmental records for some of this book's cases. While the bulk of *The Murder Squad* is based on primary sources, I was fortunate to be able to consult the work of three writers that covered some of the same territory. They were: Richard Evans's *The Pyjama Girl Mystery* and *W.J. MacKay and the NSW Police, 1910–1948: A Dangerous Man*; Tanya Bretherton's *The Killing Streets*, which is about the Eric Roland Craig case; and the late Peter Corris's *Mad Dog,* which covered the Moxley case in a blend of historical narrative and historical fiction.

References

A full bibliography and detailed source notes can be found at
https://forgottenaustralia.com/the-murder-squad-source-references/

Acknowledgements

A big shout out to all *Forgotten Australia* listeners. Your support over the years has helped make this book a reality. With special thanks to Clare and Ava, and to our wonderful families. Also Mic Looby, who's always there. Martin Hughes, Kevin O'Brien, Laura Franks, Dana Anderson, Susie Kennewell and Alistair Trapnell at Affirm Press, and Julian Welch and Tim Graham, for getting this ye olde underworld epic out into the modern world. Brad Argent and Jennifer Dodd at Ancestry.com.au, and Guy Scott-Wilson at Acast, for supporting *Forgotten Australia*. Thanks also to Stephen Davis, Rich Williams, Laurie Turtle, Mercedes Maguire, Jordon Lott, Olivia O'Flynn, Richard Glover, Stephen Peters, David Caesar, Stephen Gibbs, Meshel Laurie and Emily Webb of the *Australian True Crime* podcast, Paul Verhoeven and John Verhoeven of the *Loose Units* podcast, and Jen Kelly of the *In Black and White* podcast.